RESEARCH HANDBOOK OF WOMEN'S ENTREPRENEURSHIP AND VALUE CREATION

Dedicated to this wonderful World our beautiful home. — Shumaila

Dedicated to all aspiring, established and growing women entrepreneurs. Remember, that entrepreneurship occurs when there is nothing; in the beginning when you start from scratch and everything is messy, uncertain and ambiguous. This is when you need to have faith in yourself, and in doing so, you encourage others to have faith in you and in your entrepreneurial vision. — Colette

To my wonderful husband, who always supports me and pushes me to not give in, and to all those women in the world who have been told they couldn't do something and went on to prove those people wrong. — Monique

Dedicated to all the women who were, are and will be. — Shandana

To my mother Krystina and my father Pierre who educated me emphasizing gender equality. — Alain

Research Handbook of Women's Entrepreneurship and Value Creation

Edited by

Shumaila Yousafzai

Nazarbayev University, Kazakhstan and Cardiff University, UK

Colette Henry

Griffith University, Queensland, Australia

Monique Boddington

University of Cambridge, UK

Shandana Sheikh

Avicenna Medical and Dental College, Pakistan

Alain Fayolle

Center for Innovation and Entrepreneurship Activities, University of Cagliari, Italy

 Edward Elgar
PUBLISHING

Cheltenham, UK • Northampton, MA, USA

Published by
Edward Elgar Publishing Limited
The Lypiatts
15 Lansdown Road
Cheltenham
Glos GL50 2JA
UK

Edward Elgar Publishing, Inc.
William Pratt House
9 Dewey Court
Northampton
Massachusetts 01060
USA

Paperback edition 2023

A catalogue record for this book
is available from the British Library

Library of Congress Control Number: 2022931080

This book is available electronically in the **Elgar**online
Business subject collection
http://dx.doi.org/10.4337/9781789901375

ISBN 978 1 78990 136 8 (cased)
ISBN 978 1 0353 2365 4 (paperback)
ISBN 978 1 78990 137 5 (eBook)

Printed and bound by CPI Group (UK) Ltd, Croydon, CR0 4YY

Contents

v

About the editors

Shumaila Yousafzai is Associate Professor at Nazarbayev University, Kazakhstan where she teaches entrepreneurship, marketing and consumer behavior. After her undergraduate studies in Physics and Mathematics (University of Balochistan), and an MSc in Electronic Commerce (Coventry University, UK), she finished her PG Diploma in Research Methods from Cardiff University. Shumaila received her doctoral degree in 2005 from Cardiff University. In her research, Shumaila focuses mainly on topics linked to contextual embeddedness of entrepreneurship, firm performance, institutional theory and entrepreneurial orientation. She has published articles in various international journals, such as *Entrepreneurship Theory and Practice, Journal of Small Business Management, Industrial Marketing Management, Technovation, Journal of Business Ethics, Psychology & Marketing, Journal of Applied Social Psychology*, and *Computers in Human Behavior*. She has co-edited a special issue on women's entrepreneurship for *Entrepreneurship & Regional Development* and six edited volumes on entrepreneurship with Edward Elgar Publishing and Routledge.

Colette Henry is Head of Department of Business Studies at Dundalk Institute of Technology, Ireland, and Adjunct Professor – Department of Business Strategy & Innovation – at Griffith University, Queensland, Australia. Her previous roles include Adjunct Professor at UiT – The Arctic University of Norway; Norbrook Professor of Business & Enterprise at the Royal Veterinary College, London; President of the Institute for Small Business & Entrepreneurship, UK, and Head of School of Business & Humanities, DkIT. She chairs the *Global Women's Entrepreneurship Research Network* (Global WEP) and is Founder and Editor in Chief of the *International Journal of Gender and Entrepreneurship*. She has published on entrepreneurship education, gender, the creative industries and veterinary/rural business, with over 50 journal articles and 14 books. Colette also hosted the Royal Irish Academy's 'Rural Conversations Workshop' in Dundalk in 2019. In 2015 she received the Diana International Research Project Trailblazer Award, and in 2017 received the Sten K Johnson European Entrepreneurship Education Award from Lund University, Sweden. Colette is a fellow of the Royal Society, the Higher Education Academy, the Academy of Social Sciences, and the Institute for Small Business & Entrepreneurship.

Monique Boddington is Associate Faculty at Cambridge Judge Business School, and Deputy Director of the MSt in Entrepreneurship. Monique's research includes the study of strategy formation in early stage ventures, pivoting, gender and diversity, and the use of sociological approaches to broaden our understanding of entrepreneurial activity. Monique leads the EVER project, which is a longitudinal qualitative study of early stage ventures which aims to understand the strategic decision-making of early ventures and how teams pivot over time. Monique has a PhD from the University of Cambridge and her thesis focused on applying philosophy to archaeology to look at the nature of knowledge creation of the past. Previously, she worked on multiple EU-funded projects focused on understanding the impact of entrepreneurial education.

Shandana Sheikh received her Doctorate in Entrepreneurship from Cardiff Business School, Cardiff University. Her research particularly focuses on women entrepreneurship and value creation that accrues within it. Besides, Shandana is interested in disabled entrepreneurship and transgender entrepreneurship, particularly in the context of developing economies. Prior to her Doctoral studies, Shandana received her MBA in Marketing from Lahore School of Economics, Pakistan and an MSc in Marketing and Strategy from Warwick Business School, University of Warwick, UK.

Alain Fayolle is Professor of Entrepreneurship at CREA – Center for Innovation and Entrepreneurship Activities, University of Cagliari, Italy. He has been Distinguished Professor and the Director of the Entrepreneurship Research Centre at emlyon business school, France. Alain has published forty-five books and over two hundred articles. In 2013, Alain Fayolle received the 2013 European Entrepreneurship Education Award and was elected Chair of the AOM Entrepreneurship Division for the 2016–2017 academic year. In 2015, he was awarded the Wilford L. White Fellow by ICSB.

Contributors

Abigail Knox is a Sustainability Consultant at Three Consulting, South Africa. Her work focuses on sustainable and renewable electricity generation, markets and regulation, to development policy for the informal economy. Abigail pursues a PhD in energy value chains in South Africa. Through research, strategic policy development, consultation and implementation management, her projects set to contribute to poverty alleviation and sustainable development in South Africa.

Angela Hamouda is a Lecturer of Entrepreneurship, Creativity and Innovation. Her research interests include entrepreneurship education, female entrepreneurship and social enterprise. Her main objective is that of driving the entrepreneurship agenda. Her commitment to teaching excellence was rewarded in being the winner of the prestigious international Innovation and Entrepreneurship Teaching Excellence Awards in Aveiro, Portugal (2018).

Anne Kamau is a Researcher at the Institute for Development Studies (IDS), University of Nairobi, Kenya. She obtained her Doctorate in Public Health from the School of Public Health, University of Bielefeld, Germany. She researches on social protection, gender and transport and health systems. She has published a book chapter on 'Bridging entrepreneurial gender gap through social protection among women small scale traders in Kenya' in an edited book on *Women's Entrepreneurship and the Myth of 'Underperformance'* published in 2018 by Edward Elgar Publishing. She recently participated in an international research project authored by Tessa Wright on 'The Impact of the Future of Work for Women in Public Transport' published in 2018.

Annie Roos is a Doctoral Candidate at the Department of Economics, Swedish University of Agricultural Sciences in Uppsala, Sweden. Her research revolves around gender, context and entrepreneurship. Previously, she has published a book chapter on gender and methodology, as well as research articles in journals such as *Entrepreneurship and Regional Development*, and *Gender in Management*.

Atsede Tesfaye Hailemariam is an Assistant Professor at School of Commerce, College of Business and Economics, Addis Ababa University, Ethiopia. She has a Master's degree in mathematics from Addis Ababa University, Ethiopia; Masters of Business Administration from Open University, UK and PhD from Tilburg University, the Netherlands. Her research focuses on understanding motivation, challenges and business growth of women entrepreneurs in Ethiopia.

Brigitte Kroon is Assistant Professor in Human Resource studies, School of Social and Behavioral Sciences, Tilburg University, the Netherlands. She is affiliated to the Tilburg Institute of Family Business. Her research focuses on extending HRM systems theory to work contexts that are less standard in Human Resource Management research, such as small entrepreneurial (family) businesses, cooperative organisations, and HRM for low-skilled (migrant) workers.

Caren Scheepers is an Associate Professor in Contextual Leadership, Organisational Development and Change, and Strategic Implementation on the MBA programme at the Gordon Institute of Business Science (GIBS), University Pretoria, South Africa. She holds a PhD in Psychology and is a Professional Credentialed Coach with the International Coaching Federation. She has authored and co-edited books, numerous academic journal articles and case studies. Her latest books include *Women Leadership in Emerging Markets* (2017, Routledge) and *Change Leadership in Emerging Markets* (2020, Springer). She has been consulting on several large-scale organisational development interventions in international consulting environments and served as an internal management consultant in the financial services industry. She received The Case Centre's Outstanding Contribution to the Case Method Award in 2020.

Debbie Sparks holds a Doctorate in Environmental and Geographical Science from the University of Cape Town, South Africa, and has 20 years of research and teaching experience at her alma mater. Her broad research interests are in the areas of energy, the environment and climate change. She has an historical interest in climate change mitigation and the water–energy nexus, and a more recent interest in the effects of climate change on the youth as well as gender and energy. She has published in the area of the water-energy nexus and climate change.

Doaa Althalathini is a Lecturer in Business and Enterprise at the Faculty of Business, Oxford Brookes University, UK. She worked in her home country, Palestine, with different local and international NGOs in humanitarian and development programmes aimed to reduce poverty, empower women and enhance economic development through entrepreneurship. This experience inspired her to do a PhD at the University of Plymouth where she researched the resilience of entrepreneurs and gender in the conflict zones of Afghanistan, Iraq and Palestine.

Ethne Swartz is Professor of Management at the Feliciano School of Business, Montclair State University and serves as a Research Associate at the University of Pretoria's Gordon Institute of Business Science. She was a 2018–2019 Fulbright Scholar in South Africa. Her research interests include gender and entrepreneurship, business continuity management and business ethics. She has co-authored two books and published in peer-reviewed entrepreneurship and strategy journals.

Frances Amatucci is an Associate Professor in the School of Business, Slippery Rock University of Pennsylvania, U.S.A. She is a strong advocate of field-based and experiential learning in business education. She teaches courses related to strategic management, sustainability, and entrepreneurship and does research in these areas.

Gry Agnete Alsos is Professor of Innovation and Entrepreneurship at Nord University Business School, Bodø, Norway, where she currently also serves as co-director of Engage – Centre for Engaged Education through Entrepreneurship. She obtained her PhD in Business in 2007, focusing on knowledge transfer of portfolio entrepreneurs. Her research interests include new venture start-up processes, entrepreneurship and innovation policy, and gender perspectives to entrepreneurship and innovation. She has published several journal articles on these areas as well as contributed to several books.

Hans Bressers is Professor of Policy Studies and Environmental Policy at the University of Twente in the Netherlands and founder of the CSTM, the Department of Governance and Technology for Sustainability, one of the departments of the Faculty of Behavioural, Management and Social Sciences. He has been researcher and project leader of numerous externally funded projects, including several projects funded by EU research frameworks, the Dutch national science foundation, national priority research programmes, Dutch ministries, etc. As a PhD advisor, he has led 50 researchers to their graduation until 2018.

Hans Lundberg is Senior Lecturer in Entrepreneurship and Innovation at the School of Business and Economics, Linnaeus University, Sweden. His research focuses on early stage entrepreneurship in practices constituted of hybrid logics. His work is published in about 35 books and book chapters with leading publishers (i.e. Routledge, Edward Elgar Publishing, Springer Nature) and in various journals including *Journal of Management Studies* and *International Journal of Entrepreneurship and Innovation Management*.

Hayfaa Tlaiss an Associate Professor of Management and the Chair of the Management Department at the College of Business, Alfaisal University, KSA. She obtained her PhD from Alliance Manchester Business School, UK. Her research interests include gender in management and entrepreneurship in the Arab/ Middle East region, the influence of religion, religiosity and spirituality in the workplace and various topics in Human Resources Management and organisational behaviour. She has published in several journals, including *Journal of Business Ethics*, *Entrepreneurship and Regional Development*, *International Small Business Management*, *Journal of Small Business Management* and the *International Journal of Human Resource Management*. Her research has received significant international attention and has been widely recognised through various awards.

Jiska de Groot is a Senior Researcher in Energy and Development and is based at the University of Cape Town's African Climate and Development Initiative, South Africa. Her work focuses on the human dimension of sustainable energy access, energy poverty, gender and capacity building. Jiska has published her work in several journals including: the *Journal of Global Entrepreneurship Research*, *Energy Research & Social Science*, *Energy Policy*, and *Development Southern Africa* and has contributed to several edited books in the field of energy and development.

Kate Johnston is a Lecturer in Business at Dundalk Institute of Technology. Her research interests are in the areas of financial management, crowd funding and entrepreneurship. Kate has authored and co-authored numerous articles in refereed journals including the *Journal of Small Business and Enterprise Development, Applied Financial Economics, Journal of International Bank Marketing* and *The International Review of Retail Distribution and Consumer Research.* She has also contributed to a number of books in the area of financial management and entrepreneurship. Kate is currently supervising a number of research students in the area of crowd funding, entrepreneurship and banking and finance.

Khizran Zehra is Lecturer at Tilburg School of Economics and Management, the Netherlands. She obtained her PhD in 2018. Her research interests include women's entrepreneurship, informal entrepreneurship and resourcefulness.

Klavs Ciprikis is a PhD Researcher of labour economics at Technological University Dublin (Ireland). His research interests include an examination of labour market outcomes of marginalised groups. His current research focuses on the examination of employment and wage gaps between transgender and non-transgender persons, and between individuals with mental health problems and those without.

Konjit Hailu Gudeta is currently a post-doctoral researcher at the Faculty of Arts and Social Sciences at Maastricht University, the Netherlands. She has been working as an assistant professor at School of Commerce at Addis Ababa University, Ethiopia. She received her PhD from the Department of Human Resources Studies at Tilburg University, the Netherlands. Her primary research interests are in the areas of work–life boundary management, women entrepreneurship, women employees and precarious work situations, family businesses and savings groups.

Leona Achtenhagen is Professor at Jönköping International Business School, Sweden. She is also Director of its Media, Management and Transformation Centre (MMTC). Her research interests include women's entrepreneurship, business growth and entrepreneurship in different contexts.

Maria Villares-Varela (PhD/FHEA) is an Associate Professor in Sociology at the University of Southampton. Her research explores international migration processes and work and employment relations in migrant firms, with a particular focus on gendered and classed-based experiences of work. She has published extensively in these areas of research in journals such as *Sociology, Work Employment & Society* and *Entrepreneurship and Regional Development.*

Marloes van Engen is an Associate Professor at the Center for Strategy, Organizaton and Leadership, Nyenrode Business University, the Netherlands, and also works at the Department of Human Resource Studies, School of Social and Behavioral Sciences, Tilburg University, the Netherlands. Her passion in research is in understanding and managing diversity, equality and inclusion in organisations, and in sustainability in combining work and care. In both fields she initiated research-based interventions to increase diversity, equality and inclusion.

Mary Barrett is a Professor of Management at the University of Wollongong, Australia. Her research interests include women's entrepreneurship, and family business and leadership, especially those two in combination.

Marzieh Nasiri is an Adjunct Professor at Shahid Beheshti University (formerly known as the National University of Iran) and Ershad University. She has a PhD in marketing from Shahid Beheshti University, Iran. Her doctoral thesis was focused on entrepreneurial marketing.

Milka Kwiatek is a PhD Candidate in Sociology and Social Policy at the University of Southampton. Her research investigates the experiences of Polish migrant women entrepreneurs in the UK at the time of the dynamically shifting socio-political context wrought by the Brexit vote.

Mirela Xheneti is a Senior Lecturer in Entrepreneurship and Small Business at the University of Sussex Business School, UK. Mirela holds a PhD from the University of Bristol, UK. Prior to joining Sussex, Mirela worked as a researcher at the Small Business Research Centre, Kingston University. Mirela has a long-standing interest in how institutional change and enterprise policies affect entrepreneurial behaviour. This particular interest has been followed by the successful coordination of a number of recent projects that focus on the intersection of the informal economy and gender in developing country contexts. Mirela's work has appeared in numerous journal articles and book chapters. Most recently, her work has been published in the *Entrepreneurship and Regional Development Journal*, the *Strategic Entrepreneurship Journal*, and *International Journal of Management Reviews*.

Musarrat Jabeen is a Professor of International Relations at National Defence University (NDU) Islamabad, Pakistan. She received her PhD from the University of Karachi, in 2004, titled, 'International Institutions and the Challenge of Sustainable Development in Balochistan Since 1990'. She has several research publications and has participated in various international conferences.

Nadeera Ranabahu is a Lecturer in Entrepreneurship and Innovation at University of Canterbury, New Zealand. She obtained her PhD in 2018 from University of Wollongong, Australia. Her research interests include entrepreneurial learning and development, innovative practices and process in small businesses, responsible innovation and design thinking, microfinance accountability, and effects of microfinance on women.

Nadia Arshad is a Doctoral Candidate at Jönköping International Business School, Sweden. Nadia writes about crowdfunding in entrepreneurial ventures.

Naomi Birdthistle is Associate Professor of Entrepreneurship and Business Innovation at Griffith University. Naomi has studied in Scotland (Stirling University), Ireland (University of Limerick) and Boston (Babson College and Harvard University). Her research covers many areas within the entrepreneurship discipline, including entrepreneurship education, minority groups and entrepreneurship and women-owned and

-led businesses and has published three books, 29 peer-reviewed papers and 11 book chapters on the areas.

Nthabiseng Mohlakoana holds a Doctorate in Innovation and Governance for Sustainable Development from the Department of Governance & Technology for Sustainable Development at the University of Twente, the Netherlands. She has more than 15 years of experience in research focusing on energy access and use, gender and development in the low-income urban and rural areas, mainly in Southern Africa. Her research emphasises the importance of gender equality in planning and implementation of energy and other basic services interventions dictated by policies.

Rebecca Nevins is a Master of Business graduate from Dundalk Institute of Technology specialising in Marketing and Entrepreneurship. This is where her love for entrepreneurship research grew and in particular female entrepreneurship. Rebecca's main goal for the future is to progress with her research in the area of female entrepreneurship and strive to influence the development of support to help young female entrepreneurs.

Renuka Vyas is a Doctoral student at Cardiff University. She holds an MSc in Social Research from Birkbeck, University of London, which she earned with a distinction in 2016. Her current research is on lean entrepreneurship, gender and social value creation. Her research is published in the *International Review of Entrepreneurship* and *Technology Innovation Management Review.*

Robyn Eversole is a Professor at the Centre for Social Impact, Swinburne University, Melbourne, Australia. She is an anthropologist known for her practice-focused research on regional and community development in Latin America and the Asia-Pacific. Her books include *Knowledge Partnering for Community Development* (2015, Routledge), *Regional Development in Australia: Being Regional* (2016, Routledge), and *Anthropology for Development, From Theory to Practice* (2018, Routledge).

Roshni Narendran currently works at the University of Tasmania. She has more than 10 years' experience teaching Human Resource Management and Entrepreneurship related subjects. Roshni initially started her career working for an organisation that undertook projects in restructuring public sector units in India. This motivated her to research the role of the state and public sector in minority groups' entrepreneurial ventures (i.e. transgender entrepreneurs and women entrepreneurs). Currently, her research focuses on transgender women entrepreneurs. She has received a grant from the University of Wollongong to investigate transgender women entrepreneurs in India.

Ruta Aidis is a Senior Fellow at the Schar School for Policy and Government, George Mason University, Arlington, VA. She obtained her PhD in Economics from the University of Amsterdam in 2003 and has authored over 50 publications. Her research interests include women's entrepreneurship, SMEs, gender, value creation, institutional development and public policy.

Sadia Arshad is Visiting Researcher at Jönköping International Business School's MMTC, Sweden. Sadia is interested in researching entrepreneurship in challenging contexts.

Sanaa Talha is a PhD Candidate in the Department of Innovation and Entrepreneurship at Nord University Business School, Bodø, Norway. She started her position in March 2018. Her area of research focuses on immigrant women entrepreneurship. Her interests in the field include entrepreneurial identity formation from the perspective of nascent entrepreneurs. Other interests include studies on embeddedness, intersectionality, and entrepreneurial learning.

Shova Thapa Karki is a Senior Lecturer in Entrepreneurship and Sustainability at the University of Sussex Business School. She obtained her PhD in Ecological Economics from the Science and Technology Policy Research (SPRU), University of Sussex. Her research interests lie in the nexus of sustainability and entrepreneurship. This interest originated from her previous work on women entrepreneurs and micro-credit programmes for biodiversity conservation in protected areas of Nepal. She is currently involved in a number of research projects exploring the role of entrepreneurship in contributing to sustainable development goals.

Siavash Aein Jamshid is a Research Assistant in the Faculty of Management and Accounting at the University of Hormozgan, Iran. He holds a Master's degree in Business Management with Strategic Orientation from the University of Hormozgan. His research interests focus on entrepreneurship, innovation management, and business and sustainability. Also, working as a research assistant provides him hands-on opportunities to learn more about research methods. Besides working as a research assistant, he also advises an early-stage environmental technology company, Aria Plasma Gostar Co, on business development and strategy.

Sylvia K. Gavigan is a PhD Researcher on Entrepreneurship Training and Rural Female Entrepreneurs at Technological University Dublin, Ireland. Her research is focusing on the contribution of entrepreneurship training to the perceived emancipation of nascent rural female entrepreneurs in Uganda. Her interests include women entrepreneurs, education for girls and trade in African economies.

Thomas M. Cooney is Professor of Entrepreneurship at the Technological University Dublin (Ireland), Visiting Professor at the University of Turku (Finland) and Academic Director of the Institute for Minority Entrepreneurship (TU Dublin). He is also a former president of both the International Council for Small Business and the European Council for Small Business. Thomas works with governments, the European Commission, OECD and other international organisations on the development of entrepreneurship policies and programmes. He has published widely on the topic of entrepreneurship (including nine books) and full details of his career can be found at www.thomascooney.ie.

Vahid Makizadeh is an Assistant Professor in the Faculty of Management and Accounting at the University of Hormozgan, Iran. He has a Master's degree in

Business Management and a PhD in Strategic Management from Shahid Beheshti University (formerly known as the National University of Iran), Tehran, Iran. His main area of interest is strategic management and entrepreneurship, particularly entrepreneurship among disadvantaged people. He has spent several years working for businesses within a consultative role.

Vinita Godinho served as the General Manager Advisory at Good Shepherd Microfinance from February 2016 to December 2019 and is now the Managing Director of Financial Resilience Australia, an independent consulting firm that advises the government, industry and community on practical ways to enhance financial inclusion, resilience and wellbeing. Her PhD from RMIT University explored Indigenous worldviews on money, financial capability and wellbeing. A Fulbright scholar, Vinita proactively contributes to public/academic discourse and publications on financial inclusion and wellbeing in Australia and overseas.

Winnie V. Mitullah is a Professor of Research at the Institute for Development Studies (IDS), University of Nairobi, Kenya. She obtained her PhD in Political Science at the University of York, UK in 1993. Her research interests include service delivery, institutions and governance. Mitullah has researched and published in the areas of para-transit, and non-motorised transport. Her most recent publications include an edited Routledge volume, *Non-Motorised Transport Integration into Urban Transport Planning in Africa* (2017) and a chapter on 'Parking in Nairobi', in an edited Elsevier volume *Parking 1st Edition: An International Perspective* (2019).

Zara Lasater is Head of Program Design and Advisory Services at Good Shepherd Microfinance, a research/consultancy team focusing on building financial inclusion through co-design, strategic research and capability building. Zara is a specialist in qualitative and quantitative research and evaluation with twenty years of experience in initiating, leading, and managing multiple projects across all levels of government in Australia and within the not-for-profit sector at peak body and agency levels. She has lectured at the University of Melbourne, RMIT, and Swinburne University of Technology in Australia. As an academic, consultant, and researcher she has written extensively in the grey literature on a range of topics including social enterprise.

Introduction to the *Research Handbook of Women's Entrepreneurship and Value Creation*

Shumaila Yousafzai, Colette Henry, Monique Boddington, Shandana Sheikh and Alain Fayolle

Entrepreneurship is a multi-faceted concept in which several factors, including the entrepreneurial *context*, the *individual entrepreneur*, the *entrepreneurial environment*, and the *entrepreneurial product or service*, combine to create the *outcomes* of the entrepreneurial process. Entrepreneurial outcomes have been mostly studied in terms of financial performance, wealth creation, firm survival, improvement in the quality of life (McMullen and Warnick, 2015), and promotion of economic growth in developed and developing economies and across industries (Audretsch et al., 2006; Baumol, 1986). Although evaluation of entrepreneurial activity in these terms is important, it often results in a one-sided analysis in which entrepreneurship is evaluated and appraised solely in monetary terms, without reference to its social impact (Zahra et al., 2009), that is, without mention of other kinds of value that come from it. Although, the focus on financial outcomes excludes social entrepreneurship, which is based primarily on fulfilling a community's unmet needs and creating social value. Nevertheless, restricting the discussion of non-monetary value creation in entrepreneurship to social entrepreneurs further limits the full scope of value created by all entrepreneurs, not just social entrepreneurs. It also limits the contribution of entrepreneurial activity that is initiated by disadvantaged and marginalized groups like women, ethnic minorities, the disabled, and youth (Welter, 2011), even though these groups often create significant value beyond financial value. Such value takes multiple forms and occurs at various levels, so it must be documented if the full contribution that entrepreneurs make to the economy and society is to be recognized.

This edited volume aims to present a collection of studies that would further explore, rethink, and recognize the value created through women's entrepreneurship and will co-create useful knowledge and expertise that can feed joint learning, innovative practices and evidence-based policy-making for successful women's entrepreneurship promotion and gender-just inclusive growth around the globe. Such studies would highlight the importance of women as agents of change for society and the economy and would have important implications for policy-making in that they would direct attention to and provide evidence for the positive contribution of women entrepreneurs to the economy, regardless of their businesses' size and formal status, thus, acknowledging women entrepreneurs' efforts and supporting their value-creation activities. Through these studies, we hope that the researchers would challenge the underperformance hypothesis associated with women entrepreneurs and present evidence that women do not underperform in their businesses but that they add value, even in constrained environments. The chapters that we seek to include in the edited volume may direct future researchers to shift the focus of research from questions like "what do entrepreneurs do?" to "how do they do it?" (in order to focus on the unique ways in which each woman entrepreneur creates value), and "for whom do they do it?" (in order to focus on the multiple value outcomes women entrepreneurs create and the beneficiaries of that value) (Zahra et al., 2009). Figure I.1 illustrates some examples of the multiplicity of value creation that this edited volume aims to explore in the context of women's entrepreneurship.

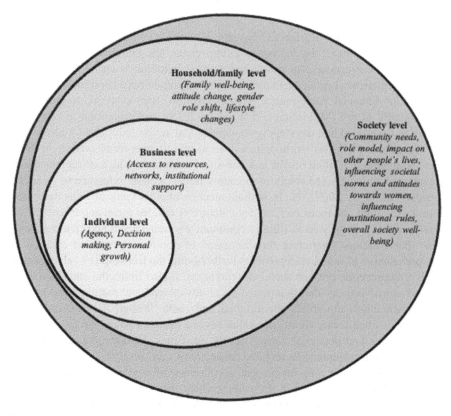

Source: Authors.

Figure I.1   *Multiple levels of value creation through women's entrepreneurial activity*

Although women entrepreneurs are often seen as the rising stars of the economy (Vossenberg, 2013) and the way forward (World Economic Forum, 2012), the disconnect between the performance of women-owned enterprises compared to those of their male counterparts still holds (Ahl, 2006; Marlow et al., 2008; Powell and Eddleston, 2008) largely because of an inequitable performance evaluation that disregards value-related outcomes beyond the financial that accrue at multiple levels and have a long-term impact on the *creators* (women entrepreneurs) of this value, as well as on the *recipients* who are affected by it. We acknowledge that it is difficult to define the multiple realms of value that result from women's entrepreneurial activity (WEA), as entrepreneurs and their contexts differ widely. Nevertheless, scholars have suggested that the extent to which the value from an entrepreneurial venture is created depends on the concept (i.e., the business idea), the resources available, and the *ability and the skills* of the entrepreneur to execute and implement the idea (Zahra et al., 2009). Therefore, we argue that not all entrepreneurs are cut out for or aspire to high growth and performance. While women entrepreneurs are often labelled *"underperformers"* in business for low growth and low success rates, and are, therefore, under-recognized in the sphere of value creation, these criteria are what society expects women to achieve, not necessarily what women themselves expect or want to achieve.

THE CHAPTERS IN THIS VOLUME

In response to the limitation in the current entrepreneurial literature regarding the full impact of and value creation through women's entrepreneurial activity, we seek to fill part of the resulting gap by inviting researchers to take a woman's perspective on value creation in entrepreneurship and explore the lived experiences of women entrepreneurs by documenting the value they create across various frontiers. We invited researchers to study performance and success from a woman's perspective and acknowledge that these women may not have high profit margins but may be satisfied with the balance between their businesses and personal lives; they may not have high-tech firms or a physical presence on the high street but may contribute to their families' and households' needs and wants. Hence, we asked the researchers to look beyond standard measures of performance and success and focus on what success and performance means to the woman entrepreneur. Each woman has her own story and offers her own unique value to add to her entrepreneurial environment. This edited volume called for opening the debate on women as creators of value in entrepreneurship and encourages researchers to advance this debate by exploring unconventional value outcomes in multiple contexts, business sectors, industries, and countries. This approach also called for challenging the "otherness" of women entrepreneurs as inferior, not fit for business, and underperforming.

This refocusing will help to cultivate a debate that emphasizes *social capital* as an *enabling resource, the social environment* as a *context*, and *social benefit* as an *outcome* of any type of entrepreneurial activity. Evaluating the outcome dimension with a social lens across various forms of entrepreneurship facilitates a multi-dimensional analysis of the growth and performance of women entrepreneurs' enterprises (Korsgaard and Anderson, 2011). This line of research has the potential to initiate a break from dominant methods of positivistic research to more exploratory ones that involve qualitative techniques that help to capture the real impact of entrepreneurship at multiple levels. Our goal is to co-create expertise that can feed joint learning, innovative practices and evidence-based policy-making for the gender-just promotion of women's entrepreneurship promotion and inclusive growth around the globe. In doing so, we highlight what influences and restrains the growth of women's entrepreneurship and offer useful insights into women's entrepreneurship as they apply to specific contexts.

In particular, contributions were sought from researchers in geographic regions that are not sufficiently represented in the women's entrepreneurship literature. We received chapters based on data from Afghanistan, Canada, Ethiopia, Guatemala, Honduras, India, Iran, Ireland, Kenya, Mexico, Nepal, Norway, Pakistan, Palestine, Saudi Arabia, South Africa, Sweden, Uganda, United Kingdom, USA and multi-country studies based on the Global Entrepreneurship Monitor (GEM) dataset. Collectively, these studies make a substantial contribution to the value creation literature through women's entrepreneurial activity, provide numerous insights and provoke fruitful directions for future research on the important role of the context in which women's entrepreneurial activity takes place.

Part I: Value Creation at the Individual Level

Despite the barriers faced by women and the constraints on their performance and growth in business, entrepreneurship may not only give women independence to follow their career choices but also empower them with control over their wealth, assets and decisions regarding this wealth, which can promote their personal growth and development and improve their overall well-being and quality of life (Beath et al., 2013; Haneef et al., 2014; Haugh and Talwar, 2014; Kantor, 2003). Value accumulated from increased agency at the individual level can contribute to elevating women's status in their entrepreneurial environment and to building positive self-perceptions among them.

In Part I we wish to represent and encourage broader engagement with the aspects of value creation at the individual level that are due to a women's engagement in entrepreneurial activity. This broader engagement will illustrate the diversity of thought that has yet to be applied to the ideas of value creation at the individual level. Amongst others, these aspects can include *enhanced agency, increased involvement in decision-making, and enriched personal growth and development*. Agency includes factors like management and control over family assets, mobility outside the home, involvement in household and family decisions, and investment- and property-related decisions (Schuler et al., 2010). Entrepreneurship and business ownership can provide women with increased agency and control over their lives, which can lead to empowerment (Kantor, 2003). Women's engagement in entrepreneurial activities and contributions towards household income can lead to increased involvement in decision-making regarding family, income and household matters (Haugh and Talwar, 2014) and it may increase her say in issues related to reproductive health, such as child spacing and fertility (Kabeer, 2001; Mayoux and Mackie, 2007), and decisions related to their children's education and marriage, particularly for female children. They may also have greater control in decisions regarding what is spent on food, housing, clothing, medicine and leisure activities (Beath et al., 2013).

Business ownership may also encourage women to fight for their rights and against injustices perpetrated against them. By owning and managing a business, women may gain in confidence and self-esteem, which positively influences their psychological and emotional well-being (Haugh and Talwar, 2014). Moreover, despite being limited in their opportunities and resource bases, women entrepreneurs may enhance their knowledge by learning to run the business and to deal with clients and suppliers and by equipping themselves with skills like marketing, financial, leadership, management and social skills. Improvement in all these aspects of life tends to elevate their status, leading to overall development and growth for women in general (Sahab et al., 2013). Beyond knowledge and skills, entrepreneurship may also result in growth in terms of the self-perception and confidence that may motivate women to develop their businesses despite the hostile entrepreneurial environment (Haugh and Talwar, 2014).

Development economists acknowledge that value creation through enterprising has a positive impact on development indicators that go beyond economic growth, in particular for women entrepreneurs (Duflo, 2012; Minniti and Naudé, 2010). Building on this notion, in **Chapter 1** *Atsede Tesfaye Hailemariam, Konjit Hailu Gudeta, Brigitte Kroon and Marloes van Engen* provide the narrative accounts of three women entrepreneurs in Addis Ababa, the capital city of Ethiopia, and highlight the challenges and opportunities women encounter as well as the values they create. They further explore the value that women entrepreneurs in Ethiopia create for their sense of self through their entrepreneurial activity within a constrained socio-economic environment. Specifically, their study gives an insight into how the women's entrepreneurial activities help in building capability to exercise agency, self-confidence, decision-making autonomy, well-being and personal growth and learning. Formal and informal support may strengthen the resilience of women entrepreneurs among which investing in education of girls and improving accessibility to financial loans. They further suggest that, initiatives aimed at nominating, navigating and changing constraining gender roles both for women and men may facilitate change and enhance social value creation.

In **Chapter 2** *Sylvia K. Gavigan, Thomas M. Cooney and Klavs Ciprikis*, following the research of Bruton et al. (2013) and Tobias et al. (2013), make a case to support the argument that women engage in entrepreneurship at the grassroots level to effectively generate individual value creation, overcome poverty and to enhance their societal and economic advancement. Taking the context of rural entrepreneurship in the Kiryandongo region of North-Western Uganda, they further suggest that as productive sources in business, rural female entrepreneurs are both direct and indirect leaders in their communities who pursue a diverse range of value creation targets to support their communities (Stephan and Pathak, 2016). In trying to understand the contribution of entrepreneurship training towards perceived emancipation and value creation at an individual level, this chapter demonstrates the importance of appropriate training as a catalyst in improving business knowledge and perceived emancipation when the women make their own decisions, when they are being independent and have freedom to start their own businesses, when they support their families, achieve equality and feel capable of taking ownership of their own businesses.

In **Chapter 3** *Jiska de Groot, Nthabiseng Mohlakoana, Abigail Knox, Debbie Sparks and Hans Bressers* remind us that while self-employment in the informal economy provides women with the independence and flexibility to balance domestic and business responsibilities, the income generated contributes to food, shelter and children's education, and many entrepreneurs express ambitions to grow their business (Fasoyiro, 2011; Knox et al. 2019). Yet, evaluations of the sector are often based only on the financial aspects of the enterprise, demonstrating the narrow conceptualization within which informal sector enterprises are assessed (Jones et al., 2017). They further argue that this approach is especially detrimental for female entrepreneurs because even though the sector is crucial for the livelihoods of many women, these informal enterprises are often inaccurately labelled as 'survivalist' enterprises that do not aspire to invest in business growth or hire staff. It is therefore often concluded that they add limited value to the economy, leading to development policies that remain fixated on monetary value creation and give priority to so-called growth-oriented enterprises. In doing so, they fail to recognize other forms of value-creation from informal entrepreneurship that extends beyond the financial gains of the enterprise. Examples of the non-monetary value added are empowerment processes and the numerous ways in which income generated through the enterprise flows back into the economy, resulting in positive social impacts, agency and self-worth, or meeting other unmet needs in society. By highlighting women's empowerment as creation of value in informal food enterprises, this chapter sets out to contribute to the evidence base, the multitude of ways in which value is created through women's entrepreneurship. Value creation, in this context refers to the success in financial and non-financial terms brought about by women's enterprises, as the value created for women by running an enterprise can encompass a range of aspects of their lives. This chapter focuses on South Africa and specifically considers the ways in which entrepreneurship in the informal sector functions as a driver of women's empowerment, proposing this as a way of creating individual value. The findings of this study show that in addition to providing a major source of income, significant additional value is created from women's entrepreneurship as their enterprises produce important empowerment benefits. These include increased capacity to make decisions, the freedom to spend income and determine one's own future, and the satisfaction and benefits that the enterprises bring to the many women who had significant reproductive responsibilities. Unlike traditional approaches to enterprise development which favour growth in firm size, profits and market penetration; this research shows that an alternative approach to development based on individual value creation linked to women's empowerment is worth pursuing.

Despite its recent economic success, India has a significant gender imbalance in entrepreneurship, underscoring the considerable odds against female entrepreneurial success in the country. Many Indian women, nonetheless, continue to take to entrepreneurship and create significant value for themselves. In an attempt to rebalance a male-centred and wealth, profit and economic growth focused scholarly discourse in entrepreneurship, in **Chapter 4** *Renuka Vyas* presents the narratives of individual-level value creation by four women entrepreneurs from different geographies and markets in India. These narratives shed light on the emancipatory power of entrepreneurship which sets free, constructs new meanings in lives, builds new futures and enhances the human agency of these individuals. They highlight how entrepreneurship, in conjunction with the value share focus of these women, sets in motion a value multiplier greatly benefitting their immediate families. They also show how entrepreneurship transforms these women into independent, assertive, evolved and empowered individuals. Entrepreneurship impacts them profoundly as it enhances their ability to look after their welfare as well as that of their family. Cleverly leveraging social media and positive testimonies of satisfied customers, these seemingly inconspicuous women, propelled by the power of entrepreneurship are slowly traversing their paths as independent, assertive, evolved and empowered individuals, leaving behind their unique female footprints in the Indian marketplace.

Part II: Value Creation at the Business Level

Beyond the value for the individual entrepreneur, a woman's engagement in the entrepreneurial activity can also add value to the business domain. The chapters included in Part II focus on factors such as access to resources, networks and institutional support that a female entrepreneur can accrue by being in business and gaining knowledge and experience with it.

Female entrepreneurs gain access to resources mainly by using their social networks to help identify opportunities in terms of new markets, customers, suppliers and processes that enhance value creation in business. By developing relationships with business and personal contacts, female entrepreneurs can build strong networks that can help them to serve new markets and customers. Networks can also be an integral source of financial capital for entrepreneurial women (Bruderl and Preisendörfer, 1998; Waldinger et al., 1990). Beyond social networks, human capital – the combination of education, experience and learning – can help female entrepreneurs to access resources like financing and markets. In economies where women have low levels of education and negligible experience in employment, the vicarious learning that is acquired when women gain information and knowledge from observing others, including other entrepreneurs (Santarelli and Tran, 2013; Shane, 2000), helps women sustain and develop their businesses. Learning by doing plays a significant role in enhancing entrepreneurs' intellectual development, adds to their human capital throughout the entrepreneurial process and helps them make sound decisions and take wise action in times of uncertainty (Malerba, 2007; Minniti and Bygrave, 2001; Schumpeter, 1934; Shane and Venkataraman, 2000). Therefore, even when women have limited access to resources, their human capital, knowledge base and social networks help them to obtain access to key resources for their businesses and so add value to their enterprises. Consequently, while an adequate resource base is a pre-requisite for entrepreneurship, the opposite may be true in the context of women's entrepreneurial activity, as women initiate an entrepreneurial idea from their homes, build, and use their networks and knowledge bases to access resources that help their businesses to grow and develop.

Women may also gain institutional support because of their entrepreneurial efforts, particularly their economic contributions through their business activities. Moreover, experience and reputation in business may help female entrepreneurs build contacts and gain access to institutional support. Differences in the context of entrepreneurial activity determine the extent of institutional access and support that women may be able to secure for their businesses. For example, women in developing countries may face strict barriers against accessing institutional support because of gendered institutions and bias in the distribution of resources among entrepreneurial actors. Moreover, the socio-cultural norms that prevail in the society may cause difficulties for women who operate within institutional voids by restricting entrepreneurial activity and, thus, the value-creation process.

In **Chapter 5** *Khizran Zehra, Leona Achtenhagen, Sadia Arshad, and Nadia Arshad* contribute to the literature on non-economic value creation by exploring micro firms founded by female entrepreneurs in the context of adversity. The authors highlight that despite the enormous effort that entrepreneurial endeavours entail for women in adverse contexts, entrepreneurship scholars frequently portray female entrepreneurs as underperforming – focusing mainly on economic growth rather than overall value creation (Marlow and McAdam, 2013). They further remind us that this strand of literature does not always consider the complexities and gender-specific challenges that women entrepreneurs face in founding and establishing businesses in contexts that are different to the mainstream western context predominant in entrepreneurship research (Amha and Ademassie, 2004). To understand the constrained economic performance of women entrepreneurs, in relation to their broader socio-economic contexts, the authors draw upon the experiences of three ethnic Hazara women entrepreneurs from Pakistan. They outline the non-economic value created by them through collaborative activities that are typically aimed at jointly improving the life situation of Hazara women. The women entrepreneurs studied in this research displayed different types of collaborations to start and grow their ventures. These collaborations were not just effective for the women's business activities but served as a synergistic mechanism from which the different stakeholders participating in the collaboration benefitted. Their informal ventures closely work with external stakeholders to manage the flow of resources and transform these resources into exchanges between customers and suppliers. They advance a view of collaborative value creation that is informal, dynamic and recognizes the importance of non-financial value creation (i.e., entrepreneurial readiness, informal training and skill transfer, resource transferability, and cultural narrative of resilience) through informal training, resources and social legitimacy in constrained contextual settings (Sarfraz, 2017).

In **Chapter 6** *Annie Roos* argues that research on entrepreneurship has a strong tendency to see value creation solely as an economic outcome, thus limiting how we envision entrepreneurship, and who is performing well, according to this standard. Women entrepreneurs almost always come out as second best in this comparison and are thus labelled as underperforming. She challenges the underperformance hypothesis surrounding women entrepreneurs by drawing upon the narratives of two women entrepreneurs from a rural Swedish community, whose experiences and successes are in direct juxtaposition with the familiar notion of the underperforming woman entrepreneur. Their stories allow us to see value created in processes that are usually neglected or missed in more conventional research and policy. Annie discusses two main observations: (1) On a business level, value accrued is used to create new value, and (2) that there is a circular flow between value adding and creating. Focusing on the business level means that the women entrepreneur interacts directly with her business, cultivating value through accumulating and creating a multiplicity of value. Focusing on both accruing and creating value, hence the process, becomes crucial in understanding how to foster further engagement with women in entrepreneurship and gender equality in regard to entrepreneurship. This cyclical relationship, when cultivating value at a business level, implies that a more holistic view of value and women entrepreneurship is needed to fully grasp the complexity of the phenomena. It highlights the fact that we can enhance value creation by focusing on accruing specific value. If the focus was solely on the value the women create, important links to how they accrued that value are missing. This chapter provides an excellent example of moving beyond the economic measures of entrepreneurship, through focusing on value as a process and not solely as an outcome.

In **Chapter 7** *Doaa Althalathini* sheds light on the experiences of women entrepreneurs in conflict zones by exploring their value creation through engaging in entrepreneurial activities. Violent conflict can intensify conservative gender ideologies and restrict women's mobility and freedom to engage in social, political, economic and enterprise activities (Bullough and Renko, 2017). Nevertheless, women could have the opportunity to participate in economic activities and break the traditional gender roles which could lead to changes in the gendered division of the labour market. This study uses in-depth narrative interviews to elicit detailed stories with three successful women entrepreneurs in Afghanistan and Palestine. It shows that while women in such a context face additional challenges aggravated by the conflict situation such as limited resources, societal constraints, larger domestic burdens and insecurity, nevertheless, these women entrepreneurs are resourceful and they look for new opportunities to start a business or keep making changes to their business when they face a bad situation or unexpected event. In doing so, they also create value in terms of access to resources and institutional support, which enables them to sustain their business despite the challenges. Acknowledging the success of those women provides a base of knowledge upon which policies can be designed to support women's 'safe' entrepreneurship. Raising awareness regarding the programs and social services available to women entrepreneurs is important to the growth of their businesses. However, and due to security concerns, women could face difficulties to improve their skills and access resources even though they have intention to start a business. This reflects the importance of understanding conflict-specific challenges that women experience and integrating a gender and conflict approach to program design.

Blended value creation occurs when businesses develop social and environmental value beyond financial value, benefitting society as well as the owners of the businesses. In **Chapter 8** *Nadeera Ranabahu and Mary Barrett* analyse narratives collected from three women entrepreneurs in rural Sri Lanka who used microfinance loans to start and develop their ventures. The results demonstrate that the women created not only economic wealth but important social-economic and economic–environmental outcomes. They also created personal value beyond financial outcomes, improved their business processes, and created benefits for their families, employees and the wider society. While all three women valued business viability and aspired to run profitable businesses, they also clearly wanted to progress beyond survival. Training activities, although not directly linked to profit, enhanced individual skills which were later used to modify business methods. For example, they learnt to negotiate and established long-term partnerships, enabling them to better manage their raw materials and supply of finished product. They increased and diversified their customer base by attending trade exhibitions. Nadeera and Mary were surprised to see the extent to which these women were alert to social or environmental outcomes and the need to manage environmental resources responsibly (Stewardship, Eco-efficiency). For example, the entrepreneurs were concerned about the reliability of their business associations and were committed to maintaining product quality and standards. They also strived to create social legitimacy by participating in local small business association meetings, learning from and exchanging ideas with other business people. All three wanted to ensure the longevity of their businesses (sustainability). They acquired assets, hired employees, found new markets, and created new products. The authors conclude that a blended value lens produces insights into outcomes often overlooked in women-owned businesses. They suggest using entrepreneurial women's perceptions about the non-economic impacts their businesses create, such as increased personal agency and higher levels of human capital in the community, to create ways of measuring blended value. Measuring these outcomes more precisely, consistently and creatively would help public policy makers understand the true value of women entrepreneurship.

Developing countries have long focused on providing specific support to enhance women's economic development through entrepreneurship, yet this is relatively new in the Australian context. In **Chapter 9** *Zara Lasater, Vinita Godinho, Robyn Eversole and Naomi Birdthistle* explore how, in Australia, non-traditional actors in the business support ecosystem are designing female-centric supports to empower latent entrepreneurs to self-realize as entrepreneurs, and, in so doing, to recognize the business value they generate. They remind us that the emerging scholarship exploring holistic or "multi-dimensional" business level value creation instead of the more restrictive notions of economic growth and financial measures of success challenges gendered assumptions and perceptions about women entrepreneurs as underperforming. In doing so, these alternative narratives of entrepreneurial success are exploring business level value created by women entrepreneurs within both developed and developing economies. In this chapter, the authors focus on women who are emerging, but not yet visible or self-identifying as entrepreneurs. They are not necessarily "reluctant" entrepreneurs; rather, their entrepreneurship is "latent". This study posits that "latent entrepreneurs" are present as entrepreneurs, but still largely invisible due to the part-time or informal nature of their entrepreneurial activities, their positioning at the margins of business support ecosystems, and their reluctance to self-identify as entrepreneurs. A grounded theory approach reveals that reframing business level value creation as social value creation is central to this actualization process, supported by three conditions: (1) Female-centric ecosystems best facilitate women entrepreneurs' access to resources, networks, and institutional support; (2) The personal knowledge and experience gained by women when supported over their business journey, empowers them to proactively build their own capabilities and help others; and (3) Being part of a "tribe" enables women to create social and economic value. The narratives reported in this study reveal a "bubbling up" of emergent female-centric ecosystems of support for "latent" women entrepreneurs in Australia, particularly those from disadvantaged and marginalized backgrounds. These ecosystems are designed to empower latent entrepreneurs to self-realize as entrepreneurs.

The public transport sector forms a large part of Kenya's informal economy in which most women work. Being a female worker in Kenya's public transport sector is challenging and it takes great resilience and persistence for the women to remain in the sector. In most cases, negative perceptions regarding women's entrance in the male dominated transport sector persist. Nevertheless, the male dominated sector is beginning to open doors for women whose entry into the sector is unearthing women's abilities. In **Chapter 10** *Anne Kamau and Winnie V. Mitullah* provide a glimpse of women's value creation drawing from narratives of 10 women workers in the public transport sector in Kenya. The chapter explores the value that women create in public transport enterprises as own-account operators or employees. Despite limited numbers and poor working conditions, women have exploited opportunities in the sector to earn their livelihoods and are creating value at individual, business, household and societal levels. The salient presence of women workers in the transport sector is beginning to change the character of the sector and the way women are perceived in public space. Overall, women's resilient participation in the sector is challenging hegemonic notions of male dominance and societal perceptions about women's work in the public sphere and in public transport. This is driven by the fact that women are incrementally building their agency through alliances and leveraging other opportunities for upward mobility. Apart from earning income for their households, their decision-making roles are improving through participation in associational life and engagement with external actors, including unions, workers' federations and capacity-building NGOs. These external engagements advance their image as role models and impact on other women and society at large, thereby changing the preconceived patriarchal conception of women's work. This is also increasing women's visibility in the public sphere. These connections are extending women's networks which are relevant for advancing their position not only in the transport sector but also in other spheres of life. They are able to save, leverage resources and invest in transport business, and support the survival of public transport businesses as workers. In their households they are taking care of their families, supplementing household income and changing the patriarchal conception of female gender.

Part III: Value Creation at the Household and Family Level

Value creation at the household and family level is a critical factor in explaining women's entrepreneurial development and social change. In Part III, the contributors present narrative and examples where women's engagement in entrepreneurial activities has led to significant changes in the domain of household dynamics. The positive impact of increased income from entrepreneurial activity on the household members can improve overall well-being and quality of life and improve their attitudes towards women so they are viewed as independent and entrepreneurial (Dsizi and Obeng, 2013; Haugh and Talwar, 2014; Kabeer, 2001). A woman's engagement in entrepreneurial activity may also have a positive influence on attitudes and gender roles in the household. Scholars have discussed the spill-over effects of work on family (Greenhaus and Powell, 2006), including the respect for participation in paid work (Hammer et al., 2002), improvement in women's status, sharing of domestic responsibilities, and reduced instances of genital mutilation, domestic violence and abuse, polygamy and early marriages. According to resource theory (Blood and Wolfe, 1960), access to resources like education and employment tend to be good predictors of women's participation in decision-making. Another area in which women's engagement in entrepreneurial activities can potentially add value is in women's decision-making role in the household (which we also discussed at the individual level of value creation), for example decisions related to the number of children to have, child spacing, and the use of contraception and abortion and decisions related to the children's education, choice of school and selection and timing of children's marriages (Haneef et al., 2014; Haugh and Talwar, 2014).

Nascent entrepreneurs develop their entrepreneurial identity, as part of the process of becoming entrepreneurs, through social interaction with their environments. As identity forms the basis of action, the identity of the entrepreneur provides implications for strategies and value created by new firms. In **Chapter 11** *Sanaa Talha and Gry Agnete Alsos* examine how immigrant women entrepreneurs develop their initial entrepreneurial identities. Building upon the founder's identities framework (Fauchart and Gruber, 2011), they examine social motivations, self-assessment measures, and the frame of reference for immigrant women entrepreneurs. They conclude that immigrant women only partly relate to identity types in this framework. Their identities are more strongly linked to their concerns for their families, and they seldom focus on economic self-interest. Furthermore, many immigrant women are motivated by the needs of their ethnic community or detected problems in society related to immigrants or other disadvantaged groups. Based on this group of entrepreneurs, they present a refined framework to include self-/family-focused entrepreneurs, immigrant communitarians, and social missionaries.

Responding to this handbook call, in **Chapter 12** *Milka Kwiatek and Maria Villares-Varela* address the reconceptualization of value by giving voice to UK-based migrant women entrepreneurs. They discuss how the growing attention to the contribution that migrants make tends to be slanted towards their financial return, while overlooking their influence on job creation, cushioning competition with native workers, and setting role models for migrant communities. They further point out how the gender-blindness of the field concealed patriarchal domination sustaining the ethnic economy. Drawing on four in-depth biographical narratives and a selection of participants' produced photographs, this study provides an academic platform for migrant women entrepreneurs to express their experiences of entrepreneurship and value creation. This chapter presents the voices of migrant women entrepreneurs in the UK in relation to the impact of their ventures on creating a meaningful input beyond the economic dividend. Although migrant businesses are generally characterized by being of small size and located in what is considered "low low value" activities, the authors argue that these assumptions are based on a circumscribed conceptualization of value creation. Narratives of the interviewees and their visual production show how becoming a businesswoman in the ethnic economy can be seen as a means of leadership in the community, solidarity with other women entrepreneurs and generating value beyond the economic dividend for both British society and countries of origin, in the realms of production and reproduction.

The final chapter in this section is contributed by *Vahid Makizadeh, Shumaila Yousafzai, Siavash Aein Jamshid and Marzieh Nasiri*. They propose that despite institutional constraints female entrepreneurs in Iran experience their entrepreneurial activities as a source of value for themselves and other stakeholders, especially their family. Drawing upon the narrative reports of female entrepreneurs in Bandarabbas, the capital city of Hormozgan province in the south of Iran, Based on the notion that the authors put forward the argument that beyond economic values, female entrepreneurs in Iran create immense values for the family including positive intra-family dynamics, the positive impact of female income on the family members, and change of attitudes towards females, who may now be perceived as an agent of change. The authors also suggest that ethics of care and enacting a supportive role for all family members in females can enhance desired family values such as respect, love, and empathy. In other words, these female entrepreneurs' traits create a favourable family atmosphere around female entrepreneurs that finally lead to deeper positive emotions in the family.

Part IV: Value Creation at the Societal Level

Female entrepreneurs can become agents of social change by promoting the society's overall development and growth through entrepreneurship. Social outcomes in this regard pertain to local community development through increased employment for the local population (Birch, 1979; Haugh, 2006) and providing and increasing the choice of goods and services that meet the community's needs. In societies with strict religious and traditional norms that restrict a woman's mobility outside the home, a female-based enterprise like a health service may be a significant source of services to other women in the community, thus contributing to value creation at the community level.

The impact of women's entrepreneurship at the societal level has been discussed in several research domains, including those of economic vitality, stability and the availability of goods and services. In terms of social impact, the society's security, values, attitudes, lifestyles and norms may be influenced. Furthermore, addition of value in terms of contributing to the community's overall development and growth may include increased well-being, raising the quality of life, creating employment, promoting gender equality and improving satisfaction with life (Haugh and Talwar, 2014; Nicholls, 2009; Welter and Xheneti, 2015; Zahra and Wright, 2015). Women's entrepreneurial activity can also change the perceptions of and attitudes towards women in a society, resulting in greater support for female entrepreneurs. These changes include influencing gender norms and traditions, enhancing the status of and respect for women in the society, and inculcating positive motivation to become entrepreneurs and increase their independence in others through role models (Haugh and Talwar, 2014; Mayoux and Mackie, 2007).

In the presence of social constraints on women in a society, entrepreneurship can bring about social change by empowering women to fight for their rights and to change gendered assumptions about women. Through entrepreneurial efforts, women can show that they can be agents for social change and justify their increased freedom and mobility. They may exercise agency, have control over their life decisions and overcome societal resistance to pursue their goals in their personal and professional lives. Moreover, women in business can increase society's respect and recognition of women (Haugh and Talwar, 2014). Similarly, women may influence gendered institutions in their entrepreneurial environments because of their entrepreneurial efforts and contributions to value in their societies. In this regard, women may gain access to entrepreneurial resources from institutions that were once available only to male entrepreneurs. Being in business can also help women gain knowledge about the ways of doing business, the rules and regulations regarding business activity in various markets and strategies with which to overcome institutional voids. Entrepreneurship empowers women and enables them to overcome injustices that may hamper business performance and affect their personal lives (Kabeer, 2001; Mayoux and Mackie, 2007; Tankard and Paluck, 2016; Zahra and Wright, 2015).

There has been a great deal written and said about the barriers and challenges that Arab women entrepreneurs face. However, studies that attempt to explore and understand the importance of women entrepreneurs as agents of change in Arab society, including how they deliver and support value-creation activities, are noticeably scarce. In **Chapter 14** *Hayfaa Tlaiss* explores the unique ways in which Saudi Arabian women entrepreneurs create value within a constrained, patriarchal society. In doing so, she challenges mainstream studies that focus only on obstacles. Instead, she celebrates Arab women's agency and acknowledges their success as value creators. Her findings demonstrate how entrepreneurial success is a subjective concept within which entrepreneurs have their own understanding and conceptualizations of what success means to them. The women in this study assessed their entrepreneurial success from within broader perspectives, whereby they factored in their conceptualizations of value creation at the societal level. They portrayed personal agency and capitalized on a feminist perspective to Islamic teachings in order to construct their own entrepreneurial identity within a conservative, masculine context rather than accepting patriarchal interpretations. These women negotiated their entrepreneurial choices and navigated through religious and patriarchal societal structures and constraints. In doing so, they created value at the societal level through being role models for young women and agents for change in Saudi society. Hence, Hayfaa proposes that Arab women, even those operating within a dominant masculine patriarchy, have agency and the ability to emancipate themselves and give their entrepreneurial ventures and activities an alternative meaning that is based on value creation and success.

Research has consistently shown that the informal economy provides alternative means to livelihoods and reduces poverty, offers a creative and transitional space to test capability, and is a vehicle for social mobility amongst the urban poor (Adom and Williams, 2012; Gough et al., 2003; Langevang and Gough, 2012; Timilsina, 2011). In **Chapter 15** *Mirela Xheneti and Shova Thapa Karki* explore how informal women entrepreneurs in a developing country context create value through nurturing social relations in their communities. Focusing on the rich narratives of three women entrepreneurs in three cities in Nepal, they illustrate the richness of life experiences and the economic and socio-cultural characteristics with implications for societal value creation. Particularly, they highlight three different ways through which women entrepreneurs are creating value – by changing perceptions about women's work, supporting other women in the community by providing employment opportunities, and acting as role models in their communities. By focusing on a narrative approach, the authors are able to make visible the processes through which these different societal value outcomes were achieved. A processual view of value creation allows to understand how women's agency develops over time together with the constraints and enablers of this agency.

Along the lines of the theme of this volume, in **Chapter 16** *Ruta Aidis* highlights the important economic and social contribution made by female entrepreneurial activities. Ruta points out that previous studies often focus on solo women entrepreneurs and the benefits accrued to them and their communities. In her chapter, she expands on the blended value conceptual framework and explores the significant non-financial value that is created by women entrepreneurs for women as their employees or as women workers. The six women entrepreneurs, all small and medium-size enterprise owners profiled in this chapter, operate in diverse sectors and country contexts in the Americas and exemplify a blended value approach highlighting a broader range of value creation through entrepreneurship beyond economic gains. All show that added value for women (as employees and workers) can be compatible with successful business development. Ruta's findings support the female oriented value system of the ethics of care that focuses on the interconnectedness among parties involved and nurturing behaviour. The issues addressed in each of the six case studies of women entrepreneurs operating in the Americas vary, ranging from specific safety needs for women workers and supporting working mothers re-entering the workforce to providing an inclusive business model that focuses on "quality of life" and gender equity in male-dominated sectors. Yet an overarching commonality in these case studies is the commitment to providing added value as part of their everyday business operations. They are all examples of a blended values approach to entrepreneurship and their added value activities are related to the ethics of care, a nurturing behaviour towards other women, which supports the notion of a female oriented value system introduced by Gilligan (1982). Ruta suggests that working together with the media, governments should increase awareness and visibility of the instrumental role SMEs play in providing additional value to women workers as a strategy to incentivize additional SMEs to adopt similar practices.

In the unique context of South Africa, where entrepreneurs see opportunity in social needs spawned by apartheid, *Ethné Swartz, Caren Scheepers and Frances Amatucci* in **Chapter 17** contribute to the discussion on value creation by extending our understanding on how women entrepreneurs in South Africa create value at the societal level and how the South African political and historical context influences this value creation. Using illustrative case studies of four employer firms across a range of industries, they discuss how social value creation began with women exerting influence on the content of the constitution that enshrines legal and property rights for women. The authors further explore how these women create new institutional forms by seizing on regulatory system changes to build investment companies for financial inclusion. This mindset is vital to how "shared value" is perceived in countries undergoing fundamental transformations. At the cognitive and the normative levels, these female entrepreneurs demonstrate the agency and choice required to create opportunities for previously disadvantaged groups by offering jobs in hospitality, digital services, education, and facilities management. They have also influenced the normative system by providing new role models and setting new gender role expectations through scaling and growing companies. Overall, this chapter offers a deeper understanding of the human agency contribution of women and points to a heightened awareness of women's role in democratic change in South Africa. The authors have successfully managed to demonstrate how South Africa's political and historical context created the environment for the emergence of these women-founded enterprises that contribute to a multiplier effect of social value creation. Government and policy makers should note the important role of women entrepreneurs, and offer encouragement and recognition for their efforts, and where appropriate, funding to assist in scaling their services.

For more than three decades, studies on women's entrepreneurship have focused on cisgender heterosexual male and female entrepreneurs who act within narrowly gendered spaces (Al-Dajani et al., 2015; Marlow and Martinez Dy, 2018). Thus, the call by mainstream scholars for equality between men and women in entrepreneurial spaces has focused on the conventional binary of the two genders at the expense of others. Others are considered to be an "out-group" of gender identities, such as gay, lesbian, transgender, asexual, intersex, and queer – all of which are quite often excluded from mainstream visibility in discussions of gender and entrepreneurship (Marlow and Martinez Dy, 2018). In **Chapter 18**, *Roshni Narendran* highlights the need to go beyond the socially accepted binary sexes when considering female entrepreneurship. In culturally rich countries like India, the transgender community faces barriers which prevent them from breaking free from the socially assigned roles for men and women. Even though India has a long history with the transgender community, there are still reports of abuse. In this chapter, Roshni shares insights into two transgender women entrepreneurs in South India who create social value to help others who, despite the bullying and discrimination against their nonconforming gender and sexual identities, have created successful enterprises in South India and provided platforms to fight against discrimination, showcase their talent, and develop skill sets, all of which help to bring the transgender community into the mainstream. This chapter examines the process by which they identified opportunities through witnessing and experiencing harassment and shows how this provided them with knowledge and access to stakeholders to create social value for others in the community. It shows how disclosing their gender identity gave them an opportunity to build resilience to create and share value with other members of the community. Members of the transgender community face many problems; however, it is important to understand how such barriers contribute to their resilience and the creation of social value for other members of the community. This is one of the few works within the scholarship on female entrepreneurship that moves beyond the mainstream studies of male and female entrepreneurs.

As discussed in previous chapters, value creation is central to any discussion on entrepreneurship. For the most part these discussions focused on the potential economic impact, particularly job creation, innovation and new business development. The emergence of research in the area of female entrepreneurship in the 1980s suggests that any discussion on value creation needs to move beyond this traditional economic model to include a broader societal value creation approach. The emergence of the Millennial generation has reignited the debate on value creation and entrepreneurship, as this new generation of young and technologically savvy individuals have a stronger motivation towards social responsibility and making an impact on the world. In **Chapter 19** *Angela Hamouda, Kate Johnston and Rebecca Nevins* provide new insights into this new cohort of entrepreneurs and the implications for the development of appropriate training and supports. The authors envisage that this new wave of entrepreneurs are challenging our typical view of entrepreneurs and in turn are calling into question the supports needed to encourage growth among this cohort.

In **Chapter 20** *Hans Lundberg* proposes to reconceptualize the idea of social value creation as social constraint alleviation. Hans refers to social as the limitations of a system that keep it from attaining its goal, system refers to systems consisting of people (i.e., a specific social stratum) and social constraint alleviation is based on the distinction between organizations that bypass or exploit a social constraint and organizations that absorb it. Hans argues that this distinction is fundamental, as according to Sinkovics et al. (2015, p. 341), organizations "that design their business models in such a way that their day-to-day operations absorb a social constraint [...] achieve a significant development impact on the communities in which they are embedded". His second main argument is that it is not enough to consider only the internal system of an organization and its stakeholders; equally needed is to be able to measure, estimate, analyze and compare social value creation on societal level. Following a case study approach, Hans focuses on data from an under-represented geographical context (Mexico) and highlights the importance of women entrepreneurs as social value creators with high societal impact. The findings highlight that women entrepreneurs generate value via leadership traits *normally* assigned to women (i.e., dialogical, relational, relating, authentic, caring). It further provides insight into the art of complexity reduction via management of paradoxes by women entrepreneurs. Hans concludes that *social value is something tangible emanating out of concrete practices*, rather than an abstraction or "something fluffy".

Conflict destroys infrastructure, damages the social fabric, and drives down socio-economic strength of individuals. In the context of post-conflict countries, entrepreneurship seems to be the best option for countries to tie their hopes for accelerated economic development In **Chapter 21** *Musarrat Jabeen and Shandana Sheikh* investigate the experiences of women entrepreneurs in a post-conflict development context by exploring their value creation at the individual and society level through the narrative accounts of two women entrepreneurs in Swat, Pakistan. The authors suggest that women entrepreneurs create value by realizing enhanced entrepreneurial intentions, entrepreneurial skills and experiencing greater recognition in the community as an entrepreneur by virtue of their skills and capability. The women entrepreneurs moved their businesses to counter anti-women empowerment militant organizations. The results of this research identify women entrepreneurs as a significant source of value creation in the under-researched contexts of post conflict development and militancy. Accordingly, it highlights the knowledge on entrepreneurship in post conflict development context; so that the state and society can build sustainable peace based on women entrepreneurship.

MOVING FORWARD

The process of value creation depends on the environment in which it is created (Zahra et al., 2009). While some policies support women in business, most are targeted at high-growth and profit-oriented businesses (Aslund and Bäckström, 2015) and ignore the micro-women entrepreneurs who may not be high-profit-oriented but may be important contributors of social value. Concluding the discussion from the previous sections, the chapters presented in this edited volume present the case that the contexts in which entrepreneurs operate present them with unique challenges, so an entrepreneur's performance should be judged from a broad environmental perspective. Knowledge of the context helps to define a need or entrepreneurial idea that can result in an outcome of value. More important, legitimization of value is a key aspect in it being validated across the public sphere, for all concerned agents. Authorization of value through women's entrepreneurial activity is a key to its creation and facilitation. Such authorization entails a double responsibility: to legitimize women entrepreneurs, such as those in the informal economy and micro businesses, and to legitimize the multiple aspects of value that result from such activity. Efforts are required across a variety of frontiers to achieve this goal. For example, governments can play an active role in validating, recognizing and appreciating the value outcomes of women entrepreneurs in creating public value. As for the business sector, it can support women by providing support services, including business skills, training and financing. The non-profit sector and the community can also play an active role in legitimizing the value of women entrepreneurs. Through their businesses, women meet the needs of their communities and add value to it, so appreciation of women's entrepreneurial efforts by fellow community members, citizens, and household and family members can encourage women to become more entrepreneurial.

CLOSING REMARKS

We extend a special thanks to Edward Elgar and its staff, who have been most helpful throughout this entire process. We also warmly thank all of the authors who submitted their manuscripts for consideration for this book. They showed their desire to share their knowledge and experience with the book's readers and a willingness to present their research and their views for possible challenge by their peers. We also thank the reviewers, who provided excellent independent and incisive consideration of the anonymous submissions.

We hope that this compendium of chapters and themes stimulates and contributes to the ongoing debate surrounding the contextual embeddedness of women-owned enterprises. The chapters in this book can help to fill some gaps in what we know while stimulating further thought and action.

REFERENCES

Adom, K. and Williams, C.C. (2012). Evaluating the motives of informal entrepreneurs in Koforidua, Ghana. *Journal of Developmental Entrepreneurship*, Vol 17(1), p. 1250005.

Ahl, H. (2006). Why research on women entrepreneurs needs new directions. *Entrepreneurship Theory and Practice*. Vol 30(5), pp. 595–621. doi:10.1111/j.1540-6520.2006.00138.x.

Al-Dajani, H., Carter, S., Shaw, E. and Marlow, S. (2015). Entrepreneurship among the displaced and dispossessed: Exploring the limits of emancipatory entrepreneuring. *British Journal of Management*, Vol 26(4), pp. 713–730.

Amha, W. and Ademassie, A. (2004). Rural financial intermediation program and its role in strengthening the rural financial system in Ethiopia. *Journal of Microfinance Development Review*, Vol 3(2), 230–365.

Aslund, A. and Bäckström, I. (2015). Creation of value to society – a process map of the societal entrepreneurship area. *Total Quality Management & Business Excellence*, Vol 26, pp. 385–399.

Audretsch, D.B., Keilbach, M.C. and Lehmann, E.E. (2006). *Entrepreneurship and Economic Growth*. New York: Oxford University Press.

Baumol, W.J. (1986). Entrepreneurship: Productive, unproductive, and destructive. *Journal of Business Venturing*, Vol 11(1), pp. 3–22.

Beath, A. Christia, F. and Enikolopov, R. (2013). Empowering women through development aid: Evidence from a field experiment in Afghanistan. *American Political Science Review*, Vol 107(3), pp. 540–557.

Birch, D.G. (1979). *The Job Generation Process*. Cambridge, MA: MIT Program on Neighborhood and Regional Change.

Blood, R.O. and Wolfe, D.M. (1960). *Husbands and Wives*. New York: Free Press.

Bruderl, J. and Preisendörfer, P. (1998). Network support and the success of newly founded businesses. *Small Business Economics*, Vol 19, pp. 213–225.

Bruton, G.D., Ketchen Jr, D.J. and Ireland, R.D. (2013). Entrepreneurship as a solution to poverty. *Journal of Business Venturing*, Vol 28, pp. 683–689.

Bullough, A. and Renko, M. (2017). A different frame of reference: Entrepreneurship and gender differences in the perception of danger. *Academy of Management Discoveries*, Vol 3(1), pp. 21–41.

Dsizi, S. and Obeng, F. (2013). Microfinance and the socio-economic wellbeing of women entrepreneurs in Ghana. *International Journal of Business and Social Research*, Vol 3(11), pp. 45–62.

Duflo, E. (2012). Women empowerment and economic development. *Journal of Economic Literature*, Vol 50(4), pp. 1051–1079.

Fasoyiro, S.B. (2011). Assessment of hazards in local soy-cheese processing: Implications on health and environment in Oyo state, Nigeria. *WIT Transactions on Ecology and the Environment*, Vol 152, pp. 37–44.

Fauchart, E. and Gruber, M. (2011). Darwinians, communitarians, and missionaries: The role of founder identity in entrepreneurship. *Academy of Management Journal*, Vol 54 (5), pp. 935–957.

Gilligan, C. (1982). *In a Different Voice*. Cambridge, MA: Harvard University Press.

Gough, K.V., Tipple, G. and Napier, M. (2003). Making a living in African cities: The role of home-based enterprises in Accra and Pretoria. *International Planning Studies*, Vol 8(4), pp. 253–277.

Greenhaus, J.H. and Powell, G.N. (2006). When work and family are allies: A theory of work–family enrichment. *Academy of Management Review*, Vol 31(1), pp. 72–92.

Hammer, L.B., Cullen, J.C., Caubet, S., Johnson, J., Neal, M.B. and Sinclair, R.R. (2002). *The Effects of Work–Family Fit on Depression: A Longitudinal Study*. Paper presented at the 17th Annual Meeting of SIOP, Toronto.

Haneef, C., Pritchard, M., Hannan, M., Kenward, S., Rahman, M. and Alam, Z. (2014). *Women as entrepreneurs: The impact of having an independent income on women's empowerment*. http://www.enterprise-development.org/wp-content/uploads/Women-as-Ent repreneurs_The-impact-of-having-an-independent-income-on-womens-emp owerment_August-2014.pdf. Accessed on 20 February 2020.

Haugh, H. (2006). Social enterprise. Beyond economic outcomes and individual returns. In Mair, J., Robinson, J., and Hockerts, K. (eds), *Social Entrepreneurship*. New York: Palgrave Macmillan, pp. 180–205.

Haugh, H.M. and Talwar, A. (2014). linking social entrepreneurship and social change: The mediating role of empowerment. *Journal of Business Ethics*, pp 1–16.

Jones, P., Jones, A. and Williams-Burnett, N. (2017). Let's get physical: Stories of entrepreneurial activity from sports coaches/instructors. *International Journal of Entrepreneurship and Innovation*, Vol 18(4), pp. 219–230.

Kabeer, N. (2001). Conflicts over credit: Re-evaluating the empowerment potential of loans to women in rural Bangladesh. *World Development*, Vol 29(1), pp. 63–84.

Kantor, P. (2003). Women's empowerment through home-based work: Evidence from India. *Development and Change.* Vol 34(3), pp. 425–445.

Knox, A.J., Bressers, H., Mohlakoana, N. and De Groot, J. (2019). Aspirations to grow: When micro- and informal enterprises in the street food sector speak for themselves. *Journal of Global Entrepreneurship Research*, Vol 9(1), p. 38.

Korsgaard, S. and Anderson, A.R. (2011). Enacting entrepreneurship as social value creation. *International Small Business Journal*, Vol 29(2), pp. 135–151.

Langevang, T. and Gough, K.V. (2012). Diverging pathways: Young female employment and entrepreneurship in sub-Saharan Africa. *The Geographical Journal*, Vol 178(3), pp. 242–252.

Malerba, F. (2007). Innovation and the dynamics and evolution of industries: Progress and challenges. *International Journal of Industrial Organization*, Vol 25, pp. 675–699.

Marlow, S., Carter, S. and Shaw, E. (2008). Constructing female entrepreneurship policy in the UK: Is the US a relevant benchmark? *Environment and Planning C: Government and Policy*, Vol 26(2), pp. 335–351.

Marlow, S. and Martinez Dy, A. (2018). Annual review article: Is it time to rethink the gender agenda in entrepreneurship research? *International Small Business Journal*, Vol 36(1), pp. 3–22.

Marlow, S. and McAdam, M. (2013). Gender and entrepreneurship: Advancing debate and challenging myths; exploring the mystery of the under-performing female entrepreneur. *International Journal of Entrepreneurial Behavior & Research*, Vol 19(1), pp. 114–124. https://doi.org/10.1108/13552551311299288.

Mayoux, L. and Mackie, G. (2007). *Guide to gender integration in value chain development, "making the strongest links"*. International Labour Organization. http://www.ilo.org/wcmsp5/groups/public/@ed_emp/@emp_ent/documents/instructionalmaterial/wcms_106538.pdf. Accessed on 19 August 2020.

McMullen, J.S. and Warnick, B. (2015). The downside of blended value and hybrid organizing. *Journal of Management Studies*, Vol 53(4), pp. 630–662.

Minniti, M. and Bygrave, W. (2001). A dynamic model of entrepreneurial learning. *Entrepreneurship Theory and Practice*, Vol 25, pp. 5–16.

Minniti, M. and Naudé, W. (2010). What do we know about the patterns and determinants of female entrepreneurship across countries? *European Journal of Development Research*, Vol 22, 277–293.

Nicholls, A. (2009). We do good things, don't we? Blended value accounting in social entrepreneurship. *Accounting, Organizations and Society*, Vol 34(6), pp. 755–769.

Powell, G.N. and Eddleston, K.A. (2008). The paradox of the contented female business owner. *Journal of Vocational Behavior*, Vol 73(1), pp. 24–36.

Sahab, S., Thakur, G. and Gupta, P.C. (2013). A case study on empowerment of rural women through micro entrepreneurship development. *Journal of Business Management*, Vol 9(6), pp. 123–126.

Santarelli, E. and Tran, H.T. (2013). Growth of incumbent firms and entrepreneurship in Vietnam. *University of Bologna – Department of Economics Working Paper* # 785.

Sarfraz, H. (2017). A restaurant in Quetta's Hazara Town is by women, for women, *The Express Tribune*, 13 November 2017, https://tribune.com.pk/story/1534555/1-a-restaurant-in-hazara-town-is-for-women-by-women/. Accessed on 13 December 2019.

Schuler, S.R., Islam, F. and Rottach, E. (2010). Women's empowerment revisited: A case study from Bangladesh. *Development in Practice*, Vol 20(7), pp. 840–854.

Schumpeter, J.A. (1934). *The Theory of Economic Development: An Inquiry into Profits, Capital Credit, Interest and the Business Cycle*. Cambridge, MA: Harvard University Press.

Shane, S. (2000). Prior knowledge and the discovery of entrepreneurial opportunities. *Organization Science*, Vol 11(4), pp. 448–469.

Shane, S. and Venkataraman, S. (2000). The promise of entrepreneurship as a field of research. *Academy of Management Review*, Vol 25(1), pp. 217–226.

Sinkovics, N., Sinkovics, R.R., Hoque, S.F. and Czaban, L. (2015). A reconceptualisation of social value creation as social constraint alleviation. *Critical Perspectives on International Business*, 11 (3/4), 340–363.

Stephan, U. and Pathak, S. (2016). Beyond cultural values? Cultural leadership ideals and entrepreneurship. *Journal of Business Venturing*, Vol 31(5), pp. 505–523.

Tankard, M.E. and Paluck, E.L. (2016). Norm perception as a vehicle for social change. *Social Issues and Policy Review*, Vol 10(1), pp. 181–211.

Timilsina, K.P. (2011). An urban informal economy: Livelihood opportunity to poor challenges for urban governance. *Global Journal of Human Social Science*, Vol 11(2), 25–31.

Tobias, J.M., Mair, J. and Barbosa-Leiker, C. (2013). Toward a theory of transformative entrepreneuring: Poverty reduction and conflict resolution in Rwanda's entrepreneurial coffee sector. *Journal of Business Venturing*, Vol 28(6), pp. 728–742.

Vossenberg, S. (2013). Women entrepreneurship promotion in developing countries: *What explains the gender gap in entrepreneurship and how to close it?* file:///Users/shandanasheikh/Downloads/MSM-WP2013-08%20(7).pdf. Accessed on 5 April 2020.

Waldinger, R.D., Aldrich, H. and Ward, R. (1990). *Ethnic Entrepreneurs: Immigrant Business in Industrial Societies*. Newbury Park, CA: Sage.

Welter, F. (2011). Contextualizing entrepreneurship – conceptual challenges and ways forward. *Entrepreneurship Theory and Practice*, Vol 35(1), pp. 165–184.

Welter, F. and Xheneti, M. (2015). Value for whom? Exploring the value of informal entrepreneurial activities in post-socialist contexts. *Exploring Criminal and Illegal Enterprise: New Perspectives on Research, Policy and Practice*, Vol 5, pp. 253–275.

World Economic Forum. (2012). *Global gender gap report*. http://www3.weforum.org/docs/WEF_GenderGap_Report_2012.pdf. Accessed on 12 May 2020.

Zahra, S.A., Gedajlovic, E., Neubaum, D.O. and Shulman, J.M. (2009). A typology of social entrepreneurs: Motives, search processes and ethical challenges. *Journal of Business Venturing*, Vol 24, pp. 519–532.

Zahra, S.A. and Wright, M. (2015). Understanding the social role of entrepreneurship. *Journal of Management Studies*, Vol 53(4), pp. 610–629.

PART I

VALUE CREATION AT THE INDIVIDUAL LEVEL

1. Women in Ethiopia: creating value through entrepreneurship

Atsede Tesfaye Hailemariam, Konjit Hailu Gudeta, Brigitte Kroon and Marloes van Engen

INTRODUCTION

Globally, women are increasingly entering into entrepreneurship for a variety of reasons. According to the Global Entrepreneurship Monitor (GEM) survey (Elam et al., 2019) women in sub-Saharan Africa (SSA) recorded the highest entrepreneurial activity in the year 2018. Women's entrepreneurship, particularly in these regions, is often believed to contribute to poverty alleviation by creating economic opportunities for the enterprising women and through helping as well as creating employment opportunities to others (De Vita, Mari, & Poggesi, 2014). Studies also report that women's entrepreneurship contributes to a country's economic development (Minniti & Naudé, 2010) as well as the entrepreneur's family's wellbeing as the women will invest in their children's health, food and education through their enhanced economic freedom (Duflo, 2012).

Existing studies on women entrepreneurship report that women who engage in entrepreneurship in SSA are mostly necessity-based entrepreneurs (Amorós & Bosma, 2014) operating in the informal sector (De Vita et al., 2014) for survival. However, recent studies show that women entrepreneurs go into business for numerous different reasons other than for survival such as a need for autonomy, learning opportunities, achievement, independency, and to fulfill dreams beyond economic growth (Hailemariam & Kroon, 2018; Jennings & Brush, 2013; Katongole, Ahebwa, & Kawere, 2013; Mitchell, 2004). This variation in reasons beyond economic goals makes it difficult to identify a distinct criterion for measuring their business success. More importantly, the diversity in the goals and drives of women entrepreneurs indicates that there is no such thing as 'the female entrepreneur'. Women entrepreneurs may be operating at different levels (micro, small, medium, or large), may have different demographic characteristics, may differ in the reasons that sparked their choice to enter entrepreneurship and may be motivated by different needs and aspirations (Vossenberg, 2016). This sheer diversity translates in a diversity in individual value creation of women entrepreneurs. Policy makers and research on women entrepreneurs could therefore benefit from a better understanding of individual value creation. Recent studies engaging in the value creation perspective that transcend the often-reported economic measures, identified the benefits of this perspective to understand entrepreneurial activity in general and female entrepreneurship in particular (Al-Dajani & Marlow, 2013; Gries & Naudé, 2011). A number of studies on diversity in value creation for female entrepreneurs highlight individual values such as empowerment, decision-making agency and personal wellbeing.

A number of studies document the role of entrepreneurship in empowering women, especially for those coming from disadvantaged backgrounds including poverty, gender inequality and domestic violence (Al-Dajani & Marlow; 2013, Kabeer, 2012; Vossenberg, 2016). Empowerment is defined as the processes of creating the ability to make a choice for individuals who have otherwise been denied such options previously (Haugh & Talwar, 2016; Kabeer, 1999). Women empowerment in particular involves 'access to finance' which, in turn, may result in enhanced confidence, a better status of women in their community, improved wellbeing as a result of spending money to taking care of themselves and active participation in public life, to name a few (Haugh & Talwar, 2016; Mayoux, 2000).

Furthermore, women's empowerment attained through entrepreneurship is also reported to benefit women by increasing their decision-making agency. Agency, women's ability to define their own goals and to act up on them (Kabeer, 1999), widens up women's life choices and contributes to their improved self-identity (Al-Dajani & Marlow, 2013). The benefits of enhanced decision-making agency include the power of women to make choices that improve their and their family's wellbeing, their increased control over resources as well as granting them the freedom to escape from the risk of violence (Kabeer, 1999). In general, these findings indicate that there exist values in entrepreneurship that go beyond increasing the financial freedom of women entrepreneurs.

In recent years, there is an increasing interest to identify differences in motivations to engage in businesses, as well as in the contribution of enterprising on human development. This acknowledges the contribution of women's businesses to value creation at different levels, apart from emphasizing economic value indicators. Sheikh and colleagues (2018) highlight the importance of studying women's entrepreneurship through the 'value creation lens' as it helps understand the different ways how women's businesses result in positive changes towards family, society and the country at large. The approach identified four different levels at which women create through their entrepreneurial activities. This includes individual level values (values for the women themselves through increased decision-making ability, opportunity for personal growth, etcetera), household level values (contribution to the family, such as using the increased income to improve family's wellbeing), business level values (that include contribution to the business through increased access to networks, resources, etcetera) and community level values (that involve positive changes in the community, such as changing the attitudes and perceptions towards women in the community). Their study also highlights that women's businesses create a number of values that may distinctly vary among enterprises in different contexts (Sheikh et al., 2018, pp. 23–24). Thus, it is key to explore and identify these values, certainly in a context that is less researched, in order to enhance our understanding of the contribution women's businesses make in different societies. It is also important to start from women's own meaning/conceptualization of business success and performance, as this may substantially differ from the mainstream definitions in the entrepreneurship literature. Women often create their own peculiar values through their businesses, for instance, by the contribution their business operation has for the social wellbeing of communities or even society at large, or how well it contributes to the family/household rather than the profit margin. In this contribution, we concentrate on how women find personal value for themselves in doing business.

Therefore, this study aims to explore individual value creation of women entrepreneurs in a developing SSA country. By using the narrative accounts of three women entrepreneurs from Addis Ababa, Ethiopia, we show how women create value for themselves through entrepreneurship. We contribute to the field of women entrepreneurship by documenting how successful women entrepreneurs in Ethiopia empower and benefit themselves through enterprising.

THE CONTEXT FOR WOMEN ENTREPRENEURS IN ETHIOPIA

Ethiopia is a densely populated SSA developing country with an estimated population of 110 million. In the decade from 2005/2006 to 2015/2016, the Ethiopian economy had a GDP average growth of 10.5% per year, which is nearly double the sub-Saharan regional average of 5.4% (World Bank, 2017). However, the country is falling behind in terms of credit to the private sector. Only 6.9% of small businesses in Ethiopia were financed by banks during 2014, which is below the average for SSA countries of 9.1% (World Bank 2016). Collateral requirements – mostly property – is the largest barrier in acquiring a loan from banks. While this barrier is common to both men and women entrepreneurs, for women entrepreneurs this is often exacerbated, because properties are usually registered in the husband's name, and major decisions including finance and property are often made by husbands, making access to finance without the support of a husband difficult (Hailemariam, Kroon, Van Engen, & Van Veldhoven, 2019, World Bank 2009). Overall, in a patriarchal society such as Ethiopia where men dominate societal institutions and hold authority over women (Milazzo & Goldstein, 2017), women do not have equal economic rights as men (Hallward-Driemeier & Gajigo, 2013). Consequently, women-owned micro and small enterprises are constrained from inadequate capital investments and women thus more often than not run their businesses with no or insufficient access to loans (Drbie & Kassahun, 2013; Wasihun & Paul, 2010).

Without easy access to loans from banks, Ethiopian women find alternative resources to finance their business. The main source is the government-led microfinance institution, established to provide small loans to poor self-employed individuals operating micro businesses in different regions of the country. Next to this institution there are some financing initiatives specifically created to provide loans to women entrepreneurs. One of these initiatives is the organization for Women in Self Employment (WISE) that provides saving and credit services to economically disadvantaged women. Another two initiatives are the Women Entrepreneurship Development Project (WEDP) backed by the World Bank fund, and the 'Enat Bank'

– founded by (women) investors in Ethiopia. These two initiatives target the 'missing middle': women entrepreneurs who are neither served by microfinance institutions due to small size loans nor by banks requiring excessive collaterals. These organizations offer access to loans for the group of women who do not have the financial capacity and assets to submit collaterals. However, these initiatives target a small group of women entrepreneurs in some selected urban areas only. Therefore, many women entrepreneurs depend on their own savings, their family and an indigenous rotating saving and credit association known as '*Equb*' (or '*iqqub*') (Kedir & Ibrahim, 2011; Solomon, 2010; Stevenson & St-Onge, 2005). However, such funds are often very small, making growth and success quite challenging.

Next to financial challenges, women entrepreneurs operating their businesses in Ethiopia face challenges due to the traditionally subordinate position of women in the patriarchal societies. In particular, societal expectations of fulfilling domestic responsibilities and community roles (such as attending funerals and comforting the bereaved) all bear on the shoulders of women (Gudeta & Van Engen, 2017; 2018). These societal expectations about women reflect in the way women entrepreneurs are socially treated. In addition, women entrepreneurs may face domestic violence when their entrepreneurial activities threaten the traditionally dominant position of men in the family. Such domestic violence restricts women entrepreneurs' decision-making autonomy and freedom of choice on what, how, and when to operate their enterprises, their control over financial resources as well as their opportunities to participate in networking activities relevant to their business (Hailemariam et al., 2019).

However, despite the challenges and constraints Ethiopian women face, worldwide reports show that 13% of the female population in Ethiopia is engaged in entrepreneurial activity (GEM, 2013). A considerable proportion of women entrepreneurs in the country is engaged in the informal sector, operating petty trades (Triodos-Facet, 2011). However, women are increasingly engaging in entrepreneurial activity in the formal sector of the economy as well. For example, there are women entrepreneurs who have been able to move from the informal to the formal sector by growing their micro enterprise into a small business. In addition, more educated women have entered entrepreneurship by building on their previous work experience. A final example are women entrepreneurs who have better access to finance and resources due to their own societal background (Solomon 2010; Stevenson & St-Onge, 2005; World Bank, 2009). Women entrepreneurs who engage in entrepreneurial activity by choice stated that they enjoy entrepreneurship not purely as a means for income, but because it allows them to do what they love to do, to fulfil their dreams, to be independent as a woman and to give back to their families (Hailemariam & Kroon, 2018). Hence, the values put forward by Ethiopian women entrepreneurs are various and extend well beyond wealth creation. This chapter presents three example cases of how Ethiopian women entrepreneurs who operate their businesses in the formal economy of Ethiopia create value for themselves through engaging in entrepreneurial activity.

SAMPLE AND ANALYSIS

The cases presented in this chapter are based on interviews with three women entrepreneurs in Addis Ababa, the capital city of Ethiopia. The interviews were conducted as part of a larger project on motivation, work–family boundary management experiences and socio-cultural contexts of women entrepreneurs in Addis Ababa, Ethiopia's capital (Gudeta, 2018; Hailemariam, 2018). For this larger project, a purposive sampling strategy was applied to include participants who vary considerably in terms of the lines of business/industry they are operating in, age of their business, family characteristics (marital status, number of children) as well as age and educational background of the interviewees. More specifically, snowball sampling techniques and referrals through friends and already interviewed women entrepreneurs were used. In this contribution, we present the narrative accounts of three of the women entrepreneurs who were interviewed for the larger study. We selected three diverse accounts of individual value creation: For the first entrepreneur her business meant empowerment though poverty alleviation, for the second entrepreneur her business meant the transition to a meaningful life after repatriation, and for the third entrepreneur her gradual transition from participating in a business to becoming a business woman was the means for her emancipation. The interviews were voice recorded after receiving the consent of the participants, transcribed in Amharic (the government's working language) and later translated in English. The interviews are paraphrased by the researchers to prepare the narrative accounts of three successful women entrepreneurs with different walks of lives: Zahara, Elsa and Tinbit. Zahara started her business from almost nothing. To her, starting a business meant overcoming strong resistance and violence from her ex-husband who was not supportive of her going into the business. Elsa chose to return to the country after living abroad for a number of years (known as a 'diaspora' in Ethiopia) and began a tourism business on her family's estate. The third participant is Tinbit, who initially was pushed to do business by her husband but who later felt empowered to take over the business and run it on her own. Their narratives show how women's businesses help to create a number of values for the women themselves.

NARRATIVE 1: ZAHARA – FROM POVERTY TO EMPOWERMENT

Zahara started a business 15 years ago with a loan of ETB 500 (approximately US $61 then) that she received from an organization for women in self- employment (WISE) that trains and provides loans for poor girls and women. The income generated from the business was used to support living expenses and education of her siblings.

Her mother passed away when she was in 6th grade. Her father then remarried but she said 'what happened after that is just beyond words. I don't want to talk about it'. She had to drop out of school in 10th grade to take care of her three brothers and one sister. When she joined the training offered by the organization, Zahara was married and had two children. Her husband-at-the-time was not happy about it. She said 'I got into the marriage due to my economic problems, so, you face a lot of nasty things when you move in with such terms'. She was even beaten by her ex-husband when she insisted on attending the training.

After completion of the training and receiving the ETB 500 loan, she started selling spice. She was involved in both preparing the spice and selling it to customers around her village, and distributing to small shops. She said 'to be honest, the spice business is profitable but it was not the kind of business I wanted to do in the long-term and it was very tiring'. Meanwhile she completed a hairdressing training after which she quit her spice selling business and started a beauty salon business. At present, her brothers are running the hairdressing business and they are no longer dependent on her. She was also engaged in collecting garbage, but later she transferred the ownership of this business to her employees. Zahara is currently involved in the café and restaurant business and owns a construction-equipment rental business with her friend. Moreover, she is in the process of acquiring a flour-producing factory.

Making her own decisions and accessing a loan is no longer a challenge to Zahara. She said, 'Now I might have a lot of people who could guarantee my collateral. I also can use my house or my car as collateral. But in the past as you know, when you don't have money, people don't give you much regard; hence, the situation then was not good'. Further she said:

> I wouldn't have been able to talk to you like this in the past. I was not able to talk in public. I used to think I was inferior, and I used to be scared. I did not have self-esteem. So, a change of your inner self is the real success; even more than money! Because when you raise your kids, you don't show them your past weaknesses but your current strength.

NARRATIVE 2: ELSA – SEEKING A MEANINGFUL LIFE IN BUSINESS

Fifty-two-year-old Elsa left Ethiopia when she was seventeen years old. She got her degree in education and was working in the United States of America (USA) for about 28 years where she came to develop a sense of an Ethiopian identity. At first, she did not have any plan of what to do when she decided to come back to her country. However, she was articulate about her motive in contributing to society: 'I have always been seeking a meaning for life'.

Elsa is a single woman who has enjoyed travelling and adventures ever since she was young. Specifically, her travels around Ethiopia made her discover what she really loves and what she has to do to live a meaningful life. Her experience as a tourist around the world has also helped her to develop the idea of a guesthouse business. She started the business with her own capital at her grandparent's place where she grew up before she left for the USA and where she currently resides. She is proud that she left her status and assets abroad to come back home to live and run her business at her grandparent's place. She said 'since my grandfather was the first child everybody (brothers, in-laws, cousins) used to come here. And that was my joy.' She used to miss this joy of living together with a big family of about 16 while she was living abroad. The creation of the business at this sentimental place was also important to keep the history and belongings of her grandfather who worked hard for his country.

The guest house is decorated with antiques belonging to her grandparents. She said 'when tourists come to stay at my place, eager to learn about the different cuisines, cultural ornaments, and lifestyles of Ethiopia, it gives me immense satisfaction. I see myself as contributing to my country.' Moreover, she provides a tour guide service for the people who stay at the guesthouse, as well as yoga and meditation training for women. Currently she is running the business with six employees. Her own task is to pick up the guests and serve as a tour guide. She said 'I met so many beautiful people. Beautiful people who bring their own wisdom. When you live together, when you talk, you intimately connect with people. This business is my life. Also, the fact I created a business for myself is more important.' Moreover, she stresses, 'I'm very happy that I moved back and I'm very happy all the family members are getting what I wanted to give out and they love it'.

NARRATIVE 3: TINBIT – FROM EMPOWERMENT TO EMANCIPATION

Tinbit, aged 36, is a mother of three children aged 16, 9, and 7. She first went into business by selling spare parts with her husband. After a while, they switched to a pharmacy business that did not succeed as they expected. After spending six years in these two businesses, she then moved to her current business: a stationery materials retail business. She has now worked for nine years running this successful retail business.

She describes her entrepreneurial engagement as a mere coincidence that brought her to do business. The business was established by her husband and she just needed to do something at the time, something that would make her economically productive. At first, she was reluctant to join her husband in running the business but later she was convinced that she had to do something. With no prior experience in business, she admits that she found running a business difficult. However, she also says that she is happy that she is involved in it and that she enjoys the experience and the challenge that comes with entrepreneurship. She also highlights how being in business teaches oneself that one can achieve anything that one puts their heart to, and that this is even truer for women. Being in business, as she puts it, 'helps women realize to achieve the same kind of success others have reached'. She expresses engaging in business has helped her build her confidence, as she puts it saying, 'I don't feel incapable because I am a woman. I work with men at equal footing. I am confident and I work hard. That is how I perceive the whole thing.'

Through engaging in business, Tinbit has grown to become increasingly empowered to make her own choices. For example, it allowed her to explore options of how to expand her business and identify ventures that are more profitable. Although she admits that she seeks advice from her husband and brothers-in-law, she is now the one that makes the ultimate decision of running her business.

Tinbit also points out that other women should be encouraged to go into business. She strongly argues that traditional gender roles ascribed to women in Ethiopian society should not prescribe their behavior as subordinate to men. Tinbit believes that women should not be limited to only taking care of domestic responsibilities; they can do other productive activities as well. She says, for a woman in this society, being involved in a business (however small it is) rather than staying at home taking care of domestic responsibilities, makes a woman more careful of what she wears and how she presents herself to others. Caring for herself like this will ultimately make her lead a happy life, feeling good about herself and giving her an increased self-worth. However, if she stays home, she will be bound to care less for herself and that will highly affect her self-esteem. She highly appreciates her husband's support and encouragement that pushed her into business, as it paved the way to where she is now. Nevertheless, she notes that not many husbands in the society are as positive towards encouraging their wives to go out and work.

Tinbit appreciates how the experience of going into business has contributed to broadening her thinking. It has also given her a chance to meet more people and build a good network, which contributed to widening her horizon. Moreover, she believes that it is her responsibility to take care of her husband's and children's wellbeing while shouldering the (sole) responsibility for supervising domestic help in taking care of household chores. When asked about her business goal, she said 'currently there are a lot of things going on. I have to raise my children well and we have to improve our lives and we have to help our fellow countrymen. It's now that I have grown and matured that I know the value of everything I am doing.'

PERSONAL VALUE CREATION THROUGH ENTREPRENEURSHIP

The narratives of Zahara, Elsa and Tinbit illustrate how engaging in entrepreneurial activity contributes to personal value creation. When synthesizing the life stories of the women, the first thing that strikes the eye is how in each of the selected narratives entrepreneurship comes forward as a vehicle for learning and personal growth.

Although the entrance to entrepreneurship is different for each of the three women, each encountered a learning experience that is unique to entrepreneurship. The entrepreneurial activity induced a need to develop entrepreneurial skills such as strategic thinking, networking and exploring business opportunities. Life resources – a project for poor women, financial means and cultural awareness gained abroad, or an encouraging husband – empowered these women to start and grow a successful business of their own. Yet, the values they attribute to their experience go further than the success of their businesses and tell of changes in how these women perceive and value themselves. These values can be grouped into the value of autonomy, emancipation and personal wellbeing.

A central personal value that comes forward in the narratives is the development of autonomy. Gaining experience as an entrepreneur made all women value their personal decision-making autonomy, gaining financial independence as well as their autonomy in relating to others beyond their private family networks. This autonomy is expressed through enhanced self-esteem and a strong sense of personal agency over their personal life choice. In a study by Al-Dajani and Marlow (2013) among women entrepreneurs in Jordan, a similarly patriarchal society, it is reported that women's empowerment through entrepreneurship enabled them to gain more freedom and independence from their often restrictive environment. The increase in autonomy reflects how women entrepreneurs create value beyond their role of women in a traditional patriarchal society such as Ethiopia. Having gained confidence in their entrepreneurial ventures, the women now realize how they enact a role that was traditionally ascribed to men. Each one of them is proud about their emancipation into a domain that is traditionally considered a male bastion. Their emancipation shows in both social and material notions. The social notion is related to the change from a dependent position in a household to a bread-winning position. Their pride in being able to take care of children, siblings and extended families is omnipresent in the stories. Their emancipation also shows in substantive matters such as the increased ability to independently obtain loans and decide on business investments. This finding is in line with other studies that show how women's entrepreneurship shapes the power relations in the family as they get more financial freedom and thereby increased ability to make decisions on their investment (Al-Dajani & Marlow, 2013; Haugh & Talwar, 2016).

Eventually, each of the women tells the story that the personal growth experienced through becoming an entrepreneur was intrinsically satisfying. Each narrative in this study tells a story of increased personal wellbeing. For all of the women, entrepreneurship was a vehicle for self-fulfilment: they relate their happiness and content, their pride about their achievements, and their personal wellbeing engaging in doing business. Indeed, establishing a business is often reported to benefit women through enhancing their self-esteem, happiness and satisfaction with their lives (Sheikh et al., 2018). This underlines the potential of entrepreneurship as a path for women in developing countries to live a life that is personally meaningful and motivating.

To sum up, the narratives of three Ethiopian women underline that individual value creation of entrepreneurship is partly material (a better financial position) but, through gaining capacity and a sense of self-confidence to negotiate and influence decisions (Rowlands, 1997), individual value creation most importantly is a story of personal growth and wellbeing. The individual values ascribed do not seem to be unique to developing countries. Despite warnings about transferring Western values without contextualization to developing countries, some universalistic human motives seem to come to the fore, such as finding value in personal development, in having decision agency and in being able to invest in relations with others (Hailemariam, 2018). Fundamentally however, these universal motives are embedded in socio-cultural norms, leading women to describe these values in coherence with their understanding of their position in society as (primary) care-givers (Gudeta, 2018). Future research could further investigate the interaction between individual, household, communal, social, cultural and governmental levels that impact and contextualize positive personal values for women entrepreneurs.

CONCLUSION AND POLICY IMPLICATIONS

The individual value that women in SSA find through engaging in entrepreneurship provides a strong intrinsic drive to keep putting effort in their enterprises. In this contribution, we highlighted individual values like learning, empowerment, decision-making agency, personal wellbeing and confidence associated with the experiences of women entrepreneurs in Addis Ababa. Such intrinsic, personal values are revealed in the behavior and persistence of women, who by their behavior could act as a role model to their children, their families and their local communities.

The empowerment that individual women experience through engaging in entrepreneurship may envision that entrepreneurship is a fruitful route for the emancipation of women in patriarchal societies and a way to accelerate women's potential to contribute to developing economies. However, this contribution also illustrates restraints women find in their path while enacting their personal values. Traditional expectations on women's role in society and structural problems in the access to loans could frustrate women with entrepreneurial ambitions such that they withdraw from their plans. Hence, although this contribution highlights the importance of individual value creation, it also emphasizes the need to consider the constraints in which personal value creation can develop.

Policy implications following from our understanding of the importance of personal value creation in entrepreneurship are numerous. From our narratives it was evident that formal and informal support has played an important role to boost the resilience of the women in rough times. For Zahara, it was the material support of small loans, practical support with running a business, paired with the role modelling that other women entrepreneurs provided her that helped her in her quest for a better existence. For Elsa, the chance to have lived and travelled in many cultures and countries made her realize the unique beauty of her home country and its people. Her entering the hospitality industry helped her to create a business from her experiences and connectedness to the community, and in the process create personal value in a meaningful life. For Tinbit, it was being exposed to entrepreneurship paired with her husband's support that eventually evolved in her emancipation and strong sense of the need for societal change towards gender equality for all women in society.

Hence, policy recommendations are equally diverse. A first recommendation is to invest in the education of girls, as education is not only imperative in raising skill levels, but also results in developing confidence and in changing women's perceptions of themselves. Their self-perceptions are of paramount importance, given that they have to go against the tides of cultural values and attitudes to become entrepreneurs. A second recommendation is to develop initiatives for nominating, navigating and changing existing socio-cultural norms about gender roles in society (Poelmans, 2012), in a direction of social norms that reflect gender equality. For sustainable results, such initiatives that aim to create awareness on normative gender roles and the disproportional burden women face in the society should involve both males and females. This would contribute in changing male attitudes to be more involved in providing care and domestic support while it helps change the normalized expectations of females that often lead them to believe they should solely shoulder care and domestic roles. A third recommendation is a need to make available and accessible loans to a large number of women entrepreneurs that have no savings and access to collateral, to facilitate business creation by women.

In the end, the value of such higher-level initiatives is imperative to remove barriers for women to engage in activities that can provide them with values that are important to themselves.

REFERENCES

Al-Dajani, H., & Marlow, S. (2013). Empowerment and entrepreneurship: A theoretical framework. *International Journal of Entrepreneurial Behaviour and Research, 19*(5), 503–524.

Amorós, J. E., & Bosma, N. (2014). Global Entrepreneurship Monitor 2013. Retrieved from https://www.gemconsortium.org/report/48772.

De Vita, L., Mari, M., & Poggesi, S. (2014). Women entrepreneurs in and from developing countries: Evidences from the literature. *European Management Journal, 32*(3), 451–460.

Drbie, M., & Kassahun, T. (2013). Deterrents to the success of micro and small enterprises in Akaki-Kality Sub-City. *Journal of Business and Administrative Studies, 5*(2), 1–33.

Duflo, E. (2012). Women empowerment and economic development. *Journal of Economic Literature, 50*(4), 1051–1079.

Elam, A. B., Brush, C. G., Greene, P. G., Baumer, B., Dean, M., & Heavlow, R. (2019). Global Entrepreneurship Monitor: 2018/2019 Women's Entrepreneurship Report. Retrieved from https://www.gemconsortium.org/report/gem-20182019-womens-entrepreneurship-report.

GEM (2013). Global Entrepreneurship Monitor 2012: Women's Report. Retrieved from www.babson.edu/Academics/centres/blank-center/global-resarch/gem/pages/reports.aspx.

Gries, T., & Naudé, W. (2011). Entrepreneurship and human development: A capability approach. *Journal of Public Economics, 95*(3–4), 216–224.

Gudeta, K. H. (2018). *Managing Boundarylessness Between Work, Family and Community: The Experiences of Women Entrepreneurs in Ethiopia*. Dissertation, Tilburg University.

Gudeta, K. H., & Van Engen, M. L. (2017). The omnipresent community in the work–life boundary management experiences of women entrepreneurs in Ethiopia. In Les Heras, M., Chinchilla, N., & Grau, M. (Eds.), *The Work–Family Balance in Light of Globalization and Technology* (pp. 181–201). Newcastle, UK: Cambridge Scholars Publishing.

Gudeta, K. H., & Van Engen, M. L. (2018). The work–life boundary management styles of women entrepreneurs in Ethiopia: Choice or imposition? *Journal of Small Business and Enterprise Development, 25*(3), 368–386.

Hailemariam, A. T. (2018). *Women Entrepreneurs in Sub-Saharan Africa: A Self-Determination Theory Perspective. The Case of Ethiopia*. Dissertation, Tilburg University.

Hailemariam, A. T., & Kroon, B. (2018). Redefining success beyond economic growth and wealth generation: The case of Ethiopia. In Yousafzai, S., Fayolle, A., Lindgreen, A., Henry, C., Saeed, S., & Sheikh, S. (Eds.), *Women Entrepreneurs and the Myth of*

'*Underperformance*': *A New Look at Women's Entrepreneurship Research* (pp. 1–19). Cheltenham, UK and Northampton, MA, USA: Edward Elgar Publishing.

Hailemariam, A. T., Kroon, B., Van Engen, M. L., & Van Veldhoven, M. (2019). Dreams and reality: Autonomy support for women entrepreneurs in Ethiopia. *Equality, Diversity and Inclusion: An International Journal, 38*(7), 727–742.

Hallward-Driemeier, M., & Gajigo, O. (2013). Strengthening economic rights and women's occupational choice: The impact of reforming Ethiopia's family law. *Policy Research Working Paper* [6695], The World Bank.

Haugh, H. M., & Talwar, A. (2016). Linking social entrepreneurship and social change: The mediating role of empowerment. *Journal of Business Ethics, 133*(4), 643–658.

Jennings, J. E., & Brush, C. G. (2013). Research on women entrepreneurs: challenges to (and from) the broader entrepreneurship literature? *The Academy of Management Annals, 7*(1), 663–715.

Kabeer, N. (1999). Resources, agency, achievements: Reflections on the measurement of women's empowerment. *Development and Change, 30*(3), 435–464.

Kabeer, N. (2012). Women's economic empowerment and inclusive growth: Labour markets and enterprise development. *International Development Research Centre, 44*(10), 1–70.

Katongole, C., Ahebwa, W. M., & Kawere, R. (2013). Enterprise success and entrepreneur's personality traits: An analysis of micro- and small-scale women-owned enterprises in Uganda's tourism industry. *Tourism and Hospitality Research, 13*(3), 166–177.

Kedir, A. M., & Ibrahim, G. (2011). ROSCAs in Urban Ethiopia: Are the characteristics of the institutions more important than those of members? *Journal of Development Studies, 47*(7), 998–1016.

Mayoux, L. (2000). Micro-finance and the empowerment of women: A review of the key issues. *International Labour Organization*. Retrieved from https://www.ilo.org/wcmsp5/groups/public/---ed_emp/documents/publication/wcms_117993.pdf.

Milazzo, A., & Goldstein, M. (2017). Governance and women's economic and political participation. Retrieved from https://openknowledge.worldbank.org/bitstream/handle/10986/27267/116405_WDR17_BP_Governance_and_Womens_Participation-Milazzo_Goldstein.pdf.

Minniti, M., & Naudé, W. (2010). What do we know about the patterns and determinants of female entrepreneurship across countries? *The European Journal of Development Research, 22*(3), 277–293.

Mitchell, B. C. (2004). Motives of entrepreneurs: A case study of South Africa. *The Journal of Entrepreneurship, 13*(2), 167–183.

Poelmans, S. (2012). The 'Triple-N' model: Changing normative beliefs about parenting and career success. *Journal of Social Issues, 68*(4), 838–847.

Rowlands, J. (1997). *Questioning Empowerment: Working with Women in Honduras*. Oxford: Oxfam.

Sheikh, S., Yousafzai, S., Sist, F., Ar, A. A., & Saeed, S. (2018). Value creation through women's entrepreneurship. In Yousafzai, S., Fayolle, A., Lindgreen, A., Henry, C., Saeed, S., & Sheikh, S. (Eds.), *Women Entrepreneurs and the Myth of 'Underperformance': A New Look at Women's Entrepreneurship Research* (pp. 20–33). Cheltenham, UK and Northampton, MA, USA: Edward Elgar Publishing.

Solomon, D. (2010). *Desk review of studies conducted on women entrepreneurs of Ethiopia*. Private Sector Development Hub/Addis Ababa Chamber of Commerce and Sectoral Associations.

Stevenson, L., & St-Onge, A. (2005). Support for growth-oriented, women entrepreneurs in Ethiopia, Kenya, and Tanzania: An overview report. *International Labour Organization*. Retrieved from https://www.ilo.org/public/libdoc/ilo/2005/105B09_30_engl.pdf.

Triodos-Facet. (2011). *Ethiopian Women Entrepreneurship Capacity Building Studies*. The Netherlands: Triodos Facet B.V and BMB Mott MacDonald B.V.

Vossenberg, S. (2016). Gender-aware women's entrepreneurship development for inclusive development in sub-Saharan Africa. INCLUDE knowledge platform on inclusive development policies. Retrieved from https://includeplatform.net/wp-content/uploads/2016/01/INCLUDE-GRF-Vossenberg-Gender-Aware-Women%E2%80%99s-Entrepreneurship-Development.pdf.

Wasihun, R., & Paul, I. (2010). Growth determinants of women operated micro and small enterprises in Addis Ababa. *Journal of Sustainable Development in Africa*, *12*(6), 233–246.

World Bank (2009). *Ethiopia – toward the competitive frontier: Strategies for improving Ethiopia's investment climate*. Report No. 48472-ET, The World Bank, Washington, DC.

World Bank (2016). *World Bank Groups Enterprise Surveys*. Retrieved from http://www.enterprisesurveys.org/data/exploreeconomies/2015/ethiopia.

World Bank (2017). *The World Bank in Ethiopia: Overview updated October 2017*. Retrieved from http://www.worldbank.org/en/country/ethiopia/overview.

2. Evaluating the contribution of entrepreneurship training, perceived emancipation and value creation for rural female entrepreneurs in Uganda

Sylvia K. Gavigan, Thomas M. Cooney and Klavs Ciprikis

INTRODUCTION

Although research in entrepreneurship training has expanded in modern times, it remains primarily focused on developed countries (Bruton et al., 2013), with relatively few studies having been undertaken on the topic within the context of Africa. Rural female entrepreneurs play a key role in Africa, since they are critically important contributors to value creation for themselves, their families and the economy. Entrepreneurship training serves as a mechanism for changing the behaviour and attitudes of individual female entrepreneurs. Offering appropriate entrepreneurship training to female entrepreneurs in rural areas may improve their lives (Kyrgidou and Petridou, 2013), but there is little research available on this topic relating to Africa. This dearth of information is surprising given that international organisations such as the World Bank and the United Nations, as well as governments and enterprise agencies across the globe, have consistently highlighted the benefits of female entrepreneurs (Chell et al., 2010; Urban and Kujinga, 2017) and their impact on economic growth in emerging economies (Lepoutre et al., 2013).

This chapter examines the impact of an entrepreneurship-training programme on perceived emancipation in the Kiryandongo region of North-Western Uganda. A sample of 266 rural women participants in the training programme were surveyed before and after entrepreneurship training in order to investigate the impact of training on their levels of perceived emancipation. This study follows the definition of emancipation as proposed by Rindova et al. (2009) which states that emancipation is an act of seeking autonomy, authoring and pursuit of individual freedom. The level of emancipation for each individual in this study is derived from a 13-item questionnaire presented in Table 2.3. The questionnaire is based on the primary literature in the area of emancipation, which is presented in Table 2.1. Singh (2017) suggests that education and training play a vital role in raising the living standards and improving the quality of life for individual women. Therefore, training is an emancipation tool through which an individual may improve their social standards and wellbeing. Furthermore, the roles of education and training are inherent in seeking autonomy, decision-making, and individual freedom which are also supported by the literature in Table 2.1.

The emancipation levels were measured as an index and the results indicate that entrepreneurship training improves perceived emancipation by approximately 4 points. The results emphasise the importance of appropriate training in improving business knowledge and perceived emancipation of rural women in Uganda. As a result, improvements in emancipation lead to personal value creation which may improve the lives of people in the region. This chapter will discuss the context of rural female entrepreneurs in Uganda, the importance of entrepreneurship training, and the relationship between emancipation and entrepreneurship. Thereafter, the chapter will detail the methodology used in this study, provide an analysis of the results and present key findings of the study.

RURAL FEMALE ENTREPRENEURS

In Uganda, agriculture is the main economic activity, employing two-thirds of the population and generating 25 per cent of the gross domestic product in 2014 (UBOS, 2014). Despite its current significance, the sector is projected to become less important as the country moves towards a more industrialised economy, which will significantly increase challenges facing rural female entrepreneurs. According to Minniti (2009) and Laguía et al. (2019), when informal sectors are taken into consideration, women are contributing an even greater role to rural entrepreneurship than previously envisaged or understood. Further, Jaffee and Hyde (2000) contended that greater priority must be given to promoting entrepreneurial activity and value creation goals amongst rural female entrepreneurs because women tend to emphasise society values and act on an ethic of care because of gender socialisation, thus leading to certain levels of entrepreneurial activity. However, Lassalle and McElwee (2016) suggested that many rural female entrepreneurs, particularly in emerging economies like Uganda, have become entrepreneurs because of the need to survive or to enhance their livelihood, rather than through opportunity recognition. It has also been determined that the perceptions women hold about themselves and their human capital (e.g. education and work experience) will affect their entrepreneurial activity (Bird and Sapp, 2004). Despite these factors influencing nascent rural female entrepreneurial activity in Uganda, little is known about the relationship between entrepreneurship training and perceived emancipation of nascent rural female entrepreneurs. Given the substantial challenges facing rural female entrepreneurs in Uganda, it has been suggested that more tailored entrepreneurship training programmes must be provided for this target group (Lourenço et al., 2014).

While the number of women involved in entrepreneurial activities has grown in Uganda, significant disparities remain with respect to poverty levels, the lack of entrepreneurship training, the lack of employment opportunities and women's access to productive resources and land (Kyrgidou and Petridou, 2013). Furthermore, women are much more likely than men to lack skills for business and women tend towards necessity-driven enterprises rather than exploiting market opportunities (GEM Report, 2012). Arguably, entrepreneurship is gender-biased as females face considerably greater challenges in their entrepreneurial endeavours than their male counterparts (Marlow and McAdam, 2013). For example, Lourenço et al. (2014) list multiple barriers to entrepreneurship for rural female entrepreneurs in Uganda, such as lack of access to credit, gender inequality and lack of access to knowledge and training.

Gorgievski et al. (2011) examined some of the factors associated with entrepreneurial value creation at an individual level. Psychological factors such as self-efficacy, confidence and motivation towards achieving social goals have also contributed to value creation at an individual level (Miller et al., 2012; Smith and Woodworth, 2012). Other factors include issues such as cultural norms regarding commercial ventures (Terjesen et al., 2016), social enterprise (Stephan et al., 2015) and environmental businesses (Vazquez-Brust et al., 2014). Stephan et al. (2015) have suggested that a deficit in entrepreneurial attainment and self-employment of rural female entrepreneurs is likely due to barriers faced by women in a society. Perceptions and social prejudices concerning gender roles, deficiencies in basic child-care facilities, gender-based inequalities accessing developmental resources and a lack of training affect value creation amongst nascent rural female entrepreneurs (Driga et al., 2009). Furthermore, Sheikh et al. (2018) argued that female entrepreneurs may not set growth as the primary goal of a business due to their family commitments and life–work balance. In a rural setting, this balance may be important and opportunities for targeting business growth is less likely. However, to generate wealth requires value creation by leveraging innovation to exploit new opportunities and creating a new product-market domain (Hitt et al., 2011). Therefore, generating wealth through value creation is an entrepreneur's central function (Gustafson, 2019).

ENTREPRENEURSHIP TRAINING

Entrepreneurship training can equip women with knowledge and skills to start a business (Katz, 2014) as it is regarded as a practical means to promote entrepreneurship (Peterman and Kennedy, 2003). Further, Martin et al. (2013) suggest that entrepreneurship training is effective in promoting cognitive and individual motivational outcomes that result in increased entrepreneurial activity. However, a theoretical understanding of how and why entrepreneurship training exerts a positive influence on entrepreneurial competencies is still limited (Gielnik et al., 2015). There is a need for research examining in what ways training makes a difference for female entrepreneurs (Martínez et al., 2010). In addition, McKenzie and Woodruff (2014) have argued that the long-term impact of entrepreneurship training seems to be limited, because entrepreneurial success is not the result of a single entrepreneurial action, but constant training and development of new ideas and opportunities. Shane and Venkataraman (2000) also stated that training results in short-term changes in entrepreneurial behaviour and that it does not lead to long-term entrepreneurial success.

Therefore, it is critical that training is undertaken throughout the entrepreneurial process (Gielnik et al., 2017). Balan and Metcalfe (2012) argued that entrepreneurship training is not only about the transfer of knowledge, but also about the ability to discover new opportunities and master venture creation processes to create value at an individual level.

Research in entrepreneurship portrays entrepreneurs as innovative and creative individuals who search for new solutions in order to create value (Kirzner, 2009). Therefore, they are important contributors to economic growth in Africa. Entrepreneurs require business knowledge to be able to organise and coordinate resources, which in turn leads to value creation and better business opportunities. Hence, entrepreneurship training is considered to be a key instrument in enhancing entrepreneurial attitudes in potential and nascent entrepreneurs (Ahmad, 2013). Further, Mani (2018) found that participants in entrepreneurship training programmes accumulate many benefits in terms of skill improvements, but little research has been undertaken regarding the relationship between entrepreneurship training and perceived emancipation within an African context.

THE RELEVANCE OF EMANCIPATION TO ENTREPRENEURSHIP

The link between entrepreneurship and emancipation was established by Rindova et al. (2009). This perspective is a worthy development as it moves entrepreneurship theory into a domain that has long been a concern for organisational scholars (Steyaert, 2007). The focus on emancipation broadens concerns about the role of organisation processes in the production of, and resistance to, inequalities of power (Garavan et al., 2010). Shane (2003) suggested that the success of the entrepreneurial process is determined by an entrepreneur's ability to make decisions and to navigate through the internal and external factors that affect individual value creation. In addition, the emancipatory approach highlights the freeing or emancipatory process, and the results of becoming a new venture creator (Rindova et al., 2009). Importantly, this approach emphasises an entrepreneur as evolving oneself, just as new agencies emerge and propagate in the external world (Lindbergh and Schwartz, 2018).

However, the role of the agent remains unique, because the pertinent term 'emancipation' (which refers to the act of setting free from the power of another) is critical for women starting a business (Rindova et al., 2009). For example, the majority of small-scale entrepreneurs in Uganda are women and they are seen as agents of change and value creators for themselves and their families. This is because they are often marginalised and improving their lives involves a significant impact on themselves and their families (Singh and Belwal, 2008). Uganda's female entrepreneurs are frequently motivated to start their own businesses in order to become independent, achieve job satisfaction, gain economic independence and to have an opportunity to be more creative (Tibbits and Kandasaami, 1995). Some literature has suggested that the greater participation of women in entrepreneurial activity is increasingly being viewed as one of the prime contributors to individuals benefiting from economic growth (Singh and Belwal, 2008; Shastri et al., 2019).

Rural female entrepreneurs can use business as a tool to create value for oneself and one's community, which can also make a difference to wider society (Nguyen et al., 2014). It has been further observed that women, through increased participation in income-generating activities, can contribute to the stability and reduction of social problems, hence the need for independence in business start-up activity (Tesfaye and Lundström, 2019). Table 2.1 highlights 13 key elements that are central to the emancipatory process. These elements are used as a basis for the investigation of entrepreneurship training and emancipation of rural nascent female entrepreneurs in Uganda.

The emancipatory elements that are discussed in Table 2.1 indicate an overarching framework that brings together individuals (women entrepreneurs), opportunities (environmental conditions), modes of organising (new ventures) and increased networks of new customers (value creation). The concept of emancipation is a phenomenon that is quite complex. Overall, the examination of value creation through perceived emancipation in this study occurs at an individual level since it involves women seeking to improve their knowledge and skillsets regarding effectively managing a business, as well as growing through personal development.

METHODOLOGY

The data for this study comes from two surveys of a cohort of 266 randomly selected female entrepreneurs in small-scale businesses in informal sectors in the Kiryandongo region of Uganda who took part in an entrepreneurship training programme. The training programme was designed and implemented by an international development and advocacy organisation (the Deutsche Stiftung Weltbevoelkerung) using a blended learning approach and it was funded by the World Food Programme in Uganda. The organisation invited a random sample of rural women from the region who were already in small-scale informal businesses and who had no prior business knowledge to participate in the entrepreneurship training programme. The women who responded to the invitation form the cohort of this study. As suggested by Schneider (2017), the training programme was aimed at supporting rural women to build confidence, motivation and value creation during the early stages of their businesses.

Participants in the training programme learned about important aspects of business, such as business plans, financial management and marketing techniques. The programme was implemented in a way that would improve women's awareness, perception, flexibility, emotional stability, authority, equality, knowledge, autonomy, education, independence, decision-making and freedom. The principal goal of the programme was to improve business performance, but also an individual's perceived level of emancipation.

All women who participated in the training programme were surveyed before the entrepreneurship training module started and after the training module finished,

Table 2.1   *Key sources of emancipation typology*

Dimension of Emancipation	Source	Description
Independence	Freire, 1996	Independence entails allowing rural women to use their own judgement as opposed to blindly following the assertions of others. In order for emancipation to be realised when making entrepreneurial decisions, women (individuals) need to recognise that oppression exists and that it is negative.
Seeking autonomy	Delmar et al., 2013	The need to develop emancipation theory is the expressed motivation for autonomy from the existing structures of authority, income reliance and resource constraints
Authoring	Goss et al., 2011; Kozan & Akdeniz, 2014; Oe & Mitsuhashi, 2013	To be a successful entrepreneur, one has to forge networks and relationships with other actors of power while starting an enterprise.
Equality	Ranciere, 2009; Bourdier, 1999	One of the most interesting pieces of work was Ranciere's radical premise of equality between beings. Ranciere did not disagree with the existence of power struggle, work division or unequal access to resources, nor did he deny the exploitative nature of wage relations or the 'deskilling' of workers that the labour process theory highlights.
Education	Singh, 2017	Education as emancipation is a solution to liberate oneself from any kind of bondage. The idea of emancipation is to recognise problems and challenge the status quo. An educated person is emancipated when she is consciously aware of her rights and freedom.
Decision-making	Beijing, 1995	Discriminatory laws and practices hold women back in many ways. However, the Beijing Conference Agreement, which is known as a platform for action, referred to women involved power and decision-making as one of the main critical areas for the emancipation of women.
Flexible environment	Kalischuck and Thorpe, 2002; August-Brady, 2000	A flexible environment can also be described as one that is responsive to change, leading to personal benefits for individuals and society. It increases choice and thereby enhances self-esteem and understanding.
Personal knowledge	Berragan, 1998; Polanyi, 1958	This is described as the ability to understand oneself. Personal knowledge influences everything one does, because it involves being aware of one's own feelings.
Perception	Ranciere, 1998	This is the mental space that is used to order the perception of the world and how we connect sensible experiences to intelligible modes of interpretation.
Emotion	Verduijn et al., 2014	Emotions constitute factors in the decisions that people make in personal and professional relationships.
Declarations	Bird & Schjoedt, 2017; Weber & DeSoucey, 2008	Making declarations refers here to the intentions and acts of creating change as a necessary component of the business. Through a declaration, an entrepreneur may position the new enterprise in a way that stakeholders might perceive as meaningful and valuable.

Dimension of Emancipation	Source	Description
Reflection	Romyn, 2000; Wittmann-Price, 2004	Reflection or cognitive awareness is seen as developing a perception of questioning practices that are based solely on the tradition of emancipation or authority.
Freedom	Rindova, 2009	The role of the agent remains unique, because the pertinent term 'emancipation', which refers to the act of setting free from the power of another, is critical for women starting businesses and therefore value creation.

Source: Author, from literature review.

independent from the training programme organisers. The training module was carried out for a week during the month of February 2019. The instruments for the data collection consisted of a questionnaire aimed at collecting information about entrepreneurship training and perceived emancipation amongst nascent rural female entrepreneurs in Uganda. The questionnaire consisted of 21 items divided into four categories: (1) Introduction; (2) Business Training and Skills; (3) Emancipation; and (4) Demographics. Individual emancipation was derived from a 13-item questionnaire which asked respondents to 'strongly disagree', 'disagree', 'undecided', 'agree' or 'strongly agree' with each item. The list of 13 questions asked is presented in Table 2.2. The list of questions used to measure perceived emancipation was derived from a thorough literature review as presented in Table 2.1. From the review of the literature, the main areas for consideration were identified, which helped to formulate questions regarding the level of perceived emancipation. An index of the level of perceived emancipation for each individual is estimated from the 13-item questionnaire, which is the dependent variable in this study. The emancipation index is constructed from a 5-point Likert scale (0 = 'strongly disagree'; 1 = 'disagree'; 2 = 'undecided'; 3 = 'agree'; 4 = 'strongly agree') before and after the training programme. The sum of the responses to each question indicates the level of perceived emancipation for each individual. An index of 52 indicates the highest level of perceived emancipation, while 0 is the lowest level of emancipation.

In terms of the explanatory variables, training is included as a dummy variable, representing the entrepreneurship training programme in each survey period. Other demographic characteristics such as age (18 to 24 years, 25 to 34 years, 35 to 44 years, 45 to 54 years, 55 to 64 years, and over 65 years); highest level of education achieved (primary, secondary, vocational, university, and other); marital status (single, married, separated, divorced, and widowed); job type (agriculture, shop owner, road vendor, and other); number of children (no children, 1 to 2 children, 3 to 5 children, 6 to 10 children, and more than 10 children) were also considered.

In order to examine the impact of training on perceived emancipation the data set combines before and after training periods for each individual, which yields a panel of data of 532 observations. Hausman's (1978) test indicates that a random effects regression is the most appropriate method of investigating the relationship between perceived emancipation and sociodemographic variables in this study. Similarly,

Audretsch et al. (2019) have employed a random effects regression model to examine the impact of training on entrepreneurship performance. The random effects model is also the most applicable because the model generates random slopes in variables and reduces standard errors, and it assumes a normal distribution in variables (Bell et al., 2019). The following random effects regression equation is utilised to examine the impact of training and demographic characteristics on perceived emancipation of individual i in time period t:

$$Y_{it} = \beta_0 + \beta_1 T_{it} + \beta_n X_{it}.$$

In this formula, Y is the perceived emancipation index, T is training, X represents individual demographic characteristics, β are their coefficient estimates, while t refers to time before and after training. The Heckman sample selection test indicates that there is no sample selection bias in the data sample.

DATA ANALYSIS

The analysis of the data generated from the primary research provides very interesting insights regarding the relationship between entrepreneurship training and the increased levels of perceived emancipation amongst the programme participants. Table 2.2 shows that the women surveyed on average report low levels of education attainment. For example, approximately 34 per cent of the sample report no education and 56 per cent report only primary education. Many women in Uganda experience lack of access to education, employment opportunities and reproductive resources (Kyrgidou and Petridou, 2013). In terms of family characteristics, approximately 72 per cent of the sample are married and 42 per cent have 3 to 5 children, while a further 40 per cent of the sample have 6 to 10 children. The results also indicate that 77 per cent of the women are working in agriculture. Many households live off subsistence agriculture which agrees with Kristensen et al. (2016) who previously highlighted that 70 per cent of the land area in Uganda is used to produce locally consumed food crops.

The average rating for the emancipation factors are listed in Table 2.3. The results indicate that most of the emancipation scores have improved after training. The results suggest that the entrepreneurship training programme may be effective in improving emancipation of women towards expanding their business knowledge and competencies, as well as enhancing their personal development attributes.

Regression results indicating the statistical significance and the effect of each variable in the emancipation model regression are presented in Table 2.4. Regression results reveal that the training had a positive and statistically significant effect on emancipation. This means that participating in the entrepreneurship training programme improves the emancipation level by approximately 4 points. Rae (2010) stated that entrepreneurship training is vital for creating an understanding of entre-

Table 2.2   *Descriptive statistics of variables in the emancipation equation*

	Mean	Std. Dev.
Emancipation	33.57	(8.063)
Age		
18–24	0.13	(0.334)
25–34	0.30	(0.461)
35–44	0.25	(0.433)
45–54	0.20	(0.400)
55–64	0.10	(0.300)
Over 64	0.02	(0.129)
Education		
None	0.34	(0.474)
Primary	0.56	(0.496)
Secondary	0.07	(0.261)
Vocational	0.01	(0.114)
University	0.01	(0.075)
Marital Status		
Single	0.04	(0.204)
Married	0.72	(0.450)
Separated	0.05	(0.212)
Divorced	0.03	(0.171)
Widowed	0.16	(0.367)
Work Type		
Agriculture	0.77	(0.421)
Small Business	0.35	(0.477)
Road Vendor	0.08	(0.273)
Other	0.03	(0.176)
Children		
None	0.02	(0.129)
1–2	0.14	(0.350)
3–5	0.42	(0.493)
6–10	0.40	(0.490)
Over 10	0.02	(0.155)

Note: Mean emancipation scores and demographic characteristics are reported. The number of observations in the panel data set is 532.

Table 2.3   Means of key emancipation factors before and after training

	Means	
Key factors of emancipation	Before	After
1. Capable of making decisions without approval of others	2.06	2.05
2. Have the ability to start own business	2.60	2.74
3. Independent and choose my own life	1.83	1.93
4. Can run own business without other people telling me what to do	2.32	1.96
5. Can use personal knowledge of business to grow enterprise	2.47	2.70
6. Flexible environment is key to start own business	2.26	3.10
7. Have ability to start own business to support family	2.62	2.60
8. Capable of declaring changes for own business	2.65	2.86
9. Have complete autonomy in everything I do	1.83	3.00
10. Very good at controlling my emotions	3.02	2.88
11. Capable of taking ownership of my business	2.61	2.66
12. Confident that starting own business will help to achieve equality	2.77	3.31
13. Important to continue educating self	2.83	3.48
Total mean	**2.45**	**2.71**

Note: Mean emancipation scores for the whole sample for each element are calculated from a 5-point Likert scale (0-1-2-3-4). Higher scores are indicative of better emancipation level.

preneurship, developing entrepreneurial capabilities and contributing to entrepreneurial identities and cultures at an individual level.

In terms of other demographic characteristics in the study, older women experienced greater effects on their levels of perceived emancipation. For example, women between 25 and 34 years of age had a 2.5 times greater impact on emancipation than adult women under 25, and women between 45 and 54 years of age had the highest impact (4.8 increase in index) on emancipation compared to women under 25. Although skill development (Kuratko and Morris, 2018) and education (Gartner, 1994) may improve emancipation, the results of this study suggest that apart from vocational training, education has no statistical effect on emancipation. This may be due to fewer women reporting education levels greater than primary education. Vocational education leads to a positive and statistically significant 5.9 increase in the emancipation index compared to women without education. Married women experienced a negative and statistically significant impact on their emancipation levels. Marriage leads to a 5.6 reduction in the emancipation index compared to single women, while other marital status variables have an insignificant effect on the emancipation index. This may be due to cultural and psychological factors that many women are often marginalised because of societal barriers. Working in agriculture and in other jobs yields 2.4 and 4.7 greater positive impact on emancipation respectively when compared to housewives. Having children does not have a statistically significant effect on emancipation.

Table 2.4   *Random effects regression of the emancipation equation*

	Coef. Std.	Err.
Training	3.96	(0.639)***
Age		
25–34	2.49	(1.269)**
35–44	4.24	(1.412)***
45–54	4.78	(1.471)***
55–64	3.47	(1.715)**
Over 64	0.89	(2.943)
Education		
Primary	0.68	(0.807)
Secondary	0.47	(1.458)
Vocational	5.94	(3.238)*
University	6.20	(4.602)
Marital Status		
Married	-5.64	(1.644)***
Separated	-2.56	(2.197)
Divorced	-1.14	(2.539)
Widowed	-1.78	(1.846)
Work Type		
Agriculture	2.42	(0.866)***
Small Business	0.36	(0.777)
Road Vendor	-1.20	(1.299)
Other	4.70	(1.871)**
Children		
1–2	-0.54	(2.750)
3–5	-1.25	(2.712)
6–10	-1.80	(2.759)
Over 10	-2.15	(3.515)
R-squared	0.1751	

Note: Dependent variable is emancipation index. Omitted categories are age, 18 to 24; education, none; marital status, single; work type, housewife; children, none. ***Indicates significance at the 0.01 level or better; **indicates significance at the 0.05 level or better; *indicates significance at the 0.10 level or better.

CONCLUSION

The aim of this chapter is to examine the impact of entrepreneurship training on the perceived emancipation of women in Uganda. The design of the entrepreneurship training module targeted early nascent female entrepreneurs in Uganda and sought to consider how this training improves their emancipation. Hence, for many rural women, the primary benefit of their entrepreneurial activities is in the form of family responsibility, including the education and health of their children and the care of elders. Between working in their informal businesses and taking care of their families, rural female entrepreneurs were perceived as dependent on a number of forms of assistance at different stages of their entrepreneurial activity.

The key findings of this study indicate that entrepreneurship training has a positive and significant effect on emancipation. Entrepreneurship training may increase the emancipation index by approximately 4 points. Ahmad (2013) found that entrepreneurship training is considered one of the key instruments to enhance the entrepreneurial attitude of both potential and nascent entrepreneurs. Older female entrepreneurs also experience a greater impact on their emancipation and individual value creation. One possible reason for this is because women who are in those categories of age are independent, capable of making their own decisions, capable of taking ownership for their business, have freedom and a lot of experience (Gross, 2010). The finding that married women experience lower levels of emancipation than single women was confirmed by Bantebya-Kyomuhendo and McIntosh (2006).

This study fills the gap in literature regarding the impact of training on emancipation of female entrepreneurs in Uganda and their increased personal value. Whether women are starting or already in business, the main goal of entrepreneurship training may work as a catalyst to increase women's perceived emancipation by making their own decisions, being independent, having freedom to start their own businesses, supporting their families, offering flexibility in their work and with their families, as well as achieving equality and making them capable of taking ownership of their own businesses. Therefore, this chapter has clearly demonstrated that entrepreneurship training can lead to increased value creation at an individual level for rural female entrepreneurs in Uganda.

REFERENCES

Ahmad, S. Z. (2013). The need for inclusion of entrepreneurship education in Malaysia lower and higher learning institutions. *Education + Training, 55*(2), 191–203.

Audretsch, D. B., Belitski, M., & Desai, S. (2019). National business regulations and city entrepreneurship in Europe: A multilevel nested analysis. *Entrepreneurship Theory and Practice, 43*(6), 1148–1165.

Balan, P., & Metcalfe, M. (2012). Identifying teaching methods that engage entrepreneurship students. *Education + Training, 54*(5), 368–384.

Bantebya-Kyomuhendo, G., & McIntosh, M. K. (2006). *Women, Work and Domestic Virtue in Uganda 1900–2003*. Oxford: James Currey.

Bell, A., Fairbrother, M., & Jones, K. (2019). Fixed and random effects models: making an informed choice. *Quality and Quantity, 53*(2), 1051–1074.

Bird, S. R., & Sapp, S. G. (2004). Understanding the gender gap in small business success: Urban and rural comparisons. *Gender & Society, 18*(1), 5–28.

Bruton, G. D., Ketchen Jr, D. J., & Ireland, R. D. (2013). Entrepreneurship as a solution to poverty. *Journal of Business Venturing, 28*(6), 683–689.

Chell, E., Nicolopoulou, K., & Karataş-Özkan, M. (2010). Social entrepreneurship and enterprise: International and innovation perspectives. *Entrepreneurship & Regional Development, 22*(6), 485–493.

Driga, O., Lafuente, E., & Vaillant, Y. (2009). Reasons for the relatively lower entrepreneurial activity levels of rural women in Spain. *Sociologia ruralis, 49*(1), 70–96.

Garavan, T., Birdthistle, N., Cinnéide, B. Ó., & Collet, C. (2010). Entrepreneurship education in the Republic of Ireland: Context, opportunities and challenges. In Fayolle, A. (Ed.), *Handbook of Research in Entrepreneurship Education: International Perspectives*, Volume 3. Cheltenham, UK and Northampton, MA, USA: Edward Elgar Publishing, pp. 225–247.

Gartner, W.C. (1994). Image formation process. *Journal of Travel & Tourism Marketing, 2*(2/3), 191–216.

GEM Report (2012). 2012 Report on women and entrepreneurship. *Global Entrepreneurship Monitor*, 16.

Gielnik, M. M., Uy, M. A., Funken, R., & Bischoff, K. M. (2017). Boosting and sustaining passion: A long-term perspective on the effects of entrepreneurship training. *Journal of Business Venturing, 32*(3), 334–353.

Gielnik, M. M., Frese, M., Kahara-Kawuki, A., Wasswa Katono, I., Kyejjusa, S., Ngoma, M., ... & Oyugi, J. (2015). Action and action-regulation in entrepreneurship: Evaluating a student training for promoting entrepreneurship. *Academy of Management Learning & Education, 14*(1), 69–94.

Gorgievski, M. J., Ascalon, M. E., & Stephan, U. (2011). Small business owners' success criteria, a values approach to personal differences. *Journal of Small Business Management, 49*(2), 207–232.

Gross, S. (2010). Inequality and emancipation: An educational approach. *Journal of Education and Research, 2*(1), 9–16.

Gustafson, A. B. (2019). Is risk taking beneficial?: An analysis of John Hobson's 'The Ethics of Gambling' (1905) and Frank Knight's Risk, Uncertainty, Profit (1921).

Hausman, J. A. (1978). Specification tests in econometrics. *Econometrica: Journal of the Econometric Society*, 1251–1271.

Hitt, M. A., Ireland, R. D., Sirmon, D. G., & Trahms, C. A. (2011). Strategic entrepreneurship: Creating value for individuals, organizations, and society. *Academy of Management Perspectives, 25*(2), 57–75.

Jaffee, S., & Hyde, J. S. (2000). Gender differences in moral orientation: A meta-analysis. *Psychological Bulletin, 126*(5), 703.

Katz, J. A. (2014). Education and training in entrepreneurship. In Gielnik, M. M., Cardon, M. S., & Frese, M. (Eds.), *The Psychology of Entrepreneurship*. London: Psychology Press, pp. 241–268.

Kirzner, I. M. (2009). The alert and creative entrepreneur: A clarification. *Small Business Economics, 32*(2), 145–152.

Kristensen, S. B. P., Namatovu, R., & Dawa, S. (2016). Rural youth entrepreneurship in eastern Uganda. In Gough, K. V., & Langevang, T. (Eds.), *Young Entrepreneurs in Sub-Saharan Africa*. London: Routledge, pp. 132–145.

Kuratko, D. F., & Morris, M. H. (2018). Corporate entrepreneurship: A critical challenge for educators and researchers. *Entrepreneurship Education and Pedagogy, 1*(1), 42–60.

Kyrgidou, L. P., & Petridou, E. (2013). Developing women entrepreneurs' knowledge, skills and attitudes through e-mentoring support. *Journal of Small Business and Enterprise Development, 20*(3), 548–566.

Laguía, A., García-Ael, C., Wach, D., & Moriano, J. A. (2019). 'Think entrepreneur-think male': a task and relationship scale to measure gender stereotypes in entrepreneurship. *International Entrepreneurship and Management Journal, 15*(3), 749–772.

Lassalle, P., & McElwee, G. (2016). Polish entrepreneurs in Glasgow and entrepreneurial opportunity structure. *International Journal of Entrepreneurial Behavior & Research*, *22*(2), 260–281.

Lepoutre, J., Justo, R., Terjesen, S., & Bosma, N. (2013). Designing a global standardized methodology for measuring social entrepreneurship activity: The Global Entrepreneurship Monitor social entrepreneurship study. *Small Business Economics*, *40*(3), 693–714.

Lindbergh, J., & Schwartz, B. (2018). Entrepreneurship in societal change. In Berglund, K., & Verduyn, K. (Eds.), *Revitalizing Entrepreneurship Education: Adopting a Critical Approach in the Classroom*. London: Routledge, Chapter 2.

Lourenço, F., Sappleton, N., Dardaine-Edwards, A., McElwee, G., Cheng, R., Taylor, D. W., & Taylor, A. G. (2014). Experience of entrepreneurial training for female farmers to stimulate entrepreneurship in Uganda. *Gender in Management: An International Journal*, *29*(7), 382–401.

Mani, M. (2018). Entrepreneurship education: A students' perspective. In Information Resources Management Association (Ed.), *Business Education and Ethics: Concepts, Methodologies, Tools, and Applications*. Hershey, PA: IGI Global, pp. 526–540.

Marlow, S., & McAdam, M. (2013). Gender and entrepreneurship: Advancing debate and challenging myths; exploring the mystery of the under-performing female entrepreneur. *International Journal of Entrepreneurial Behavior & Research*, *19*(1), 114–124.

Martin, B. C., McNally, J. J., & Kay, M. J. (2013). Examining the formation of human capital in entrepreneurship: A meta-analysis of entrepreneurship education outcomes. *Journal of Business Venturing*, *28*(2), 211–224.

Martínez, A. C., Levie, J., Kelley, D. J., SÆmundsson, R. J., & Schøtt, T. (2010). Global entrepreneurship monitor special report: A global perspective on entrepreneurship education and training. Strathclyde: University of Strathclyde, Elsevier.

McKenzie, D., & Woodruff, C. (2014). What are we learning from business training and entrepreneurship evaluations around the developing world? *The World Bank Research Observer*, *29*(1), 48–82.

Miller, T. L., Grimes, M. G., McMullen, J. S., & Vogus, T. J. (2012). Venturing for others with heart and head: How compassion encourages social entrepreneurship. *Academy of Management Review*, *37*(4), 616–640.

Minniti, M. (2009). Gender issues in entrepreneurship. *Foundations and Trends® in Entrepreneurship*, *5*(7–8), 497–621.

Nguyen, C., Frederick, H., & Nguyen, H. (2014). Female entrepreneurship in rural Vietnam: An exploratory study. In Lewis, K., Henry, C., Gatewood, E. J., & Watson, J. (Eds.), *Women's Entrepreneurship in the 21st Century*. Cheltenham, UK and Northampton, MA, USA: Edward Elgar Publishing, Chapter 4.

Peterman, N. E., & Kennedy, J. (2003). Enterprise education: Influencing students' perceptions of entrepreneurship. *Entrepreneurship Theory and Practice*, *28*(2), 129–144.

Rae, D., Martin, L., Antcliff, V., & Hannon, P. (2010, November). The 2010 survey of enterprise and entrepreneurship in higher education. In 33rd ISBE Conference, pp. 3–4.

Rindova, V., Barry, D., & Ketchen Jr, D. J. (2009). Entrepreneuring as emancipation. *Academy of Management Review*, *34*(3), 477–491.

Schneider, K. (2017). Entrepreneurial competencies of women entrepreneurs of micro and small enterprises. *Science Journal of Education*, *5*(6), 252–261.

Shane, S. A. (2003). *A General Theory of Entrepreneurship: The Individual–Opportunity Nexus*. Cheltenham, UK and Northampton, MA, USA: Edward Elgar Publishing.

Shane, S., & Venkataraman, S. (2000). The promise of entrepreneurship as a field of research. *Academy of Management Review*, *25*(1), 217–226.

Shastri, S., Shastri, S., & Pareek, A. (2019). Motivations and challenges of women entrepreneurs. *International Journal of Sociology and Social Policy*, *39*(5/6), 338–355.

Sheikh, S., Sist, F., Akdeniz, A., & Yousafzai, S. (2018). Developing an understanding of entrepreneurship intertwined with motherhood: A career narrative of British Mumpreneurs. In Yousafzai, S., Lindgreen, A., Saeed, S., & Henry, C. (Eds.), *Contextual Embeddedness of Women's Entrepreneurship* (pp. 219–232). London: Routledge.

Singh, G., & Belwal, R. (2008). Entrepreneurship and SMEs in Ethiopia. *Gender in Management: An International Journal, 23*(2), 120–136.

Singh, V. (2017). Education and emancipation of Dalits children: Analysing human development in lens of capability approach perspective. *Social Work Chronicle, 6*(a), 28–38.

Smith, I. H., & Woodworth, W. P. (2012). Developing social entrepreneurs and social innovators: A social identity and self-efficacy approach. *Academy of Management Learning & Education, 11*(3), 390–407.

Stephan, U., Uhlaner, L. M., & Stride, C. (2015). Institutions and social entrepreneurship: The role of institutional voids, institutional support, and institutional configurations. *Journal of International Business Studies, 46*(3), 308–331.

Steyaert, C. (2007). 'Entrepreneuring' as a conceptual attractor? A review of process theories in 20 years of entrepreneurship studies. *Entrepreneurship and Regional Development, 19*(6), 453–477.

Terjesen, S., Hessels, J., & Li, D. (2016). Comparative international entrepreneurship: A review and research agenda. *Journal of Management, 42*(1), 299–344.

Tesfaye, B., & Lundström, A. (2019). Engaging successful migrant entrepreneurs in socially responsible causes: A case from Sweden. In Farache, F., Grigore, G., Stancu, A., & McQueen, D. (Eds.), *Responsible People*. Cham: Palgrave Macmillan, pp. 15–38.

Tibbits, G. E., & Kandasaami, T. (1995). An empirical investigation of women small business owner. *The International Journal of Accounting and Business Society, 3*(1), 41–56.

UBOS (2014). 2014–2015 Statistical abstract, Uganda government ministry of finance and economic development.

Urban, B., & Kujinga, L. (2017). The institutional environment and social entrepreneurship intentions. *International Journal of Entrepreneurial Behavior & Research, 23*(4), 638–655.

Vazquez-Brust, D., Smith, A. M., & Sarkis, J. (2014). Managing the transition to critical green growth: The 'Green Growth State'. *Futures, 64*, 38–50.

3. Creating value in the margins: rethinking value creation, empowerment and women's entrepreneurship in South Africa's street food sector

Jiska de Groot, Nthabiseng Mohlakoana, Abigail Knox, Debbie Sparks and Hans Bressers

INTRODUCTION

Entrepreneurship in the informal sector provides an important source of income for many in developing economies (ILO, 2018). Globally, more than 60% of employed men and women earn their livelihoods in the informal economy. The informal food sector, the focus of this chapter, is part of this proliferating sector and provides an important source of income for women in Africa, who own and operate enterprises in the sector. The informal economy's ability to absorb semi-unskilled labour and the low barriers to entry are often cited as reasons for women's high participation in the informal sector (Muzaffar et al., 2009). But entrepreneurship in this sector can do more: self-employment in the informal economy may provide women with the independence and flexibility to balance domestic and business responsibilities (Kabeer, 2012). The income generated contributes to food, shelter and children's education (Fasoyiro, 2011), and many entrepreneurs express ambitions to grow their business (Knox et al., 2019). Yet, evaluations of the sector are often based only on the financial aspects of the enterprise (Jones et al., 2017), demonstrating the narrow conceptualization within which informal sector enterprises are assessed.

This is especially detrimental for female entrepreneurs because even though the sector is crucial for the livelihoods of many women, these informal enterprises are often inaccurately labelled as 'survivalist' enterprises that do not aspire to invest in business growth or hire staff (Knox et al., 2019). It is therefore often concluded that they add limited value to the economy, leading to development policies that remain fixated on monetary value creation and give priority to so-called growth-oriented enterprises. In doing so, they fail to recognize other forms of value-creation from informal entrepreneurship that extends beyond the financial gains of the enterprise. Examples of the non-monetary value added are empowerment processes and the numerous ways in which income generated through the enterprise flows back into the economy, resulting in positive social impacts (see, e.g. de Groot et al., 2017; Zahra et al., 2009), agency and self-worth (Mohlakoana et al., 2018), or meeting other unmet needs in society. By highlighting women's empowerment as creation of value in informal food enterprises, this chapter sets out to contribute to the evidence base, the multitude of ways in which value is created through women's entrepreneurship. Value creation, in this context, will refer to the success in financial and non-financial terms brought about by women's enterprises, as the value created for women by running an enterprise can encompass a range of aspects of their lives. This chapter focuses on South Africa and specifically considers the ways in which entrepreneurship in the informal sector functions as a driver of women's empowerment, proposing this as a way of creating individual value. The chapter is structured as follows: Section 2 discusses the key literature on this topic, Section 3 briefly describes the study's methods and introduces the study area. Section 4 presents the study's findings followed by a discussion section (Section 5) which brings together the elements of women's empowerment to discuss individual value creation in informal food enterprises. Section 6 highlights the study's main findings and makes policy suggestions for a more holistic approach to value creation in the sector.

WOMEN ENTREPRENEURS IN THE INFORMAL SECTOR AND THE VALUE THEY CREATE

The entrepreneurial activities of the majority of women in developing countries are focused on the informal sector (Clancy and Dutta, 2005; ILO, 2018). Informal enterprises are broadly defined as enterprises that are not formally registered, which keep no accounts, and in which its employees are not formally registered (Chen, 2012). Women are often driven into the informal end of the economy for three reasons: low barriers to entry (Muzaffar et al., 2009), fewer registration regulations, and the need for limited start-up capital (Berner et al., 2012; Gomez, 2008; Grant, 2013; Gurtoo and Williams, 2009); less stringent requirements for skills or qualifications; and women's domestic responsibilities.

As a result, women's informal activities are often located in the least profitable end of the economies in which they operate, in highly saturated, low-income activities, frequently in the production and sales of food items (ENDA, 2010; Osei-Boateng and Ampratwum, 2011). This places most women's informal microenterprises beyond the reach of common development policies and programmes supporting entrepreneurship, since they tend to support enterprises falling within the traditional/ mainstream conceptions of drivers of economic growth (Berner et al., 2012; Choto et al., 2014; Skinner and Haysom, 2016). Informal microenterprises are also at times penalized through punitive policies and regulations.

Considering the serious challenges outlined above the question can be posed – what, if any, value do women derive from entrepreneurship in the informal sector? The existing literature is divided, with Monteith and Giesbert (2017), for example, reporting that informal workers in Uganda, Burkino Faso and Sri Lanka valued a combination of instrumental features of work relating to income, survival and health, freedom and independence, trust and relationships at work, alongside social recognition and respect. Self-employment in the informal economy was also found to provide women with the independence and flexibility to balance domestic and business responsibilities (Kabeer, 2012). Similarly, Mohlakoana et al. (2019) reported that female entrepreneurs in Senegal, Rwanda and South Africa felt positive about their personal situation and value was derived from their enterprise in a variety of ways, including increased self-esteem, better financial circumstances and more respect among family and friends. In contrast, Temkin (2009) reported that informal entrepreneurs in Mexico tended to be poorer, older and less educated than their formally employed counterparts and less satisfied with their household's financial circumstances.

Value creation in enterprises is generally studied from the narrow perspective of financial performance, wealth creation and firm growth and survival (McMullen and Warnick, 2015). Women-owned businesses tend to be smaller, slower growing, and less profitable than those owned by men (Greene et al., 2003). Furthermore, some authors including Berner et al. (2012) and Temkin (2009) argue that few women's enterprises are 'growth' oriented in the sense of favouring risk-taking and business expansion through employees over diversification and low-risk approaches. This view is based on the outdated perception that entrepreneurship depicts a form of masculinity (see, e.g. Mirchandani, 1999; Knox et al. 2019) in which a masculine view of entrepreneurship is dominant, with men's value systems, mindsets and behavioural patterns employed when studying and evaluating women's businesses.

Entrepreneurship is often constructed through a masculine lens and this has received considerable critique (see, e.g. Andersén, 2011; de Groot et al., 2017; Knox et al., 2019). This is despite evidence indicating that women's and men's businesses have different business characteristics, motives of entrepreneurial endeavour, barriers and opportunities, management styles and even areas of entrepreneurship (see, e.g. Huarng et al., 2012). The masculine lens also overlooks the multiple dimensions of value creation in enterprises by not moving beyond a narrow view of monetary value creation to encompass other types of value creation such as agency, independence, quality of life, flexibility and the ability to respond to social needs (Zahra et al., 2009; Mahmud et al., 2012). Women were found to derive satisfaction that is equal to men from their entrepreneurial careers, yet also placed greater emphasis on socio-emotional career satisfaction derived through interpersonal relations with employees and customers, self-realization of goals (Walker et al., 2011), freedom to take risks and define one's own work style (Bennett and Dann, 2000) and the pursuit of social and family-related goals and responsibilities (Bird and Brush, 2002; Mohlakoana et al., 2019).

WOMEN'S EMPOWERMENT AND VALUE CREATION

This chapter focuses specifically on empowerment as a non-monetary value arising from informal entrepreneurship. Women's empowerment is a key aspect of the social dimension of value creation and growth, and as a concept it is a transformative process of value creation. Empowerment can span a range of dimensions, including the economic, sociocultural, familial/interpersonal, legal, political, and psychological (Kabeer, 1999; Mahmud et al., 2012). It affects individuals, households and the community and operates on a sliding scale from disempowerment to empowerment. The literature distinguishes five key elements of empowerment. First, the contextual factors in a women's life, including educational opportunities, culture and religion that affect the opportunities available to her (Mahmud et al., 2012). Others include personal circumstances, for example being head of household with economic decision-making capacity, and mobility (Downing and Daniels, 1992). The second is a woman's access to resources, including material, human and social resources (Kabeer, 1999), and her ability to exercise control over these (Mahmud et al., 2012), both of which can be important pre-conditions for empowerment. Third, the ability to define her goals and act upon them is referred to as agency (Mahmud et al., 2012) and represents both observable and non-observable empowerment processes, such as the motivation to act upon a goal or the ability to negotiate in a range of contexts (Kabeer, 1999). The fourth is a woman's achievements. Her existing achievements reflect the outcomes of the transformation processes of empowerment and the (in) equality of the choices that affect these outcomes (Kabeer, 1999). Fifth, women's transformative processes, which represent the shift from being disempowered to being empowered. It is here where context, access to resources, agency and achievements come together to bring about change. The empowerment process shares many characteristics of value creation in enterprises, through a combination of concept (consisting of the business idea or the niche), the resources available to the entrepreneur, and the ability and the skills of the entrepreneur to execute and implement the idea (Zahra et al., 2009). These synergies and the way they are interlaced provide an excellent starting point to explore women's empowerment as value creation. Next, we will consider each factor in more detail and how they individually and together create value in women's lives.

METHODOLOGY

This study consists of qualitative interviews conducted with female entrepreneurs in the informal food sector in South Africa. Between 2015 and 2018, a total of 49 semi-structured interviews were conducted with informal food traders in Cape Town and Durban. These traders were sourced at transport hubs, marketplaces, road-side and home-based enterprises using purposive sampling to ensure a wide range of food enterprises.

Face-to-face semi-structured interviews lasted between 30 and 60 minutes each, and covered areas including: demographics and business characteristics; energy use in the enterprise; empowerment and entrepreneurship. A range of entrepreneurship types were selected to cover different aspects of the informal sector including food preparation, processing and vending, both home-based and outside of the home. The qualitative interviews were transcribed, coded and thematically analysed using a deductive strategy following Kabeer's elements of empowerment.[1]

Many of South Africa's inhabitants live below the poverty line and due to its Apartheid legacy, South Africa remains one of the most unequal societies in the world (World Bank, 2018). Informal businesses are essential for the livelihood strategies of many to escape poverty or unemployment, which averages 27.6% nationally (Trading Economics, 2019). Through entrepreneurship, many women seek to expand their skill set and use their experience to earn an income and make the most of opportunities to gain control over their destiny whilst fulfilling family responsibilities.

In South Africa in 2012, roughly 2.1 million people operated in the informal economy, of which about 57% were men and 41% women. However, the South African government views the informal economy as a 'second economy' that perpetuates Apartheid's system of inequality and marginalization, leading to a tense relationship between authorities and the informal sector. Nevertheless, the sector is acknowledged and even supported through a range of national and local government policies, regulations and byelaws.

WOMEN'S EMPOWERMENT AS A MEANS TO CREATE VALUE IN THE INFORMAL FOOD ENTERPRISES

The five elements of empowerment identified in the previous sections align closely with scholars that suggested that value creation in enterprises happens through a combination of concept, the resources available to the entrepreneur, and the ability and skills of the entrepreneur to execute and implement the idea (Zahra et al., 2009). This suggests important synergies between value creation and empowerment, in which women's empowerment itself can be seen as a form of value creation. The following sections will relate the relevant aspects of empowerment to value creation in an enterprise, considering the first four elements of empowerment. The fifth element (women's transformative processes) links the other elements and will be discussed in Section 5.

Concept and the Contextual Factors that Affect Value Creation in Women's Enterprises in South Africa's Informal Food Sector

Zahra et al. (2009) identify concept as a key factor for value creation in enterprises, including business idea or niche. Individual value is created in the informal food sector niche, where a range of contextual factors create and hinder opportunities. South Africa's struggling economy, high levels of poverty and unemployment provide the context in which a large informal sector has emerged and in which the entrepreneurs operate. Most study respondents had low levels of education, generally up to high school level. Despite these disempowering circumstances, they managed to become entrepreneurs and create value.

Sego, a respondent from Cape Town selling cooked meat, stated:

> People always want it [barbequed meat], so it is easy to start. You just need to find a good spot. (Sego, Cape Town, married with children)

She is one of several respondents who illustrate that the informal food sector has low barriers to entry. Existing studies in this area confirm that the sector provides a relatively 'easy' way to generate an income when there is a lack of formal jobs and one's level of education is low (Clancy and Dutta, 2005; Khamata-Njenga and Clancy, 2003).

Some women operated in the informal sector because they were unsure how long they would be active in the food sector as they felt this depended on business success. Haan (2016) notes that because of this they did not feel obliged to register their business.

A woman's personal circumstances, including her position as head of household, partner with equal decision-making power or being economically dependent will affect her empowerment process (Mahmud et al., 2012). Many entrepreneurs in the informal food sector in Africa are main breadwinners (Mohlakoana et al., 2019). We found a large percentage of single, divorced and widowed entrepreneurs (28 out of 49 interviewees), which can aid individual empowerment processes born out of necessity. For example, Tenday is a single mother who started her business to provide for her family. She expresses that she is very happy about this, as her business gives her the freedom to do whatever she wants. She uses the money generated to pay her workers, and whatever remains is for her to spend based on her own judgement. She likes the fact that she does not need to discuss with anybody (or ask permission) on what to do with her money and can make her own life choices. She expresses that:

> it is empowering to have a business; and it is better than sitting at home. (Durban, single mother)

There appears to be a link between head of household and increased agency evident in our study, as women expressed that their position as head of household has increased agency which, albeit born out of necessity, has created an environment that allowed the empowerment process to unfold. This is a significant finding as the increase in female-headed households in South Africa, combined with high unemployment and low levels of education, may result in an increase of women that turn to the informal food sector as a means to improve livelihoods. Their position as informal entrepreneur may also create additional personal value in the form of increased agency and enable the empowerment process to unfold.

Access to Resources

Access to resources is the second critical element of both empowerment (Kabeer, 2005) and value creation (Zahra et al., 2009). This was discussed extensively by participants, with only a few having some sort of access and many expressing a desire to have better access to finances. Nqobile (a 54-year-old respondent from Durban), indicated that although she is interested in growing her business to become more profitable, she would need money. As she expressed:

Without money it won't grow. (Durban, married with children)

Similarly, Lesego, a widow from Durban, selling traditional hot meals, indicated that what she needs the most in order to grow, is money. She can then buy enough stock and more equipment to make her stand look more presentable. However, she also indicated that she would never take a loan because she wouldn't be able to pay it back.

The literature supports the need resource access, with Mahmud et al. (2012) and Kabeer (2005) stating that agency and the transformative process are strongly related to a woman's access and control over material, human and social resources, whether acquired through the market, community or family. Furthermore, Kabeer (2005) indicates that if a woman's main access to resources is as a dependent member of her family, her capacity to make strategic life choices is likely to be limited, whilst the previous section has shown that being household head may create opportunities for empowerment.

In general, informal entrepreneurs have access to few resources which hinders the value that can be created from their enterprise: they will not be able to get a bank loan or access to other formal finance, access to municipal services, alongside enterprise assistance such as business accelerators. They are often actively oppressed by restricting urban planning policies and police harassment and are not accounted for in development policies (Choto et al., 2014; Skinner and Haysom, 2016). Although the informal food sector is very visible on the street, it remains overlooked by formal planning and policy processes. This is arguably intentional due to selective non-planning, benign neglect and tolerance of 'grey space' (see, e.g. Yiftachel, 2009), forcing women to buy small quantities of goods that, if confiscated or stolen, would not sink the business. Yet, this prevents them from reaching economies of scale and decreases the monetary value that they can create from their enterprise. Because women dominate the informal food sector in South Africa, the lack of access to resources severely limits business operation and growth.

The effect of a lack of access to resources and how it affects value creation was discussed by most respondents and we found that if entrepreneurs had access to resources, however modest, they would use this to grow their businesses. These findings are supported by those from a quantitative survey among this group of entrepreneurs (see Knox et al., 2019). We found that despite an entrepreneur's ability to identify a niche from which to operate and create value in her enterprise, her lack of access to financial resources hampers her ability to pursue this. However, the limited resources the women had access to, were used to improve their lives, creating value in the margins.

Respondents identified several ways in which they tried to overcome their lack of resources and manage the informality of their enterprise. Peer-to-peer informal saving schemes were mentioned by several interviewees as a way to access money. Wendy, an entrepreneur in Cape Town, for example, stated:

> I put my money in the bank or use a bit for a gooi gooi. (Cape Town, single)

A *gooi gooi* is an informal financing scheme that provides entrepreneurs with the opportunity to access larger sums of money needed for business investment, for example a barbeque or new appliance. This is an important way of accessing credit and allowing for informal savings, especially among women (Mashigo and Schoeman, 2012). An important element of women's alternative ways of accessing funding is that it demonstrates their ability to source resources for business improvement, increasing the value and potential of their businesses.

While access to finances as a resource was the most prominent issue for entrepreneurs in our study, a second was access to a suitable enterprise location. The informal food sector targets commuters and passersby. Municipal interventions, however, often affect access to locations or resources in those locations. Beatrice, for example, indicates that:

> I operate my stand with a few other women at the same trading spot ... The trading area which provides a shade and protection for us ... that is nice. (Cape Town, single with children)

She indicates that the area also has electricity, which traders are expected to use. Although at first glance this is a supportive intervention by the municipality, the traders are not allowed to use other fuels such as gas, wood or charcoal for their enterprises. This causes a lack of access to essential resources because it prohibits entrepreneurs from preparing their best selling or most profitable products. Similarly, forced relocation of traders to centralized vending locations may result in decreased access to customers they may have had at popular vending spots. Thus, a lack of access to financial resources and location-related resources affects value creation in the enterprises studied, limiting the potential of the entrepreneurs and hindering the empowerment process.

Agency

Agency creates value as it provides entrepreneurs with the ability to implement their idea(s) (Zahra et al., 2009). The previous sections showed how contextual factors such as the position as female-headed household, appropriate locations and access to finance increased entrepreneurs' agency in their enterprises. The majority of interviewees expressed a positive ability to make decisions and act on their own life choices. Most felt very strongly that operating a business gave them a sense of freedom, pride and achievement, and financial freedom and independence. Thus, in itself entrepreneurship is creating individual value and positively affected the way in which people saw themselves, that is, agency. For example, Thuli from Cape

Town expressed that she is able to purposefully plan for her future since starting her business:

> ... my own business, it gives me a steady income that I can work with, and that is good. You see, I can make plans for the future because it gives me a budget. (Cape Town, married)

Similarly, Karabo from Cape Town saw a business opportunity for selling meat and used her agency to start a business. She prefers to be self-employed than joining formal employment as she gets more money than she would in a formal job and because it creates value at a personal level, for example through the freedom to operate and flexibility of working hours. Correspondingly, Amanda expressed that she feels that:

> women are now more independent and self-reliant; they no longer depend on men to earn a living. (Cape town, single with children)

Hence in addition to the ability to make decisions, there is evidence that, for the women above, their sense of agency increased by operating their own business, and the purpose that they brought to their actions changed, for example by planning for the longer term, or deciding to stay in the informal sector. Thus, in addition to monetary value, non-monetary value in terms of autonomy and freedom is generated, as well as a sense of purpose. This becomes even more evident in the next section, where individual achievements are discussed.

Achievements and Value Creation

Whilst resources and agency make up our capabilities and reflect our opportunity to live our desired lives (Kabeer, 2005), the closely intertwined concept of 'achievements' refers to 'the extent to which this potential is realised or fails to be realised; that is, to the outcomes of people's efforts' (Kabeer, 2005, p. 15). It is here where the difference between the empowering effect of an enterprise for a woman's independence and meaning, and the barriers needing to be overcome to reach full potential are visible. Our study shows that both are present since many women were empowered in some areas but not necessarily in others.

Some entrepreneurs stated that selling food in the informal sector resulted from a lack of alternatives and choice (e.g. wage labour), even if they enjoyed having the enterprise and felt empowered. Cecelia, for example, started her business out of necessity to sustain her family when her husband died and she was unemployed. She said it was easy to start this business, since all it requires is a barbeque and a good location. Although she feels happy to run a business and expressed ambitions for her enterprise to grow, women's activities to take up entrepreneurship would be 'far more likely to be empowering if it contributes to women's sense of independence, rather than simply meeting survival needs' (Kabeer 2005, p.15).

Most respondents, however, reported the sense of independence and self-worth they experienced from being an entrepreneur. Karabo, for example, describes her realization of potential when stating that:

> Because I work for myself, I earn my own income and I can budget the amount I want for income and do things that I want to do … compared to someone who has a job and wait for wages. I can push my income the way I want. I can easily make decisions. (Karabo, married with children)

Karabo started her business because she saw an opportunity and she felt a desire for independence, rather than a lack of alternatives. Most women interviewed stated that they do the work, making their own decisions, and they expressed a sense of pride that they were able to turn their passion for cooking into an income-generating activity, creating a sense of achievement and pride. Furthermore, many respondents that used to seek formal employment expressed that because their business is successful, they have chosen not to return to the formal sector, which suggests that sufficient monetary and non-monetary value was created through their enterprise.

The majority of women felt that women were successful in their sector, and many respondents reported that, often after starting a family, they chose to join the informal sector. This has important implications for individual value creation. First, because enterprises were found to contribute to a sense of independence and self-reliance, for both single-headed households and those in partnerships. Second, the enterprises provided the flexibility needed to allow women to combine reproductive responsibilities with income generation, creating value that extends far beyond the individual into much broader societal benefits such as education and welfare of children. Sipu from Cape Town, for example, is married, has one child, and started her business after she graduated from school but was unsure about her career path. Now, eight years later, she owns an enterprise with four employees. She feels like a 'real entrepreneur', as she started with nothing, but now has established a name because of the variety and quality of her food. This demonstrates Sipu's ability to lead the life that she has chosen and realize her potential. She has full autonomy over her business and its profit, which she wants to use to buy a house together with her husband, but most importantly to pay for her child's education. Education has also been mentioned by other respondents such as Karabo, who highlighted that she wanted her children to complete tertiary education so that they can make their own life choices.

However, the empowerment benefits resulting from an informal food enterprise were not present for all. The data show that some women entered the sector in desperate need for an income and remained in the sector out of necessity rather than choice. Among these women, there seemed to be less of a sense of agency and self-determination compared to the majority of respondents who took up entrepreneurship by choice (even if they entered the sector out of necessity). Here, value was created in the process, which moves beyond (financial) gain, and encompasses independence, freedom of choice and movement, confidence, and pride in their endeavours as an important benefit of operating in the informal food sector. Specifically, the informal food sector seems to gain traction in its empowerment benefits when enterprises become successful and provide financial independence and decision-making power. An important caveat, however, is the risk that once the entrepreneurs see the potential of their enterprise and want to realize this full potential (by increasing business size or joining the formal sector), they may face a range of new and/or ongoing constraints such as funding limitations (often gender-related), as well as restrictive policy and planning environments.

DISCUSSION: ACCESS TO RESOURCES, AGENCY AND ACHIEVEMENTS: INDIVIDUAL VALUE CREATION AND THE TRANSFORMATIVE PROCESS

This section will discuss how informal entrepreneurship in the food sector has created value at an individual level and contributes to the transformative process. The interrelations between agency, access to resources and achievements are explored as the pathways that contribute to the transformative process and ultimately value creation. The narratives have shown a range of empowerment aspects, particularly the ability of the women to make their own decisions, be financially independent, and have a sense of achievement and pride. The aspect of choice is more complicated, and many authors (see, e.g. Kishor and Gupta, 2004; Kabeer, 2005) stress that empowerment really revolves around the ability to make choices, which we found to be the case too. Importantly, being empowered means that there must be alternatives. In this study, the majority of respondents discussed their ability to make choices alongside the alternatives they have had (e.g. sitting at home, formal employment or other career paths). The question is whether these are real choices or choices borne out of necessity, or both, as their entrepreneurship was sometimes a result of their role as head of household or the absence of formal employment. Importantly, pathways of change are context-dependent, and even within the same context women's empowerment experiences may differ within the same dimension (Mahmud et al., 2012). Our study supports this since for some, entering the informal food sector has been a real choice, whereas for others it initially was necessity but has become a choice over time through the monetary and non-monetary value it has created for the women. Nevertheless, assuming that everybody enters the informal sector out of a lack of choice or necessity, is biased and reproduces structures of inequality.

The second pre-condition for the transformative process of empowerment discussed by Kabeer (2005) is that 'alternatives must not only exist, they must also be seen to exist' (p. 14). Power relations are most effective when they are not perceived as such and gender inequality persists through the unquestioned acceptance of this power balance. A good example is shown by Pamela's story. Pamela is married and started her business because she has a love for cooking and didn't want to stay at home after the birth of her second child. Pamela's business is part of her husband's slaughterhouse, and she indicates that even though she runs it, he is the boss and has the final say over her business. She would like to grow her business, but indicates it is up to her husband to decide and did not question this power relation, suggesting a deeper embeddedness of her and her enterprise in patriarchal structures than many of the interviewees faced. Those with partners often mentioned that both share the decision-making power in the house or that they were the sole decision-maker in the enterprise. Kabeer (2005) describes the phenomenon of women who internalize their lesser claim on household resources or decision-making power, being because behaving otherwise is considered outside the realm of possibilities. As she stresses, these forms of behaviour: 'are really based on the denial of choice' (Kabeer, 2005, p. 14), and as a result limit women's empowerment. Thus, in the example above, although the enterprise creates individual value for the women in relation to satisfaction and self-worth, her empowerment journey is more complicated.

Moreover, the empowerment experienced by the women in this case study is sometimes aided by living in a society that faces serious challenges with regard to family structures and domestic problems, resulting in many female-headed households. Although this may create value at an individual level, this value is not synonymous with empowerment. As empowerment is a relational transformative process, it means that a person's surrounding must also be part of this transformation (e.g. husbands, broader family relations and society as a whole). Compared to a similar sample of interviewees in Rwanda and Senegal, the rates of marriage were far lower in South Africa (Mohlakoana et al., 2019), which contributes to explaining the large number of female-headed households in this study. Because several women interviewed were the head of household, they likely have no husband and fewer other relatives that claim this position, easing the personal sense of empowerment and agency-related processes, but that may contribute less to the long-term societal transformation that accompanies personal agency and achievements.

The above findings have important synergies with the literature on individual value creation through entrepreneurship (see, e.g. Zahra et al., 2009) in which value creation is described as a combination of concept, access to resources and the entrepreneur's ability to implement the idea. The findings show that several entrepreneurs identified a niche in which to operate and used their agency and skillset to implement their idea.

Most respondents demonstrated increased agency as a result of their enterprise. Although this is partly related to their *context* (a large informal economy, few other job opportunities and a high number of female, single-headed households) the micro-narratives of the entrepreneurs highlight motivation and drive as well as the personal value they derive from being able to make their own decisions or the sense of self-worth of becoming an entrepreneur.

In the data presented, there are various cases of transformative agency, even if small, that in the long term may transform a system (particularly in the case of South Africa) that is increasingly characterized by female-headed households. The transformative process, however, should also extend to the financial and regulatory environment to ensure that enterprises are appreciated and considered an asset to the economy. The business support and integration in spatial planning that such business status attracts and deserves would further enhance the transformative process.

Changes in any one dimension of empowerment can lead to changes in others. For instance, 'achievements' such as business success in one sphere of life and the monetary and non-monetary value they derive from business success, can form the basis on which women seek improvements in other spheres. Similarly, policy changes that provide women with access to new or improved resources may be the result of their collective action for change, for example public vending spaces, better access to finances or education in the long term. Such changes may occur over the life course of an individual or group or across generations, but all are important contributors to both women's empowerment and value creation.

CONCLUSIONS

This chapter set out to contribute to the evidence base on the multiple kinds of individual value that are created through women's entrepreneurship in the informal food sector and its synergies with women's empowerment processes. The study found that even in the context of the informal economy, significant value was created at an individual level. Examples are personal growth through increased capacity to make decisions, the freedom to spend income and determine one's own future, as well as the satisfaction and benefits that the enterprises brought to the many women who had significant reproductive responsibilities.

The cases of transformative agency presented not only create individual value for the entrepreneurs, but may transform the system in the long term, if they are nurtured and extended to the financial and regulatory environment and receive business support. Despite the long hours, low profits and high odds in the informal sector, women are able to create individual monetary and non-monetary value and achieve their own empowerment. The positive value created in one sphere of a woman's life can form the basis on which they seek improvements in other spheres. A woman's success and achievements are related to financial independence, ability to make her own decisions, freedom to spend her own money, ability to support her family financially, increased sense of self-worth and agency, and by balancing productive and reproductive responsibilities. Unlike traditional approaches to enterprise development which favour growth in firm size, profits and market penetration; this research shows that an alternative approach to development based on individual value creation linked to women's empowerment is worth pursuing.

This chapter therefore calls for greater attention to alternative measures of value generated by informal economic activities. Relevant stakeholders need to consider a much broader range of entrepreneurship types in the provision of micro-finance to enable women's informal enterprises to also benefit. In addition, economic development and planning policies need to start working with the sector in order to contribute to an environment in which women entrepreneurs in the informal food sector can increase the individual value created from their enterprises and realize their full potential.

NOTE

1. All names have been anonymised.

REFERENCES

Andersén, J. 2011. Strategic resources and firm performance. *Management Decision*, 49:1, 87–98.

Bennett, R., & Dann, S. 2000. The change experience of Australian female entrepreneurs. *Graduate Business School of Queensland University*, 7:2, 75–83.

Berner, E., Gomez, G., & Knorringa, P. 2012. Helping a large number of people become a little less poor: the logic of survival entrepreneurs. *European Journal of Development*, 24, 382–396.

Bird, B., & Brush, C., 2002. A gendered perspective on organizational creation. *Entrepreneurship Theory and Practice*, 26:3, 41–65.

Chen, M.A., 2012. *The informal economy: definitions, theories and policies*. Cambridge, MA; Manchester UK: WIEGO.

Choto, P., Tengeh, R. K., & Iwu, C. G. 2014. *Daring to survive or to grow? The growth aspirations and challenges of survivalist entrepreneurs in South Africa*. Retrieved from: http://hdl.handle.net/11189/4920.

Clancy, J., & Dutta, S. 2005. Women and productive uses of energy: some light on a shadowy area, in Paper presented at the UNDP Meeting on Productive Uses of Renewable Energy. Bangkok, Thailand 9–11 May 2005.

de Groot, J., Mohlakoana, N., Knox, A., & Bressers, H. 2017. Fuelling women's empowerment? An exploration of the linkages between gender, entrepreneurship and access to energy in the informal food sector. *Energy Research & Social Science*, 28, 86–97. https://doi.org/10.1016/j.erss.2017.04.004.

Downing, J., & Daniels, L. 1992. The growth and dynamics of women entrepreneurs in Southern Africa. GEMINI Technical Report No. 47. Washington, DC: United States Agency for International Development.

ENDA, 2010. Rapport provisoire de l'enquête de base sur l'alimentation de rue dans la région de Dakar. ENDA.

Fasoyiro, S. B. 2011. Assessment of hazards in local soy-cheese processing: implications on health and environment in Oyo State, Nigeria. *WIT Transactions on Ecology and the Environment*, 152, 37–44.

Gomez, G. 2008. *Do micro-enterprises promote equity or growth?* Gorinchem: Woord en Daad Institute of Social Studies.

Grant, R. 2013. Gendered spaces of informal entrepreneurship in Soweto, South Africa. *Urban Geography*, 34:1, 86–108.

Greene, P. G., Hart, M. M., Gatewood, E. J., Brush, C. G., & Carter, N. M. 2003. Women entrepreneurs: moving front and center: an overview of research and theory. White Paper Series. U.S. Boca Raton, FL: Association for Small Business & Entrepreneurship. http://www.usasbe.org/knowledge/whitepapers/greene2003.pdf.

Gurtoo, A., & Williams, C. C. 2009. Entrepreneurship and the informal sector: some lessons from India. *The International Journal of Entrepreneurship and Innovation*, 10:1, 55–62.

Haan, B. 2016. *Energy and women's empowerment: a study on modern energy services and women's empowerment in the informal food sector in Cape Town, South Africa*. Amsterdam: IVM Institute for Environmental Studies, Vrije Universiteit Amsterdam.

Huarng, K. H., Mas-Tur, A., & Yu, T. H. K. 2012. Factors affecting the success of women entrepreneurs. *International Entrepreneurship and Management Journal*, 8:4, 487–497.

ILO. 2018. *Women and men in the informal economy: a statistical picture* (Third Edition). Geneva: International Labour Organization.

Jones, T., Ram, M., & Villares-Varela, M. 2017. Injecting reality into the migrant entrepreneurship agenda, pp. 125–145. In C. Essers, P. Dey, D. Tedmanson, & K. Verduyin (Eds.), *Critical perspectives on entrepreneurship: challenging dominant discourses on entrepreneurship* (Routledge Rethinking Entrepreneurship Research). Abingdon: Routledge.

Kabeer, N. 1999. Resources, agency, achievements: reflections on the measurement of women's empowerment. *Development and Change*, 30:3, 435–464.

Kabeer, N. 2005. Gender equality and women's empowerment: a critical analysis of the third Millennium Development Goal. *Gender and Development*, 13:1, 13–24.

Kabeer, N. 2012. Women's economic empowerment and inclusive growth: labour markets and enterprise development (SIG 887 Working Paper). UK: School of Oriental and African Studies.

Khamata-Njenga, B., & Clancy 2003. Concepts and issues in gender and energy: the gender face of energy. *ENERGIA*, 1–82.

Kishor, S., & Gupta, K. 2004. Women's empowerment in India and its states: evidence from the NFHS. *Economic and Political Weekly*, 39:7, 694–712.

Knox, A.J., Bressers, H., Mohlakoana, N., & De Groot, J. 2019. Aspirations to grow: when micro- and informal enterprises in the street food sector speak for themselves. *Journal of Global Entrepreneurship Research*. https://doi.org/10.1186/s40497-019-0161-7.

Mahmud, S., Shah, N. M., & Becker, S. 2012. Measurement of women's empowerment in rural Bangladesh. *World Development*, 2012. 40:3, 610–619.

Mashigo, P., & Schoeman, C. 2012. Stokvels as an instrument and channel to extend credit to poor households in South Africa. *Journal of Economic and Financial Sciences*, 5:1, 49–62.

McMullen, J. S., & Warnick, B. 2015. The downside of blended value and hybrid organizing. *Journal of Management Studies*, 5:4, 630–661.

Mirchandani, K. 1999. Feminist insight on gendered work: new directions in research on women and entrepreneurship. *Gender, Work and Organization*, 6:4, 224–235.

Mohlakoana, N., Knox, A. De Groot, J., & Bressers, H. 2018. Determinants of energy use in the informal food sector. *Development Southern Africa*, 1–15.

Mohlakoana, N., Knox, A., Ranzanici, A., Diouf, M., Bressers, H., De Groot, J., Pailman, W. & Sanfelice, V. 2019. Productive uses of energy and gender in the street food sector in Rwanda, Senegal and South Africa. Research report RA2, ENERGIA.

Monteith, W., & Giesbert, L. 2017. When the stomach is full we look for respect: perceptions of 'good work' in the urban informal sectors of three developing countries. *Work, Employment and Society*, 31:5, 816–833. doi.org/10.1177/0950017016650606.

Muzaffar, A. T., Huq, I., & Mallik, B. A. 2009. Entrepreneurs of the streets: an analytical work on the street food vendors of Dhaka City. *International Journal of Business and Management*, 4:2, 80. https://doi.org/10.5539/ijbm.v4n2p80.

Osei-Boateng, C., & Ampratwum, E. 2011. *The informal sector in Ghana*. Ghana: Friedrich Ebert Stiftung.

Skinner, C., & Haysom, G. 2016. The informal sector's role in food security: a missing link in policy debates? Working Paper No 44. Cape Town: PLAAS, UWC and Centre of Excellence on Food Security.

Temkin, B. 2009. Informal self-employment in developing countries: entrepreneurship or survivalist strategy? Some complications for public policy. *Analyses of Social Issues and Public Policy*, 9:1, 135–156.

Trading Economics. 2019. *South Africa Unemployment Rate*. tradingeconomics.com/south-africa/unemployment-rate.

Walker, L. S., Webster, M., Jr., & Bianchi, A. J. 2011. Testing the spread of status value theory. *Social Science Research*, 40:6, 1652–1663.

World Bank, 2018. *South Africa*. http://data.worldbank.org/country/south-africa.

Yiftachel, O. 2009. Theoretical notes on 'Gray Cities': the coming of urban apartheid? *Planning Theory*, 8:1, 88–100. https://doi.org/10.1177/1473095208099300.

Zahra, S. A., Gedajlovic, E., Neubaum, D. O., & Shulman, J. M. 2009. A typology of social entrepreneurs: motives, search processes and ethical challenges. *Journal of Business Venturing*, 24:5, 219–532.

4. Emancipation and value share: the individual-level value creation by women entrepreneurs in India

Renuka Vyas

Entrepreneurs are perceived as heroic creators of value in modern times (Lazear, 2004). However, due to a legacy of male focussed perception of entrepreneurship (Ahl, 2006), a profit-driven assessment of its value (Korsgaard & Anderson, 2011) and an economic-growth centric measurement of its impact (Schumpeter, 1934), the conventional entrepreneurship discourse continues to lean heavily 'on the economic value creation by men'. In her seminal work on female entrepreneurship, Ahl (2006:595), calls for research 'that do(es) not reproduce women's subordination but capture(s) more and richer aspects of women's entrepreneurship'. One such aspect is the value creation by female entrepreneurs at an individual level. To recalibrate the aforementioned skewed worldview within the extant entrepreneurship discourse, pursuing a broad research question, 'how women in India use entrepreneurship as an instrument to create value at the individual-level' and deploying a qualitative narrative approach, this chapter presents the stories of four women entrepreneurs in India from this perspective. These narratives underscore the transformational power of entrepreneurship that has empowered these women to shape independently their destinies through 'enhanced agency, increased involvement in decision-making and enriched personal growth and development' (Yousafzai, Henry, Boddington & Sheikh, 2019:3). The evidence on the individual value creation by these women is extracted from their personal stories presented here as 'rich descriptions' in the voice of the protagonists and validated in light of the above articulation of value creation at the individual level by Yousafzai et al. (2019). These narratives shed light on the emancipatory power of entrepreneurship which sets free, constructs new meanings in lives, builds new futures and thereby enhances the human agency of the individuals involved.

India, home to 1.3 billion people, is the largest democracy in the world. Its economy, until recently, the world's fastest-growing large economy, is now the third biggest in the world in purchasing power parity (World Bank, 2018). Gender equality, however, is poor in India and it is ranked close to the bottom of the world gender gap hierarchy (World Economic Forum, 2018). A powerful indicator of this inequality is that though girls in India now outperform boys at every level of education (Desai & Vanneman, 2018), women still lag far behind men in formal employment. In 2018, their participation rate in the labour force was 24% against 79% for men (ILO, 2019).

This inequality is reflected in entrepreneurship too. Female business ownership ratio in India is just 14% (Government of India, 2016) and in the small and medium enterprises (SMEs), this proportion is a paltry 5% (Government of India, 2019). In contrast, Global Entrepreneurship Monitor reports a much higher, 60%, average female/male total early-stage entrepreneurial activity (TEA) ratio for 2001–2018, higher than what it is in many developed countries (F/M TEA in UK and Germany is about 50%) and only slightly lower than the global average (68%). As TEA measures percentage of people who have either started a business in the last 42 months or who are actively preparing to start a business (Vyas & Vyas, 2019), a 5% SMEs ownership rate against a 60% TEA, makes this obvious that female entrepreneurial aspirations in India are extremely hard to be translated into eventual business creation. An interesting fact here is that the average female/male opportunity-driven TEA in India for 2013–2018 was close to 95%. Opportunity-driven entrepreneurship involves spotting an opportunity and setting up an enterprise to exploit it (Sternberg & Wennekers 2005) and is considered a qualitatively superior form of entrepreneurship than necessity entrepreneurship (Acs, 2006) which the individuals resort to due to the lack of employment opportunities. This means that in terms of the quality of early-stage entrepreneurship, women are almost on par with men in India.

This implies that India, notwithstanding its size and recent economic success, is the largest and the most visible symbol of gender entrepreneurial opportunity imbalance in the world. It has been argued that '…norms governing women's roles in society limit (Indian) women's perceptions about what is achievable…' (Field, Jayachandran & Pande, 2010). However, some of them transcend these limits through entrepreneurship and create significant value, against formidable odds, for themselves and their families. It is therefore especially interesting to understand why and how some Indian women, disregarding entrenched social norms, cross the limits placed on their aspirations and set themselves free through entrepreneurship. To present their narratives to the wider world and to rebalance the skewed economic-outcome-focussed worldview within the extant entrepreneurship research (Korsgaard & Anderson, 2011), this work charts the value created by four women entrepreneurs in India at the individual level. These women operate in areas as diverse as fashion, art, beauty and gift and through the transformational power of entrepreneurship emerge as the empowered agents of change, independently shaping their destinies (Yousafzai et al., 2019).

VALUE, VALUE CREATION AND SOCIAL VALUE CREATION

Value in Use and Exchange

What constitutes value and how we measure it are highly subjective both in everyday practice as well as in the scholarly discourse (Lepak, Smith & Taylor, 2007). The Greek philosopher Plato was the first to delve on the idea of value, underscoring the difference between value-in-exchange and value-in-use (Sewall, 1968). The former determined by the forces of the market and the latter by what matters to us as humans. Adam Smith (1776), reiterating the contrast between the two, showed that things with great value-in-use often have little value-in-exchange and vice versa. The tension between the two has persisted and continues to weigh in on the contemporary debate on the value creation by entrepreneurs.

Economic and Social Value

As entrepreneurship emerged from the shadows of economics in the early twentieth century (Hébert & Link, 2009) it could not shake off the baggage of market-driven yardsticks of exchange for quantification of value and their primacy over judgements on what matters to us, aka, the social value (Korsgaard & Anderson, 2011) oblivious to the more benevolent traditions in other fields such as ethics that emphasise capacity to provide a benefit as a true value of what we do (Baier, 1985; Haksever, Chaganti & Cook, 2004). However, as entrepreneurship asserts itself as an independent social science (Shane & Venkataraman, 2000), it must also contemplate the full diversity of perspectives within business and organisation literature when it comes to conceptualising or quantifying value (Lepak et al., 2007).

Measurement of Value Creation

It has been argued that the true magnitude of value creation can only be measured from the subjective positions of its targets and sources who could be individuals, organisations or the whole society (Bowman & Ambrosini, 2000). Even though entrepreneurship is 'socially enacted', owing to the roots of its thought processes in economics, it has traditionally assigned growing profits precedence over 'realized self-actualization, a sense of achievement and a sense of being' (Korsgaard & Anderson, 2011:136). Driven by such 'growth ideology' (Stanworth & Curran, 1976), 'unstated growth assumptions' (Gartner, 2001) and a focus on 'the wealth creation' (Welter, Baker, Audretsch & Gartner, 2017) entrepreneurship discourse continues to undervalue the spiritual dimensions of what it means to be a human (Schumacher, 1973) oblivious to the fact that creation and extraction of social value is at the heart of entrepreneurship (Anderson, 1998). Having said that, the intertwined nature of economic and social value should not be overlooked as the profit motive neither excludes nor negates social motives and often the ability of entrepreneurs to share social value hinges on their ability to create economic value (Acs, Boardman & McNeely, 2013).

Value and Gender

A key aspect of plurality in the conceptualisation of value has its gendered dimensions. Men perceive value from a *justice* outlook seeking 'autonomy, objectivity, positivistic rationality, reductionism, and universality' (Hechavarría et al.,

2017:228). In contrast, women's value judgements are underpinned by *care* and they treasure 'empathy, sympathy, compassion, loyalty, discernment, love, benevolence, community, and promotion of a civil society' (Hechavarría et al., 2017:228). However, these two divergent perspectives to value are *gender pronounced* rather than *gender-specific* and it is not that men value justice to the exclusion of care or that women's care concerns impede justice. It is just that most women prioritise care over justice (Baier, 1985). This has vital consequences to how women perceive their roles as entrepreneurs and as the narratives charted below show, for value-creating women, value sharing has primacy over value capture (Cherrier, Goswami & Ray, 2018; Hlady-Rispal & Servantie, 2018). Another key aspect of value creation at the individual level is that it renders irrelevant the distinction between value-in-use and value-in-exchange as the created value accrues to its creator without an exchange through the market. A further crucial dimension of value creation through entrepreneurship at the individual level is its emancipatory role. '...the act of setting free ...' (Rindova, Barry & Ketchen, 2009:478) '...to construct new meaning in life and new social roles and connections that provide a platform for building a new future...' (Chandra, 2017:657) or as Yousafzai et al. (2019:3) call it 'the enhancement of agency'.

METHODOLOGY

Churchill and Bygrave (1989:18) suggest that '...at the beginnings of a paradigm... exploratory, empirical research may be more useful...'. Individual-level value creation through entrepreneurship being a developing paradigm, an exploratory inquiry was, thus, considered appropriate for this work. Narrative analysis, which explores the stories told by people about their lives and helps in understanding what they make out of their experiences (Bailey-Rodriguez, Frost & Elichaoff, 2018) was deemed a fitting tool to capture this.

The exploration started with informal inquiries with people in India with expert domain knowledge. These included a social worker, a leading mentor to female entrepreneurs and an entrepreneurship academic. They recommended a score of potential subjects. From these, five cases were chosen to draw insights from a broad spectrum of diversity of female entrepreneurship in India. In-depth one-to-one telephone interviews of these entrepreneurs were subsequently conducted, which lasted between 45 minutes to an hour. Interviews were transcribed and sent to the respondents for verification as well as for modification. Remarkably, all of them made some additions to what they had already said to reinforce the points that were closer to their hearts. Their modifications were added to their narrations and then sent back to them for the final approval. Five narratives were first recorded. However, one of these was subsequently excluded as it did not adequately reflect the value creation at the individual level.

In the tradition of the classical unstructured narrative approach (De Fina & Georgakopoulou, 2019), the interviews allowed the women to tell their stories with the minimum intervention by the researcher. The interviews began with an open question (Flick, 2013) about these women's current business, followed by questions on why and how they started, what help they received, what problems they faced, what level their business was at that point and what their plans were. As the respondents narrated their stories, supplementary questions were asked only to seek clarity. Each of the resultant narratives is distinct and charts these women's unique journeys that communicate their perspectives to the value that they have created for themselves.

This work, thus, explores the individual-level value creation by four Indian women entrepreneurs, personally very dissimilar from one-another, functioning in diverse milieus in three different states of India. The spectrum extends from the highly educated, technologically savvy and well-off to the barely literate, poor and vulnerable. Despite such extreme polarity of their circumstances, none of them is driven, principally, by the economic value outcomes and they all perceive entrepreneurship as an avenue to realise value at the individual level as well as to share it with their family.

NARRATIVE – 1

Kruti[1] grew up in Kenya and as a child, she was highly creative and was called, 'Kruti the artist'. Her teachers recognised and appreciated her talent and encouraged her to hone it. She believes that God has given her boundless imagination and a great artistic talent to pass it on to society and not to keep it to herself.

She came to live in a small town in Western India as a teenage student to study advanced accountancy and auditing, fields quite distant from the art. Following her graduation, she settled down in the same town with her husband, an engineer, leading a quiet and inconspicuous life as a wife, mother and a part of a big family carrying out mundane household chores. However, whenever she would get time, she would work on her art.

Slowly and gradually the word of her artistic endeavours spread and people started asking her to formally exhibit it. She held her first exhibition at home in her garden. It proved a success and her subsequent exhibitions were in neighbouring large cities and then in the various parts of India. When a well-known architect-builder advised her to have a permanent art gallery, she started it in her father's 60-year-old large house. It was her first step into the art market. Her gallery and her work at display were greatly appreciated. However, there was criticism too. She was told that an art gallery in a small backward town, where hardly anybody understood art, was out of place and that using such a big house for something as insignificant as art was a waste. However, she continued to receive support from her husband as well as from her late mother-in-law. Her children were young and did not understand the true meaning or the value of what she was doing but they were always with her and often helped her arranging the artwork in the gallery.

Her gallery continued to attract attention with people from far-off places coming to the town to see it. Her fame slowly spread and magazines and newspapers started writing about her. Her mother-in-law who used to live in a village will take out cuttings and would proudly show them to folks in the village. Her late father too was immensely proud of her.

Today, she markets her art, along with through her gallery, on the internet as well as through Google. Her work now has a substantial international market and she has conducted over 100 exhibitions in various parts of the world. She has received significant social recognition and numerous awards, both as a female entrepreneur and as an artist. Academic institutions and universities invite her to speak at conferences and articles have appeared on her work in magazines and newspapers. For her success, she gives credit to her customers who appreciate her art.

NARRATIVE – 2

Akanksha, from a business family, wanted to be an entrepreneur from an early age. However, her life as a child was not easy. She lost her mother when she was 13. Her father remarried and she had to live with her stepmother. She was not allowed to pursue even her post-graduation and her marriage was arranged immediately after her graduation. She faced marital discord from the very beginning and spent her early married life just as a housewife taking care of her child.

After seven married years, she had her second child, who was – luckily for her – a girl. Akanksha started designing clothes for her daughter, calling tailors to her home for the task. Her husband did not like this. One day he got quite upset about the time she was spending on designing dresses for her daughter and told her to do it for others also so that they will be at least earning something. In response, she said, 'OK if this is what you want then I will start a business.' He thought she was making fun of him but she was serious and as soon as he told her this, she hired one tailor and one embroiderer and started her business in April 2011. Her husband gave 50,000 rupees to her to start the business. This was the only help she got from her family. With this money, she bought a sewing machine, an embroidery machine, art for the embroidery and all other material needed and started.

From that day she has been growing her business continuously. She believes that whatever success she has achieved is because of her persistence. Though her family gave her early monetary support, along with running her business, she also had to do all the household work and had to take care of her children. Only if she did all this that she was permitted to pursue her business. That is how she worked for her business in the early years.

She received good support from her friends who helped her by spreading the good word of mouth. Her early customers came by such publicity and that has continued until now. Initially, she had support from her husband too. However, he did not expect her business to grow this much. He thought, for her, it was just a hobby but when her business started growing, it led to problems and arguments. Her husband would shout in front of customers. He also tried to persuade her workers to stop working for her and even tore down customers' clothes. He told her that what she had done was enough and she should now stop. However, she did not give up. She thought that now I have a chance to do what I always wanted to do and I will not stop. By this time, she had created a good customer base. She also had trustworthy employees working for her. She therefore persevered and made it clear that whatever happens, she will continue with her business.

Before she started her business all her life was inside the four walls of her home. She started going out and met many of her relatives for the first time. With these contacts, her social circle grew and she greatly cherishes her social growth that her business had facilitated. With time, she became increasingly confident as she started earning a decent income from her business, enough to support herself and her children. This was a big boost for her and it is what keeps her going.

The success of her business has brought about a change in her attitude and her social life. She had never imagined that she could have so many friends and she would meet so many people. She has gained confidence because she is economically independent. Even though she is now separated from her husband, she can take care of her children on her own. She has also started travelling to other states which she could not have thought possible even in her dreams. Now she goes to other cities in India for procurement of items for the expansion of her business. When she started, it was only tailoring but now it is much more. When she started, she had only one tailor now she has 10 people working on four or five machines. Currently, she has a customer base of around 800 to 900 people, who do not go anywhere else and keep coming back to her. She also has many customers who are settled in other countries and who recommend her products and services to their friends and acquaintances.

In the last six months, she has started helping other women as well. She goes to slums and colonies and speaks to women living there. She educates them on the importance of a woman earning for herself and taking care of herself. They see her as a role model and this makes her happy.

She says 'only after establishing myself, I realised that I have the right to live happily. I can live in a way which I decide and that I need not live just to please all the relationships around me. My business has given me this confidence. So, for me, life started after 40 years.'

NARRATIVE – 3

Jyotsna

When her husband died, Jyotsna was young and in her early twenties. She was pregnant with her second child and had no support. To survive and sustain her young family, she first started asking the people whom she knew for work.

Though she got work this way, she invariably had to leave it soon as men tried to take advantage of her vulnerability. The first job that she got was in a children's care centre. However, the men in charge of the centre tried to abuse her and she had to leave the job. In another instance, she was employed to cook in the home of a working woman. When she would go for cooking, the woman in the house would have gone to work, the children to their schools and only the husband would be in the house. Once, he tried to molest her. She resisted and left this work too. She did not tell anybody at that time of these experiences because she thought that people would blame her rather than the men. She finally told one of her friends and she advised her not to be silent and raise the matter with the family, but she decided not to get into an unnecessary conflict with a rich and powerful family. As a young widow alone with small children she was happy to do any work, to earn a living. She worked at grocery stores and cooked at people's homes. However, she was not treated with respect often and had to leave work to maintain her dignity.

On advice from a friend she learned the work of a beautician and started working in that role. Once, when she was working for a women's welfare centre, a priest saw her work, was impressed with her skills and advised her to start her own business doing it. With his help and a small bank loan, she started a small beauty parlour eight years ago.

When she started, she was very shy and would not ask for payments from her customers after she had completed her work. Some of them would just walk away without paying, behaving as if she was doing this for free as a friend. Now she has become more confident and asks for the payments. Some customers do not like this.

Her business is in a small town in western India. She lives in another small nearby small town from where she commutes, first by bike, then a used scooter and now a new scooter. She does particularly well during October, November and December when Indians living abroad visit India.

She has two sons. Due to the income from her business, she was able to first send them to good schools and private colleges. Now, one of them is working in another country and she is happy that her investment in her children's education has paid off. Through her entrepreneurship, she not only escaped the indignity of abuse at the workplace, but she also supported herself and her children, her brothers and her mother. She even organised and paid for her brothers' weddings. She did not do anything for herself. Her children are now educated and in employment. Her brothers are also settled with their families and living independently.

Now, she wants to help others in a situation like her previous situation. One of her cousins has recently died leaving behind a young wife. She feels a keen sense of empathy for her and wants to help her to start her own business. For this, she is providing her free training. She is also trying to help other similar women who need help. She wants to expand her business if she can find some partner, maybe, using a fresh loan from the bank. Earlier people used to look down upon her, but now, they praise her for what she has done for her children, her mother and her brothers.

NARRATIVE – 4

Maitri

Maitri has a master's in commerce from a leading university in India. She worked in her father's foreign trade business for about five years, which she did not enjoy. She was always inclined towards fashion and so went to the UK and did her master's in fashion. When she came back, she worked near Delhi, buying houses for her company, for six years and then she worked in her home city for a well-known brand for two years. One of the reasons for her to turn to entrepreneurship was that there were very few fashion-related jobs in her city.

Maitri subsequently started a gifting business with a friend. They curate gift boxes as per the requirements of their customers. They do single boxes as well where they have their own designs. They have tied up with several suppliers for a variety of gift products. If anyone wants to give somebody a birthday gift or anniversary gift, then they give them their budget and accordingly, Maitri and her friend curate and provide options of the gift boxes and also courier them on their behalf. They also do corporate gifting during Diwali and other occasions.

Maitri always wanted to start her own business. She has a friend with whom she had studied in the UK. Her friend came up with the idea of their current business and at that time, Maitri was not working, having taken a break. She found the idea attractive and so they started it two years ago.

They had an easy start. She feels they were lucky that just by advertising on Instagram and other social media they got good word-of-mouth publicity. They also met with good suppliers with excellent products. Now that they have a settled business and are trying to scale up, they are finding it a little bit difficult as it requires significant financial investment. Another issue now is that they both are new mothers. Managing the home and business together is becoming a little tricky right now. But she thinks once they come out of this initial phase, they will be fine.

When they started, they both received some basic directions from their husbands on things such as the paperwork, company registration and other relevant processes. They also guided them to the right people to contact but other than that, she believes it is just two of them who have done everything. Right from looking for suppliers, setting up a company, designing the boxes, everything they have done themselves. Right now, they are just a two-member team.

Maitri believes that her business has created great personal value for her. The kind of response that they got in the first two years has been fantastic. Every Diwali – they had two Diwalis by now – they got orders of 500 to 600 boxes per season, which is particularly good for them considering how new they are and they have achieved this just based on social media without any advertisement. She thinks it is a great achievement for her as a person.

DISCUSSION

There is significant overlap, concurrent with noticeable diversity, in the motives and drivers that pulled these women into entrepreneurship. Akanksha and Maitri always wanted to be entrepreneurs though the circumstances that eventually allowed them to achieve this aspiration were quite different. Kruti and Akanksha had a strong passion for, and exceptional talents in, the fields in which they set up their enterprises. Jyotsna's[2] circumstances forced her to start her business. However, it was her skill as a beautician that opened to her the doors of her enterprise. This highlights the obvious link between the entrepreneurs' knowledge, skills and talents and their ability to create value (Locke & Fitzpatrick, 1995).

Contrary to the perception that obstacles to entrepreneurship for women in India start at the family level, these narratives provide evidence divergent from such a worldview. It must also be noted that support for such a perception cannot be in the stories of those who succeed in their entrepreneurial efforts and may reside in the tales of those who failed to make the grade. However, these accounts do demonstrate the key role of familial support. Except for Jyotsna who lost her husband while still in her twenties, all others had help from their husbands which they specifically mention. Akanksha's story is unusual where her husband who provided the seed capital, subsequently turned hostile and tried to sabotage her business once it started growing.

Jyotsna, a young widow, pregnant with her second child, started from a position of the greatest relative disadvantage. She also had to endure distressing behaviours while working for others. However, though her entrepreneurial journey was not smooth, she soon achieved success. Her story is a testimony of the emancipatory power of entrepreneurship and transformation, through it, of a life of misery and dependence into that of significant promise and empowerment (Chandra, 2017; Yousafzai et al., 2019). Though she thinks of her achievements only in terms of what she did for her family, how entrepreneurship altered her own life is the most noteworthy part of her narrative. Her story also highlights the primacy of care over justice in the choices that women make at the individual level (Baier, 1985, Hechavarría et al., 2017). When she faced molestation, she just quietly retreated and continued to focus on providing care to her family rather than try and bring to justice the perpetrators.

In all these narratives, there is a strong undercurrent of pride and an unmistakable sense of self-actualisation through entrepreneurship at the individual level (Korsgaard & Anderson, 2011; Yousafzai et al., 2019). Kruti is content that she could follow her passion and made her family happy and proud of her achievements. For Akanksha and Maitri the mere fact of being entrepreneurs gives them a tremendous sense of fulfilment. Kruti has achieved significant social recognition and is invited by premier Indian academic and commercial institutions as a key-note speaker and a resource person.

The value created by these women, thus, is most obvious and most substantial at their personal levels. Driven either by their aspirations or in search of redemption from their predicaments, as in the case of Jyotsna and Akanksha, they all are followers of a strong inner voice of women seeking more meaningful lives for themselves.

Jyotsna's case is the most dramatic. However, for Akanksha, underscoring the emancipatory power of entrepreneurship (Rindova et al., 2009; Chandra, 2017), the most prized outcome of her entrepreneurship is her ability to give her daughter a life not constrained by the forces that kept her trapped in unhappiness for decades. For Kruti, who was advised to keep her flights of fancy to herself because 'in her town nobody understood or cared about art', to be a symbol of her town's identity as a place of art is the most cherished achievement, a powerful enunciation of the agency enhancement at the individual level by entrepreneurship (Yousafzai et al., 2019:3). Maitri is happy that she is doing a work of her choosing and is free to raise a child without the constraints of salaried employment. For each of these women, entrepreneurship is the instrument through which life-changing value at the personal level is created (Chandra, 2017). These narratives highlight a less-discussed aspect of value creation through entrepreneurship at the individual level. It is only at this level that both the source and the target of value creation (Bowman & Ambrosini, 2000) is the same.

As is obvious, the people who benefit first and the most, when the value is created by a woman at the individual level, is the family. The most significant beneficiaries that emerge from these narratives are in Jyotsna's family. Similarly, Akanksha's son is now being educated at a premium institute. However more important, from her perspective, is that her daughter is destined to a life far more liberated than her own early life. Kruti's enterprise based on her art is a matter of pride for both her parents and her in-laws.

THE VALUE MULTIPLIER AT WORK

There is an obvious intent to 'share the value' in all these narratives (Hlady-Rispal & Servantie, 2018). The interconnectivity of the entrepreneurial value creation process is also obvious here, particularly the nexus of value created at the personal level and the welfare of the family. Education is the mechanism that leverages and intensifies this influence. Most of these women mention children's education as their top priority and so a value multiplier is visible in these narratives. Women setting up an enterprise to educate their children and employing other women who in turn use the money earned to educate their children.

These narratives answer the question, why and how some Indian women defying social norms and the limits set by others to their aspirations (Field et al., 2010), can create significant value at the individual level, quite unambiguously. In the multitude of Indian women living the roles scripted by others, a few make a deliberate choice for a life lived differently. They leverage their knowledge, skills and talents (Locke & Fitzpatrick, 1995), no matter whether exceptional or mundane, to realise their true potential through entrepreneurship. In the process, they achieve emancipation (Rindova et al., 2009), freedom (Chandra, 2017) and enhanced agency (Yousafzai et al., 2019). The lesson from their narratives for the other women in gender-imbalanced India is clear and obvious. It is a choice that they have to make themselves. It cannot – and will not – be made by others. However, if they too, like Kruti, Maitri, Akanksha and Jyotsna, opt to dream differently, no matter what their circumstances are, and if they appropriately deploy their knowledge, skills and talents, whatever they may be, they too can create significant value for themselves and can achieve emancipation through entrepreneurship.

CONCLUSION

These narratives show how driven by their passion and utilising their talents (Locke & Fitzpatrick, 1995), women create value at the individual level asserting their power as entrepreneurs to transform and enhance their stature. Entrepreneurship impacts them profoundly as it enhances their ability to look after their welfare as well as that of their family. Cleverly leveraging social media and positive testimonies of satisfied customers, these seemingly inconspicuous women, propelled by the power of entrepreneurship, are slowly traversing their paths as independent, assertive, evolved and empowered individuals, leaving behind their unique female footprints in the Indian marketplace.

LIMITATIONS AND FUTURE RESEARCH DIRECTIONS

Limitations of this work mainly come from its narrative-driven data and method. Bearman, Greenhill and Nestel (2019:377) observe, '…the narrative nature of the data is (often) both strength and limitation'. Though it provides 'a holistic understanding of the phenomenon', there is no scope to verify the respondent assertions. Further, the qualitative nature of analysis necessitates a small sample which renders the resultant insights non-generalisable. The narrative approach deployed here, at the same time, balances the disadvantage of size and scale with a nuanced understanding of the individual circumstances and highlights very well the individual-level value creation by the participants. At the same time, being based on a small sample, its conclusions remain tentative and suggestive. For a more complete picture of the phenomenon to emerge, many further such qualitative studies would be needed, eventually paving the way for larger confirmatory studies.

NOTES

1. Not her real name. All names are changed to protect the identity of subjects.
2. Jyotsna seems to be a necessity entrepreneur (Block, Kohn, Miller & Ullrich, 2015). However, she is not. She took to entrepreneurship not because she did not find work. She took to it to escape the workplace abuse that she encountered in paid employment.

REFERENCES

Acs, Z. (2006). How is entrepreneurship good for economic growth? *Innovations*, 1(1), 97–107.

Acs, Z. J., Boardman, M. C. & McNeely, C. L. (2013). The social value of productive entrepreneurship. *Small Business Economics*, 40(3), 785–796.

Ahl, H. (2006). Why research on women entrepreneurs needs new directions. *Entrepreneurship Theory and Practice*, 30(5), 595–621.

Anderson A. R. (1998). Cultivating the Garden of Eden: Environmental entrepreneuring. *Journal of Organizational Change Management*, 11(2), 135–144.

Baier, A. C. (1985). What do women want in a moral theory? *Nous*, 19(1), 53–63.

Bailey-Rodriguez, D., Frost, N. & Elichaoff, F. (2018). Narrative analysis. *Doing Qualitative Research in Psychology: A Practical Guide*, 209.

Bearman, M., Greenhill, J. & Nestel, D. (2019). The power of simulation: A large-scale narrative analysis of learners' experiences. *Medical Education*, 53(4), 369–379.

Block, J. H., Kohn, K., Miller, D. & Ullrich, K. (2015). Necessity entrepreneurship and competitive strategy. *Small Business Economics*, 44(1), 37–54.

Bowman, C. & Ambrosini, V. (2000). Value creation versus value capture: Towards a coherent definition of value in strategy. *British Journal of Management*, 11(1), 1–15.

Chandra, Y. (2017). Social entrepreneurship as emancipatory work. *Journal of Business Venturing*, 32(6), 657–673.

Cherrier, H., Goswami, P. & Ray, S. (2018). Social entrepreneurship: Creating value in the context of institutional complexity. *Journal of Business Research*, 86, 245–258.

Churchill, N. & Bygrave, W. D. (1989). the entrepreneurship paradigm (I): A philosophical look at its research methodologies. *Entrepreneurship Theory and Practice*, 14(1), 7–26.

De Fina, A. & Georgakopoulou, A. (2019). *The Handbook of Narrative Analysis*. Wiley-Blackwell.

Desai, S. & Vanneman, R. (2018). *India Human Development Survey-India*, 2011–12. Ann Arbor, MI: Inter-university Consortium for Political and Social Research [distributor], 8 August 2018. https://doi.org/10.3886/ICPSR36151.v6.

Field, E., Jayachandran, S. & Pande, R. (2010). Do traditional institutions constrain female entrepreneurship? A field experiment on business training in India. *American Economic Review*, 100(2), 125–129.

Flick, U. (Ed.). (2013). *The Sage Handbook of Qualitative Data Analysis*. Sage.

Gartner W. B. (2001). Is there an elephant in entrepreneurship? Blind assumptions in theory development. *Entrepreneurship Theory and Practice*, 25(4), 27–39.

Government of India (2016). *Study of Working Women and Privileges in the Unorganized Sector*. Ministry of Women & Child Development, New Delhi.

Government of India (2019). *Annual Report, 2018–19*. Ministry of Micro, Small and Medium Enterprises, New Delhi.

Haksever, C., Chaganti, R. & Cook, R. G. (2004). A model of value creation: Strategic view. *Journal of Business Ethics*, 49(3), 295–307.

Hébert, R. F. & Link, A. N. (2009). *A History of Entrepreneurship*. Routledge.

Hechavarría, D. M., Terjesen, S. A., Ingram, A. E., Renko, M., Justo, R. & Elam, A. (2017). Taking care of business: The impact of culture and gender on entrepreneurs' blended value creation goals. *Small Business Economics*, 48(1), 225–257.

Hlady-Rispal, M. & Servantie, V. (2018). Deconstructing the way in which value is created in the context of social entrepreneurship. *International Journal of Management Reviews*, 20(1), 62–80.

ILO (2019). *ILOSTAT database*, International Labour Organization. Data retrieved in April 2019.

Korsgaard, S. & Anderson, A. R. (2011). Enacting entrepreneurship as social value creation. *International Small Business Journal*, 29(2), 135–151.

Lazear, E. P. (2004). Balanced skills and entrepreneurship. *American Economic Review*, 94(2), 208–211.

Lepak, D. P., Smith, K. G. & Taylor, M. S. (2007). Value creation and value capture: A multilevel perspective. *Academy of Management Review*, 32(1), 180–194.

Locke, E. & Fitzpatrick, S. (1995). Promoting creativity in organizations. In C. Ford & D. Gioia (Eds), *Creative Action in Organizations*, 115–120. Sage.

Rindova, V., Barry, D. & Ketchen Jr, D. J. (2009). Entrepreneuring as emancipation. *Academy of Management Review*, 34(3), 477–491.

Schumacher E. F. (1973). *Small Is Beautiful: Economics as if People Mattered*. Bland and Briggs.

Schumpeter, J. A. (1934). *The Theory of Economic Development*. Harvard University Press.

Sewall, H. R. (1968). *The Theory of Value before Adam Smith* (Augustus M. Kelley Publishers, 1901, Reprint).

Shane, S. & Venkataraman, S. (2000). The promise of entrepreneurship as a field of research. *Academy of Management Review*, 25(1), 217–226.

Smith, A. (1776). *An Inquiry into the Nature and Causes of the Wealth of Nations (Cannan Ed.)*. Online Library of Liberty.

Stanworth, M. J. K. & Curran, J. (1976). Growth and the small firm: An alternative view. *Journal of Management Studies*, 13(1), 95–110.

Sternberg, R. & Wennekers, S. (2005). Determinants and effects of new business creation: Investigations using Global Entrepreneurship Monitor data. *Small Business Economics*, 24(3), 193–203.

Vyas, V. & Vyas, R. (2019). Entrepreneurship and economic growth: A review and synthesis of conceptual arguments and empirical evidence. *International Review of Entrepreneurship*, 17(3), 231–256.

Welter, F., Baker, T., Audretsch, D. B. & Gartner, W. B. (2017). Everyday entrepreneurship: A call for entrepreneurship research to embrace entrepreneurial diversity. *Entrepreneurship Theory and Practice*, 41(3), 311–321.

World Bank (2018). *World Development Indicators*. The World Bank Group.

World Economic Forum (2018). *The Global Gender Gap Report 2018*, 17 December.

Yousafzai, S., Henry, C., Boddington, M. & Sheikh, S. (Eds) (2019). Call of chapters. *Research Handbook of Women's Entrepreneurship and Value Creation*. Edward Elgar Publishing.

PART II

VALUE CREATION AT THE BUSINESS LEVEL

5. Collaborative value creation in a highly adverse context: experiences of Hazara women entrepreneurs in Balochistan

Khizran Zehra, Leona Achtenhagen, Sadia Arshad, and Nadia Arshad

Hamida[1] opened a restaurant in the heart of Hazara Town in August 2017 with the goal of generating skills and income for women affected by repeated attacks against their community. If a woman lost the breadwinner of her family to anti-Hazara attacks, or was victimized herself, she could come to the restaurant, work in a safe place, earn money, and support her family. That simple, altruistic project turned out to be far more controversial – and, ultimately, dangerous – than she could ever have anticipated. (Roads&Kingdoms, 2018)

The above quote and Hamida's further story below stem from a news article reporting on her attempt at entrepreneurial activities in a ghetto of the Hazara community in Quetta, Pakistan, which after many violent attacks is protected by several security checkpoints. The story continues to tell about Hamida's recent political career and the controversy that had emerged with the landlord owning the building of her restaurant. Continuing on the development of her entrepreneurial endeavour, she tells how women "would show up to interviews accompanied by supportive mothers. But after a month or two on the job, a father or brother would show up at the restaurant complaining of Hamida's disregard of the family's honour." The attention she had received in Pakistani media (e.g. Sarfraz, 2017) came at a price: "While many supported the project, others – mostly men – objected. They would say: 'Why are women stepping out of their homes? What's the need? They can stay at home and do needlework'", Hamida recalls. She would respond: "This is not the needlework generation." The harassment began when a photo of a male politician served by a female staff member was published by BBC Urdu, triggering a smear campaign on social media. "They said I was shameless, without honour", Hamida said, reading aloud from print-outs of Facebook pages. "In the name of running a hotel, immorality is spread" read one. Another included a photograph of Hamida: "Dear sisters, be vigilant of your purdah, as some agents of infidels are leading you towards immodesty with their slogans of freedom and culture." A third read, "On the pretext of earning a livelihood, our mother's and sister's modesty is being snatched… Men only come to this restaurant to leer at women." And the story continues: "Tensions came to a head on a cold night in November 2017. Hamida, Ali [her husband], and their sons were closing the restaurant when a pair of assailants, hidden in shadow outside, opened fire with a silenced pistol. They missed – but only barely" (Roads&Kingdoms, 2018).

This introductory anecdote illustrates the experiences of a woman entrepreneur in the highly conservative, patriarchal Hazara community in Pakistan – a context not only characterized by antiquated gender roles but also by a high level of violence against this ethnic minority group and the general lack of perspectives for its youth (NCHR, 2018). While Hamida has her husband's support, many women have lost their male chaperone in violent attacks, leaving them with few other options than turning to entrepreneurial activities as a last resort for livelihood.

Despite the enormous effort that such entrepreneurial endeavours entail for these women in adverse contexts, entrepreneurship scholars frequently portray female entrepreneurs as underperforming – focusing mainly on economic growth rather than overall value creation (Marlow & McAdam, 2013). This strand of literature does not always consider the complexities that women entrepreneurs face in founding and establishing businesses in contexts that are different to the mainstream US context predominant in entrepreneurship research (cf. Amha & Ademassie, 2004). Indeed, gender-specific challenges that are created by patriarchal norms, culture, religion, and traditions can largely restrict the opportunities for women's entrepreneurial value creation (Zehra & Achtenhagen, 2018). Therefore, the constrained economic performance of women entrepreneurs should be understood in relation to their broader socio-economic contexts (Hailemariam & Kroon, 2018).

Such contextualization of women's entrepreneurship implies acknowledging the social and economic challenges faced by women entrepreneurs in creating not only economic, but also social benefits (Porter & Kramer, 2006). In particular, micro businesses run informally by women entrepreneurs should be understood in relation to prevailing patriarchal and traditional social norms (Williams & Nadin, 2012; Zehra, 2018) along with entrepreneurship's societal effects on both an individual and community level (Welter & Xheneti, 2015). However, what defines such overall value creation varies across social, cultural and economic contexts. For example, activities that offer certain entrepreneurial potential and job opportunities are considered important for informal value creation in transition economies (Welter & Xheneti, 2013). Branzei and Abdelnour (2010) point to the role of entrepreneurship to move beyond the disruption caused by terrorism.

Hamida's story above also points to another important aspect of value creation, namely collaborative activities. She received support for her entrepreneurship from her husband and children and could leverage her public recognition, as a politician, for her activities. However, the main purpose underlying her entrepreneurial activities is based on Hazara women helping each other to elevate their status (Sarfraz, 2017). This chapter aims to further explore non-economic value creation through collaborative activities as an important factor in creating sustainable entrepreneurial activities in adverse contexts.

The remainder of this chapter is structured as follows. Next, we outline relevant aspects of non-economic as well as collaborative value creation. Then, we present the highly constrained context of our study, the conservative and patriarchal Hazara community in the city of Quetta in Balochistan, Pakistan. Terrorist attacks have targeted the Hazara community in the past years and resulted in brutal killings, leaving many Hazara women without a male chaperone often expected in such patri-archism, forcing them into entrepreneurship as a last resort for livelihood. Regional disparities, as well as social and gender inequalities, add additional complexity to their constrained entrepreneurship environment, as illustrated by Hamida's story above. After a brief description of our method and introduction to the Hazara women entrepreneurs in our sample, we present our findings and analysis. We conclude the chapter with a discussion.

NON-ECONOMIC VALUE CREATION

The notion of non-economic value created at the business level is the focus of this chapter. Non-economic value creation is an important part of the true value of businesses (Korsgaard & Anderson, 2011), especially in underprivileged situations and constrained entrepreneurial contexts (cf. Godfrey, 2011; Webb et al., 2009), calling for the consideration of entrepreneurial activities in their broader socio-economic context (Hailemariam & Kroon, 2018; Porter & Kramer, 2006).

The concept of non-economic business value is rather vaguely defined, though entrepreneurship literature makes reference to business value in non-economic terms. Sometimes, value refers rather statically to input variables, such as non-economic resources like prior education. In other cases, value refers to outcomes of business development, such as the social value of businesses assessed in their contribution to alleviating poverty or inequality. The non-economic side of business value can also address issues of human achievement and satisfaction, opening up to narratives of entrepreneurs' experiences and creativity.

Understanding non-economic value creation at micro enterprise level requires an understanding of micro businesses and acknowledgment of a range of non-economic business needs and activities. In Pakistan, micro enterprises are defined as "projects or businesses in trading/manufacturing/services/agriculture that will lead to liveli-hood improvement and income generation, who are either self-employed or employ few individuals not exceeding 10 (excluding seasonal labor)" (SBP, 2012, p. 1). Most of the micro enterprises in Pakistan start as informal enterprises and enjoy social legitimacy and acceptability. Micro entrepreneurs operate in numerous fields such as food stalls, livestock, and the service sector and contribute to solving social problems and creating value that is unique to their contexts. Nonetheless, micro enterprises in Pakistan often lack financial services (SBP, 2012) and are typically constrained due to insufficient resources, especially human and financial capital (Webb et al., 2009). Micro businesses, therefore, rely mostly on locally available resources, such as local networks, cultural resources and natural amenities (Welter & Xheneti, 2013; Welter et al., 2017).

Prior research has shown that non-economic value can comprise of multiple dimensions which can coevolve and coexist, and this value creation can in turn, act as an enabling and reinforcing mechanism for entrepreneurial activities (Korsgaard & Anderson, 2011). For example, entrepreneurship can be a means of self-identification and status symbol in particular groups of society (Hytti, 2015). Abetti (2004) found that entrepreneurs can be motivated to participate in micro businesses to give free reign to their entrepreneurial mindset, viewing bureaucratic set-ups as restrictive to their creativity and potential success. At a business level, non-economic outcomes may be the enhanced skills, knowledge and experience of entrepreneurs (Korsgaard & Anderson, 2011) – and research has established a positive relation of knowledge, information, and education with successful economic and entrepreneurial activities (e.g. Davidsson & Honig, 2003; Hambrick, 2007). Prior knowledge and experience gained through entrepreneurship increase the likelihood of success and experienced entrepreneurs may deal better with uncertain situations (Elfring & Hulsink, 2003).

Informal workers are important for the social cohesion of their communities, having both formal and informal linkages (Broembsen, 2019). Local trust-based networks are another non-economic outcome. Such local structures can promote social capital benefits, for example, an increased customer base, smooth resource transfer, skilled manpower, and event information (Dana, 2001; Zehra, 2018).

When entrepreneurs are constrained, they create value using entrepreneurial knowledge for creative problem-solving, such as combining existing resources with new ones in novel ways (Sirmon & Hitt, 2003) to allow for success with limited resources (Baker et al., 2003; Baker & Nelson, 2005). Another route for value creation in constrained new ventures is via networks (Hoang & Antoncic, 2003) and social resourcing (Sarasvathy et al., 2008) to access instrumental resources such as social capital to obtain scarce resources (Gedajlovic et al., 2013). Gathered resources are recombined and used to pursue opportunities (Shane & Venkataraman, 2000). The acquisition of skills, material, and labour, facilitated via business relationships and business networks, is crucial in creating competitive products and services (Baker & Nelson, 2005; Davidsson & Honig, 2003). Different elements of this process of value creation through relationships and collaborations among different stakeholders are non-economic. The non-economic value and process of non-economic value creation have impacts on both focal business and connected relationships (Mandják & Durrieu, 2000). We consider that the business collaboration approach could contribute to advancing the understanding of non-economic value creation.

BUSINESS COLLABORATIONS FOR NON-ECONOMIC VALUE CREATION

Collaborations between businesses can play an important role in achieving social and economic business goals (Ahlström & Sjoström, 2005; London & Hart, 2011) and value creation (Austin, 2010). Micro entrepreneurs benefit from collaborations in order to mitigate resource scarcity. Researchers have long argued that social relations and the structure of an entrepreneur's social networks may facilitate the mobilization of valuable resources (e.g. Gedajlovic et al., 2013). Prior literature shows the importance of collaborations for business success also in developing-economy contexts, especially for informal entrepreneurs (Bhagavatula, 2009; Bhagavatula et al., 2010;

Mair & Marti, 2007, 2009). Resources created through collaborations can facilitate innovation, skill development, and set industry standards (Yaziji, 2004).

Previous literature (e.g. Bhagavatula et al., 2010; Davidsson & Honig, 2003), showed that the bulk of the start-up capital for women entrepreneurs typically comes from the immediate family, personal savings, or friends. In order to expand the scope of value creation, women entrepreneurs seek resources from informal sources, such as contracting, community involvement, and collaborations. Sometimes, an extra layer of powerful local government or business contacts is added, as demonstrated by Zehra (2018). In informal micro enterprises in Pakistan, different types of business relations and collaborations build upon one another depending upon resource needs and value creation goals (Zehra, 2018). Previous research confirmed that micro entrepreneurs in emerging economies such as Pakistan and India use collaborations prominently to secure resources for short-term goals and survival, but as soon as the ventures grow, entrepreneurs need to rely on business collaborations beyond closed networks to co-create and sustain value creation in constrained situations (Bhagavatula et al., 2010; Zehra, 2018). Together, different types of collaborations appear to provide the best possibilities for value creation, and trust among collaborators and act as a catalyst to speed up social-economic value creation (Bhagavatula et al., 2010). Trust-based networks have led to the growth of micro-entrepreneurs, who work in collaborations based on trust and friendship (Starr & MacMillan, 1990; Zehra, 2018). Collaborations among businesses are a continuous process and change over time depending on resource needs and business goals (Austin & Seitanidi, 2012). These collaborations accumulate trust over time and in return accumulated trust further nurtures collaborations and networks (Coleman, 1988). Trust refers to the belief and confidence in other agents to behave as expected, in spite of uncertainties, risks, and the possibility of them acting opportunistically (Lyon, 2000). Collaborations and exchanges between networks based on trust build on social relationships that proceed according to unwritten yet well-understood rules specifying the norms and direction of a particular collaboration (Kranton, 1996). Trust in collaborations is also related to the strength of collaboration (Granovetter, 1973). In the context of women entrepreneurs, particularly in constrained and transition contexts, this trust is mostly lacking, resulting in fewer collaborations and fewer opportunities for women. For example, women's unequal position in Cameroon limits their equal access to resources compared to male entrepreneurs (Mayoux, 2001). Similar findings were shared from a study on women entrepreneurs in Indonesia by Silvey and Elmhirst (2003).

However, there remains a lack of knowledge particularly about the nature and dimensions of non-economic value creation and how collaborations can contribute to the non-economic business value creation among micro businesses (Austin & Seitanidi, 2012). This chapter addresses this question to promote an understanding of collaborations as a mechanism for non-economic value creation.

THE HAZARA

The Hazara are a Shi'ite ethnic minority of Mongolian and Central Asian descent that make up about 500,000 of Quetta's 2.3 million people. Quetta is the capital of Pakistan's province of Balochistan. Over the past years, the Hazara have frequently been targeted by militant and terrorist groups, such as the Pakistani Taliban, the Islamic State and the Lashkar-e-Jhangvi (LeJ) group (RFE, 2019; see also Ali, 2015). According to Al Jazeera, LeJ issued a letter reading:

> It is our mission in Pakistan that every city, village and other place, every corner be cleansed of the Shia and the Shia Hazara. (…) And, as before, in all of Pakistan, especially Quetta, we will continue our successful jihad against the Shia Hazara and Pakistan will become a graveyard for them. (Hashim, 2013)

According to a recent report by the National Commission for Human Rights, 509 members of the Hazara community were killed and 627 injured in various incidents of terrorism in Quetta between January 2012 and December 2017 (NCHR, 2018). In order to enhance the protection of the Hazara community, two guarded neighbour-hoods, Hazara Town and Mari Abad, have been implemented in Quetta, protected by soldiers and security checkpoints. While these checkpoints were established for the security of the Hazara, they also tend to cut them off from other communities, dra-matically isolating them and confining their business activities (*Independent*, 2019). According to NCHR (2018):

> the ongoing persistent violent situation, fear, restricted mobility and socio-economic prob-lems have seriously impacted the psychological well-being of Hazaras. They feel isolated as they cannot mingle freely with other communities to share their sorrows and joys. This isolation has created frustration, disappointment and psychological problems as being a Hazara seems to be a crime. Things have come to a level that even the slightest noise causes panic amongst them, being perceived as a suicide attack or remote control bomb. This feeling of insecurity has created anxiety amongst the community, compelling them to the use of narcotics for relief. Community members are also showing signs of paranoia and delusional behavior, they claim.

The violence against the Hazara has particularly targeted women and girls (UN Women, 2016), though it must be noted that violence against women is generally a widespread problem in Pakistan (Bath, 2011). For example, Hilaly (2011) claims that 80% of Pakistani women experience domestic violence. To make matters worse, the Hazara face a malfunctioning infrastructure with scarce water resources and electricity running only five hours per day (Sarfraz, 2017).

Despite all these challenges, there is increase in entrepreneurial activity in the Hazarvi community (Collins, Watson & Skoko, 2017). This is not because they would have an entrepreneurial culture, but they are necessity-based entrepreneurs who lack even the most basic resources to start their businesses (Collins et al., 2017). This is an interesting context to understand entrepreneurial actions under constraints,

Table 5.1   *Profiles of women entrepreneurs in our study*

Name of Entrepreneur	Gul	Mariam	Jalila
Age	37	29	33
Education	Intermediate	Matriculation	Bachelors
Marital status	Widowed	Single	Single
Children	2	0	0
Type of business	Traditional hand embroidery business	Boutique and tailoring	Gym
Previous experience	Nil	Nil	Trainee
Duration of business	8	5	2
Number of employees	Outsources (6–10 workers on wages)	No employees but help from mother and sister	2 (her sister, watchman)

emerging against all odds. This narrative of resilience and human agency can help us in understanding non-economic value creation in constrained scenarios.

METHOD

In order to understand the lived experiences of Hazara women entrepreneurs in this constrained environment, local researchers from the Quetta University in Pakistan collected data through interviews with three local women entrepreneurs from this ethnic minority community in Quetta. The entrepreneurs were identified through personal contacts and snowballing technique.

The interviews were based on an interview pro forma, covering seven topic areas: the entrepreneur's personal background, the emergence of the venture idea and start-up process, the core characteristics and activities of the venture, local resources used, networks and collaborations, implications of the informality of the venture, and finally specificities of the Hazara community context in relation to the entrepreneurial venture. The personal interviews were transcribed and sent to the authors of this chapter. Given the difficult situation of these women entrepreneurs, familiarity with the local context was a prerequisite to gain access. The interviewed entrepreneurs were between 29 and 37 years of age: Gul has a business of traditional hand-embroidered garments, Mariam has a boutique mainly providing tailoring services, and Jalila has a gym only for women (see Table 5.1).

The interview transcripts were read several times by the researchers and themes emerging from this reading were manually colour coded to facilitate within-case analysis and to identify common patterns across the cases (Griffee, 2005).

FINDINGS

Constrained Dynamics of Women's Entrepreneurship in Hazara

All three businesses are located in Hazara Town and face similar constraints. Some of these emerge from within the community, triggered by patriarchal, conservative Hazara men attempting to confine women, and others emerge from the overshadowing threat by militant groups, targeting all Hazaras. As a result, it is not easy for the women to leave the house to go to work and to market their products. For example, the women entrepreneurs complain that men look at them with disapproval, suggesting that they should stay home: "There are men sitting on my way to the gym. They look at me in a weird way as they have a mentality that women should sit at home. This makes it uncomfortable and tense sometimes, but often I simply ignore them and move on" (Jalila).

All three women entrepreneurs find this male behaviour challenging. As their businesses are small scale, their marketing activities and customers relationships demand that they leave the house a lot, as other types of sales and advertising would be too costly. A constant challenge they face is the security situation, and with it, the fear of falling victim to terrorism. As outlined above, there is an extra layer of security for their area, as every person entering Hazara Town is searched and some may not be allowed to enter. However, as it is not easy for non-community members to enter the area, many people avoid visiting that part of town. Thereby, this extra layer of security has become a barrier restricting the market size of the women entrepreneurs to Hazara Town – though reducing the risk of terrorist attacks this measure also limits the number of potential customers and restricts the opportunity to grow. Also, human resources need to be recruited locally. As a consequence of this constrained environment, many Hazara have moved abroad and support their families financially through remittances.

Gul and Her Business of Embroidered Garments

Gul is running a business selling hand-embroidered clothes. Her entrepreneurial activities were triggered out of need in the aftermath of her husband's death in a terrorist attack. She reflects:

> You have no control over the situation. When a dear one is gone, it is the most difficult phase of your life. But you cannot die with the deceased ones, and I had to live for my children. We were an ideal happy family, but then ... there was no source of income. I needed money to survive, and this was the only skill I had. So, I actually started for my own and my children's survival, but now it is not only my source of income, it is my passion. (Gul)

Gul's value proposition is to promote unique and traditionally embroidered garments hand-made for women. Given her initial lack of financial resources, she started the business based on pre-orders, where the customers upfront provided the fabric, threads, and beads, while Gul only had to invest her time and skills. Once she had acquired enough capital through her sales, she started making garments using her own resources in addition to pre-ordered garments. As high-quality hand embroidery requires well-developed skills, she quickly started to rely on skilled women as her primary resource. In order to accommodate the increasing number of customer orders, Gul leverages her network to outsource embroidery tasks to other women. Promoting this intricate skill and bringing recognition to the women working for her became as important for Gul as creating financial value for the community. As the designs and patterns used in the embroidery are an important part of the workers' cultural heritage, it also helps to foster a sense of pride in an otherwise constrained context. By now, Gul has dedicated a room in her home to her business, where her customers – women only – can visit and select garments. Though she is not directly involved in international activities, some of her customers export the garments to Australia, Europe and the USA.

Mariam and Her Tailoring Business

Mariam also started her business out of necessity in response to the results of a violent attack against the Hazara:

> After my father's martyrdom in a targeted killing, we had a financial crisis as he was the only bread earner. We got 15,000 rupees per month from the Shuhada's Fund, but that was not sufficient for making a living for my family. My mother had taught me sewing, but her old machine was broken. (Mariam)

The value proposition of Mariam's business is to provide women with an opportunity to get their dresses fitted and made in their neighbourhood. She realized that women were not comfortable in giving their body size to men, while talking more freely to a woman when selecting the design and size of their dress. Forced by the need to provide an income for her family, Mariam reflected on which valuable skills she had that could be leveraged in entrepreneurial activities. Her mother had taught her how to sew, but Mariam needed a sewing machine to start her business and did not have enough money to buy one. Luckily, she received a machine through a donation. Similar to Gul, Mariam initially needed to ask her customers to provide the fabric and materials, as she lacked the financial resources to be able to hold fabrics in stock. Thus, she simply combined her available resources, that is, her sewing skills and the sewing machine, in creating the end product. While Mariam had learned sewing from her mother, she now informally trains her sister. Both her mother and sister now help her with sewing as well as dealing with the customers.

Jalila and Her Gym for Women Only

Jalila runs a gym where only women can become members and exercise. Jalila observed that there were many women in her community who were interested in going to a gym and exercise, but who felt impeded by societal restrictions to go to a gym also frequented by men:

> I love to exercise, and I believe in healthy life and healthy body. There are several other gyms in the city, but there was none only for women. I wanted to start a gym exclusively for the women of the Hazara community, where they could exercise without any tension, fear or shyness, as no men could come to the gym. Though restricting it only to women lowers the profits, that does not matter for me as I like women exercising and adopting a healthy lifestyle. (Jalila)

Thus, the value proposition of Jalila's business is to provide Hazara women with an opportunity to have a healthy lifestyle in a socially acceptable setting. The initial financial resources were provided by her sister who lives in the USA, and these were used to buy equipment, pay rent for the business, and a salary to the watchman. By now, the business has become profitable. The sister is now her business partner and feels emotionally attached to the business. In addition, Jalila receives help from another gym member, who has become a friend and works with her on a voluntary basis.

ILLUSTRATING COLLABORATIVE NON-ECONOMIC VALUE CREATION

The women entrepreneurs studied in this research displayed different types of collaborations to start and grow their ventures. These collaborations were not just effective for the women's business activities but served as a synergistic mechanism from which the different stakeholders participating in the collaboration benefitted. We identified different dimensions of non-economic value creation in this study. These dimensions illustrate different aspects of collaborative non-economic value creation and are introduced below, labelled as entrepreneurial readiness, informal training and skill transfer, resource transferability, and cultural narrative of resilience.

Entrepreneurial Readiness

The three entrepreneurs are necessity-based entrepreneurs and are highly resource constrained. All the resources that they gathered were from their connections or through different collaborations. We see them as well-connected with their peers as well as other women of the Hazara community because of the presence of the trust inherent in their social relationships. The women in our study were creative and alert in collaborating by developing strong relations with family, friends, stakeholders, and local peers. Collaborating with local peers helped the entrepreneurs to make their services more appealing by adding local cultural and traditional aspects to their products and services. These collaborations helped in mobilizing and utilizing local knowledge, culture, labour, and networks for their entrepreneurial activities. These relationships and collaborations acted as a synergistic mechanism that provided female entrepreneurs with increased entrepreneurial readiness, alertness and confidence to create services for local women despite the constraints faced. For example, Gul's embroidery service addresses women's restricted roles and local cultural taboos in the Hazara community by facilitating their access to traditional clothing: "It is easy for the women of my community to visit my home and leave their dresses for embroidering. They feel more comfortable when talking about the fitting of their dresses compared to men tailors, and they can get their desired designs" (Gul). Jalila tells about how her business is affected by working women's struggles to fulfil dual roles: "Many local working women join this gym. They are local teachers and lecturers who typically join during the vacation period, as with their home and work duties, vacation is the best time to get involved in the gym without affecting their household chores" (Jalila).

These women entrepreneurs accessed and utilized local resources, such as fabrics, labour, information, and historical knowledge to their benefit. For example, Mariam tells:

> In the beginning, I worked with preorders, where the local fabrics, local embroidery patterns and raw material such as thread and mirrors were provided by the local customers and retailers, as this cost less money. You know, cloth is quite cheap in Quetta, so when I saw the potential market for my work after filling preorders, I bought some local raw material like cloths and threads, prepared some unstitched dresses and started selling them on the local market. (Mariam)

The entrepreneurs used traditional crafts (such as local embroidery) and traditional cultural taboos (that women should only serve women) to arrange for customers, sponsors, and obtaining cheap materials. Local wage labour is employed because it is cheap and available due to the mobility restrictions posed on Hazara women. Collaboration with local women and closed relationships are common ways of gaining local knowledge, thereby improving the relational conditions of female entrepreneurs and contributing to the overall readiness of micro entrepreneurs in the Hazara community. Similar to Hamida in the opening story, for the three entrepreneurs in our study the aspect of helping other women to elevate their status is very important. Entrepreneurial readiness in this study is illustrated as an ongoing and emerging phenomenon that allows informal women entrepreneurs to be innovative in problem-solving (Sarasvathy, 2001) and alert to the possibility of using resources readily available to them (Baker & Nelson, 2005). Entrepreneurial readiness allows these informal women entrepreneurs to be resourceful through their adaptive responses to the challenging environments (Harmeling, Sarasvathy & Freeman, 2009). The collaborations of informal entrepreneurs with the local community enhance their alertness to local conditions and traditions and allow these women entrepreneurs to expand their businesses and develop positive reputations, as exemplified by Gul: "The embroidery patterns are traditional and antique. However, I use creativity in those patterns and the customers respond positively" (Gul).

Informal Training, Skill Development, and Skill Transfer

During their enterprising activities, women entrepreneurs in our sample gained valuable local information about social capital, culture, and human resources. Launching and managing the enterprises allowed them to better connect locally and they established collaborations with experienced entrepreneurs and other stakeholders. Collaborations with other locally anchored female entrepreneurs help these Hazara women entrepreneurs to explore the market and to share and transfer their skills and human capital collaboratively among local women. Literature shows that experienced entrepreneurs may deal better with uncertain situations, which is why new entrants prefer to affiliate with existing women entrepreneurs (Elfring & Hulsink, 2003), for example to get advice.

Along the same lines, we observed in this study that the female entrepreneurs were frequently involved in activities where they could both develop their own skills and transfer these skills within their networks. For example, our participants were homemakers before they started their necessity-based businesses. This means that they had no formal skills or training in running and managing a business. However, their informal training and collaborative strategies allowed them to gain sector-relevant experience and important knowledge about how the market works. This is a unique way of gaining relevant human capital for constrained entrepreneurs. The existing literature on entrepreneurship and human capital acknowledges the role of pre-start-up experience and certifications, however, we also need to appreciate this type of informal training that can not only contribute to human capital but can also enhance business activity in constrained regions.

The Hazara entrepreneurs in our study learned different communication skills and about business regulations, marketing and selling, bargaining, negotiating and planning activities whilst actually running their businesses. They also showed that they intentionally contributed to further skill transfer for the purpose of continuing local women-based business activities. As Mariam tells:

> For my business, the only resource I started with was my embroidery skill. In the beginning I used to make simple designs. With practice and my mother's supervision, now I can make complicated designs. (…) Now, we are teaching embroidery to my sister as well. This is a skill which can empower women even to work from home.

This skill transfer is not just limited to different crafts, but it extends to informal business training. The micro entrepreneurs in our study did not have any formal training, but they gained business insights through their small-scale business activities and by collaborating with other local entrepreneurs. As told by Jalila:

> I used to exercise in other gyms, and from there I learned about the fitness equipment to be used. There was mostly heavy equipment more suitable for men. Exercising in other gyms was my only source of learning about gym equipment. I learned about gym equipment particularly for women from the sellers of such equipment on Jinnah Road.

Therefore, informal micro business activities were observed as a means of obtaining knowledge about the local market, clients, resources and services. Out of necessity, the women entrepreneurs opted for informal micro business activities that required limited resources to test their ideas and developed social relationships and local cohesive networks as well as their resource base over time. During this entrepreneurial experience, the women gained valuable local information, social capital, and cultural resources. Informal skill enhancement through small-scale business activities and their local networks improved their business acumen to allow them to utilize resources effectively.

In relation to non-economic value, informal training comes across as an important aspect in gaining necessary business skills and market knowledge for informal micro entrepreneurs. As they are lacking formal education, the female entrepreneurs in this study have limited skills, which restrict their opportunities to develop a more diverse business profile. Professional training is a challenge to obtain for these entrepreneurs due to the adverse conditions they face as women in Hazara Town. Gul, for example, tells how she has informally acquired the skill employed in her business: "Traditional embroidery is our cultural heritage and I have learned it from my mother and aunts. (…) I became more creative in my embroidery patterns and skills over time. I can now combine antique and traditional patterns with modern embroidery skills." Thus, informal skill transfer and skill enhancement from peers can increase these entrepreneurs' likelihood of success.

Resource Transferability

The entrepreneurs' resource gathering activity started with personal resources at hand, and then extended to internal and external collaborations, that is, from close family and friends to local stakeholders (mostly local female entrepreneurs and female customers). The entrepreneurs mainly gathered resources through personal ties such as family members and friends. For example, Gul tells how "In the start of my business, local friends helped in getting orders and spreading the information about my business" and Mariam appreciates that "[i]f there is a heavy workload, my mother and sister also help voluntarily". The second collaboration dimension was through business networking, mostly between entrepreneurs and local female customers, as exemplified by Gul: "Now my customers are further selling my products to Australia, the USA, and Europe, as they have their families and networks out there. This results in increased sales and growth of my business."

Collaborations of both types played important roles in resource gathering among the micro entrepreneurs. Their collaborative ties tend to be based on mutual trust. Social collaborations provide financial, cultural, moral, and physical resources, and most importantly credibility and social legitimacy to the women entrepreneurs. All these resources are important, but the goodwill and social legitimacy provided through social collaborations are especially crucial for socio-economic value creation through entrepreneurial activities.

Cultural Narrative of Resilience

As outlined above, the situation of the Hazara community in Quetta, and for women in particular, is harsh, but even more so for its youth who lack the perspective of a better future (Sarfraz, 2017). Thus, entrepreneurial experiences such as the ones outlined in this chapter can bring a fresh air of hope to the local community. The particular cultural narratives observed in the cases not only concern the physical or material use of local resources, but extend to the traditions, feelings, and emotions of resilience, safety and survival in the local community. For example, Jalila tells: "Non-community members find it frustrating to enter the area due to high security checks. This has an adverse effect on our potential customers, and it lowers the profit, but we have to take care of our security and safety ourselves." Thus, women entrepreneurs appear to play an important role in developing cultural resources, such as stories and narratives, to mobilize strength and survival in the local market and to also gain legitimation for their enterprise (Lounsbury & Glynn, 2001). For example, Jalila, who runs the gym, promotes a health awareness, fitness and strength narrative and has also taken special measures to secure her local customers. Only local females from the community can join the fitness activities because of security concerns. Gul wants to keep traditional and antique embroidery patterns alive and recognized as a source of cultural identity. Mariam wants to transfer her sewing skills and embroidery skills to local women also with the aim for them to have a means to earn their living. To maintain this narrative of fighting against the odds, these women rely on their personal skills, commitment and most importantly local collaborations with close and expanded networks. They believe that their ambitions combined with their skills and local networks will help them to survive and grow in this challenging situation for the Hazara ethnic community and to deal with the gender-based harassment that demands strength and resilience from them. These findings resonate with Bullough et al. (2014) who found that even under conditions of war, individuals develop entrepreneurial intentions if they are able to grow from resilience and believe in their entrepreneurial abilities.

DISCUSSION

The experiences of the Hazara women entrepreneurs in our study illustrate the multidimensionality of non-economic value creation: Social relationships and collaborations provided them with resources such as local knowledge, raw materials, advice, legitimacy, and social viability for their entrepreneurial activities. In return, the women entrepreneurs displayed a strong commitment to non-economic value creation in the form of entrepreneurial readiness, trust, narratives of resilience among locals, skill enhancement for improving the product offering, and transferability of services and resources. Also striking in our findings is how the entrepreneurial activities of all three women entrepreneurs attempted to improve other women's lives, thereby playing an important role in easing their chores in an adverse context. This impact was not only evident for the female customers, but also by providing skills and income to other women, improving their chances of small-scale emancipation.

Entrepreneurial readiness as the willingness and confidence of entrepreneurs improves because of relational conditions of entrepreneurs (Bygballe et al., 2016), that is, through social networks and local stakeholders (such as labour, community, and peers), allowing the entrepreneurs to handle their entrepreneurial activities. The Hazara women entrepreneurs' social connectedness improved their confidence and ability to judge the availability and utilization of resources to exploit certain opportunities (Westlund & Bolton, 2003). Entrepreneurial readiness promotes the willingness of entrepreneurs (Lau et al., 2012) and the resource perceptions of entrepreneurs (Schillo et al., 2016) to direct entrepreneurial behaviours towards adapting a product or service for use in a specific location or market.

Trust accumulates and strengthens social relationships and improves the chances of value creation among small-scale entrepreneurs in constrained contexts (e.g. Aldrich, Elam & Reese, 1997; Elfring & Hulsink, 2003). Trust-based collaborations with members of the community provide business legitimacy (Feldman, 2004; Feldman et al., 2011). Informal micro-entrepreneurship cannot exist without tolerance or legitimacy in local ecosystems (De Castro et al., 2014) and legitimacy within a constrained context for informal entrepreneurs seems to be crucial in shaping opportunities.

Our findings are consistent with Powell and Baker (2014), who found that groups and society can be used as a forum of shared interest to promote ventures and gain market share. The Hazara micro entrepreneurs relied on relations and collaborations to avoid uncertainties (Heinström, 2010) and to create unique dimensions of non-economic value. They created value through the involvement and participation of local collaborations. Such collaborations act as the mechanism that nurtures the process of economic and non-economic value creation, because of the presence of high tolerance of ambiguity (Bhatti, 2013; Birtchnell, 2011; Kumar, 2011), and they allow for survival and progress even with a low resource base (Birtchnell, 2011). Rich social ties substitute for a lack of formal governance mechanisms and influence economic and non-economic value creation (cf. Mair, Marti & Ventresca, 2012). This trend of collaboration is positive for the entrepreneurial activities of the Hazara, as a high frequency of collaboration of small businesses in a region can open up for new entrepreneurial opportunities and aspirations, and foster an acceptance of entrepreneurial activity (Kangasharju, 2000). In the constrained context of the Hazara ethnic minority, non-economic value creation can translate into encouragement for business start-ups among local women, and also men, and can elevate their status and eventually result in innovation and diversity (cf. Audretsch, Bönte & Keilbach, 2008).

The women entrepreneurs in our study were extremely challenged and constrained, however, they worked against all odds and contributed to collaborative non-economic value by co-creating their social and business environment. Wiltbank et al. (2006) suggest that entrepreneurs in unpredictable markets co-create their future not through prediction but instead through self-selected stakeholders. However, in our study, our participants frequently predict their environment and are skilfully developing and transferring their collaborations to fight resource constraints and yet complement each other for missing resources. This essence of resilience to transform with changing circumstances (Welter & Xheneti, 2015) is remarkable in Hazara women entrepreneurs. Though the history and challenges of Hazara women entrepreneurs are unique, their entrepreneurial responses to these constraints reflect on entrepreneurial agency that works at both individual and collective level (Skerratt, 2013). Therefore, we believe that this scope of entrepreneurial action organized at the collaborative level can help in understanding different dimensions of non-economic value creation. This entrepreneurial agency can be understood and translated into policy agendas in regions with constrained scenarios. Policy makers in Pakistan can highlight the importance of learning (Terjesen, 2007) and can work towards stability of this region to provide and guide entrepreneurial actions.

NOTE

1.   All names have been anonymized.

REFERENCES

Abetti, P. A. (2004). Informal corporate entrepreneurship: Implications from the failure of the Concorde alloy foundry and the success of the Toshiba laptop. *International Journal of Entrepreneurship and Innovation Management*, 4(6), 529–545.

Ahlström, J. & Sjoström, E. (2005). CSOs and business partnerships: Strategies for interaction. *Business Strategy and the Environment*, 14(4), 230–240.

Aldrich, H. E., Elam, A. B. & Reese, P. R. (1997). Strong ties, weak ties, and strangers: Do women owners differ from men in their use of networking to obtain assistance? In: Birley, S. & Macmillan, I. (eds), *Entrepreneurship in a global context*, London: Routledge, 1–25.

Ali, Z. (2015). Identity as a form of human insecurity: The case of religious minorities in Pakistan. *Journal of Human Security Studies*, 4(2), 108–126.

Amha, W. & Ademassie, A. (2004). Rural financial intermediation program and its role in strengthening the rural financial system in Ethiopia. *Journal of Microfinance Development Review*, 3(2), 230–365.

Audretsch, D. B., Bönte, W. & Keilbach, M. (2008). Entrepreneurship capital and its impact on knowledge diffusion and economic performance. *Journal of Business Venturing*, 23(6), 687–698.

Austin, J. E. (2010). From organization to organization: On creating value. *Journal of Business Ethics*, 94(Suppl. 1), 13–15.

Austin, J. E. & Seitanidi, M. M. (2012). Collaborative value creation: A review of partnering between nonprofits and businesses: Part I: Value creation spectrum and collaboration stages, *Nonprofit & Voluntary Sector Quarterly*, 41(5), 726–758.

Baker, T., Miner, A. S. & Eesley, D. T. (2003). Improvising firms: Bricolage, account giving and improvisational competencies in the founding process. *Research Policy*, 32, 255–276.

Baker, T. & Nelson, R. E. (2005). Creating something from nothing: Resource construction through entrepreneurial bricolage. *Administrative Science Quarterly*, 50(3), 329–366.

Bath, A. (2011). Violence against women in Pakistan, Master's thesis University of San Francisco 1122, Fall 16 December 2011, retrieved from https://repository-usfca.edu/thes/ 1122 on 17 January 2020.

Bhagavatula, S. (2009). Weaving social networks. Performance of small rural firms in India as an outcome of entrepreneurs; social and human capital. PhD thesis, Vrije Universiteit Amsterdam, retrieved from https://research.vu.nl/en/publications/weaving-social-networks on 5 December 2019.

Bhagavatula, S., Elfring, T., Van Tilburg, A. & Van De Bunt, G. G. (2010). How social and human capital influence opportunity recognition and resource mobilization in India's hand-loom industry. *Journal of Business Venturing*, 25(3), 245–260.

Bhatti, Y. (2013). Jugaad innovation: Think frugal, be flexible, generate breakthrough growth. *South Asian Journal of Global Business Research*, 2(2), 279–282.

Birtchnell, T. (2011). Jugaad as systemic risk and disruptive innovation in India. *Contemporary South Asia*, 19(4), 357–372.

Branzei, O. & Abdelnour, S. (2010). Another day, another dollar: Enterprise resilience under terrorism in developing countries, *Journal of International Business Studies*, 41(5), 804–825.

Broembsen, V. M. (2019). The European Regulation of Bulgarian Homeworkers: Regulating Informal Labour in Global Production Networks. Working Paper (Law) No. 40. Retrieved from https://www.wiego.org/publications/european-unions-commodification-bulgarian -homeworkers-regulating-informal-labour on 19 December 2019.

Bullough, A., Renko, M. & Myatt, T. (2014). Danger zone entrepreneurs: The importance of resilience and self-efficacy for entrepreneurial intentions, *Entrepreneurship Theory & Practice*, May, 473–499.

Bygballe, L. E., Swärd, A. R. & Vaagaasar, A. L. (2016). Coordinating in construction projects and the emergence of synchronized readiness. *International Journal of Project Management*, 34(8), 1479–1492.

Coleman, J. S. (1988). Social capital in the creation of human capital. *American Journal of Sociology*, 94, S95–S120.

Collins, J., Watson, K. & Skoko, B. (2017). From boats to businesses. The remarkable journey of Hazara refugee entrepreneurs in Adelaide. Full report retrieved from https://www.uts.edu .au/sites/default/files/2017-10/From%20Boats%20to%20Businesses%20Full%20Report %20-%20Web.pdf on 5 February 2020.

Dana, L. P. (2001). The education and training of entrepreneurs in Asia. *Education + Training*, 43(8/9), 405–416.

Davidsson, P. & Honig, B. (2003). The role of social and human capital among nascent entre-preneurs. *Journal of Business Venturing*, 18(3), 301–331.

De Castro, J. O., Khavul, S. & Bruton, G. D. (2014). Shades of grey: How do informal firms navigate between macro and meso institutional environments? *Strategic Entrepreneurship Journal*, 8(1), 75–94.

Elfring, T. & Hulsink, W. (2003). Networks in entrepreneurship: The case of high-technology firms. *Small Business Economics*, 21(4), 409–422.

Feldman, M. S. (2004). Resources in emerging structures and processes of change. *Organization Science*, 15(3), 295–309.

Feldman, M., Worline, M., Cameron, K. & Spreitzer, G. (2011). *Oxford handbook of positive organizational scholarship*. New York: Oxford University Press.

Gedajlovic, E., Honig, B., Moore, C. B., Payne, G. T. & Wright, M. (2013). Social capital and entrepreneurship: A schema and research agenda. *Entrepreneurship Theory and Practice*, 37(3), 455–478.

Godfrey, P. C. (2011). Toward a theory of the informal economy. *Academy of Management Annals*, 5(1), 231–277.

Granovetter, M. S. (1973). The strength of weak ties. *American Journal of Sociology*, 78(6), 1360–1380.

Griffee, D.T. (2005). Research tips: Interview data collection, *Journal of Developmental Education*, 28(3), 36–37.

Hailemariam, A. T. & Kroon, B. (2018). Redefining success beyond economic growth and wealth generation: the case of Ethiopia. In: Yousafzai, S., Fayolle, A., Lindgreen, A., Henry, C., Saeed, S. & Sheikh, S. (eds), *Women entrepreneurs and the myth of 'underperformance': A new look at women's entrepreneurship research*, Cheltenham, UK and Northampton, MA, USA: Edward Elgar Publishing, 3–19.

Hambrick, D. C. (2007). Upper echelons theory: An update. *Academy of Management Review*, 32(2), 334–343.

Harmeling, S. S., Sarasvathy, S. D., & Freeman, R. E. (2009). Related debates in ethics and entrepreneurship: Values, opportunities, and contingency. *Journal of Business Ethics*, 84(3), 341–365.

Hashim, A. (2013). Pakistan's Hazara Shia living under siege, Al Jazeera, 18 January 2013, retrieved from https://www.aljazeera.com/indepth/features/2013/01/201311 7124512947691.html, on 6 December 2019.

Heinström, J. (2010). *From fear to flow: personality and information interaction*. Amsterdam: Elsevier.

Hilaly, Z. (2011). The dismal state of women in Pakistan, *The Express Tribune*, 22 June 2011, retrieved from https://tribune.com.pk/story/193434/the-dismal-state-of-women-in -pakistan/ on 5 November 2019.

Hoang, H. & Antoncic, B. (2003). Network-based research in entrepreneurship: A critical review. *Journal of Business Venturing*, 18(2), 165–187.

Hytti, U. (2015). Gendered understanding of recruitment processes: Applications and résumés. In: Broadbridge, A. M. & Fielden, S. L. (eds), *Handbook of gendered careers in management*. Edward Elgar Publishing, 74–89.

Independent (2019). Fear and persecution in Pakistan's Hazara community. *The Independent*, 2 August 2019, written by Akhtar Soomro, retrieved from https://www.independent.co .uk/arts-entertainment/photography/pakistan-hazara-ethnic-minority-community-quetta -a8995466.html on 14 October 2019.

Kangasharju, A. (2000). Growth of the smallest: Determinants of small firm growth during strong macroeconomic fluctuations. *International Small Business Journal*, 19(1), 28–43.

Korsgaard, S. & Anderson, A. R. (2011). Enacting entrepreneurship as social value creation. *International Small Business Journal*, 29(2), 135–151.

Kranton, R. E. (1996). Reciprocal exchange: A self-sustaining system. *The American Economic Review*, 830–851.

Kumar, M. (2011). Jugaad: Its antecedents and consequences, *DSM Business Review*, 3(2), 83–105.

Lau, V. P., Dimitrova, M. N., Shaffer, M. A., Davidkov, T. & Yordanova, D. I. (2012). Entrepreneurial readiness and firm growth: An integrated etic and emic approach. *Journal of International Management*, 18(2), 147–159.

London, T. & Hart, S. L. (2011). *Next generation business strategies for the base of the pyramid: New approaches for building mutual value*. Upper Saddle River, NJ: Pearson Education.

Lounsbury, M. & Glynn, M. A. (2001). Cultural entrepreneurship: Stories, legitimacy, and the acquisition of resources. *Strategic Management Journal*, 22(6–7), 545–564.

Lyon, F. (2000). Trust, networks and norms: The creation of social capital in agricultural economies in Ghana. *World Development*, 28(4), 663–681.

Mair, J. & Marti, I. (2007). Entrepreneurship for social impact: Encouraging market access in rural Bangladesh. *Corporate Governance: The International Journal of Business in Society*, 7(4), 493–501.

Mair, J. & Marti, I. (2009). Entrepreneurship in and around institutional voids: A case study from Bangladesh. *Journal of Business Venturing*, 24(5), 419–435.

Mair, J., Marti, I. & Ventresca, M. J. (2012). Building inclusive markets in rural Bangladesh: How intermediaries work institutional voids. *Academy of Management Journal*, 55(4), 819–850.

Mandják, T. & Durrieu, F. (2000, September). Understanding the non-economic value of business relationships. *16th IMP Conference*, retrieved from https://www.impgroup.org/uploads/papers/89.pdf on December 8, 2019.

Marlow, S. & McAdam, M. (2013). Gender and entrepreneurship: Advancing debate and challenging myths; exploring the mystery of the under-performing female entrepreneur. *International Journal of Entrepreneurial Behavior & Research*, 19(1), 114–124.

Mayoux, L. (2001). Tackling the downside: Social capital, women's empowerment and microfinance in Cameroon. *Development and Change*, 32(3), 435–464.

NCHR (2018). Understanding the agonies of ethnic Hazaras, Islamabad: National Commission for Human Rights Pakistan, retrieved from https://nchr.gov.pk/wp-content/uploads/2019/01/HAZARA-REPORT.pdf on 8 December 2019.

Porter, M. E. & Kramer, M. R. (2006). The link between competitive advantage and corporate social responsibility. *Harvard Business Review*, 84(12), 78–92.

Powell, E. E. & Baker, T. (2014). Creating slack: Institutional constraints and entrepreneurial discretion. *Frontiers of Entrepreneurship Research*, 34(14), 1.

RFE (2019). 'Down with terrorism': Pakistan's minority Hazara protest for third day after attack, Radio Free Europe/Radio Liberty, 14 April 2019, retrieved from https://www.rferl.org/a/down-with-terrorism-pakistan-s-minority-hazara-protest-for-third-day-after-attack/29880241.html on 14 October 2019.

Roads&Kingdoms (2018). A Hazara woman opened a restaurant in Quetta to help her Shia-Hazara community. Then the threats began, retrieved from https://roadsandkingdoms.com/2018/hazara-restaurant-quetta-pakistan/ on 14 October 2019.

Sarasvathy, S. D. (2001). Causation and effectuation: Toward a theoretical shift from economic inevitability to entrepreneurial contingency. *Academy of Management Review*, 26(2), 243–263.

Sarasvathy, S. D., Dew, N., Read, S. & Wiltbank, R. (2008). Designing organizations that design environments: Lessons from entrepreneurial expertise. *Organization Studies*, 29(3), 331–350.

Sarfraz, H. (2017). A restaurant in Quetta's Hazara Town is by women, for women, *The Express Tribune*, 13 November 2017, retrieved from https://tribune.com.pk/story/1534555/1-a-restaurant-in-hazara-town-is-for-women-by-women/ on 13 December 2019.

SBP (2012). Enclosure: Definition of Microenterprise & Revised Prudential Regulations No. 10 & 11. AC&MFD Circular No. 02 of 2012, retrieved from http://www.sbp.org.pk/acd/2012/C2-AnnexA.pdf on 5 February 2020.

Schillo, R. S., Persaud, A. & Jin, M. (2016). Entrepreneurial readiness in the context of national systems of entrepreneurship. *Small Business Economics*, 46(4), 619–637.

Shane, S., & Venkataraman, S. (2000). The promise of entrepreneurship as a field of research. *Academy of Management Review*, 25(1), 217–226.

Silvey, R. & Elmhirst, R. (2003). Engendering social capital: Women workers and rural-urban networks in Indonesia's crisis. *World Development*, 31(5), 865–879.

Sirmon, D. G. & Hitt, M. A. (2003). Managing resources: Linking unique resources, management, and wealth creation in family firms. *Entrepreneurship Theory and Practice*, 27(4), 339–358.

Skerratt, S. (2013). Enhancing the analysis of rural community resilience: Evidence from community land ownership. *Journal of Rural Studies*, 31, 36–46.

Starr, J. A. & MacMillan, I. C. (1990). Resource cooptation via social contracting: Resource acquisition strategies for new ventures. *Strategic Management Journal*, 79–92.

Terjesen, Siri A. (2007). Asian models of entrepreneurship: From the Indian Union and the Kingdom of Nepal to the Japanese archipelago: Context, policy & practice. *Small Business Economics*, 28(1), 105–107.

UN Women (2016). Women's economic participation and empowerment in Pakistan, retrieved from http://asiapacific.unwoman.org/en/countries/pakistan/wee on 5 February 2020.

Webb, J. W., Tihanyi, L., Ireland, R. D., & Sirmon, D. G. (2009). You say illegal, I say legitimate: Entrepreneurship in the informal economy. *Academy of Management Review*, 34(3), 492–510.

Welter, F., Baker, T., Audretsch, D. B., & Gartner, W. B. (2017). Everyday entrepreneurship—a call for entrepreneurship research to embrace entrepreneurial diversity. *Entrepreneurship Theory and Practice*, 41(3), 311–321.

Welter, F. & Xheneti, M. (2013). Reenacting contextual boundaries: Entrepreneurial resourcefulness in challenging environments. In: Corbett, A. C. & Katz, J. (eds), *Entrepreneurial resourcefulness: Competing with constraints*. Bingley: Emerald, Vol. 15, 149–183.

Welter, F. & Xheneti, M. (2015). Value for whom? Exploring the value of informal entrepreneurial activities in post-socialist contexts. In McElwee, G. & Smith, R. (eds), *Exploring criminal and illegal enterprise: New perspectives on research, policy & practice*. Bingley: Emerald, 253–275.

Westlund, H. & Bolton, R. (2003). Local social capital and entrepreneurship. *Small Business Economics*, 21(2), 77–113.

Williams, C. & Nadin, S. (2012). Tackling entrepreneurship in the informal economy: Evaluating the policy options. *Journal of Entrepreneurship and Public Policy*, 1, 111–124.

Wiltbank, R., Dew, N., Read, S. & Sarasvathy, S. D. (2006). What to do next? The case for non-predictive strategy. *Strategic Management Journal*, 27(10), 981–998.

Yaziji, M. (2004). Turning gadflies into allies. *Harvard Business Review*, 82(2), 110–115.

Zehra, K. (2018). *Resource mobilization among informal entrepreneurs: A case of event planning industry of Pakistan* (Doctoral dissertation, Jönköping University, Jönköping International Business School).

Zehra, K. & Achtenhagen, L. (2018). If policy (half-heartedly) says yes, but patriarchy says no: How the gendered institutional contexts in Pakistan restricts women entrepreneurship. In: Yousafzi, S. Y., Lindgreen, A., Saeed, S. & Henry, C. (eds), *Contextual embeddedness of women's entrepreneurship: Going beyond a gender neutral approach*. London: Routledge, Chapter 2.

6. Cultivating business value beyond economic measures: narratives from Sweden

Annie Roos

INTRODUCTION

In this chapter, I explore the life narratives (Anderson, 2008; Gherardi, 2015) of two women entrepreneurs, Mona and Paulette, who are living in the same rural community in Sweden.[1] Mona and her husband started the first business in their portfolio in 1988. While she is a multi-entrepreneur, we will focus on one stream of business in this chapter: her textile business. In short, Mona ran a textile business that failed financially. Later, she established a design company producing textiles from a historical local print. Paulette, on the other hand, administers a personal assistant business for those in need. It outgrew the local community facilities and moved its headquarters to the nearby town. However, she still has customers in the community. In 2018, the business celebrated 20 years since its first customer. Now, the business consists of 500 employees and is the second largest business, in terms of turnover, in the community.

Using the life narratives of Mona and Paulette, I aim to challenge the underperformance hypothesis surrounding women entrepreneurs. The notion that women entrepreneurs are taken to be underperforming in relation to men entrepreneurs has been well established in research (Ahl & Marlow, 2012; Marlow & McAdam, 2013). Business performance is understood as the financial outcome of the business, and not as the particular process (Marlow & Patton, 2005). As such, women entrepreneurs are at a disadvantage in obtaining capital for their business development (Marlow & Patton, 2005) and thus seen as less skilful in recognising opportunity and are stereotyped as risk adverse (Marlow & Swail, 2014). These statements are not surprising, as entrepreneurship generally, and women's entrepreneurship in particular, is seen as an instrument for economic growth (Ahl, 2006). Consequently, the perceived underperformance of women entrepreneurs is positioned as a problem within research (Ahl, 2006).

Focusing on the particular context of Sweden, we can see that, different from other countries, the research on the perceived underperformance of women entrepreneurs is explained by structural factors rather than individual (Ahl et al., 2016). The underperformance is explained, and critiqued, by the gendered business landscape (women and men work in different sectors) and the double burden of women's responsibility for family and household. Moreover, statistics show that businesses owned by women entrepreneurs in Sweden have a lower turnover and profit compared to businesses owned by men (Statistics Sweden, 2017). However, Ahl et al. (2016) critique the research, framing women as underperforming, saying that it merely adheres to entrepreneurship being seen as inherently male and individualist. Moreover, they critique the research for lacking a focus on context, structures and the family dimension of entrepreneurship. This underperforming hypothesis is the effect of research on women entrepreneurs being set as a comparison to male entrepreneurs (Marlow & McAdam, 2013).

Nevertheless, women entrepreneurs come out as underdogs compared to men, when measuring entrepreneurship as an economic phenomenon (Marlow & McAdam, 2013). However, only using the financial measures of entrepreneurship ignores the stratified value that is accrued and created through the entrepreneurship process (Korsgaard & Anderson, 2011). Instead, accumulated value can be seen as enabling access to resources, both financial and more so non-financial resources, and in particular the need for the business.

For this chapter, I look beyond the outcomes of entrepreneurship. Instead, the process of entrepreneurship is important, as it potentially captures something different than the solely male norms of entrepreneurship (Marlow & Patton, 2005). Hence, I focus on how women entrepreneurs both accrue and create value with their entrepreneurship. As policy and research use the individual entrepreneur in relation to economic development (Drakopoulou Dodd & Anderson, 2007), it becomes logical for this chapter to focus on how the individual accrues and creates value beyond economic development. Focusing on the business level means that the women entrepreneur interacts directly with her business, cultivating value through accumulating and creating a multiplicity of value. Focusing on both accruing and creating value, hence the process, becomes crucial in understanding how to foster further engagement with women in entrepreneurship and gender equality in regard to entrepreneurship.

Revisiting the aim of the chapter, to challenge the underperformance hypothesis surrounding women entrepreneurs, the guiding research question is 'How do women entrepreneurs accrue and create value on a business level?' With this guiding question in mind, I will in the next section, define value and further anchor the chapter in its Swedish context. After that, the methodology and the two cases of Mona and Paulette are further explained. The narratives of Mona and Paulette are presented in relation to how they accrue and create value in their businesses. For the analysis, their narratives are used to present a conceptual figure of how to think about value within entrepreneurship. Lastly, the discussion and the conclusion are presented, tying the chapter together with this introduction.

ENTREPRENEURIAL VALUE AND THE SWEDISH CONTEXT

When it comes to value creation from entrepreneurship it is generally seen in two different ways, the traditional business evaluation and the social value creation

(Lautermann, 2013). The traditional business evaluation is characterised by egoism, profit and being accepted in the perceived business sector. The value the entrepreneur adds to entrepreneurship is regarded as, for example, bringing in investors (Malmström et al., 2017) and providing a legitimate entrepreneur persona (Berglund et al., 2018). The value from entrepreneurship has similarly been characterised as generating more income for the entrepreneur (Korsgaard & Anderson, 2011), unleashing entrepreneurial financial potential (Berglund et al., 2018) and as an alternative income to traditional employment (Alkhaled & Berglund, 2018). The value women entrepreneurs find important with entrepreneurship does not differ substantially from the value men find important (Fagenson, 1993). They both focus on autonomy and creating worth from their personal conviction.

The other side of value creation focuses on altruism, non-profit and the social sector (Lautermann, 2013). The non-financial recourses the entrepreneur adds to entrepreneurship are, for example, networks (Datta & Gailey, 2012), using the home as a space for the business (Ekinsmyth, 2013) and embedding the business in its context (Aggestam & Wigren-Kristoferson, 2017). In turn, entrepreneurs also create importance in their entrepreneurship through personal value, such as skills, knowledge and experiences (Korsgaard & Anderson, 2011), as well as empowerment (Datta & Gailey, 2012). The value created can be linked to the satisfaction of solving a complex problem (Kokko, 2018), and the ability to balance the notion of home and work-life (Chasserio et al., 2014).

Admittedly, the value from entrepreneurs, and women entrepreneurs especially, is something that politicians consider. Entrepreneurship is seen as a way to gain freedom in self-expression (Smith, 2010; Tillmar, 2009), to provide economic welfare to society (Kenny & Scriver, 2012; Ogbor, 2000), and to help solve complex societal problems (Ahl et al., 2016; McKeever et al., 2015). Women entrepreneurs are seen as a key group to target for further development. Sweden is no different here, with politicians arguing for 'unleashing women's entrepreneurial potential so they can contribute to economic growth' (Berglund et al., 2018, p. 531). As around 30 percent of businesses in Sweden are run by women (Statistics Sweden, 2014), they are seen as an untapped pool of resources. There are no institutional laws or policies in place hindering women from starting businesses, yet gender equality in entrepreneurship is far from accomplished. The government has introduced a number of political initiatives directed towards promoting women entrepreneurship (see for example Nilsson, 1997; Pettersson et al., 2017; Roos, 2019). Nonetheless, the gap in ownership is stable and not decreasing (Statistics Sweden, 2017).

The political initiatives have given women entrepreneurs in different stages of their entrepreneurial journey the opportunity to learn more about how to run a business and the opportunity to share knowledge, visions and problems with fellow entrepreneurs (Roos, 2019). In contrast, many women entrepreneurs face financial barriers, where investors gender-characterise them (Malmström et al., 2017). The locale or setting is also crucial for shaping entrepreneurship carried out by women entrepreneurs (Roos, 2017). Local social practices shape the involvement of women in entrepreneurship, especially migrant women entrepreneurs (Webster, 2016).

Navigating these social practices is central for many entrepreneurs, taking time from value creation. Additionally, they face governmental prejudices, where the Swedish government, through policy, conveys how women entrepreneurs should run their businesses and create value similar to men (Roos, 2019). Indeed, the government argues that the women entrepreneurs in Sweden should become more 'proper entrepreneurs'.

Policies to address these inequalities argue for entrepreneurship to empower women to gain gender equality through economic development (Berglund et al., 2018). The special actions applied in many countries are, for example, start-up grants (Marlow & Patton, 2005), counselling services (Nilsson, 1997), mentorship programmes (Marlow & McAdam, 2012) and networks that target only women entrepreneurs (Roos, 2019). The value creation from these networks is a way for women entrepreneurs to circumvent the different types of structural barriers they face, such as a lack of knowledge and the lack of availability of official support (Byrne & Fayolle, 2010), as well as changing basic local gender structures (Roos, 2019). Researchers have, however, questioned the value of women entrepreneurship networks, as these networks are continuously 'othering' the women entrepreneurs by separating them from men's networks (Byrne & Fayolle, 2010; Roos, 2019).

INTRODUCING MONA, PAULETTE AND THE NETWORK

The narratives of Mona and Paulette will be discussed shortly, and I will focus on how they accrue and create value on a business level. Table 6.1 introduces Mona and Paulette and it also presents their joint involvement in the local female entrepreneurship network. The narratives were collected as part of a four-year ethnographic study from 2015 to 2018 that was part of a larger study conducted in a rural community in Sweden. I approached the community with the broad aim of understanding how people are influenced by gender structures and how they actively and passively reproduce such structures (Calás et al., 2007; Lindgren & Packendorff, 2009). In the ethnography, I used a multi-method approach (Johnstone, 2007) involving doing interviews, participating in meetings, observing meetings and seminars, and connecting with people and businesses on social media. The multi-method approach is appropriate when doing an ethnography as it provides different sources for understanding the same cultural phenomena (Brannen, 1996), in this case value.

From the wide array of interesting people I met, the entrepreneurs in this chapter were chosen based on how they contribute to the understanding of value creation by women entrepreneurs (Emmel, 2013). The businesses differ in size when it comes to employees and revenue and the women differ in the number of businesses they run. Consequently, their measured financial value varies quite a lot. They are, however, similar in their personal links with the community. Their similarities and differences were thus intriguing when talking of accruing and creating value other than purely financial results. The choice of these women was thus theoretical (Neergaard, 2007),

Table 6.1   *Presenting Mona, Paulette and the network*

Mona	Paulette
Mona started her career as a business owner as a business wife, when her husband bought his first excavator in 1988. 'I did the paperwork and I was a "business wife".' Today she is a multi-entrepreneur in the sense that she and her husband have a wide variety of businesses in their portfolio. The excavation business is still running and has several employees. They have a vacation home for rent in Spain, which they also use themselves. Additionally, they rent out portable toilets to different events around Sweden. They are one of the leading actors in this sector. Furthermore, Mona has a design business and is a seller of aloe vera products.	Paulette's business, a private personal (healthcare) assistance company, was started in 1998 when she was 22 years old. She started her business from home right out of school without an official office space. Starting in the community was logical to her since this is where she grew up, lived and where she found her clients. From day one, she had three clients, which means the business started out with seven employees. The business has now grown to about 500 employees with around 70 clients, and around 20 people working in administration. The business is now organised as a holding company with Paulette still being the CEO and owner.

Network
Both Mona and Paulette are involved in a local female entrepreneurship network. The network was funded by a Swedish government programme that was initiated to promote female entrepreneurship. The network began in 2013 and is still running (2019). The number of participants varies, ranging between three and 30 people. On average, they arrange six meetings per year. The women entrepreneurs meet and have lectures on social media and basic accounting, as well as inspirational talks where they listen to other women entrepreneurs. Together they have built a collective view on what a women entrepreneur is and developed their business relations.

as I hoped the women's narratives could tell us something interesting about how value is accrued and created in business.

I conducted three interviews with Mona and with Paulette I conducted five. The main goal of the interviews was to capture the complexity of these women's lives, hence not just the numerical part of their business or solely their perceived business-life (Doucet & Mauthner, 2008). With this in mind, the questions were broad, limited in number and our conversation was free to go in any direction appropriate at the time. The first time I interviewed the entrepreneurs, I had three guiding questions with me: tell me about yourself, your businesses and what is happening in the local community. In the following interviews, the questions focused on changes that had happened on a personal, business and community level since we met the last time. This open interview approach minimises the risk of reproducing my expectations as a researcher and any pre-set categories (Johansson, 2004). All in all, the interviews lasted from one and a half hours up to three hours. The interviews were recorded and afterwards transcribed. Additionally, I wrote eight pages of field notes with Mona, and 22 pages with Paulette. The field notes were, for example, written at the meetings of the local female entrepreneurship network where I was an observer for the duration of the fieldwork.

The material, consisting of observations and quotes, was then organised in Nvivo (Saldaña, 2009). I structured the material from the women as life narratives, focusing on their everyday practices (Anderson, 2008) and on the discursive practices around specific situations (Gherardi, 2015). Mona and Paulette both provided me with long narratives beginning with the start of their businesses in the 1990s. With a narrative, we can understand what motivates an entrepreneur and how they run their ventures, both now and when the entrepreneur tries to make sense of past events (Johansson, 2004). I organised the narratives from Mona and Paulette into two different categories: how they accrue value and how they create value. Their involvement in the network became evident when analysing their narratives and hence the network became an important category to consider. The narratives are explored below, focusing on Mona and Paulette's involvement in the network and how they accrue and create value at a business level.

WOMEN ENTREPRENEURS ACCRUING VALUE ON A BUSINESS LEVEL

Throughout this section, the focus is on how the entrepreneurs are adding value. We look at their individual businesses and involvement in the local female entrepreneurship network. Overall, the value Mona and Paulette accrue is highly linked to their experience as long-time entrepreneurs. For Mona, this capability becomes evident when she starts a second textile business, and for Paulette it is seen in her instinct when hiring new employees. When it comes to their involvement in the network, they are mainly there for social reasons: staying up to date and learning from each other. We begin with Mona and her textile businesses.

Mona

In the 1990s, when Mona became unemployed, she was entitled to receive a start-up grant from the government to open up her own store with textiles, a sewing workshop and some gift items. This was her first shop and the first time she had a business on her own, without her husband. It was a wild card, she says, but she always liked sewing and took a chance. After a couple of months, she realised it wasn't feasible to make a living off the venture. So, when the lease on the property ran out, she closed the shop and continued focusing on the other business in her and her husband's portfolio.

Most recently, Mona has returned to her roots and experience from when she had the textile store. In her new business, Mona is using community designs originating from the 1800s to produce new fabrics for table cloths and other fabric-related products. She was contacted by the local historical society because they wanted someone to start marketing these designs. Mona's long history with the community, through owning several businesses and being involved in different business networks, gave her legitimacy for being selected as the producer of the local historical prints. Without the local historical society considering Mona as a person who would handle these fabrics with respect, this business would not have happened. Here, she benefited from her relations within the community, as her social network is highly established and refined. The business was dependent on Mona's ability to embed the company within the local context (Aggestam & Wigren-Kristoferson, 2017).

Paulette

Paulette grew her business through a long history within the private personal health-care sector. When she started in 1998, the government praised private welfare businesses, though today the private caregiving sector in Sweden is under scrutiny and money is tight for all parties involved. Paulette navigates these challenges through her knowledge of the sector and her persistence in keeping the business afloat. The highest expense she is facing is salaries for her employees, 'High salaries are a way to attract competent caregivers'. Most of the employees in Paulette's business are women, even though she sees a trend towards more men becoming interested in the jobs her company provides. For Paulette, it is more important that the employees are good caregivers than that they have the proper education. Virtuous caregivers are the everyday face of her business and she builds on her conviction to attract qualified personnel within this sector.

Network

Mona was the initiating force and ran the female entrepreneurship network within the local community. In the network, she organised 20–30 meetings the first years, which involved planning the agenda and booking rooms and lecturers. Mona is involved in the network because she believes these women can help each other to think about their businesses in ways they might otherwise not without the support of other women entrepreneurs. She likes the diversity of business owners that she has met through the network and appreciates what they have to offer the group. 'The more women we are and the more different we are, the more we give each other. Being involved in and running the network took a lot of time, up to the point where Mona felt she had to say no to the network and prioritise her own businesses. When Mona stepped down from her role as organiser, Paulette took over the position. For her, the network is a good way of finding out what is happening in other's businesses and in the local community. She also receives inspiration from the members in the network, 'You get some pep talks from others who dare to do things and such.'

Even though these types of networks have been questioned for their effectiveness in changing gender structures (Byrne & Fayolle, 2010), both Mona and Paulette have personally benefited from their involvement. Through the network, Mona is able to gain new ideas for her business, and for Paulette it is a way of staying up to date with what is happening in the local business community. They bring value to their entrepreneurship through the sisterhood in business provided by this network (Datta & Gailey, 2012). Above all, Mona and Paulette are focusing on gaining new knowledge, as they experience a lack of official support in their business development (Byrne & Fayolle, 2010).

WOMEN ENTREPRENEURS CREATING VALUE AT A BUSINESS LEVEL

We now move on to how the women entrepreneurs, Mona and Paulette, create value at a business level. We see how the two women, through the network, create value crucial for local community development. First, they foster gender equality through making women entrepreneurs visible in the community. They also enable collaboration around business-related issues. In turn, Mona and Paulette are able to give advice and provide inspiration to women entrepreneurs through the network, thus helping build other women entrepreneurs' businesses. On a more personal level, Mona and Paulette take pride in creating value for their surroundings. Starting with Mona, we explore the value she creates with her textile business.

Mona

Turning to Mona's textile business, we can see that through her business she was able to inspire and shape a historical aspect of the local community. Without the history of the community, the textile designs would not be a reality. Mona's business is an outcome of the public context. When she markets the old designs, she is changing the confirmed view of the community as depleted and obsolete to an entity worth doing business with.

Starting this business also enabled her to return to her roots in textiles. Ever since she closed down her textile shop, the fabrics have been lingering in her mind. As hard as it was to fail financially at running the textile shop, she wanted to continue working with textiles and do something different this time around. As textiles are a passion for Mona, and something that she loves, she is able to carry this personal value through to her business.

Another personal advantage of how Mona runs her business is her ability to do all of this work from her home and balance it with her other businesses. As focused on by Chasserio et al. (2014), Mona's entrepreneurship is part of her professional and personal life, and thus the business clearly creates a personal value for Mona.

Paulette

Paulette is constantly working to improve the quality of services her business offers, through education and activities for employees and clients. The sectoral problems are complex and she takes satisfaction in trying to solve them (Kokko, 2018). She works hard for her business to be a serious actor within the sector, despite the difficult financial situation. She is trying to change the overall working conditions within the sector through the business. Paulette believes that one way to do this is to pay her employees a monthly salary instead of an hourly wage, which has been the norm in the sector. This gives the employees the opportunity to plan financially and a more professional status in the sector.

In 2010, Paulette expanded her holding company, adding a new business that works with education. The business produces courses developed for the caregiving sector in Sweden and sells to public and private organisations. As they educate their own personnel and other potential employees, they not only create personal value for the individual, they also secure knowledge within the sector.

In turn, Paulette, through her business activities, gains skills through the courses, as well as benefits further from the knowledge and experiences. These attainments are something that she is creating for herself through her entrepreneurship (Korsgaard & Anderson, 2011).

Network

Through the network and Mona's leadership, a collaboration between the municipality and the local business networks was initiated. The aim of the collaboration is to promote business issues in the region and to lessen the distance between business owners and the municipality officials and politicians. Consequently, Mona and the network now have the power to affect how work in the municipality is done with businesses. They can highlight issues that are important to women entrepreneurs through this collaboration and in turn, their work affects local gender structures (Hanson, 2009; Roos, 2019).

Through the network, Mona and Paulette are promoting an increase in women entrepreneurship, both through contributing to a successful governmental programme and by making women entrepreneurs more visible in the local community. Paulette and Mona both say that they are able to give back to other women entrepreneurs with ideas and advice. Paulette feels she has become a role model for others in the network. As Paulette owns one of the two largest businesses in the community, she is bound to make impressions on the other local entrepreneurs. The other women in the network praise Paulette's way of running a business, and one stated enviously, 'She can go for a holiday for two weeks without even a phone call from the office. She has an action document for everything that could happen.' Paulette has created a business persona that inspires and encourages other entrepreneurs. Through the network, the women entrepreneurs build empowerment at a business level (Datta & Gailey, 2012). Paulette is clearly empowered by her involvement in the network and she is also able to empower others.

ANALYSIS – ACCRUING AND CREATING BUSINESS VALUE

The focus of this chapter is how value accrued is used to create new value at the business level. This can be seen in both Mona's and Paulette's stories. Mona used her start-up grant from the government to launch a textile store. Later in life, she was able to continue with her textile interest and started the design business, working with the historical prints from the community. As Mona was contacted by the local historical society, it was her close connection to the community that enabled her to gain legitimacy to access the patterns. Even though I have focused on the business level, it is plain to see the aspects of value accrued and created go beyond the financial. Instead of the traditional gains brought about when bringing in investors with financial capital (Malmström et al., 2017), Mona built her business on her legitimacy to get access to the prints. Similarly, Paulette was part of the business network and gained the social relations it provided. She later decided that the network was worth carrying on and renewed it so even more women entrepreneurs could succeed in their entrepreneurship, consequently empowering herself and others (Datta & Gailey, 2012). She thus accrued the value the network provided and created new value for herself and others in the community (Fagenson, 1993).

What is noteworthy about the stories of how Mona and Paulette have cultivated value, is how the linkage can also be viewed in reverse. The value they create from their business is used for gaining even more value. Figure 6.1 captures this cyclical relationship from the narratives. In Mona's business, value was created with the textiles by preserving and keeping a historical piece of the community alive through her business. Consequently, Mona is dependent on the community for her businesses and needs to maintain social ties and trust with the people there. If Mona moved the business, or her home, from the community she would probably lose legitimacy

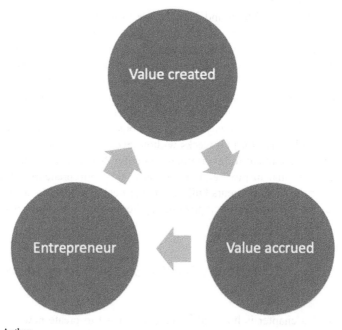

Source: Author.

Figure 6.1   *A cyclical relationship between value accrued and created at business level*

and would not be able to use the prints any longer. Being a local is essential to her success in this sense (Aggestam & Wigren-Kristoferson, 2017). In turn, this makes Mona even more tied to the community, which is a value that she accrues in her entrepreneurship when embedding the business for legitimacy. Paulette builds on her previous knowledge of the sector when running her business. This value is essential in her commercial development. With this knowledge, she is trying to create value through focusing on the complex problems (Kokko, 2018) in the sector her business is involved in. This is seen in the way she educates her own personnel and potential employees, as well as how she introduces multiple initiatives to give the sector a more professional status. In turn, she benefits from her work with education and training. As she is eager and persistent in hiring and employing good caregivers (i.e. qualified personnel), she also gains from her own created value within the sector.

This cyclical relationship, when cultivating value at a business level, implies that a more holistic view of value and women entrepreneurship is needed to fully grasp the complexity of the phenomena. It highlights the fact that we can enhance value creation by focusing on accruing specific value. If the focus was solely on the value the women create, important links to how they accrued that value are missing. As an example, if we only focus on how the network is creating value for the entrepreneurs (such as the collaboration with the municipality) we are missing how the women accrue value from the network (such as personal business development). Thus, if no value was gained, the women would probably not organise and the creation of value would not happen. Consequently, if we limit our analysis to only seeing outcomes or creations of value, we are uncertain of how to foster the creation in the first place. The advantage of seeing value through this cyclical relationship is that we can uncover the links between how women entrepreneurs accrue and create multiple forms of value at a business level.

DISCUSSION – CULTIVATING BUSINESS VALUE BEYOND ECONOMIC MEASURES

Through the narratives of women entrepreneurs, I have aimed to challenge the underperformance hypothesis surrounding women entrepreneurs. More specifically, I have investigated how women entrepreneurs accrue and create value on a business level. The two narratives in this chapter, the women entrepreneurs' experiences and successes, are in direct juxtaposition with the familiar notion of the underperforming woman entrepreneur. Instead, the narratives allow us to see value created in processes that are usually neglected or missed in more conventional research and policy. From the narratives, two main observations are evident. First, that accrued value is used to create new value, and hence second, that there is a circular flow between adding value and creating it.

The cyclical relationship shown in Figure 6.1, is an example of focusing on the process rather than purely on the outcome of entrepreneurship. Previously, research on entrepreneurship emphasised value as an outcome of entrepreneurship, with a focus on financial and economic development (Korsgaard & Anderson, 2011; Marlow & Patton, 2005). In seeing women entrepreneurs accruing and creating value as a process, we can move beyond entrepreneurship as something masculine and individualistic (Ahl et al., 2016). The value process becomes important to envision entrepreneurship as something other than based on a male interpretation (Marlow & Patton, 2005). Moreover, with this process, concepts such as context, structure and family can be acknowledged in the entrepreneurship process. Women entrepreneurs, and perhaps also male entrepreneurs, accrue and create value in relation to these concepts. These concepts have been previously missed in research on women entrepreneurship (Ahl et al., 2016).

The analysis of the women entrepreneurs in this chapter is an example of expanding the value concept by showing how value is cultivated. In essence, the expanded value concept, seen as a process, is in an opposing position to the underperforming prejudice around women entrepreneurs. Since focusing on an economic assessment of entrepreneurship simply ignores other value (Korsgaard & Anderson, 2011), a more expanded value concept means that women entrepreneurs would get credit for all the value they create, not solely those measured in financial terms.

Expanding the value concept is of particular importance in Sweden, which has a strong financial valuation of entrepreneurship (Pettersson et al., 2017). As there are no institutional laws or policies in Sweden that hinder women from running businesses, there are other structures and practices in place holding back gender equality (Malmström et al., 2017; Roos, 2017, 2019; Webster, 2016). These structures and practices lead to the prejudice that women entrepreneurs are underperforming in their entrepreneurship in comparison to male entrepreneurs (Ahl et al., 2016). With Swedish politicians arguing for 'unleashing women's entrepreneurial potential so they can contribute to economic growth' (Berglund et al., 2018, p. 531), there is no doubt that the value concept attached to entrepreneurship needs expansion.

This chapter is anchored in other research critiquing the underperforming of women entrepreneurs in comparison to their male counterparts (such as Ahl & Marlow, 2012; Marlow & McAdam, 2013). This chapter contributes to this body of literature by focusing on value as a process and not purely an outcome. Through focusing on how value is cultivated, the link between accruing and creating, I show how the business level has multiple forms of value and how accruing value can foster the creation of value. I thus argue that research and policy need to move away from seeing entrepreneurship, and perhaps even more so women entrepreneurship, as solely an economic endeavour (Ahl, 2006). A holistic view of value, involving the process of accruing and creating, is needed to better grasp the complexity of women entrepreneurship. For policy, a holistic view of value is of particular importance since policy recreates women entrepreneurs as secondary compared to men entrepreneurs (Ahl & Nelson, 2015). With a more holistic view of value, policy could better grasp the full process of value creation in entrepreneurship and target specific areas of development. As I have focused on value at the business level, it may not be the same within other levels of the business life of women entrepreneurs. Future research could focus on how women entrepreneurs accrue and create value within different levels of their business. As these cases are rural, embeddedness in different local structures (Roos, 2019) could be crucial in how these women accrue and create value.

NOTE

1. Names have been anonymised.

REFERENCES

Aggestam, M., & Wigren-Kristoferson, C. (2017). How women entrepreneurs build embeddedness: A case study approach. *International Journal of Gender and Entrepreneurship*, *9*(3), 252–268.

Ahl, H. (2006). Why research on women entrepreneurs needs new directions. *Entrepreneurship Theory and Practice*, *30*(5), 595–621.

Ahl, H., Berglund, K., Pettersson, K., & Tillmar, M. (2016). From feminism to FemInc.ism: On the uneasy relationship between feminism, entrepreneurship and the Nordic welfare state. *International Entrepreneurship and Management Journal*, *12*(2), 369–392.

Ahl, H., & Marlow, S. (2012). Exploring the dynamics of gender, feminism and entrepreneurship: Advancing debate to escape a dead end? *Organization*, *19*(5), 543–562.

Ahl, H., & Nelson, T. (2015). How policy positions women entrepreneurs: A comparative analysis of state discourse in Sweden and the United States. *Journal of Business Venturing*, *30*(2), 273–291.

Alkhaled, S., & Berglund, K. (2018). 'And now I'm free': Women's empowerment and emancipation through entrepreneurship in Saudi Arabia and Sweden. *Entrepreneurship & Regional Development*, *30*(7–8), 877–900.

Anderson, E. R. (2008). 'Whose name's on the awning?' Gender, entrepreneurship and the American diner. *Gender, Place and Culture*, *15*(4), 395–410.

Berglund, K., Ahl, H., Pettersson, K., & Tillmar, M. (2018). Women's entrepreneurship, neoliberalism and economic justice in the postfeminist era: A discourse analysis of policy change in Sweden. *Gender, Work & Organization*, *25*(5), 531–556.

Brannen, M. Y. (1996). Ethnographic international management research. In B. J. Punnett & O. Shenkar (Eds), *Handbook for international management research* (pp. 115–143). Blackwell Business.

Byrne, J., & Fayolle, A. (2010). A feminist inquiry into entrepreneurship training. In D. Smallbone, J. Leitao, M. Raposo, & F. Welter (Eds), *The theory and practice of entrepreneurship: Frontiers in European entrepreneurship research* (pp. 76–100). Edward Elgar Publishing.

Calás, M. B., Smircich, L., & Bourne, K. A. (2007). Knowing Lisa? Feminist analyses of 'gender and entrepreneurship'. In D. Bilimoria & S. K. Piderit (Eds), *Handbook on women in business and management* (pp. 78–105). Edward Elgar Publishing.

Chasserio, S., Pailot, P., & Poroli, C. (2014). When entrepreneurial identity meets multiple social identities: Interplays and identity work of women entrepreneurs. *International Journal of Entrepreneurial Behavior & Research*, *20*(2), 128–154.

Datta, P. B., & Gailey, R. (2012). Empowering women through social entrepreneurship: Case study of a women's cooperative in India. *Entrepreneurship Theory and Practice*, *36*(3), 569–587.

Doucet, A., & Mauthner, N. (2008). Qualitative interviewing and feminist research. In P. Alasuutari, L. Bickman, & J. Brannen (Eds), *The Sage handbook of social research methods* (pp. 328–343). Sage.

Drakopoulou Dodd, S., & Anderson, A. R. (2007). Mumpsimus and the mything of the individualistic entrepreneur. *International Small Business Journal, 25*(4), 341–360.

Ekinsmyth, C. (2013). Managing the business of everyday life: The roles of space and place in 'mumpreneurship'. *International Journal of Entrepreneurial Behavior & Research, 19*(5), 525–546.

Emmel, N. (2013). *Sampling and choosing cases in qualitative research: A realist approach.* Sage.

Fagenson, E. A. (1993). Personal value systems of men and women entrepreneurs versus managers. *Journal of Business Venturing, 8*(5), 409–430.

Gherardi, S. (2015). Authoring the female entrepreneur while talking the discourse of work–family life balance. *International Small Business Journal, 33*(6), 649–666.

Hanson, S. (2009). Changing places through women's entrepreneurship. *Economic Geography, 85*(3), 245–267.

Johansson, A. W. (2004). Narrating the entrepreneur. *International Small Business Journal, 22*(3), 273–293.

Johnstone, B. A. (2007). Ethnographic methods in entrepreneurship research. In H. Neergaard & J. P. Ullhoi (Eds), *Handbook of qualitative research methods in entrepreneurship* (pp. 97–121). Edward Elgar Publishing.

Kenny, K., & Scriver, S. (2012). Dangerously empty? Hegemony and the construction of the Irish entrepreneur. *Organization, 19*(5), 615–633.

Kokko, S. (2018). Social entrepreneurship: Creating social value when bridging holes. *Social Enterprise Journal, 14*(4), 410–428.

Korsgaard, S., & Anderson, A. R. (2011). Enacting entrepreneurship as social value creation. *International Small Business Journal, 29*(2), 135–151.

Lautermann, C. (2013). The ambiguities of (social) value creation: Towards an extended understanding of entrepreneurial value creation for society. *Social Enterprise Journal, 9*(2), 184–202.

Lindgren, M., & Packendorff, J. (2009). Social constructionism and entrepreneurship: Basic assumptions and consequences for theory and research. *International Journal of Entrepreneurial Behavior & Research, 15*(1), 25–47.

Malmström, M., Johansson, J., & Wincent, J. (2017). Gender stereotypes and venture support decisions: How governmental venture capitalists socially construct entrepreneurs' potential. *Entrepreneurship Theory and Practice, 41*(5), 833–860.

Marlow, S., & McAdam, M. (2012). Analyzing the influence of gender upon high-technology venturing within the context of business incubation. *Entrepreneurship Theory and Practice, 36*(4), 655–676.

Marlow, S., & McAdam, M. (2013). Gender and entrepreneurship: Advancing debate and challenging myths; exploring the mystery of the under-performing female entrepreneur. *International Journal of Entrepreneurial Behaviour & Research, 19*(1), 114–124.

Marlow, S., & Patton, D. (2005). All credit to men? Entrepreneurship, finance, and gender. *Entrepreneurship Theory and Practice, 29*(6), 717–735.

Marlow, S., & Swail, J. (2014). Gender, risk and finance: Why can't a woman be more like a man? *Entrepreneurship & Regional Development, 26*(1–2), 80–96.

McKeever, E., Jack, S., & Anderson, A. (2015). Embedded entrepreneurship in the creative re-construction of place. *Journal of Business Venturing, 30*(1), 50–65.

Neergaard, H. (2007). Sampling in entrepreneurial settings. In J. P. Ulhøi & H. Neergaard (Eds), *Handbook of qualitative research methods in entrepreneurship* (pp. 253–278). Edward Elgar Publishing.

Nilsson, P. (1997). Business counselling services directed towards female entrepreneurs: Some legitimacy dilemmas. *Entrepreneurship & Regional Development, 9*(3), 239–258.

Ogbor, J. O. (2000). Mythicizing and reification in entrepreneurial discourse: Ideology-critique of entrepreneurial studies. *Journal of Management Studies, 37*(5), 605–635.

Pettersson, K., Ahl, H., Berglund, K., & Tillmar, M. (2017). In the name of women? Feminist readings of policies for women's entrepreneurship in Scandinavia. *Scandinavian Journal of Management, 33*(1), 50–63.

Roos, A. (2017). A multiplicity of contexts: Gender and locality in a contextualized view of entrepreneurship. *Journal of Asia Entrepreneurship and Sustainability, 13*(4), 10–28.

Roos, A. (2019). Embeddedness in context: Understanding gender in a female entrepreneurship network. *Entrepreneurship & Regional Development, 31*(3–4), 279–292.

Saldaña, J. (2009). *The coding manual for qualitative researchers*. Sage.

Smith, R. (2010). Masculinity, doxa and the institutionalisation of entrepreneurial identity in the novel *Cityboy*. *International Journal of Gender and Entrepreneurship, 2*(1), 27–48.

Statistics Sweden. (2014, 17 December). *Sju av tio företagare är män*. http://www.scb.se/sv_/hitta-statistik/artiklar/sju-av-tio-foretagare-ar-man/.

Statistics Sweden. (2017, 8 March). *Färre kvinnor än män driver företag*. https://www.scb.se/hitta-statistik/artiklar/2017/Farre-kvinnor-an-man-driver-foretag/.

Tillmar, M. (2009). Societal entrepreneurs in the health sector: Crossing the frontiers. *Social Enterprise Journal, 5*(3), 282–298.

Webster, N. A. (2016). *Gender and social practices in migration: A case study of Thai women in rural Sweden* [Dissertation, Department of Human Geography, Stockholm University].

7. Value creation in conflict zones: evidence from Afghan and Palestinian women entrepreneurs

Doaa Althalathini

INTRODUCTION

In contexts of conflict and dangerous adverse conditions, entrepreneurial activities increase to substitute for limited governance institutions and labour opportunities (Ciarli, Kofol, & Menon, 2015). However, research on entrepreneurship in such contexts is still under-explored with calls for further investigation (Althalathini, Al-Dajani, & Apostolopoulos, 2021), particularly among women (Bullough & Renko, 2017). Research in conflict zones has presented women as dependents and victims while overlooking their actions, challenges and contributions to socio-economic life (El Jack, 2018), especially as entrepreneurs. Women under conflict are more likely to emerge as entrepreneurs to support their families due to the temporary or permanent loss of men's incomes (Holmén, Min, & Saarelainen, 2011), whilst experiencing more challenges than women in non-conflict affected developing countries (Ayadurai & Sohail, 2006). The limited evidence available so far suggests that women entrepreneurs in conflict zones not only have the potential to create value in monetary or economic terms, but they also create social value by empowering other women and challenging conservative gender ideologies (Lemmon, 2012). Even in the most challenging contexts, such as Afghanistan, women entrepreneurs can drive institutional change which leads to the evolution of new attitudes and norms (Ritchie, 2016). Therefore, it can be argued that conflict can empower women and promote gender egalitarianism (Anugwom, 2011).

Despite the challenges they face and the significant economic and social value they create, rigorous evidence of the role of women entrepreneurs living in conflict zones is still very scarce (Bullough & Renko 2017; Hudock, Sherman, & Williamson, 2016). Therefore, more research is needed, particularly with the wide recognition of contextual embeddedness which can either facilitate or inhibit women's engagement in entrepreneurship (Yousafzai, Fayolle, Saeed, Henry, & Lindgreen, 2019). This will contribute to our understating of how better to facilitate women entrepreneurship in war-torn areas with extreme gender inequality. Therefore, this chapter contributes to the limited research by exploring the experiences of women entrepreneurs and how they handle challenging and resource-constrained contexts in order to start, revive and grow their businesses. The chapter is doing that by investigating the narratives of three successful women entrepreneurs in Afghanistan and Palestine and discussing their efforts in value creation at the business level.

Both countries have experienced decades of intense and protracted political tension and conflict which have led to massive disruption of livelihoods and networks of social support. Trillions of dollars in foreign aid to those countries have failed to reduce poverty and foster sustainable development (Wildeman & Tartir, 2014). Women are bound by conservative cultural norms and practices, which limit their role in economic, political and social life (Ahmed-Ghosh, 2003). Although Afghan women have made great achievements since 2001, they still face considerable challenges which undermine their role in the broader society (Beath, Christia, & Enikolopov, 2013). Normative constraints and growing insecurity impair Afghan women (Holmén et al., 2011), and the range of entrepreneurial activities they can undertake are very constrained, mainly handicrafts, embroidery, jewellery, and traditional clothing (Tzemach, 2008). In the Palestinian context, women suffer from a twofold marginalisation, being part of the Palestinian society which exists under Israeli occupation and living in a male-dominated society with resulting cultural restraints (Muhanna, 2013). Despite low engagement rates in the labour market, their participation rates have risen over the past 20 years, compared to men. It reached 20.7 per cent in 2018, compared to 10.3 per cent in 2001, whereas men's participation rate has decreased (71.5 and 66.8 per cent respectively) (PCBS, 2019).

This chapter explores the success stories of three women entrepreneurs as active agents in Afghanistan and Palestine. The next section outlines the theoretical background; followed by the methodology. The section presenting the findings ensues, and finally, discussion and conclusions are presented.

VALUE CREATION AND WOMEN ENTREPRENEURSHIP IN CONFLICT CONTEXTS

Traditionally, value creation in entrepreneurship was connected to economic growth, as research found a positive correlation (Acs, 2006). However, value is a much richer concept, and concentration on economic growth might ignore the critical human and social aspects of the process (Sheikh, Yousafzai, Sist, Akdeniz, & Saeed, 2018). Porter and Kramer (2011) argued that by focusing on financial value, research might overlook societal needs and the economic distress of people, and called for creating a 'shared value'. More importantly, the narrow approach of defining value creation has overlooked the efforts of women entrepreneurs by associating them with 'underperformance' and being less successful than men (Dean, Larsen, Ford, & Akram, 2019). Significant research has been undertaken on women entrepreneurs and their challenges and achievements (Marlow & McAdam, 2013), but there is still a lack of studies with an explicit focus on women starting and operating their enterprises in conflict zones. In such contexts with weak economic development, the need to redefine value creation is important for entrepreneurship in general and for women entrepreneurship in particular.

In most fragile and conflict-affected countries, people are involved in entrepreneurial activities at the grassroots level to create value, for example, to reduce poverty (Tobias, Mair, & Barbosa-Leiker, 2013). The characteristics of conflict contexts, with their substantial institutional deficiencies, offer entrepreneurs opportunities to create value by addressing the needs and challenges of their societies (Nenova, 2004; Porter & Kramer, 2011). Entrepreneurs in such contexts can identify new and innovative products, services, processes, technologies or markets (Ahmad & Seymour, 2008), in order to resolve institutional deficiencies and compensate for inadequate government performance (Nenova, 2004). As the political and economic situation and its consequences regarding market volatility and uncertainty make marketing strategy decisions more difficult for entrepreneurs (Read, Dew, Sarasvathy, Song, & Wiltbank, 2009), finding new markets to overcome the barrier of the low purchasing power of local customers can be a strategy for the survival and growth of businesses (Aidis, Welter, Smallbone, & Isakova, 2007).

In the context of conflict, women entrepreneurs can create economic and social values through the creation or developing of economic activity. They might be pushed to entrepreneurship (Holmén et al., 2011), but they also could contribute positively to overall household and community welfare (Althalathini, Al-Dajani, & Apostolopoulos, 2020). While conservative gender ideologies can be intensified and women can have restricted freedom to engage in social, political and economic activities, conflict also opens opportunities for women to challenge socio-cultural institutions that act against gender equality (Justino et al., 2012). Several authors have argued that wars enable women to break the traditional social norms and to change the gendered division of the labour market where they secure income for the survival of their families (Fuest, 2008; Giles & Hyndman, 2004). However, women in such contexts strive to start and operate businesses, as they face additional challenges that are aggravated by the conflict situation such as limited resources, societal constraints, unsupportive regulations, larger domestic burdens and insecurity (Boros, 2008). Therefore, instead of focusing only on the value they create, it is important to understand the process of value creation and the strategies to overcome such a challenging context.

Within a context characterised by long-term adversity, political volatility and extreme levels of resource scarcity, entrepreneurs engage in bricolage activities to make the most of limited resources (Cheung & Kwong, 2017; Langevang & Namatovu, 2019). Bricolage is defined as 'making do by applying combinations of the resources at hand to new problems and opportunities' (Baker & Nelson, 2005, p. 333). Entrepreneurs adopt bricolage strategies to start and grow businesses out of nothing, and actively engage to create opportunities and innovative solutions (Baker & Nelson, 2005). They tend to do that by using human resources, learning and using undervalued, slack, or discarded resources that are often available for free or cheaply (Desa & Basu, 2013). Desa (2012) illustrated how bricolage allows entrepreneurs within restrictive institutions to function and gain access to institutional support, enhancing their resilience under uncertain conditions. Therefore, the application of bricolage can trigger entrepreneurial action in resource-constrained contexts of conflict and for women entrepreneurs who face regulative, normative and cognitive institutional challenges (Lemmon, 2012). Women entrepreneurs thus have to make use of resources available in the social environment to survive and perhaps flourish (Baker, Pollock, & Sapienza, 2010). They have to rely on their social capital to mitigate the effects of institutional deficiency (Ciarli, Parto, & Savona, 2009). Particularly, role of family is critical to support them financially, emotionally and socially in such contexts (Welsh, Kaciak, & Minialai, 2015).

However, the lack of appropriate skills and knowledge could affect women's ability to mobilise resources in conflict zones (Bullough, de Luque, Abdelzaher, & Heim, 2015). This is more important given the challenges that women entrepreneurs face regarding insecurity and lack of available finance, experts or tailored support programmes (World Bank, 2014). In particular, appropriate training and mentoring are important to compensate for the lack of knowledge during the operation of businesses for women (Ghosh & Rajaram, 2015). For example, the emergence of women entrepreneurs in Afghanistan has been made possible primarily through international aid after the fall of Taliban (Boros, 2008). In Palestine, many international aid programmes facilitate the start-up and growth of women's enterprises (Qazzaz, Mrar, & Adwan, 2005). Therefore, there is a great interest by the international community in promoting women entrepreneurship in conflict zones, either through programmes that target only women or by imposing conditions for their funding programmes to ensure women's economic participation (Fuest, 2008). Hence, international aid can be considered as a push factor for women entrepreneurs through providing loans, training, mentoring and advocacy (Beath et al., 2013). With the lack of experts, the ability to learn on a continuous basis is viewed as a key determinant in maintaining the business (Tseng, 2013). For example, learning to change businesses strategies or processes could help recovery from adverse situations (Manzano-García & Calvo, 2013), which can be supported by international aid or self-learning, for example from the internet, which could improve the entrepreneurial capabilities and creativity of women (Jiao, ogilvie, & Cui, 2010).

Overall, women entrepreneurs in conflict zones have a high resilience in adapting to and overcoming challenges, which reflects on the performance of their businesses (Anugwom, 2011; World Bank, 2014). The limited studies available have focused mainly on the challenges they face and their empowerment dimensions, for example the increase in family income and decision making (Bullough & Renko, 2017; Holmén et al., 2011; Lemmon, 2012). Therefore, we still know little about women's economic participation under conflict and how they overcome challenges to create value (Hudock et al., 2016). Studying women entrepreneurship helps to transform women's survivalist activities into more sustainable income-generating activities as this is still a central challenge in conflict settings (Esim & Omeira, 2009). Taking into account these limitations, this chapter sheds light on the women entrepreneurs' efforts to start and run successful businesses in the under-explored contexts of conflict.

Table 7.1   *Demographic data of the participants*

Participant name		Rangina	Bissan	Sanaa
Country		Afghanistan	Palestine	Palestine
City		Kandahar	Hebron	Ramallah
Education		University	University	College
Age		41	25	46
Marital status		Married	Single	Married
Business		Embroidery	Rose Production	Aluminium accessories
Start of Business		2008	2012	2002
Partnership		No	Yes, family	Yes, non-family
Number of employees at start-up	Men	0	1	0
	Women	20	0	0
Number of employees post start-up	Men	7	3	1
	Women	90	2	3

METHODOLOGY

A qualitative approach was used to investigate and interpret value creation based on women's experiences in this specific context (Langevang & Namatovu, 2019). Research on women entrepreneurship in conflict zones is still limited; therefore, an explorative narrative inquiry approach is adopted in which the life-story narratives of the women are the core for our knowledge. The depth of this process produces 'thick descriptions' of contextual detail and social relations closely linked to their experiences (Saunders, Lewis, & Thornhill, 2015). In-depth narrative interviews were used to elicit detailed narratives and stories (Muylaert, Sarubbi, Gallo, & Neto, 2014), allowing women to speak of their experiences without externally imposed constraints, and enabling sense making and identity construction (Wang & Geale, 2015).

The empirics for this chapter are part of a larger study which targeted 16 women entrepreneurs (four in Afghanistan, four in Iraq and eight in Palestine). However, three successful case studies have been chosen, one in Afghanistan and two in Palestine, due to the richness of their entrepreneurial stories. Criterion sampling was adopted to approach the participants through utilising personal networks followed by snowballing in the two countries (Patton, 2002). The women were required to be the owners and managers of their enterprises, which had been operating for over four years at the time of the interviews. Focusing on mature and sustainable enterprises that were operational within long-term conflict-affected contexts, provided rich data and in-depth insights from the participants, informing their value creation efforts. The in-depth interviews were conducted via Skype to overcome travel risks to the study's contexts (Lo Iacono, Symonds, & Brown, 2016), and were recorded after obtaining the permission of the participants. Table 7.1 presents the participants' demographic and business indicators.

Bissan (24, Hebron, Palestine) sought for independence and started her business of ornamental planting in 2012 with her father, who was working as a farmer in Israel. Sanaa (46 years, Ramallah, Palestine) used to work temporarily as a secretary and teacher in schools. She started her business of making accessories out of necessity in 2000 because of financial pressures after the martyrdom of her brother-in-law. Rangina (41, Kandahar, Afghanistan) worked for a NGO in 2003 in a project which provided income-generating activities for women by producing handmade embroidery products. Then, she started the project as a profitable business in 2008, 'Kandahar Treasure', in order to ensure its sustainability in order to help women. Her business is the first officially registered women's business in Kandahar.

The interviews were conducted in English in Afghanistan while Arabic was used in Palestine, and they lasted between 90 and 120 minutes. Interviews were transcribed and imported into MAXQDA software, where they were coded and analysed. The qualitative thematic analysis went through two phases, the descriptive level and the conceptual level (Friese, 2014). The first phase included reading the interview transcripts where initial codes were generated (Braun & Clarke, 2006). The conceptual-level analysis included exploring the data from the perspective of the study question and identifying patterns and relations between the themes and narratives (Friese, 2014). To achieve accuracy, the interviews, transcription and data analysis were conducted in the same language in order to avoid any differences in meaning if translated (Temple & Young, 2004). English translation and back trans-lation were used for the quotations included within this chapter (Van Nes, Abma, Jonsson, & Deeg, 2010). This process ensured the accuracy of the data analysis and the credibility of the findings (Maneesriwongul & Dixon, 2004).

FINDINGS

The thematic analysis reveals that the three women entrepreneurs created value by introducing new products and processes, utilising new technology and accessing international markets. The narratives also show the strategies the women adopted in order to overcome challenges and create value. They were able to mobilise resources and seek networking, knowledge and institutional support which enabled them to revive and grow their businesses.

New Products and Processes

Despite many challenges in conducting business in the two countries, where inves-tors and companies tend to eschew investments, such contexts offer great opportu-nities for local entrepreneurs to start businesses. The thematic analysis reveals that the women showed awareness of their context and its many problems which could be turned into business ideas. In a conflict context, entrepreneurs can create value by identifying gaps where they can meet the needs of their societies, utilising the internet, personal experiences and innovation such as in the case of Bissan:

> I conducted a study about the Damask rose consumption in Hebron and found that the demand is much higher than the production [...] My business is almost the only one in the West Bank to produce roses [...] We started with the production of 1,000 seedlings but now we are producing nearly 6,000 seedlings, we introduced new varieties of Damask rose, new colours and a new way of planting and distribution [...] My productivity in winter was very low due to the snow which destroyed the iron structure of the greenhouse; my loss was about 40–60 thousand Israeli shekels during the 4-months in winter [...] I worked on designing a special greenhouse which was difficult, but I wanted to increase my productivity. I don't want to exaggerate but I don't think there is a greenhouse here such as mine.

In such a problematic but opportunistic context, women entrepreneurs can create value not only by offering new products and processes but also by making necessary changes to their businesses when they face adverse situations. For example, Sanaa, who started a home-based business out of necessity, looked for new opportunities and introduced aluminium jewellery with cheaper prices than jewellery made of silver or gold:

> I had a special interest in making accessories and they were not very available at the time I started; we haven't had the Chinese accessories yet. However, the market then was saturated with cheap accessories. So, I wanted to learn something new or make unique products. I searched the internet and I learned about making aluminium jewellery, which wasn't known in our region [...] I then found a training in Italy. So, in coordination with the Palestine Trade Center, I was able to take that training and find my [business] partner, and this was the turning point because I was almost the first one in the Middle East to do that.

As value creation needs resources which are limited for women in such contexts, bricolage is considered the most effective strategy to overcome this issue. Rangina, who started her business to economically empower other women, made use of the physical and human capital as she stated:

> [...] the NGO took apart and we had all the foundation and supplies and some of the necessary tools to set up an office and the left raw materials from the donors' funding. The first months, some of the women volunteered and they didn't get a salary but we quickly produced products that are indigenous to Kandahar province and started selling.

Recently, Rangina published a book, *Embroidering within Boundaries: Afghan Women Creating a Future*, which discusses how the business started as a small women's initiative and now she and her employees are seriously committed women who are 'making history'. Using the limited available resources is particularly important for the start-up as women generally may be more constrained by a lack of capital. Sanaa gave an interesting example:

> I decided to start my business from the old accessories from my neighbours and friends. I went to shops where they have accessories which are used, damaged or old; I bought them cheaply [...] and sold them again. If there were women's gatherings then they invited me to sell my accessories or they sold them on my behalf. When I participated in exhibitions at universities, the academics gave me their old accessories and I changed them [...] to make them more modern. In 2006, I used gems. It was difficult in the beginning because

they were expensive unless I got them from others [...] when I had some capital, I started to buy new gems.

Regardless of the context, lack of finance is a significant challenge for women entrepreneurs. In conflict zones, the volatile political and economic situation, the religious practices with difficulty in meeting the conditions of financial institutions such as high interest rates and required sponsors, discourage women from applying for loans. Therefore, they rely on other financial resources. The women in this study used their family's savings and relationships with stakeholders to overcome such difficulties, as Bissan mentioned: '[w]e used personal cheques to pay the remaining money from the business profit, and that was easier than the loan's process and bank commitments'. They tend to apply for other flexible and permitted sources of finance, which contributes to the survival of their business, as Rangina did:

> We women don't have that kind of networks to be able to borrow from friends. Many women aren't wealthy in Afghanistan [...] My mom and brothers together donated money into the business to keep it alive [...] There aren't many institutions that provide microfinance, and when they consider paying loans to women, they think of a range of US$500–1000. Our monthly operation at the time that I was asking for loans was US$16,000 a month. The interest rate was high, 20%. I'm a Muslim and I know paying interest is a sin. The timeframe they gave was just 3 months, so it wasn't feasible. I applied for loans from Kiva which is interest free and they gave us more than 12 months to pay back and this happened twice.

Utilising New Technology

As both countries still suffer from institutional deficiencies and a lack of technological advancement, utilising new technology is an advantage in developing businesses further. Technology can be used to overcome many of the challenges in this context and increase productivity as indicated by Bissan:

> I always check the websites of large international companies [...] I contact them if I have any enquiries. In Jordan, I also visited 17 Damask rose farms, around 5 of them are automated. I gained information about their design and the seedlings they use. I also gained experience and ideas that I don't have to make my farm automated. I always make updates in the technology I use in seedling production so I can overcome the many challenges of importing seedlings from Israel. So, my business will be specialising in the production of roses and seedlings.

However, starting and developing the business further was particularly enhanced by financial and managerial support from international development agencies as Bissan discussed: 'I got a grant of US$17,000 which provided me with a larger cooling room. It was one of the challenges I faced. I had a small refrigerator with a capacity of maximum 2,000 roses. Now, the capacity is about 50,000 roses.' However, with insecurity issues in the two countries, women face challenges regarding their movements unless they have their family support, which was a significant reason to enable the three women to gain knowledge and manage their businesses successfully, as Bissan discussed:

> There were women who lost their places in the grant competition since their families refused to let them go to the training because of the security situation. I told my father to come with me if you are afraid. He went twice and then he allowed me to go alone [...] Intransigence will not help; as a girl you need to have a strategy to change the way your family thinks.

Access to New Markets

Because of limited local markets and competitive pressure from cheap imports, women entrepreneurs can create value by accessing international markets. Sanaa, for example, markets her products in international exhibitions in the Arab countries, the USA, and Europe. The women are not only creating economic value by introducing their products internationally. The image of businesses in conflict zones is still suspect, as indicated by the women, so that some people may have the perception that people who start businesses in impoverished nations will produce poor or low-quality products. Those women also create social value by challenging and changing such perceptions about conflict zones. They introduce high quality products and such efforts could facilitate access to international markets as Rangina stated:

> I found that our embroidery was a unique skill, and creating handmade beautiful products has a market opportunity both in the local market and internationally [...] Afghanistan continued to be a major headline around the world and this helps to market our products. By presenting them, especially made by women in Kandahar, there is social perception that brings more people to us because our story is strong. That out of a very severe conflict zone, these beautiful hand-made products are coming out and have quality. So, that contrast in itself is helping us to attract that attention that we have received so far.

The tailored training and mentoring programmes offered were important in gaining knowledge and improving the women's business acumen, as Bissan confirmed: 'This helped me to do a feasibility study in order to import to Jordan. However, I realised that this will not be profitable. Therefore, I decided to focus on the local market which is more profitable at the current stage.' This was also the case for Sana who was involved in different training programmes which enhanced her management skills and developed her business, 'The Business Women Forum brought us designers to create new ideas, and customise our products if we want to export to European markets. They gave us financial and management courses [...] they registered my business and offered tax exemption for 3 years.'

However, the women also adopted strategies to overcome the complexity and difficulties in conflict contexts to access international markets such as informal exports where they rely on their informal networks abroad to promote and market their products. In addition, the women utilise their networks to participate in local and international exhibitions where they are partially or fully funded, which could build relationships with customers abroad and develop new learning experiences, as in the case of Sanaa:

> The Chamber of Commerce keeps us updated of any new exhibition. […] The Union of Handicrafts helped me to participate in international exhibitions such the one in Algeria […] my customers there asked me twice to send them pieces [of accessories]. Today I made a request to travel to an exhibition in Sharjah […] when I go to any exhibition, I try to benefit from other experiences and get new ideas and designs, and not only to sell my accessories.

Such participation also gave the women publicity through media reports, which resulted in local and international attention. This promoted their businesses and changed the general perception about the people and women who are doing business in such contexts.

DISCUSSION AND CONCLUSION

Conflict contexts such as Afghanistan and Palestine are characterised by a lack of resources and institutional support. However, this did not deter entrepreneurship activities, instead it provided motivation to work on creating new solutions for this scarcity (Cheung & Kwong, 2017). The resources, capabilities and skills the participants gained, enabled them to control various adverse situations, in which they created ways to make use of the limited resources (Langowitz & Minniti, 2007). Their value creation cannot be understood only through measurable criteria, such as profits. Rather, it should be analysed as a process in terms of how they are able to navigate challenges and opportunities in resource-constrained contexts through access to resources, networks and institutional support.

Despite the paucity of resources and the weak institutional environment, the participants in this study created value through introducing new products and technologies and gaining access to international markets. They generated economic value but also produced value for their society by meeting needs and addressing societal challenges. The participants engaged in bricolage activities which were crucial to their business start-up and survival in such restrictive institutional environments (Desa, 2012). The women made use of the available physical, human and social capital and institutional support in order to seize opportunities (Baker et al., 2010). Because of limited local markets, the women worked on engaging in international markets (Aidis et al., 2007) through informal export, participating in international exhibitions and support from informal networks abroad. Moreover, self-learning and looking for new and innovative opportunities contribute to mitigating the lack of institutional support. They worked on enhancing their human capital through continuous learning and finding solutions to the problems they encountered by searching the internet, meeting other women entrepreneurs, training, and doing and experiencing (Jiao et al., 2010). They worked on changing and updating their products and processes in order to maintain and grow the business (Manzano-García & Calvo, 2013). The participants' networking with different NGOs, particularly women's organisations, was an enabling factor in gaining knowledge, skills and resources (World Bank, 2014).

Therefore, enhancing the human capital of women through entrepreneurship education and training programmes is critical in tackling institutional challenges and hence enhancing the ability to create value (Bullough et al., 2015). The tailored training and mentoring programmes were important for the Palestinian participants in improving their knowledge and experiences which added to their ability to create value (Ghosh & Rajaram, 2015). This sheds light on the importance of NGOs and mainly women's associations working in conflict zones where they can have an influential role in increasing women's representation and fostering social change (Fuest, 2008; Ritchie, 2016). Women's associations were the main support for the participants in Palestine which provided them with financial, managerial and legal support. This was further enabled by the international aid for women entrepreneurship (Beath et al., 2013). In addition, giving publicity to the experiences of women entrepreneurs living in war zones can play a significant role in enabling women to add value to their business (Höijer, 2004). For example, media reports can promote the businesses of women entrepreneurs and show not only the negative sides of war but also the successful stories of women who are striving and succeeding in living and producing high-quality and innovative products and services.

However, the external environment can affect the overall effectiveness of interventions aiming to promote women entrepreneurship in conflict zones. While women can have the intention and ideas to start a business, they have more obstacles than men in conflict zones in accessing resources, improving their skills and turning their ideas into reality (Holmén et al., 2011). Therefore, interventions need to be gender-responsive and contextualised, taking into consideration issues such as insecurity. Overall, this chapter answers the call for more attention to the contextualisation of women entrepreneurship research (Yousafzai et al., 2019), mainly in under-explored contexts such as conflict zones (Althalathini, Al-Dajani, & Apostolopoulos, 2021). It contributes to women entrepreneurship literature by exploring the richness of the stories of women entrepreneurs in contexts of conflict and their efforts to create value through starting and sustaining a business. Those women entrepreneurs do not fit in with the stereotypes of the position of women in wars as passive agents. Rather, the women were able to implement new business ideas and to introduce innovative solutions to the challenges they encountered through their access to financial and social capital and the ability of self-learning. Therefore, acknowledging the success of those women and their significant contributions to their businesses and societies is important in conflict zones. These findings have significant implications in informing development policies on the effective ways to support women entrepreneurs and their efforts to create value, which will result in business growth and long-term social change.

REFERENCES

Acs, Z. (2006). How Is Entrepreneurship Good for Economic Growth? *Innovations: Technology, Governance, Globalization, 1*(1), 97–107.

Ahmad, N., & Seymour, R.G. (2008). Defining Entrepreneurial Activity. Definitions Supporting Frameworks for Data Collection. OECD Statistics Working Papers 2008/01, Paris: OECD.

Ahmed-Ghosh, H. (2003). A History of Women in Afghanistan: Lessons Learnt for the Future or Yesterdays and Tomorrow: Women in Afghanistan. *Journal of International Women's Studies, 4*(3), 1–14.

Aidis, R., Welter, F., Smallbone, D., & Isakova, N (2007). Female Entrepreneurship in Transition Economies: The Case of Lithuania and Ukraine. *Feminist Economics, 13*(2), 157–183.

Althalathini, D., Al-Dajani, H., & Apostolopoulos, N. (2020). Navigating Gaza's conflict through women's entrepreneurship. *International Journal of Gender and Entrepreneurship, 12*(4), 297–316.

Althalathini, D., Al-Dajani, H., & Apostolopoulos, N. (2021). The Impact of Islamic Feminism in Empowering Women's Entrepreneurship in Conflict Zones: Evidence from Afghanistan, Iraq and Palestine. *Journal of Business Ethics.* https://doi.org/10.1007/s10551-021-04818-z

Anugwom, E. (2011). 'Wetin We for Do?' Women Entrepreneurs and the Niger Delta Conflict. *Journal of Small Business & Entrepreneurship, 24*(2), 243–293.

Ayadurai, S., & Sohail, M. (2006). Profile of Women Entrepreneurship in a War-Torn Area: A Case of North East Sri Lanka. *Journal of Developmental Entrepreneurship, 11*(1), 3–17.

Baker, T., & Nelson, R. (2005). Creating Something from Nothing: Resource Construction through Entrepreneurial Bricolage. *Administrative Science Quarterly, 50*(3), 329–366.

Baker, T., Pollock, T.G., & Sapienza, H.J. (2010). Recipes for Weak Ingredients: Human Capital Bricolage and Temporary Competitive Advantage. *Academy of Management Presentation.* Montreal, Canada.

Beath, A., Christia, F., & Enikolopov, R. (2013). Empowering Women through Development Aid: Evidence from a Field Experiment in Afghanistan. *American Political Science Review, 107*(3), 540–557.

Boros, R. (2008). Afghan Women Entrepreneurs: At the Crossroads between Globalisation and Local Traditions. *International Journal of Business and Globalisation, 2*(4), 373–402.

Braun, V., & Clarke, V. (2006). Using Thematic Analysis in Psychology. *Qualitative Research in Psychology, 3*, 77–101.

Bullough, A., & Renko, M. (2017). A Different Frame of Reference: Entrepreneurship and Gender Differences in the Perception of Danger. *Academy of Management Discoveries, 3*(1), 21–41.

Bullough, A., de Luque, M.S., Abdelzaher, D., & Heim, W. (2015). Developing Women Leaders through Entrepreneurship Education and Training. *Academy of Management Perspectives, 29*(2), 250–270.

Cheung, C., & Kwong, C. (2017). Path- and Place-Dependence of Entrepreneurial Ventures at Times of War and Conflict. *International Small Business Journal, 35*(8), 1–25.

Ciarli, T., Kofol, Ch., & Menon, C. (2015). Business as Unusual. An Explanation of the Increase of Private Economic Activity in High-Conflict Areas in Afghanistan. SERC Discussion Paper 182, Spatial Economics Research Centre, LSE, London.

Ciarli, T., Parto, S., & Savona, M. (2009). Conflict and Entrepreneurial Activity in Afghanistan: Findings from the National Risk Vulnerability Assessment Data. Working Paper 2010/08, *UNU-WIDER.*

Dean, H., Larsen, G., Ford, J., & Akram, M. (2019). Female Entrepreneurship and the Metanarrative of Economic Growth: A Critical Review of Underlying Assumptions. *International Journal of Management Reviews, 21*, 24–49.

Desa, G. (2012). Resource Mobilization in International Social Entrepreneurship: Bricolage as a Mechanism of Institutional Transformation. *Entrepreneurship Theory and Practice*, *36*(4), 727–751.

Desa, G., & Basu, S. (2013). Optimization or Bricolage? Overcoming Resource Constraints in Global Social Entrepreneurship. *Strategic Entrepreneurship Journal*, *7*(26), 26–49.

El Jack, A. (2018). Wars and Conflicts in Sub-Saharan Africa/the Middle East and North Africa (MENA): A Gender-Relational Perspective. *Journal of Global Peace and Conflict*, *6*(2), 19–26.

Esim, S., & Omeira, M. (2009). Rural Women Producers and Cooperatives in Conflicts Settings in the Arab States. Lebanon: ILO, Regional Office for Arab States.

Friese, S. (2014). *Qualitative Data Analysis with ATLAS.ti.* (2nd edn). SAGE Publications.

Fuest, V. (2008). 'This is the Time to Get in Front': Changing Roles and Opportunities for Women in Liberia. *African Affairs*, *107*(427), 201–224.

Ghosh, N., & Rajaram, G. (2015). Developing Emotional Intelligence for Entrepreneurs: The Role of Entrepreneurship Development Programs. *South Asian Journal of Management*, *22*(4), 85–100.

Giles, W., & Hyndman, J. (2004). *Sites of Violence: Gender and Conflict Zones*. London: University of California Press.

Höijer, B. (2004). The Discourse of Global Compassion: The Audience and Media Reporting of Human Suffering. *Media, Culture & Society*, *26*(4), 513–531.

Holmén, M., Min, T., & Saarelainen, E. (2011). Female Entrepreneurship in Afghanistan. *Journal of Developmental Entrepreneurship*, *16*(3), 307–331.

Hudock, A., Sherman, K., & Williamson, S. (2016). Women's Economic Participation in Conflict-Affected and Fragile Settings. Georgetown Institute for Women, Peace and Security, Washington, DC.

Jiao, H., ogilvie, d.t., & Cui, Y. (2010). An Empirical Study of Mechanisms to Enhance Entrepreneurs' Capabilities through Entrepreneurial Learning in an Emerging Market. *Journal of Chinese Entrepreneurship*, *2*(2), 196–217.

Justino, P., Cardona, I., Mitchell, R., & Müller, C. (2012). Quantifying the Impact of Women's Participation in Post-Conflict Economic Recovery. Working Paper 131, HiCN.

Langevang, T., & Namatovu, R. (2019). Social Bricolage in the Aftermath of War. *Entrepreneurship & Regional Development*, *31*(9–10), 785–805.

Langowitz, N., & Minniti, M. (2007). The Entrepreneurial Propensity of Women. *Entrepreneurship Theory and Practice*, *31*(3), 341–364.

Lemmon, G. (2012). Entrepreneurship in Post-Conflict Zones. Working Paper, The Council on Foreign Relations, USA.

Lo Iacono, V., Symonds, P., & Brown, D. (2016). Skype as a Tool for Qualitative Research Interviews. *Sociological Research Online*, *21*(2).

Maneesriwongul, W., & Dixon, J.K. (2004). Instrument Translation Process: A Method Review. *Journal of Advanced Nursing*, *48*(2), 175–186.

Manzano-García, G., & Calvo, J. (2013). Psychometric Properties of Connor-Davidson Resilience Scale in a Spanish Sample of Entrepreneurs. *Psicothema*, *25*(2), 245–251.

Marlow, S., & McAdam, M. (2013). Incubation or Induction? Gendered Identity Work in the Context of Technology Business Incubation. *Entrepreneurship Theory and Practice*, *39*, 791–816.

Muhanna, A. (2013). *Agency and Gender in Gaza Masculinity, Femininity and Family during the Second Intifada*. London: Routledge.

Muylaert, C., Sarubbi, V., Gallo, P., & Neto, M. (2014). Narrative Interviews: An Important Resource in Qualitative Research. *Rev Esc Enferm USP*, *48*(2), 184–189.

Nenova, T. (2004). *Private Sector Response to the Absence of Government Institutions in Somalia*. Washington, DC: World Bank.

Patton, M. (2002). *Qualitative Research and Evaluation Methods*. London: Sage Publications.

PCBS (2019). Palestinian Central Bureau of Statistics. Retrieved 17 October 2019, from https://www.pcbs.gov.ps/site/lang__en/1/default.aspx.

Porter, M., & Kramer, M. (2011). Creating Shared Value. *Harvard Business Review, 89* (1–2), 62–77.

Qazzaz, H., Mrar, Sh., & Adwan, Y. (2005). *Female Entrepreneurs in the West Bank and Gaza Strip: Current Situation and Future Prospects*. Ramallah, Palestine: MAS.

Read, S., Dew, N., Sarasvathy, S., Song, M., & Wiltbank, R. (2009). Marketing under Uncertainty: The Logic of an Effectual Approach. *Journal of Marketing, 73*(3), 1–18.

Ritchie, H.A. (2016). Unwrapping Institutional Change in Fragile Settings: Women Entrepreneurs Driving Institutional Pathways in Afghanistan. *World Development, 83*, 39–53.

Saunders, M., Lewis, P., & Thornhill, A. (2015). *Research Methods for Business Students*. Harlow: Pearson.

Sheikh, S., Yousafzai, S., Sist, F., Akdeniz, A., & Saeed, S. (2018). Value Creation Through Women Entrepreneurship. In S. Yousafzai, A. Fayolle, A. Lindgreen, C. Henry, S. Saeed & S. Sheikh (Eds), *Women Entrepreneurship and the Myth of Underperformance: A New Look at Women Entrepreneurship Research* (pp. 20–33). Cheltenham, UK and Northampton, MA, USA: Edward Elgar Publishing.

Temple, B., & Young, A. (2004). Qualitative Research and Translation Dilemmas. *Qualitative Research, 4*(2), 161–178.

Tobias, J., Mair, J., & Barbosa-Leiker, C. (2013). Toward a Theory of Transformative Entrepreneuring: Poverty Reduction and Conflict Resolution in Rwanda's Entrepreneurial Coffee Sector. *Journal of Business Venturing, 28*(6), 728–742.

Tseng, C. (2013). Connecting Self-Directed Learning with Entrepreneurial Learning to Entrepreneurial Performance. *International Journal of Entrepreneurial Behavior & Research, 19*(4), 425–446.

Tzemach, G. (2008). Afghan Woman is All about Business. *Christian Science Monitor, 100*(44), 7.

Van Nes, F., Abma, T., Jonsson, H., & Deeg, D. (2010). Language Differences in Qualitative Research: Is Meaning Lost in Translation? *European Journal of Ageing, 7*(4), 313–316.

Wang, C., & Geale, S. (2015). The Power of Story: Narrative Inquiry as a Methodology in Nursing Research. *International Journal of Nursing Sciences, 2*(2), 195–198.

Welsh, D., Kaciak, E., & Minialai, C. (2015). The Influence of Perceived Management Skills and Perceived Gender Discrimination in Launch Decisions by Women Entrepreneurs. *International Entrepreneurship and Management Journal, 13*(1), 1–33.

Wildeman, J., & Tartir, A. (2014). Unwilling to Change, Determined to Fail: Donor Aid in Occupied Palestine in the Aftermath of the Arab Uprisings. *Mediterranean Politics, 19*(3), 431–449.

World Bank (2014). *Striving for Business Success: Voices of Liberian Women Entrepreneurs*. Washington, DC: World Bank Group.

Yousafzai, S., Fayolle, A., Saeed, S., Henry, C., & Lindgreen, A. (2019). The Contextual Embeddedness of Women's Entrepreneurship: Towards a More Informed Research Agenda. *Entrepreneurship & Regional Development, 31*(3–4), 167–177.

8. Creating blended value: Sri Lankan women micro-entrepreneurs and their ventures

Nadeera Ranabahu and Mary Barrett

INTRODUCTION

This chapter shows how three women entrepreneurs – disadvantaged women in rural areas of a developing country, Sri Lanka – use microfinance to start and develop businesses and simultaneously create non-financial value at the individual, household, business and community levels. Probing their experience in detail is important both theoretically and practically, because the women entrepreneurship literature has so far not examined blended value generation comprehensively by taking into account the different historical, temporal, institutional, spatial and social contexts in which women operate their businesses. In this chapter we pay attention to these contextual elements. Further, using a conventional and frequently applied indicator of blended value, the triple bottom line (Elkington 1994; Cohen, Smith and Mitchell 2008), we show how some microfinance-enabled businesses generate substantial blended value. By so doing, we make some progress towards rectifying theoretical misconceptions about the relative importance of women entrepreneurship, especially as enabled by microfinance loans, and suggest how policy makers could assist women entrepreneurs in ways that better match their needs.

From here, the chapter is organized as follows. First we provide a thumbnail description of the situation of women in Sri Lanka. We then briefly review the literature on how women entrepreneurs create blended value, especially the literature on microfinance-enabled businesses, and describe our selected analytical framework. Next we outline the study's data collection and analytical methods. We present and discuss results, then outline conclusions and future research directions.

SRI LANKA

Sri Lanka is a developing country in South Asia with per capita GDP of USD 4,102 (Central Bank Sri Lanka, 2018). Its human development indicators for women, such as life expectancy at birth and years of formal schooling, are mostly equivalent to men's and higher than in most other developing countries (UNDP, 2018). However, women's labour force participation rate (36.6 percent) is significantly lower than that of men (74.5 percent) (Department of Census and Statistics: Sri Lanka, 2017). This low economic participation is also visible in the entrepreneurial sector: women are decision-makers in only 25 percent of non-agricultural businesses establishments (Department of Census and Statistics: Sri Lanka, 2015). Most of these businesses are related to education services or accommodation and food service activities.

LITERATURE REVIEW

Blended value is the creation of financial, social and environmental value that benefits society and entrepreneurs (Emerson, 2003; Zahra and Wright, 2016). This view emphasizes that businesses create financial and social outcomes that are intrinsically connected and complementary. Some previous studies implicitly focus on how Sri Lankan women entrepreneurs have created economic value through various business processes. For example, women use social networks to creatively access resources and explore business opportunities (Kodithuwakku and Rosa, 2002). They grow their businesses through social capital development (Surangi, 2018) and use business development services to diversify their businesses, improve product portfolios and market channels, and employ people (Attygalle et al., 2014).

Microfinance-enabled entrepreneurship has been promoted as a source of blended value, specifically as a route out of female poverty. Microfinance proponents seek to increase women's non-land asset base (Pitt and Khandker, 1998) and empower them in less visible ways, such as increasing their control over financial resources, their mobility, and their ability to make independent purchases and be involved in major household decisions (Li, Gan, and Hu, 2011; Rahman, Khanam, and Nghiem, 2017). Microfinance services allow women to invest in family needs leading to improved health and nutrition of children (Pitt, Khandker, and Cartwright, 2006) and better household welfare (Imai and Azam, 2012). However some of these claims have been contested (e.g., Karlan and Zinman, 2011; Roodman and Morduch, 2013) and microfinance in poor communities, especially in developing countries, is often criticized for not helping create growth-oriented businesses (Bateman, 2010; Bateman, Maclean, and Galbraith, 2017). Banerjee and Duflo (2011) go further, arguing that microfinance loans are typically spent on household or personal consumption rather than business creation. Even when a business is created, it may sustain at most one entrepreneur and her family.

However, these criticisms may be part of a more general tendency to underestimate the value created by women entrepreneurs. Historically, women-owned ventures have often been labelled as 'financial underperformers' compared to male-owned ventures (Ahl, 2006; Ahl and Marlow, 2012; Marlow and McAdam, 2013). But financial indicators often overlook the fact that women's businesses usually operate in low value-added sectors (Carter et al., 2015), leading to an unfairly low assessment of their contribution. Moreover, male-oriented normative measures of entrepreneurial achievement tend to obscure entrepreneurial contributions more specific to women (Marlow and Patton, 2005). Entrepreneurship increases women's confidence, autonomy, and assertiveness within families, alongside their personal growth, sense

Table 8.1   *Triple bottom line measurement and performance categories with example*

Measurement category	Performance category	Examples
Economic performance	Economic	Profit, Return on assets, Stock price
Promise	Social	Social image, Brand equity, Social legitimacy
Perpetuity	Environmental	Reduction of pollution, emissions
Socio-efficiency	Social + Economic	Employee development, satisfaction, or loyalty; Customer satisfaction through managing service quality or customer relationships
Stewardship	Social + Environmental	Environmental reinvestment through environmental public relations activities; Environmental protection though recycling, reuse, environmental planning and reporting
Eco-efficiency	Economic + Environmental	Selection by socially responsible investment funds; Reduced costs through energy management; Stability/ longevity through environmental risk management
Sustainability	Economic + Social + Environmental	Market effectiveness through ethical but strategic decision-making; Employee satisfaction/commitment through ethical decision-making; Increased quality of life through sustainable innovation; Customer loyalty through sustainable development

Source: Adapted from Cohen et al. (2008).

of independence, and skill levels (Al-Dajani and Marlow, 2010; Thapa Karki and Xheneti, 2018). These in turn enhance venture efficiency and effectiveness. Business activities also help women create value related to benevolence (e.g., helpful and ethical practices), universalism (e.g., social justice, environment protection, and equality), self-direction (e.g., creativity) and security (e.g., family security and sense of belonging) (Borquist and de Bruin, 2019).

THEORETICAL FRAMEWORK

The triple bottom line (TBL) perspective (Cohen, Smith and Mitchell, 2008; derived from Elkington, 1994) focuses on the need for organizations to create blended value, that is, attend to People (Social) and Planet (Environmental) as well as Profit (Economic) results. Cohen et al. (2008) set out seven TBL performance categories, adding to Elkington's original formulation by showing how business processes create interrelated and overlapping social, environmental and economic outcomes. For example, reducing pollution increases the quality of the living environment and thus quality of life, while selecting socially responsible investments contributes to employee and customer satisfaction. Table 8.1 summarizes and gives examples of Cohen et al.'s outcome categories.

Table 8.2   *Interviewees and their businesses*

Name[1]	Life stage	Product or service of the business
Kamala	Unmarried. The elder of two siblings	Making and selling bras
Lalani	Married with a toddler	Making and selling confectionery
Neelawathi	Married with three grown-up children	Making and selling Kithul[2] treacle and jaggery

Notes:
[1] Pseudonyms have been used in all cases.
[2] In Sinhalese, Kithul refers to a type of palm tree. The sap of the Kithul tree's flowers is collected, processed, and sold in liquid form as a syrup. This is called treacle and is used to make sweets and as a solvent in traditional medicine. Kithul sap is also used to make a type of unrefined palm sugar called jaggery.

Elkington (2018) points out that TBL has been part of the business lexicon for at least a decade and understanding of it has been diluted by its popularity. The difficulty of measuring types of value other than profit persists. Nevertheless, TBL's popularity reminds us that blended value is not a novel idea and that a tool, however imperfect, is available to examine its manifestation in women-run enterprises.

METHOD

Data was gathered during a larger project about Sri Lankan micro-entrepreneurs' entrepreneurial thinking. The respondents were clients of a large microfinance institution (MFI) operating in Sri Lanka. For the present study, we used data from three interviews in the larger project which used open-ended questions to examine women business owners' activities, actions and decisions when starting and developing their businesses. One author, a native speaker of Sinhalese, travelled to the respondents' business locations, explained the study, obtained consent from respondents to participate, and conducted interviews lasting 20 to 30 minutes. The businesses were in food production and manufacturing (see Table 8.2). The respondents included women at three distinct life stages: unmarried, married with small children, and married with grown-up children. We asked interviewees to say what stage their business had reached: all were at the development stage.

Using NVivo, we identified themes related to blended value creation, then applied Cohen et al.'s (2008) TBL categories to the themes to see to what extent they were reflected in the women's business stories. Using narrative style to report findings allowed us to highlight relevant context for each entrepreneur.

Kamala: A Woman Managing a Bra-Manufacturing Business

Kamala owns a bra-manufacturing business. After high school, Kamala worked in a tailor's shop at a nearby town. As her wages were minimal, she started sewing bras after work at home. Kamala learnt to make bras without formal instruction, using 'reverse engineering'. She unpicked a bra and made a pattern from it which she used to make new bras. For two years she sewed the bras by herself, selling them to neighbours, acquaintances and nearby shops. Only then did she use her savings to formally start her bra manufacturing business.

Kamala experimented and learnt from experience to develop her business skills before borrowing money. As demand increased, she needed help to make the product. First, she tried a buy-back system where she trained women to sew bras and provided them with materials to sew bras at their homes. But she soon became aware of employee theft: not all the finished items were being returned to her. So she employed people to sew bras at her home where she could supervise them. This experimental learning helped her to control her inventory and operate efficiently. As the business grew she used loans from two different MFIs to buy sewing machines, hire new employees, and gradually increase her output.

Kamala also learnt from her network how to develop a brand image. When she first supplied bras to a shop in a nearby town, she was advised to use attractive packaging for each bra. At that time Kamala was not using any packaging at all. Following the retailer's advice helped her to market her products better. She also increased sales by expanding her network, meeting shop owners, pitching her products, and establishing partnerships. It was not easy: she learnt perseverance from repeated rejection. She also had to adapt after mistakes and manage interactions with customers. For example, the first time Kamala delivered her products – 4,500 bras – to a wholesale distributor, her order was rejected because she had not packed the correct number of bras together. Explaining the incident, Kamala highlighted the packaging requirements for wholesale distribution: 'You have to have 6 bras in one plastic bag, 12 bags or 72 bras, in one set.' On that day, she had to decide immediately whether to take the huge consignment of bras back to her house, repackage them and return them later, or correct the issue on the spot. She decided on the latter:

> I could have taken the bras back [to my house] but the three-wheeler charge was [too high] around 5,000 [SLR] … So I told them, even though the packaging is not right, I cannot take them back. [...] Then and there I bought a tag [labelling] machine in Colombo [the delivery location where she was at the time] and corrected the packaging [removed all 4,500 units from their packages, repackaged them correctly and relabelled them]. When I had finished the repackaging it was around 6.30 p.m.

Kamala said that she would never forget the incident.

Currently, she supplies bras to local retailers and wholesalers in Kandy and Colombo, two major Sri Lankan cities. She secured these linkages through negotiation. She explained how she had secured an order with a wholesaler in Colombo:

> I had some carpets, which I made as a side business, priced at around 10,000 [SLR]. I told them I would give them one carpet free of charge but only on condition that they gave me a long-term delivery order for bras. They asked me to bring the carpet one day and on that day I received an order to supply 5,000 units [of bras].

Kamala also pointed out that she maintained continuous delivery which gave her a strong reputation for reliability. She also emphasized the need for communication to maintain viable networks:

> Now I have good sales. I maintain continuous supply by all means possible. I regularly contact them [wholesale buyers of her products]. The most important thing is communication; you can obtain orders by maintaining communication.

She never reduced the quality of her product even when she faced competition. One anecdote makes this clear:

> The first month after I supplied them, my products had lower sales. Then I was told that they [competitors] supplied the product at a price 10 rupees lower than mine and so sales were higher for their products. I picked up one of their [a competitor's] packages and inspected the product. I saw that the competitor had used only one layer [of fabric] whereas we use two layers. So I showed the shop owner how my competitor had used only a single layer. I told him customers would not buy these bras or if they did they would return them [as the competitor's bras were of lower quality]. From the next month onwards, I had increased sales while the sales of other suppliers diminished.

Kamala is planning to do a number of things. She currently has 12 staff working for her. A month ago she hired a manager to oversee her staff, ease her workload, and try to increase the output from her workers:

> I recruited him [the manager] because it [the production work] is too much for me now. I am planning to give staff a target this year. The output I am getting from here [staff at the current location] is not enough. One place [a particular buyer] is asking for 10,000 units. So I have to have more than 10,000 products per month. Right now, I only have around 6,000 units output. When I go offsite, I cannot supervise the work here. So, his [the manager's] role is mainly to increase the output here and manage the accounts.

She plans to ensure her staff are satisfied at work by providing additional benefits. Note that this interview took place in January, which is important in Sri Lanka as a time of new beginnings.

> This month [January] I have a number of things in the pipeline for the year. I previously paid the staff here based on the number of units they stitched. Now I am planning to have a monthly salary system and provide a target. In addition, I plan to provide an allowance for attendance. In addition, I have arranged for a uniform for all the staff – a t-shirt – to be printed with my business name and logo. That is one of my dreams: to see everyone in the same uniform. I am planning to take the staff on a trip this month. I am doing what should be done from my side to bring this business to a higher level.

Kamala is also thinking about the medium term, highlighting that she is planning for the longevity of the business. She has received requests to supply bras overseas and that will require her to make some changes:

> The order is for both panty and bra. They also want a stretchy material. So, I need to change the set-up of some machines and I also need to buy some new machines.

She is happy about her achievements and highlighted the satisfaction they have brought her:

> I am very happy. I have come a long way. I have earned these rewards for myself. I have invested all the earnings in my business. I have around 12 machines and 12 people working here. I have made the market [for the products].

Lalani: A Woman Balancing Family Responsibilities with Her Confectionery Business

Lalani, a married woman with a baby, runs her own confectionery business. Before starting her business, Lalani was employed at an insurance company, but quit after giving birth because she did not have anyone to look after the child. Around the same time, her husband lost his job so Lalani was searching for 'something to do' that would make money and allow her to stay at home. Initially, she managed a vegetable stall from home, setting this up using money borrowed from an MFI. While repaying the loan, Lalani attended a training program in confectionery making organized by the MFI. Immediately afterwards she started making sweets using profits from the vegetable stall.

Lalani had a cautious, considered approach to starting and developing her business. To begin with, she produced sweets using only one to two kilograms of ingredients and calculated the cost of the process. She compared the result with the typical selling price of similar products in the market, and realized that if she sold her products at a similar price she could earn a profit. At that point she discontinued her vegetable stall and started making and selling confectionery exclusively:

> As the amount I produced was quite small, I did not really notice that profit. So I thought that I would have to increase my production. I obtained a loan from an MFI and invested that totally in the business.

The first batch of sweets Lalani produced in bulk started melting and products were returned to her. However, she was not discouraged. She went to her trainer, got the products tested, and discussed her production technique. Using a revised production technique meant the next batches of sweets were successful and from then on demand grew.

Lalani also developed strong links with external institutions. She registered her business at the district office and joined the local small entrepreneurs' association. This increased the legitimacy of the business within the local community. Now she is the chairperson of that association, which has further increased her standing as a business person. She is proud of her achievements and her ability to develop others' skills:

In the small entrepreneurs' association, there are 72 members with many men and women. But, as for the men, they do not have other work at home. They only have their business activities to do. Their wives do the other activities. When compared to them, I feel I am well ahead of them. They also obtain many ideas from me. I am so happy. I do not know how to explain this. It's a talent, I guess.

Lalani also attended training programs organized by the small enterprise unit at the district office. The programs dealt with general business management, product marketing, labelling and related topics. These helped Lalani modify her business practices:

At first, even my product labels had a lot of mistakes. This time [when printing labels], I corrected those, as I had had training related to that.

Lalani has strong links with financial institutions – the bank as well as MFIs – and has taken out more loans. Her first loan was for her vegetable business, while she used her second loan to start her confectionery business. Since then, she has obtained a third loan to start a confectionery delivery service: her husband uses a motorbike to distribute sweets in bulk.

Despite its expansion, Lalani's business is still built around her family responsibilities. She has a three-day production cycle. She makes sweets on the first night. The next day, with the help of a worker, she sugar coats them, and then the next day they package them. Then the cycle starts again. Despite this methodical approach, she is surprised how she manages all the responsibilities:

I am surprised at how I am doing it. I know a lot of people who do not do anything [in terms of business]. They ask me how I manage everything with the baby. I wake up early and do what is required for my husband and the child. I am happy because if I was employed [in a regular organization], I might not be able to manage all the responsibilities. I have to leave at 6.30 in the morning to work and I come back around 6.30 or 7.00 in the evening. When I consider the time I used to spend at my job [the one she held before having a baby], I would not have had time to be with the child. Now, I have time to look after everything for my husband and child. I attend to all those responsibilities.

Lalani is very satisfied with how things have worked out, especially with the way being a business person allows her to improve the quality of her own and her family's life:

When I was employed, I experienced a lot of pressure and tension. I do not feel that with this business. The way I am doing the business now, I am always with my child. It is good for the baby. So, I am happy, I earn a good income and I am making a profit here.

She also explained how acquiring business experience and gaining knowledge helped her change her outlook about the entrepreneurship process:

When I started the business, I only had an idea that I wanted to 'do something'. […] I thought having something small with some income for me would be enough. But now it is different. Now, I am thinking of hiring a few people. This [business] needs to be expanded, I need to buy my own vehicle, and this business needs to be further developed. Now, I am thinking about becoming a good entrepreneur. When I started the business, I did not have any idea about those things. I am not thinking about doing a [conventional] job now. Even if I could, I would never go back to an ordinary job. I am planning to improve the business to the maximum level now.

Neelawathi: A Woman Planning to Hand Over Her Traditional Business to the Next Generation

Neelawathi, a mother of three grown-up children, was pushed by circumstances rather than a definite plan to start a Kithul treacle and jaggery business. As she explained, the product itself was part of the reason. In Sri Lanka, sap from the flowers of the Kithul tree is still harvested using traditional methods. Kithul-related businesses, such as harvesting the sap, processing it, and making treacle and jaggery, are confined to areas of Sri Lanka where the tree grows. Several years ago Neelawathi's village had been selected for a Kithul-related business development project managed by the United Nations Development Programme (UNDP). The project had had three operational units: village-level societies, a regionally based UNDP partner organization, and the UNDP office in Colombo. The village-level societies collected treacle from villagers on credit, and supplied it to the regionally based UNDP partner organization. The UNDP partner organization sold the products with support from the UNDP office in Colombo, paid the village-level societies, which in turn paid the individual villagers. Neelawathi was one of the village-level treacle suppliers and the system worked well for her for about two years.

When the project period expired, the UNDP handed over the management of buying and selling to its partner organization. However, because the partner organization lacked the UNDP's marketing contacts, the process collapsed. The partner organization, despite collecting product from the village societies, did not pay the societies and this meant that villagers producing treacle, including Neelawathi, were not paid. At first, villagers simply threw away their Kithul sap and treacle, as there were no longer any reliable sales channels. However Neelawathi's family had owned Kithul trees for generations and Neelawathi saw the potential for the product if it were managed properly:

> All the people [in the village] were asking for someone to take leadership and continue the project. But no one wanted to come together again, due to this bad experience. I went to the divisional secretary [a local government official] and told him everything. He said we would hold another meeting with the Grama Niladari [the government official for a village] and other [officials]. Then, we held a meeting [with villagers]... People said that they would not use the same process as before – providing product on credit. But if someone paid cash, they would provide treacle.

It was at that point that Neelawathi thought of starting her own Kithul sap-processing business and started production.

Marketing was Neelawathi's main concern at the beginning. She started small, selling products at nearby towns and government offices on salary days. However, sales were limited. Then, with a government official from the area, she visited the agriculture department's central office. A sample of her products was tested by the agriculture department and after that she began to supply Kithul treacle and jaggery to the agriculture department's sales outlet. Although the amount she could supply was limited, the linkage with the department proved beneficial: Neelawathi was invited to trade fairs and agriculture-related exhibitions which enabled her to create other industry linkages. Neelawathi met her main bulk buyers – a supermarket chain, a traditional medicine provider, and a sales outlet attached to a television station – at such exhibitions. Microfinance loans have allowed her to buy in bulk from her suppliers, which enables her to ensure a continuous supply to her customers.

With the growth of her business, Neelawathi is making changes. At start-up, she used her kitchen to process the Kithul sap. Now she has constructed a separate hut attached to her home to do this and bottle the syrup. At the beginning, Neelawathi only had help from her husband outside his working hours, and her elder son during school vacations, to bottle treacle and transport it to retailers. Now she has a full-time employee to help fulfil demand. The people in her village and even nearby villages have become regular suppliers: they seek her out to sell the Kithul sap they have harvested. This has helped her to develop a supplier network, making it possible to supply Kithul treacle and jaggery continuously to her buyers. She has even created income sources for other villagers.

Having the business has helped Neelawathi to pay for her children's education:

> At that time [start-up], my eldest son was studying in a technical college and my daughter was selected for university. All those expenses have been covered by this business.

Her second son is studying agriculture subjects and provides ideas to develop the venture, demonstrating its sustainable development and potential longevity. Now both sons are involved in the business and Neelawathi plans eventually to hand over her business to the older one:

> After he graduated from the technical college, he got married. He is living at Chillaw [a distant city] now. But, we [Neelawathi and her husband] are planning to ask him to come back and start a workshop using his technical skills. Then, the idea is to hand over this business to him. So we won't lose this business, we will continue it.

Although Neelawathi originally planned to develop the business more quickly, she has slowed down in order to look after her elderly mother. But she is determined to develop the business:

> I am determined to develop this no matter what problems I come across. Our parents struggled a lot to make ends meet when we were children, even though we live well now. Even at that time, we, our parents and grandfather, loved our environment. At that time, a Kithul tree was worth a lot. I do not feel like giving that up.

Neelawathi is contented and happy with her progress:

> I am happy now. It is not because I have lot of profit from the business. I have maintained a good relationship with people while doing the business. If someone asks [a business] for twenty bottles, and they can only make ten, some businesses will dilute the product. However, that is not sustainable either for my business or the environment. If I do the business my way, by protecting what comes from nature, it is enough for us. I am a very simple person.

DISCUSSION

The narratives of Kamala, Lalani and Neelawathi highlight the range of ways women entrepreneurs using microfinance create multiple types of value. Their narratives resonate with the idea of the blended value concept, specifically with Cohen, Smith, and Mitchell's (2008) TBL concept. Table 8.3 summarizes the TBL values revealed in the narratives.

Table 8.3   A summary of triple bottom line values as revealed in the narratives

Triple bottom line category	Kamala	Lalani	Neelawathi
Economic performance	Business viability & survival Business efficiency Inventory control Business image	Business viability & survival Profit Quality of products	Business viability & survival
Promise	Wholesale customer relationship management Reputation of reliability	Social legitimacy & business reputation Relationship management with formal institutions	Village-level supplier relationship management Customer/institutional relationship management
Perpetuity			Appreciating and protecting Kithul trees
Socio-efficiency	Employee satisfaction, management & retention Employment generation Employee benefits Customer satisfaction through product quality	Own and others' skill development through collective action	Reliable supplier relationships Creating income generation opportunities for others
Stewardship			Protecting Kithul trees through villagers' engagement
Eco-efficiency			Stability and longevity of traditional businesses
Sustainability	Entrepreneur satisfaction and wellbeing Employee satisfaction/ commitment Venture longevity through short and medium term decisions	Entrepreneur wellbeing Increased quality of life Enhanced intergenerational care	Entrepreneur satisfaction and wellbeing Sustainable development of business

As Table 8.3 illustrates, at the level of economic performance, all three women valued business viability. Although only Lalani used the word profit, their focus on development activities shows that they aspired to run profitable businesses. This is not unexpected as business survival is a key concern for any entrepreneur. But these women clearly wanted to progress beyond survival. Training activities, although not directly linked to profit, enhanced individual skills which were later used to modify business methods. For example, Kamala learnt to negotiate and established long-term partnerships, enabling her to better manage her raw materials and her supply of finished product. Neelawathi increased and diversified her customer base by attending trade exhibitions. What we did not expect was the extent to which these women were alert to social (Promise) or environmental (Perpetuity) outcomes. Kamala was concerned about the reliability of her business associations and was committed to maintaining product quality and standards (Promise). Lalani created social legitimacy by participating in local small business association meetings, learning from and exchanging ideas with other business people (Promise). Although these outcomes were not as frequently mentioned as economic outcomes, they still played a critical role.

Table 8.3 also illustrates different combinations of the economic, social and environmental outcomes the women created. For example, employee satisfaction and customer and supplier relationship management (Socio-efficiency) were important. Neelawathi was especially aware of the need to manage environmental resources responsibly (Stewardship, Eco-efficiency). All three wanted to ensure the longevity of their businesses (Sustainability). They acquired assets, hired employees, found new markets, created new products and, in Neelawathi's case, planned to hand over the business to a family member. Thus the owners of small, microfinanced businesses seem as committed to TBL-style blended value as any CEO of a large, complex firm. While businesses at any development stage can implement TBL goals, it has been less clear how the process happens in smaller firms. This was perhaps a result of lack of research attention to women-owned firms.

Our findings illustrate that a blended value lens produces insights into outcomes often overlooked in women-owned businesses. Our micro-entrepreneurs secured economic, social and environmental wealth by blending a range of outcomes (see Table 8.3). Thus in line with Zahra and Wright (2016) our findings highlight different ways of achieving financial, social and environmental value simultaneously. Then, by using Cohen, Smith, and Mitchell's (2008) more elaborate categorization, we made various types of blended value explicit and showed how women achieved them.

Our findings also resonate with Sheikh et al. (2018), demonstrating how entrepreneurial activities develop value beyond the business level, that is, at the individual, household and community levels. All three women mentioned having enhanced agency for themselves as individuals, achieving personal as well as business growth. All three started small, gained knowledge by conducting business tasks, and transferred the knowledge back into their businesses. Knowledge transfers and even knock-backs built their resilience, motivation, and ability to adapt. At the same time, these personal- and business-level activities created valuable trickle-down effects at household and community levels. For example, by being in business, Lalani was able to better manage family responsibilities, enhancing her child's wellbeing. Neelawathi was financing her grown-up children's education from the business's profits and planning how one of her sons might succeed her. At the village/regional level these women generated employment, disseminated knowledge, and bridged the gap between the village and regional economies. For example, Lalani's contribution to the local small business association disseminated knowledge to the wider community. Neelawathi's business created regional opportunities by linking local produce with the wider market. Far from being 'underperformers', these entrepreneurs were blended value creators at all types and levels.

CONCLUSIONS AND NEXT STEPS

Our findings have practical and theoretical implications. Following Ahl (2006), Marlow and McAdam (2013) and Marlow and Patton (2005), we suggest using entrepreneurial women's comments about the non-economic impacts their businesses create such as increased personal agency and higher levels of human capital in the community, to create ways of measuring blended value. Measuring these outcomes more precisely, consistently and creatively would help public policy makers understand the true value of women entrepreneurship. At a theoretical level, it could also alleviate one of the remaining problems of the TBL concept: the difficulty of measuring non-profit outcomes.

Responding to Welter (2011), this study developed insights into women entrepreneurship in Sri Lanka, by discussing it in terms of specific institutional, spatial and social contexts there. Future researchers could do the same in other national contexts. Moreover, looking at how women develop their businesses using microfinance raises the question of whether similar processes are followed when different financial enablers are present. The way is open for future researchers to develop testable propositions about both issues. For example, one could ask whether women in different financial and cultural contexts are more or less able to do as Lalani did and secure family financial assistance to diversify their businesses. Whatever the answers, further exploration of how blended value arises in and from particular cultures and contexts should lead to greater understanding of how to create blended value in other entrepreneurial communities.

REFERENCES

Ahl, H. (2006). Why research on women entrepreneurs needs new directions. *Entrepreneurship Theory and Practice, 30*(5), 595–621.
Ahl, H. & Marlow, S. (2012). Exploring the dynamics of gender, feminism and entrepreneurship: Advancing debate to escape a dead end? *Organization, 19*(5), 543–562.
Al-Dajani, H. & Marlow, S. (2010). Impact of women's home-based enterprise on family dynamics: Evidence from Jordan. *International Small Business Journal, 28*(5), 470–486.

Attygalle, K., Hirimuthugode, D., Madurawala, S., Senaratne, A., Wijesinha, A., & Edirisinghe, C. (2014). *Female entrepreneurship and the role of business development services in promoting small and medium women entrepreneurs in Sri Lanka.* The Institute of Policy Studies of Sri Lanka and Oxfam International Sri Lanka. http://www.ips.lk/wp-content/uploads/2017/08/female_entrepreneurship.pdf.

Banerjee, A. & Duflo, E. (2011). *Poor Economics: A Radical Rethinking of the Way to Fight Global Poverty.* New York: BBS Public Affairs.

Bateman, M. (2010). *Why Doesn't Microfinance Work? The Destructive Rise of Local Neoliberalism.* London: Zed Books.

Bateman, M., Maclean, K., & Galbraith, J.K. (2017). *Seduced and Betrayed: Exposing the Contemporary Microfinance Phenomenon.* Santa Fe: University of New Mexico Press and School for Advanced Research Press.

Borquist, B. & de Bruin, A. (2019). Values and women-led social entrepreneurship. *International Journal of Gender and Entrepreneurship, 11*(2), 146–165.

Carter, S., Mwaura, S., Ram, M., Trehan, K., & Jones, T. (2015). Barriers to ethnic minority and women's enterprise: Existing evidence, policy tensions and unsettled questions. *International Small Business Journal, 33*(1), 49–69.

Central Bank Sri Lanka. (2018). *Annual Report 2018.* https://www.cbsl.gov.lk/en/publications/economic-and-financial-reports/annual-reports/annual-report-2018.

Cohen, B., Smith, B., & Mitchell, R. (2008). Toward a sustainable conceptualization of dependent variables in entrepreneurship research. *Business Strategy & the Environment, 17*(2), 107–119.

Department of Census and Statistics: Sri Lanka. (2015). *Non-agriculture economic activities in Sri Lanka: Economic census 2013/2014.* http://www.statistics.gov.lk/Economic/Non%20agri.pdf.

Department of Census and Statistics: Sri Lanka. (2017). *Quarterly report of the Sri Lanka labour force survey.* http://www.statistics.gov.lk/samplesurvey/LFS_Annual%20Report_2017.pdf.

Elkington, J. (1994). Towards the sustainable corporation: Win–win–win business strategies for sustainable development. *California Management Review, 36*(2), 90–100. http://dx.doi.org/10.2307/41165746.

Elkington, J. (2018). 25 years ago I coined the phrase 'triple bottom line'. Here's why it's time to rethink it. *Harvard Business Review*, 25 June. https://hbr.org/2018/06/25-years-ago-i-coined-the-phrase-triple-bottom-line-heres-why-im-giving-up-on-it.

Emerson, J. (2003). The blended value proposition: Integrating social and financial returns. *California Management Review, 45*(4), 35–51.

Imai, K.S. & Azam, M.D.S. (2012). Does microfinance reduce poverty in Bangladesh? New evidence from household panel data. *The Journal of Development Studies, 48*(5), 633–653.

Karlan, D. & Zinman, J. (2011). Microcredit in theory and practice: Using randomized credit scoring for impact evaluation. *Science, 332*(6035), 1278–1284.

Kodithuwakku, S.S. & Rosa, P. (2002). The entrepreneurial process and economic success in a constrained environment. *Journal of Business Venturing, 17*(5), 431–465.

Li, X., Gan, C., & Hu, B. (2011). The impact of microcredit on women's empowerment: Evidence from China. *Journal of Chinese Economic and Business Studies, 9*(3), 239–261.

Marlow, S. & McAdam, M. (2013). Gender and entrepreneurship: Advancing debate and challenging myths; exploring the mystery of the under-performing female entrepreneur. *International Journal of Entrepreneurial Behavior and Research, 19*(1), 114–124.

Marlow, S. & Patton, D. (2005). All credit to men? Entrepreneurship, finance, and gender. *Entrepreneurship Theory and Practice, 29*(6), 717–735.

Pitt, M.M. & Khandker, S.H. (1998). The impact of group-based credit programs on poor households in Bangladesh: Does the gender of participants matter? *The Journal of Political Economy, 106*(2), 958–996.

Pitt, M.M., Khandker, S.R., & Cartwright, J. (2006). Empowering women with microfinance: Evidence from Bangladesh. *Economic Development and Cultural Change, 54*(4), 791–831.

Rahman, M.M., Khanam, R., & Nghiem, S. (2017). The effects of microfinance on women's empowerment: New evidence from Bangladesh. *International Journal of Social Economics, 44*(12), 1745–1757.

Roodman, D. & Morduch, J. (2013). The impact of microcredit on the poor in Bangladesh: Revisiting the evidence. *Journal of Development Studies, 50*(4), 583–604.

Sheikh, S., Yousafzai, S., Sist, F., Aybeniz Akdeniz, A.R., & Saeed, S. (2018). Value creation through women's entrepreneurship. In S. Sheikh, S. Yousafzai, F. Sist, A.R. Aybeniz Akdeniz, & S. Saeed (Eds), *Women Entrepreneurs and the Myth of Underperformance: A New Look at Women's Entrepreneurship Research* (pp. 20–33). Cheltenham, UK and Northampton, MA, USA: Edward Elgar Publishing.

Surangi, H.A.K.N.S. (2018). What influences the networking behaviours of female entrepreneurs? A case for the small business tourism sector in Sri Lanka. *International Journal of Gender and Entrepreneurship, 10*(2), 116–133.

Thapa Karki, S. & Xheneti, M. (2018). Formalizing women entrepreneurs in Kathmandu, Nepal: Pathway towards empowerment? *International Journal of Sociology and Social Policy, 38*(7/8), 526–541.

UNDP (United Nations Development Programme) (2018). *Human Development Indices and Indicators: 2018, Statistical update briefing note for countries on the 2018 Human Development Report: Sri Lanka.* http://hdr.undp.org/sites/all/themes/hdr_theme/country-notes/LKA.pdf.

Welter, F. (2011). Contextualizing entrepreneurship: Conceptual challenges and ways forward. *Entrepreneurship Theory and Practice, 35*(1), 165–184.

Zahra, S.A. & Wright, M. (2016). Understanding the social role of entrepreneurship. *Journal of Management Studies, 53*(4), 610–629.

9. The latent entrepreneurs: inequality and enterprising women in the lucky country

Zara Lasater, Vinita Godinho, Robyn Eversole and Naomi Birdthistle

INTRODUCTION

A central theme in this volume is the social value created by women entrepreneurs. Recent studies have argued that in order to rectify a 'male-centric' framing of entrepreneurship, female entrepreneurialism needs to be examined within the specific context of what gives rise to the entrepreneurial impulse, that is, women's interaction with their environment, framed as 'contextual embeddedness' (Yousafzai, Fayolle, Saeed, Henry, & Lindgreen 2019). While one can argue that women's entrepreneurial endeavours may be studied within mainstream, arguably male-centric understandings of entrepreneurship, there is also a gap in understanding how women's entrepreneurship might be different – for instance, when it falls outside of the growth matrix underpinning much literature on entrepreneurship and business lifecycles (Steffens & Omarova 2019). This gap is particularly pronounced in a developed country context, such as Australia.

A research project (Enterprising Women 2019) which mapped the ecosystem of supports for entrepreneurial women in Victoria, Australia, led the authors to identify a category of entrepreneurial women whom we have termed 'latent'. The choice of the term 'latent' is based on the Merriam-Webster Dictionary definition of latent: 'present and capable of emerging or developing but not now visible, obvious, or active'. Our choice of this terminology purposefully eschews the paradigm of clear business lifecycles noted above, recognising that businesses may exist in less-visible forms and without clearly defined growth trajectories. 'Latent entrepreneurs' are present as entrepreneurs, but still largely invisible due to the part-time or informal nature of their often-embryonic entrepreneurial activities, their positioning at the margins of business support ecosystems, and their own reluctance to self-identify as entrepreneurs.

In Australia, a small group of non-traditional actors from the business support ecosystem – primarily not-for-profits – are developing female-centric supports designed to empower latent entrepreneurs to self-realise as entrepreneurs, and, in so doing, to recognise the business value they generate. In this chapter, we explore how these female-centric support ecosystems are making a latent entrepreneurial population and its value-creation visible. We propose conditions that facilitate the emergence of latent female entrepreneurs.

SOCIAL VALUE CREATION AND WOMEN'S ENTREPRENEURSHIP: A CONCEPTUAL FRAMING

Entrepreneurship has been framed as an individual activity, available to all with no formal barriers to entry (Kruegar & Brazeal 1994). Contemporary scholarship (Ahl & Marlow 2012; Yousafazi, Saeed & Muffatto 2015; Yousafazi et al. 2019) offers a more nuanced perspective, positing that models of entrepreneurship in advanced economies are not value-neutral; are driven by a masculine framing of agency and 'heroism'; and are not cognisant of context. This has given rise to more attention on female entrepreneurship. Yet, despite increased academic interest, women's entrepreneurship remains understudied (de Bruin, Brush & Welter 2006; 2007; Kimakwa, Abebe & Redd 2018).

Traditional gendered assumptions regarding entrepreneurial success, and the pre-eminence of objective economic measures of business success (Carrington 2006; Korsgaard & Anderson 2011), have reinforced the notion of the 'underperforming' female entrepreneur (Yousafazi et al., 2019, p. 170; also, Ahl 2006) or the 'reluctant' entrepreneur (Ahl & Marlow 2012, p. 543). To redress this perspective, Yousafazi et al. (2019) argue that paying greater attention to the different contexts (social, political, economic and cultural) within which women entrepreneurs operate, enables research to move beyond narrow measures of success, and more fully explore women's entrepreneurial experiences and social value creation. Studies of women's entrepreneurship are beginning to make visible the different dimensions of social value creation (Bogren, von Friedrichs, Rennemo, & Widding 2013; Koorsgard & Anderson 2011; Roos 2019; Tlaiss 2019). Recognising the multiple dimensions of value creation enables a fuller understanding of women's self-identification as entrepreneurs, a central theme of this chapter.

Emerging scholarship exploring holistic or 'multi-dimensional' business level value creation (Weber & Geneste 2014) instead of the more restrictive notions of economic growth and financial measures of success (Ahl & Marlow 2012) challenges gendered assumptions and perceptions about women entrepreneurs as underperforming (Lee & Rogoff 1998; Yousafazi et al. 2019). Alternative narratives of entrepreneurial success (Tlaiss 2019) are exploring business-level value created by women entrepreneurs within both developed (Bogren et al. 2013) and developing economies (Tlaiss 2019). These narratives focus on business-related resources, networks and institutional support (Sheikh, Yousafzai, Sist, & Saeed 2018, p. 24).

Social entrepreneurship scholars including Zahra, Gedajlovic, Neubaum, & Shulman (2009) find that social entrepreneurs create both economic and social wealth and benefits. Whilst social entrepreneurship is also an important research topic in Australia (Barraket et al. 2017; Eversole 2013), the focus on social enterprises as a particular type of enterprise has limited a broader social value framing of entrepreneurship, and drawn attention away from the socio-economic characteristics of the founders themselves.

Our research focuses on women who are emerging, but not yet visible or self-identifying as entrepreneurs. They are not necessarily 'reluctant' entrepreneurs; rather, their entrepreneurship is 'latent'. Other researchers have proposed definitions of latent entrepreneurship, focusing on an as-yet unrealised desire for self-employment (Blanchflower, Oswald & Stutzer 2001; Gohmann 2012; Grilo & Irigoyen 2006) whilst Atasoy (2015) finds that latent entrepreneurs want to be self-employed, although they may still be employed by others. Latent entrepreneurs are thus in many ways the inverse of the 'reluctant' entrepreneur, as explored further in this chapter.

WOMEN ENTREPRENEURS IN AUSTRALIA: AN UNDERUTILISED RESOURCE

Australia, often referred to as the 'lucky country' with a highly developed, high-income economy, has experienced uninterrupted growth over the last three decades; yet this growth has not been inclusive. Women are 12 per cent less likely to be in the paid workforce; three times as likely to work part-time; earn 14.6 per cent less per week; and retire with 73 per cent less superannuation than men on average (ACOSS & UNSW 2018). This imbalance is also apparent in the domain of business, where the number of successful women-led businesses lags behind those led by men (Startup Muster 2018).

Women's entrepreneurial skills are arguably one of Australia's most underutilised resources. Henderickson, Bucifcal, Balaguer, and Hansell (2015) note that early-stage small to medium businesses contribute disproportionally to job creation, accounting for 40 per cent of new jobs in Australia. Yet of the 1.8 million Australians who are starting new businesses, only 38 per cent (690,000) are female (Steffens & Omarova 2019). Women-led businesses are also smaller and experience less growth (Conway 2015). The Startup Muster, the largest survey of the Australian start-up ecosystem, identified that in 2018 only 22.3 per cent of start-up founders were women, down from 25.4 per cent in 2017 (p. 6).

The global literature also suggests that women entrepreneurs are under-represented within traditional entrepreneurial ecosystems (Motoyama, Konczal, Bell-Masterson, & Morelix 2014). This under-representation reflects in part additional barriers to entry faced by women entrepreneurs such as family responsibilities (Still & Timms 1999), access to finance (Blake 2006) and networks (Moppert 2010), as well as cultural and societal expectations regarding the role of women in business (Moppert 2010). McAdam, Harrison and Leitch (2018, p. 3) have explored three critical aspects of a nurturing entrepreneurial ecosystem – 'the role of the (social) context in enabling or restricting entrepreneurship'; 'the role of the external business environment on the entrepreneur'; and 'the role of the entrepreneur in creating, maintaining and developing the entrepreneurial ecosystem' while others (Sperber & Linder 2019; Sandhu, Scott & Hussain 2016) have highlighted the need for entrepreneurial ecosystems which support all aspects of women's participation. Yet relatively few studies have further explored this field (Alsos, Haugum & Ljunggren 2017) including in Australia.

RESEARCH CONTEXT: A FEMALE-CENTRIC ECOSYSTEM OF ENTREPRENEURIAL SUPPORTS

The literature on entrepreneurship recognises that entrepreneurs require an appropriate support structure, an ecosystem conducive to entrepreneurship, to assist them to establish, operate and grow their business. Brush, Edelman, Manolova, and Welter (2019) utilise the findings of Isenberg (2011) and the World Economic Forum (2013) to identify the elements of an entrepreneurship ecosystem that can facilitate the growth and development of the entrepreneurial firm. These elements include: a conducive culture; the availability of financing; the acquisition and development of human capital; new markets for products and services; and a range of institutional and infrastructural supports.

Van de Ven (1993) and Sperber and Linder (2019, p. 533) note that ecosystems are 'a complex interlinkage of a variety of actors within a geographic region that influence the formation of the group of actors.' This supports the focus on context (Alsos et al. 2017). The Enterprising Women (2019) study, examining the ecosystem of supports for women entrepreneurs in Australia, found that of the five categories of support offered (finance; incubators/accelerators; education/training; networking/peer support/advocacy; and mentoring/coaching) the majority were not gender-specific. The research also found that many women entrepreneurs, particularly those from disadvantaged communities, are unaware of and/or not using these 'gender-blind' supports. Female-centric support was being provided by two support categories – microenterprise development programs offered by not-for-profits, and co-working spaces.

Microenterprise development programs, which support people on low incomes to start and/or grow businesses, are relatively new in developed countries such as Australia, where microfinance has, so far, focused largely on asset-building (Godinho, Eccles & Thomas 2018; Goodwin & Voola 2013; Schreiner & Woller 2003). Yet the literature on the participation of marginalised women in microenterprise development programs in Australia is limited, bar one study (van Kooy 2016). The focus instead has been on the provision of microenterprise loans,[1] and government-led programs such as business enterprise centres[2] and the New Enterprise Incentive Scheme (NEIS)[3] to support nascent entrepreneurs.

The four case studies included in this chapter include three microenterprise programs being piloted by not-for-profits in Victoria, and one female-focused co-working space (see Table 9.1). 'LaunchME' led by Good Shepherd Microfinance (2019), focuses on people on low incomes; 'Sister School' run by Global Sisters supports women from a range of backgrounds; and 'Stepping Stones to Small Business' led by the Brotherhood of St Laurence (2019), targets women from refugee, migrant and asylum seeker families. One Roof Women is a Melbourne start-up designed to foster women's entrepreneurship by providing a supportive co-working space for women.

Table 9.1   *Case study overview*

	LaunchME	**Global Sisters**	**Stepping Stones**	**One Roof Women**
Program type	Microenterprise program	Microenterprise program	Microenterprise program	B Corp certified co-working hub
Length of engagement	– Rolling enrolment (up to 20 participants at each LM site) – 12-month program	– Specific Sister School start dates (10-week course) – 3-year engagement (Incubate and Accelerate)	– Specific course start dates (15-week course) – 3-year coaching/ mentoring support post course	As per membership agreement
Eligibility	– All genders (majority women) – Postcode boundaries (1 SA location, 2 VIC locations) except all young carers (VIC wide) – Work rights (except carers)	– Female (focus on single mothers and older women) – Work rights	– Female – Postcode focus – Born overseas (refugee, migrant and asylum seeker focus) – Over 50 and/or from rural and regional Victoria	– Female focus – Paid membership

METHODOLOGY

The fieldwork for this chapter is taken from the Enterprising Women (2019) research project. The methodology encompassed two phases as briefly described below.

Phase One: Establishing the Research Context and Sample

The first phase of this study involved a desktop literature review and three roundtables held in Victoria, Australia, with fifty-one attendees. The research team sourced participants through their extended networks, holding semi-structured qualitative interviews and focus groups with selected organisations providing support to women entrepreneurs. The researchers explored women's stories about their entrepreneurial experience; their views on the capabilities and supports they require to succeed in their business objectives; and the multi-layered ecosystem that supports them in Victoria.

This phase led the team to focus on the experiences of 'latent' entrepreneurs. A subsequent exercise to map this ecosystem of support led to the identification of four specific programs of support for women entrepreneurs (see Table 9.1) which were selected as critical case studies to investigate in more detail over the second phase.

Phase Two: Deeper Understandings via a Grounded Theory Approach

Phase Two sought to explore how the four selected programs supported latent women entrepreneurs, examining how the women self-perceived the value of their businesses, as well as the types of business-related supports that facilitated their journey. The researchers adopted a loosely structured grounded theory approach as advocated by Charmaz (2006), to conduct three pieces of qualitative research: (i) Semi-structured interviews with representatives from the four organisations included in the case studies; (ii) Semi-structure interviews with twelve female participants of one case study program (LaunchME); (iii) A qualitative meta-analysis of secondary qualitative data based on a desk-top review of publicly available narratives drawn from websites and YouTube videos from women participants from the three remaining case studies (Global Sisters, One Roof Women, and Stepping Stones).

Face-to-face and/or telephone interviews with representatives of the four case study organisations and LaunchME participants enabled the researchers to develop initial themes. Rather than use a priori codes in the analysis of this qualitative data, the research team used an emergent thematic coding approach (Creswell 2007). The text was iteratively analysed to identify open codes (such as 'barriers', 'enablers', 'supports') which were then grouped based on common categories and emerging patterns (such as 'institutional support', 'self-belief', 'agency', 'tribe'). Further iterations enabled the researchers to refine these into an initial set of themes and preliminary axial codes.

These themes were then tested through the qualitative meta-analysis of secondary qualitative data including publicly available narratives (drawn from websites and YouTube videos) from women participating in the remaining three programs featured as our critical case studies. While these online stories were developed primarily to publicise these programs, hence not framed by the authors of this chapter through face-to-face research, they offered the means to move towards theoretical saturation. After refining the emerging insights into four major themes, the researchers concluded the grounded theory analysis by developing three theoretical propositions included later in this chapter. The involvement of multiple authors in the finalisation of these themes and propositions has provided investigator triangulation.

FINDINGS AND DISCUSSION

The aim of our research was to better understand how 'latent' entrepreneurs who are supported by female-centric programs are empowered to become 'visible' as entrepreneurs, and recognise the value created by their businesses. The grounded theory approach we adopted enabled us to identify four major themes emerging from the data, discussed below.

Theme One: An Entrepreneurial Ecosystem that Values and Supports Women as Much as their Businesses is More Likely to Enable Women to Create Business Value

Our research suggests that the holistic, women-centred programs offered by the four organisations featured in our case studies, provide important institutional support for entrepreneurial women that is missing in the current support ecosystem. Further, the programs being offered by these organisations are generating value for women through the very act of their participation, as the programs situate the women as being more than business owners. Instead they create an environment of holistic support, which addresses the women's personal needs and the multi-dimensional barriers they currently face, in addition to supporting their businesses.

This could manifest as paying attention to 'every stage' of the business journey as articulated by one support provider: "At every stage of their business journey we are there to support them and to design programs and events around the needs to ensure basically that they have everything they need to succeed" (ORW).

It could also include an understanding of the aspirations and barriers of specific cohorts of women, as described by another support provider: "The women described seeking greater financial independence, empowerment and increased economic participation – but were frustrated by the barriers they faced" (SS).

This focus on the women, rather than their businesses alone, is also reflected by participants in these programs, as one entrepreneur explains: "What makes the business is the person so you should focus on the person. That is really helpful for people just starting out in business. Anxiety comes hand in hand with starting a business" (LM).

Women also spoke of how acknowledging the value of their business translated into an acknowledgment of their personal value. One participant stated: "My coach helped me to see my value as a person and as a business-woman" (LM) whilst another said, "My business was seen as viable…This made me feel better and lifted my confidence" (LM).

These stories show that an entrepreneurial ecosystem which values and supports women as much as their business, is more likely to enable women to create successful businesses. It also indicates that women derive personal value from other's perception of their business value.

Theme Two: The Knowledge and Experience Gained from Developing a Business in a Supportive Environment is Enabling Women to Overcome a Lack of Self-Belief, Exercise Agency, Develop Capabilities and Take Action

A constant refrain in our conversations with both entrepreneurs and program staff was the lack of self-belief among emerging women entrepreneurs, on both personal and business levels. One support provider stated:

> I see a lot of founders with a lot of self-doubt, with a lot of fear … when we run events, programs and workshops … [it's] about having those really honest conversations about the challenges, how people are feeling, the fear, the self-confidence, how we can build that, because that at the end of the day is probably really the biggest barrier. (ORW)

The women entrepreneurs also spoke at length of the connection between self-belief, self-confidence, and taking action, as evidenced by their statements:

> This has helped me to know who I am as a professional and who I am not … I've developed confidence to back myself and to know what my weaknesses and strengths are. (LM)

> For me it's given me personal confidence … . They believed in my products which helped me to believe in my business. They knew I had a niche that wasn't out there. (LM)

The participants' comments show that the knowledge and experience they have gained from participating in the programs has enabled them to overcome their own lack of self-belief, to exercise agency, develop capabilities and take action. We also found that self-belief, which enables women to form and run a business, is not developed via a linear process – it is instead shaped by their engagement in the programs, by ongoing networking with and supporting other entrepreneurs, and through the very act of running a business.

Theme Three: Value is Created for Women Entrepreneurs by Being Part of a 'Tribe' which Provides a Source of Relational Learning, Personal/Business Support, Networks and Business Identity

A key enabler that all four programs use to build a supportive environment, albeit in slightly different ways, is the conscious creation of a community or 'tribe' to support women entrepreneurs. The 'tribe' serves to both address the social isolation these women often experience, as well as to link them to new opportunities for peer-based interaction and support. LaunchME enables community-building through participant workshops and a Facebook group. While the program admits participants on a rolling basis of around twenty at a time, the interviewees speak of belonging to a particular 'group' based upon those with whom they have interacted via face-to-face workshops and/or online forums.

One Roof Women similarly explains that their business model centres on ensuring that women are not working alone, and can build a sense of community by surrounding themselves with 'like-minded people':

> A lot of them felt isolated or were working from home. A lot of them didn't really know who to go to. A lot of them didn't really have a professional network to tap into and didn't know how to build that network … A lot of them spoke about … 'we want to be able to go to a space where we can feel comfortable … just being around likeminded people to just talk out those feelings and have very honest conversation about the journey and the challenges'. (ORW)

For Global Sisters, a strong emphasis on being part of the 'Sister tribe' is seen as core to how the organisation operates. The program staff explain how the 'Sister tribe' has acted as a way for Global Sisters to create a brand. It has also enabled women to become part of a peer network. Belonging to the 'tribe' fosters connection and provides a confidence boost for when one's own confidence is waning. Importantly, being part of the 'Sister tribe' seems to be empowering women to see themselves as 'entrepreneurs' despite their initial reluctance to brand themselves in this way. As one staff member stated: "Global Sisters is about developing a sister tribe – you can see that our sisters really want to support each other and collaborate and there is a beautiful business community" (GS).

A participant expressed this as :

> I couldn't find my place ... but of course to live you have to do something so I was think-ing why is there nothing I can offer in Australia, this makes me so sad ... . Maybe this is something I can do in here and I start making a bit more ... . It makes me independent not only financially but I feel like I have some place I can be here. (GS)

Stepping Stones program staff similarly talk about the 'Stepping Stones alumni' and women participants self-identify as having been part of this program. In addition, the women we spoke to preferred to place themselves amongst other females, rather than be depicted as a lone entrepreneur, with one woman comparing her experience to being in a mother's group, with the 'baby' being her business and the other partic-ipants able to give her perspective, advice and support.

Women also talked about preferring to learn from peer-based interaction, network-ing and mentoring support. One woman focused on informal networking:

> Initially [X] was a means for me to get up and out of the isolation of working from home. But it's become so much more than that. It's a welcoming place to put your head down and get things done while also harbouring so much wisdom and inspiration in the amazing entrepreneurs sitting around you. (ORW)

Another entrepreneur focused on the role of formal networking opportunities:

> I'm working in an environment full of strong, amazing, passionate women that fight for their goals and dreams. It brings me inspiration every day on how to grow my business. Working and networking with likeminded people with different talents makes me advance faster towards my goals. (ORW)

These examples clearly highlight that value is being generated for the women entre-preneurs by the act of learning and networking (whether formal or informal), as well as by being around other women. This theme of peer-based interaction was also discussed by another participant:

> In business you stand alone, but when you see others, you see how they put in work, see dips and troughs, it helps you to stick it out. Overall, our research shows that if women can

see other women from the 'tribe' achieve business success, they are more likely to believe in their own ability to do this too. (LM)

Overall, our research shows that if women can see other women from the 'tribe' achieve business success, they are more likely to believe in their own ability to do this too. The very nature of having a business and being around other women who are building businesses, provides inspiration.

Theme Four: When Organisations Enable Women to Pursue Confidently their Ideas, Women Entrepreneurs Create Businesses that Add Value at Social and Economic Levels

We found that irrespective of their socio-cultural or economic backgrounds, most women do not see themselves as 'entrepreneurs', yet they are comfortable in acknowledging they run an 'enterprise' or business for a variety of reasons. Some frame their business engagement as an opportunity to find paid work within the need for flexible arrangements so as to gain more work–life balance or manage caring responsibilities; some as an outlet for their 'passion' and/or talents; others as a response to survival imperatives. In all cases, the value creation is not defined in strictly financial terms. This is true both for the women's rationale for starting the business, as well as the value that they hope to generate from the business. One participant expressed this as follows:

> I wanted more clarity to make a sustainable business and to manage family life and get a work/life balance…. I've looked at my local community and where the gaps are … so I'm going to a town close by so I can focus more on helping another community. (LM)

While not all women-led businesses have a social purpose, service providers noted that many of the enterprises developed via their programs have either an explicit social purpose, or are geared toward addressing a need arising out of women's lived experience:

> They are usually passionate; they are often solving real world important problems – often ones they have experienced themselves or that someone close to them has experienced it. They want to build financially successful companies and they want to build global companies but it's not the money that necessarily drives them but also equally, not more important, is actually having compassion and building an amazing product or service that will make a difference in this world. They are also driven to build really good work cultures, to support other women and other entrepreneurs, and to give back. (ORW)

One support provider felt that entrepreneurship offers women the potential to create social value:

> Entrepreneurship allows women the ability and flexibility to build something themselves, something that is meaningful to them, it enables women to create what they want the future to be and to create products and services that solve real world problems. (ORW)

Thus, their businesses are providing a vehicle for women to create social as well as economic value, offering a pathway for enterprising women – who may not see themselves as 'entrepreneurs' – to solve problems, fill gaps, and create broader value for their communities and society. Business-level value creation can therefore be directly linked to societal value creation through the act of leading a business venture, for these latent women entrepreneurs.

EMPOWERING WOMEN TO CREATE BUSINESS VALUE: A THEORY

The latent entrepreneurs described in this chapter face a range of internal barriers including a lack of self-belief and confidence, as well as external factors specific to their gender and background. Regardless of the lifecycle stage of their business, from concept to established, many of these women do not see themselves as entrepreneurs. Their entrepreneurship is often led by necessity (van Kooy 2016) in response to barriers they face in accessing job markets (Bodsworth 2014), yet they are not 'reluctant' entrepreneurs (Ahl & Marlow 2012). Instead, our study suggests that when these women are enabled to pursue their ideas, they become 'actualised' as entrepreneurs, and create businesses that generate multiple forms of value. The grounded theory approach we adopted has enabled us to formulate the following three propositions for the conditions which we hypothesise can best enable this process of transformation:

Proposition One: Female-Centric Ecosystems Best Facilitate Women Entrepreneurs' Access to Resources, Networks, and Institutional Support

As discussed earlier, women entrepreneurs face additional barriers to entry including family responsibilities (Still & Timms 1999); access to finance (Blake 2006) and networks (Moppert 2010); and expectations on women's role in business (Moppert 2010). These challenges resonate with the experience of our participants, many of whom find the broader entrepreneurial ecosystem in Australia unsupportive. Yet the four organisations featured in our case studies have found ways to provide these women better access to resources, and supported them to create their own networks, enabling them to progress from 'latent' to fully actualised entrepreneurs.

A key enabler identified in our research is the value of building female-centric ecosystems. The framing of three critical aspects of the entrepreneurial ecosystem as suggested by McAdam, Harrison & Leitch (2018, p. 3) namely 'the role of the (social) context in enabling or restricting entrepreneurship'; 'the role of the external business environment on the entrepreneur'; and 'the role of the entrepreneur in creating, maintaining and developing the entrepreneurial ecosystem', proved very useful in our analysis, as our case studies show that by creating a positive social context and offering targeted support needed by the women entrepreneurs, which they are not able to access within the business ecosystem, these four organisations have enabled the women and their businesses to be valued.

The personalised support by these female-centred programs directly addresses the specific barriers they face as entrepreneurs in Australia. The women also feel more confident about engaging with the external business environment, which normalises their status as an entrepreneur. We therefore propose that female-centric ecosystems are best able to facilitate women entrepreneurs' access to appropriate resources, networks and supports, and enable women to become active generators of their own business value.

Proposition Two: The Personal Knowledge and Experience Gained by Women When Supported Over Their Business Journey, Empowers Them to Proactively Build Their Own Capabilities and Help Others

Agency, which can be defined as 'a person's ability to direct their own actions' (Moppert 2010, p. 39), must be contextualised within the person's wider social, cultural and political environment. An individual's internalised sense of self-belief and efficacy often reflects the values and preconceptions of their wider social and cultural community (Meyers 2002) and influences their ability to act. These insights resonated strongly with our research findings – when women entrepreneurs were supported by service providers who 'believed' in their personal and business value, and connected with other women with similar experiences, this dramatically increased their self-belief.

We also found that the women entrepreneurs who felt more empowered went on to build their own capabilities, as well as mentor others to succeed in their business journey. This insight supports earlier literature on women entrepreneurs in Australia, including a study in Victoria (Moppert 2010) which found that developing a successful business enhanced self-determination amongst women entrepreneurs, which they shared with other women. Chiang, Low and Collins's study (2013) of Chinese women entrepreneurs in Australia and Canada, and Haslam McKenzie's research (1998) exploring rural business women in Western Australia, similarly found that establishing a business enabled the women to exercise agency within their cultural context, and develop entrepreneurial capabilities for themselves and others.

Our research therefore strongly supports our second proposition that the knowledge and experience gained by women when supported over their business journey, empowers them to exercise agency which is both internalised as well as shared with others.

Proposition Three: Being Part of a 'Tribe' Enables Women to Create Social and Economic Value

Central to the two points discussed above is the placing of women outside of a singular construct as a 'solo' entrepreneur into being part of a 'tribe'. In our study the 'tribe' identification went beyond networks as a form of resource allocation and information flows. Being around other women enabled participants to overcome a lack of self-belief; exercise agency through supporting fellow participants; as well as normalise their identity as an 'entrepreneur'. Being part of a 'tribe' also enabled peer-based or 'relational learning' (Ryan, Goldberg, & Evans 2010), a form of learning based on interactions and relationships, as opposed to content-driven delivery.

The four programs we studied all explicitly promoted relationship building yet there is very little research into the role of entrepreneurial women 'tribes' or communities as complex multi-dimensional constructs. Studies exploring the role of networks (one aspect of an entrepreneurial tribe) and entrepreneurs' access to business and personal networks (McAdam et al. 2018; Bogren et al. 2013) challenge the concept of the 'solitary entrepreneur' (Korsgaard & Anderson 2011, p. 135). McAdam et al. (2018) also argues that the creation of women-only networks as a policy response may provide access to peer mentoring, role models and provide opportunities for support and learning.

Emerging studies in developing countries such as Sheikh et al. (2018) focusing on entrepreneurial outcomes for rural Pakistani women and value creation at multiple levels, find that women increase their access to resources through growing social networks and information flows. Others (e.g. van Kooy 2016) find that 'learning by doing' added significantly to women's entrepreneurial capability and capacity. Our research validated these insights. While economic outcomes from their businesses remained low, participants described increased self-confidence and empowerment, enhanced social networks, and transferring their knowledge to other women, including those still based in their home countries.

CONCLUSION

Developing countries have long focused on providing specific support to enhance women's economic development through entrepreneurship, yet this is relatively new in the Australian context. Our research reveals a 'bubbling up' of emergent female-centric ecosystems of support for 'latent' women entrepreneurs in Australia, particularly those from disadvantaged and marginalised backgrounds. As distinct from start-ups and those further along on their business journey who are accessing more mainstream support, we can clearly see that these specifically curated female-centric ecosystems are providing valuable support to less-visible women entrepreneurs. By moving beyond a narrow focus on business growth, the four organisations we have studied are offering deeper and targeted support for women entrepreneurs, which are starting to make a 'latent' entrepreneurial population visible.

The reframing of business-level value creation as social value creation is central to this actualisation process. While these emerging spaces have so far formed primarily within the context of non-profit microenterprise development programs and co-working spaces, we suggest that our findings have value for women entrepreneurs more broadly.

Our study adds to the limited research on value creation within a developed country context, documenting the creation of new types of value, and making visible both 'latent entrepreneurs' as well as emergent spaces in the entrepreneurial ecosystem which are supporting them. From a policy and practice perspective, our study contributes four themes highlighting the importance of creating female-centric programs and ecosystem supports, and puts forward three theoretical propositions about the conditions that best facilitate the emergence of latent female entrepreneurs to guide future research in this field. We advocate for the adoption of these conditions by policy makers.

We also call for more research to define further these spaces outside of the cohorts we studied, to capture a broader range of women's voices. We also believe it is important to further explore the role of relational learning, peer-based support and specific enablers of business-level social value creation within different contexts (socio-cultural, business life stage, non-gendered, and place-based). Quantification of social value creation in these contexts would advance the field.

Just as 'social constructionists' leverage opportunities for their advantage (Zahra et al., 2009), we find that 'latent' women entrepreneurs are benefiting from and proactively creating their own women-specific ecosystem. This curated ecosystem is enabling these latent entrepreneurs to pursue their ideas, and lead businesses that create both financial and social value. We find that within these co-created ecosystems, a male-centric growth construct is subsumed within the larger discourse of value creation.

NOTES

1. See for example NAB microenterprise scheme (https://www.nab.com.au/content/dam/nabrwd/documents/reports/corporate/nabs-microenterprise-loan-program.pdf) or Many Rivers (http://www.manyrivers.org.au/wp-content/uploads/2016/12/Many-Rivers-2016-Evaluation-Report-Full-Evaluation-External.pdf).
2. See https://becaustralia.org.au/.
3. See https://www.jobs.gov.au/self-employment-new-business-assistance-neis.

BIBLIOGRAPHY

ACOSS & UNSW (2018). *Supplementary report to inequality in Australia 2018: The causes and profile of income inequality.* Retrieved March 17, 2019 from https://www.acoss.org.au/wp-content/uploads/2018/07/Inequality-in-Australia-2018_supplementary-report.pdf.

Ahl, H. (2006). Why research on women entrepreneurs needs new directions. *Entrepreneurship Theory and Practice, 30*(5), 595–621.

Ahl, H., & Marlow, S. (2012). Exploring the dynamics of gender, feminism and entrepreneurship: Advancing debate to escape a dead end? *Organization, 19*(5), 543–562.

Alsos, G., Haugum, M., & Ljunggren, E. (2017). Gender equality in regional entrepreneurial ecosystems: The implementation of policy initiatives. In T.S. Manolova, C. Brush, L.F. Edelman, A. Robb & F. Welter (Eds.), *Entrepreneurial Ecosystems and Growth of Women's Entrepreneurship: A Comparative Analysis* (pp. 221–243). Edward Elgar Publishing.

Atasoy, H. (2015). Latent entrepreneurship in transition economies, *IZA World of Labour*, doi: 10.15185/izawol.155.

Barraket, J., Douglas, H., Eversole, R., Mason, C., McNeill, J., & Morgan, B. (2017). Classifying social enterprise models in Australia. *Social Enterprise Journal, 13*(4), 345–361.

Blake, M. (2006). Gendered lending: Gender, context and the rules of business lending. *Venture Capital, 8*(2), 183–201.

Blanchflower, D.G, Oswald, A. & Stutzer, A. (2001). Latent entrepreneurship across nations, *European Economic Review, 45*, 680–691.

Bodsworth, E. (2014). *Being around other women makes you brave: Evaluation of Stepping Stones, a micro-business program for women from refugee and migrant backgrounds.* Brotherhood of St Laurence. Retrieved March 17, 2019 from http://library.bsl.org.au/jspui/bitstream/1/6039/1/Bodsworth_Being_around_other_women_makes_you_brave_SteppingStones_evaluation_2014.pdf.

Bogren, M., von Friedrichs, Y., Rennemo, Ø., & Widding, Ø. (2013). Networking women entrepreneurs: Fruitful for business growth? *International Journal of Gender and Entrepreneurship, 5*(1), 60–77.

Brotherhood of St Laurence. (2019) *Stepping Stones success story: Ivan Russian Language School.* Retrieved March 17. 2019 from https://www.youtube.com/watch?v=jdtVNMwoFBE&vl=en.

Brush, C., Edelman, L.F., Manolova, T., & Welter, F. (2019). A gendered look at entrepreneurship ecosystems. *Small Business Economics, 53*, 393–408.

Carrington, C. (2006). Women entrepreneurs. *Journal of Small Business & Entrepreneurship, 19*(2), 83–94.

Charmaz, K. (2006). *Constructing Grounded Theory.* Sage.

Chiang, F., Low, A., & Collins, J. (2013). Two sets of business cards: Responses of Chinese immigrant women entrepreneurs in Canada and Australia to sexism and racism. *Cosmopolitan Civil Societies: An Interdisciplinary Journal, 5*(2), 63–83.

Conway, T. (2015). Closing the gender-funding gap. Retrieved July 3, 2018 from https://www.smh.com.au/business/small-business/closing-the-genderfunding-gap-20150305-13w2u5.html.

Creswell, J.W. (2007). *Qualitative Inquiry and Research Design: Choosing Among Five Approaches* (2nd ed.). Sage.

de Bruin, A., Brush, C., & Welter, F. (2006). Introduction to the special issue: Towards building cumulative knowledge on women's entrepreneurship. *Entrepreneurship Theory and Practice, 30*(5), 585–593.

de Bruin, A., Brush, C., & Welter, F. (2007). Advancing a framework for coherent research on women's entrepreneurship. *Entrepreneurship Theory and Practice, 31*(3), 323–339.

Enterprising Women. (2019). *Building Connections for Enterprising Women Project Final Report.* Retrieved May 10, 2019 from https://goodshepherdmicrofinance.org.au/assets/files/2019/03/DFAT-ASEAN-Report_Final.pdf.

Eversole, R. (2013). Social enterprises as local development actors: Insights from Tasmania. *Local Economy, 28*(6), 567–579.

Global Sisters. (n.d.). *Main Marketing Brochure.* Retrieved March 17, 2019 from https://globalsisters.org/wp-content/uploads/2018/03/GS180208-Main-Marketing-Brochure_v5_LR_Email.pdf.

Global Sisters. (2019). *Global Sisters Sister Pitch (short) 2018.* Retrieved March 17, 2019 from https://www.youtube.com/watch?v=qMrUoBSIIcE.

Global Sisters. (2019). *Global Sisters Social Impact Series: Business Acumen.* Retrieved March 17, 2019 from https://www.youtube.com/watch?v=Yy5w33OHCqM.

Global Sisters. (2019). *Impact Report 2019.* Retrieved May 1, 2019 from https://globalsisters.org/ImpactReport/.

Global Sisters. (2019). *Meet Yoko.* Retrieved March 17, 2019 from https://www.youtube.com/watch?v=Of80K7KOyhA.

Godinho, V., Eccles, K., & Thomas, L. (2018). Beyond access: The role of microfinance in enabling financial empowerment and wellbeing for Indigenous clients: Lessons from remote Australia. *Third Sector Review, 24*(2), 57–76.

Gohmann, S.F. (2012). Institutions, latent entrepreneurship, and self-employment: An international comparison, *Entrepreneurship Theory and Practice, 36*(2), 295–321.

Goodwin, S., & Voola, A.P. (2013). Framing microfinance in Australia – gender neutral or gender blind? *Australian Journal of Social Issues, 48*, 223–239.

Good Shepherd Microfinance. (2019). *LaunchME: Kick start your business.* Retrieved April 7, 2019 from https://www.launchme.org.au/launch-me/.

Grilo, I. and Irigoyen, J.M. (2006). Entrepreneurship in the EU: To wish and not to be. *Small Business Economics, 26*(4), 305–318.

Haslam McKenzie, F. (1998). Case studies of rural business women in Western Australia and their contribution to the region. *Rural Society, 8*(3), 257–268.

Henderickson, L., Bucifcal, S., Balaguer, A., & Hansell, D. (2015). *The Employment Dynamics of Australian Entrepreneurship.* Office of the Chief Scientist: Department of Industry and Science.

Isenberg, D. (2011, May 12). *The entrepreneurship ecosystem strategy as a new paradigm for economic policy: Principles for cultivating entrepreneurship* [Paper presentation]. Institute of International and European Affairs, Dublin, Ireland.

Kimakwa, S., Abebe, M., & Redd, T. (2018). (Disgruntled) social warriors: Toward a typology of women social entrepreneurs. *Academy of Management Proceedings, 2018*(1), 10964.

Korsgaard, S., & Anderson, A. (2011). Enacting entrepreneurship as social value creation. *International Small Business Journal: Researching Entrepreneurship, 29*(2), 135–151.

Krueger, N., & Brazeal, D. (1994). Entrepreneurial potential and potential entrepreneurs. *Entrepreneurship Theory and Practice, 18*(3), 91–104.

Lee, M., & Rogoff, E. (1998). Do women entrepreneurs require special training? An empirical comparison of men and women entrepreneurs in the United States. *Journal of Small Business & Entrepreneurship, 15*(1), 4–29.

McAdam, M., Harrison, R., & Leitch, C. (2018). Stories from the field: Women's networking as gender capital in entrepreneurial ecosystems. *Small Business Economics, 53*(2), 1–16.

Meyers, D. (2002). *Gender in the mirror – cultural imagery and women's agency.* Oxford University Press.

Moppert, K. (2010). *Gendered entrepreneurship: Australian women entrepreneurs talk gender, power and agency.* Lambert Educational Publishing.

Motoyama, Y., Konczal, J., Bell-Masterson, J., & Morelix, A. (2014). *Think locally, act locally: Building a robust entrepreneurial ecosystem.* Ewing Marion Kauffman Foundation. https://www.researchgate.net/publication/266118299_Think_Locally_Act_Locally _Building_a_Robust_Entrepreneurial_Ecosystem_-_Fostering_economic_independence _by_advancing_education_and_entrepreneurship.

One Roof Women. (n.d.). *About Us.* Retrieved March 17, 2019 from https://oneroofwomen .com/about.

One Roof Women. (2019). *Members Spotlight: Ash Navaratnam.* Retrieved March 17, 2019 from https://oneroofwomen.com/blog/members-spotlight-ash-navaratnam.

One Roof Women. (2019). *Members Spotlight: Penny Willoughby.* Retrieved March 18, 2019 from https://oneroofwomen.com/blog/members-spotlight-penny-willoughby.

One Roof Women. (2019). *Members Spotlight: Cristina de Medrano.* Retrieved March 18, 2019 from https://oneroofwomen.com/blog/members-spotlight-cristina-de-medrano.

Roos, A. (2019). Embeddedness in context: Understanding gender in a female entrepreneurship network. *Entrepreneurship & Regional Development, 31*(3–4), 279–292.

Ryan, A., Goldberg, L., & Evans, J. (2010). Wise women: Mentoring as relational learning in perinatal nursing practice. *Journal of Clinical Nursing, 19*, 183–191.

Sandhu, N., Scott, J., & Hussain, J. (2016). *Informal Finance and Growth of Women Businesses in an Emergent Entrepreneurial Ecosystem: A Case of Indian Punjab*. Academic Conferences International Limited.

Schreiner, M., & Woller, G. (2003). Microenterprise development programs in the United States and in the developing world. *World Development*, *31*(9), 1567–1580.

Sheikh, S., Yousafzai, S., Sist, F., & Saeed, S. (2018). Value creation through women's entrepreneurship. In S. Yousafzai, A. Fayolle, A. Lindgreen, C. Henry, S. Saeed & S. Sheikh (Eds.), *Women Entrepreneurs and the Myth of 'Underperformance': A New Look at Women's Entrepreneurship Research* (pp. 20–30). Edward Elgar Publishing.

Sperber, S., & Linder, C. (2019). Gender-specifics in start-up strategies and the role of the entrepreneurial ecosystem. *Small Business Economics*, *53*, 533–546.

Startup Muster. (2018). *The 2018 Startup Muster Report*. Retrieved March 17, 2019 from https://www.startupmuster.com/.

Steffens, P., & Omarova, A. (2019). *Global Entrepreneurship Monitor (GEM): 2017/2018 Australian National Report*. Entrepreneurship, Commercialisation and Innovation Centre.

Still, L., & Timms, W. (1999). *Why So Small: Women-Owned Businesses: Barriers to Growth*. University of Western Australia, the Graduate School of Business, Centre for Women and Business.

Tlaiss, H. (2019). Contextualizing the career success of Arab women entrepreneurs. *Entrepreneurship & Regional Development*, *31*(3–4), 226–241.

van de Ven, H. (1993). The development of an infrastructure for entrepreneurship. *Journal of Business Venturing*, *8*(3), 211–230.

van Kooy, J. (2016). Refugee women as entrepreneurs in Australia. *Forced Migration Review*, *53*, 71–73.

Weber, P.C., & Geneste, L. (2014). Exploring gender-related perceptions of SME success. *International Journal of Gender and Entrepreneurship*, *6*(1), 15–27.

World Economic Forum. (2013). *Entrepreneurial Ecosystems Around the Globe and Company Growth Dynamics*. World Economic Forum.

Yousafzai, S., Fayolle, A., Saeed, S., Henry, C., & Lindgreen, A. (2019). The contextual embeddedness of women's entrepreneurship: Towards a more informed research agenda. *Entrepreneurship & Regional Development*, *31*(3–4), 167–177.

Yousafzai, S., Saeed, S., & Muffatto, M. (2015). Institutional theory and contextual embeddedness of women's entrepreneurial leadership: Evidence from 92 countries. *Journal of Small Business Management*, *53*(3), 587–604.

Zahra, S., Gedajlovic, E., Neubaum, D. & Shulman, J. (2009). A typology of social entrepreneurs: Motives, search processes and ethical challenges. *Journal of Business Venturing*, *24*(5), 519–532.

10. Women entrepreneurs creating value in informal public transport enterprises in Kenya

Anne Kamau and Winnie V. Mitullah

Kenya's transport sector comprises of road, air, rail, water and sea (KIPPRA, 2017) and it contributes between 5% and 15% of the national gross domestic product (RoK, 2018; KNBS, 2019a). The sector provides seasonal and short-term employment in public transport, hauling and digital platforms (MacKellar, 2009). Kenya does not have a state-owned public transport system. Instead, informal privately owned vehicles commonly known as matatus or paratransits provide public transport services, and constitute more than 80% of Kenya's public transport services (Behrens et al., 2017; Salon and Gulyani, 2019). Paratransits are small-scale business enterprises (Cervero, 2000) that include buses, mini-buses and smaller 14-seater vehicles (McCormick et al., 2016). Matatus are recognized in Kenya's law and are described as public service vehicles with a seating capacity of not more than 25 passengers excluding the driver (RoK, 2012) even though, in practice, some matatu's like the mini-buses have a higher passenger carrying capacity. In addition, three- and two-wheeler motorcycles that provide public transport services mainly in areas where matatus do not reach (Nyachieo, 2015).

It is estimated that there are over 100,000 registered public service vehicles (PSVs) in Kenya (Spooner and Whelligan, 2017) with Nairobi alone having over 8,000 matatus operating close to 70 routes and carrying about 400,000 passengers daily (Wright, 2018). In 2018 about 106,676 mini-buses and buses were registered and about 57,949 licenses were issued to PSV operators (KNBS, 2019b). Williams and Kedir (2018) noted that informality is higher when there is inadequate state intervention, for instance in Kenya's public transport. It is only recently that the government invested in a state-owned and financed rail transport system known as the Standard Gauge Railway (Wissenbach and Yuan, 2017; Oluochi, 2018). There are also plans to roll out a state supported Bus Rapid Transit (BRT) system in Nairobi (GLI, 2018; Wright, 2018). In the meantime, matatus remain the main mode of public transport in Kenya, providing commuter service to about 70% of Nairobi's population (Bailey and Duggan, 2020).

The informal sector employs about 80% of Kenya's workforce with the paratransit sector being the fourth largest employer of informal economy workers (Maina, 2016; Kamau et al., 2018). Matatus enterprises employ over 300,000 people directly and indirectly (GLI, 2018) and are operated for profit, charging commercial rates to users. The direct beneficiaries are the vehicle owners and employees (Kempe, 2014) and there are many small businesses that indirectly depend on transport businesses (GLI, 2017).

The sector is a complex and multi-layered entrepreneurial undertaking (Khayesi and Nafukho, 2016) with a diverse complex web of actors who have divergent interests. It is structured at different levels of the informal hierarchy intertwined with formal modes of social and economic agency (Heinze, 2018; Kamau, forthcoming). The diverse interests include government agencies and traffic authorities, vehicle owners and operators, stage managers and SACCO officials, political class, cartels and other stakeholders (Oira and Makori, 2015).

WOMEN PARTICIPATION IN INFORMAL PUBLIC TRANSPORT ENTERPRISES

The public transport sector in Kenya is male dominated and in Nairobi, women constitute only about 6.7% of the sector workers (GLI, 2018). Nationally these figures could be higher, although Nairobi County has the highest number of paratransit modes. Women participate in the sector mainly as employees and not vehicle owners (Wright, 2018) and work mainly as conductors, passenger callers, with few working as drivers and fleet managers (GLI, 2017). The Kenyan case is similar to the global trend where few women are involved in public transport enterprises and constitute only one in seven transport workers (Wright, 2018). Nonetheless, women are increasingly entering the sector and changing the outlook of the sector as demonstrated in this chapter.

Kenya lacks reliable data on ownership of public transport vehicles thus it is difficult to comprehend the complexity of the industry (Graeff, 2013), and the numbers of women and men who have invested in the sector. Nonetheless, there are women investors in the sector, including some who own fleets of vehicles. Like the case of men, some of these women are absentee owners (Graeff, 2013). Nonetheless, the higher echelons of the sector are dominated by male gender that pioneered investment in the sector. Owning a public transport business requires large capital for vehicle purchase, fitting parts and mechanical work, and obtaining required licensing and registration documents. Hence, matatu owners are high net-worth individuals (Maina, 2016) who invest their own finances in the businesses or have access to asset financing and repay through a work-and-pay system (Oira and Makori, 2015).

Women's unequal participation in Kenya's public transport is linked to the history of matatus that dates back to early 1960s (Klopp, 2012; Mukabana, 2016). Matatus emerged to serve the segregated African populations (Mutongi, 2017) after restrictions barring movement of Africans to Nairobi were lifted. Men were then allowed to migrate to the city to provide labour in the industries and serve the colonial government (Mwangi, 2014). The women remained in rural areas and were locked out of urban areas by the capitalist enterprises, policies and patriarchy, which controlled women's mobility in order to maintain the family order (Kinyanjui, 2014). In particular, single women were discouraged from moving to cities due to fear that they might become prostitutes and transmit venereal diseases. Women found in the city were charged for 'loitering in a public place for immoral purposes' under Section 19(m) of the Nairobi General Nuisance by-laws which stated that 'any person who in any street – loiters or importunes for purposes of prostitution is guilty of an offence' (FIDA, 2008; KELIN, 2016).

It is only later, and with enhanced urban–rural connections provided by matatus, that women increasingly migrated to the city mainly to join their husbands. However, pre-colonial and colonial patriarchal practices placed obstacles for women (Zeleza, 1988) that restricted their entry into wage labour and hence they had a slow start (Kinyanjui, 2014). Women's social place was restricted to the private domain of the 'home' while men belonged to the public sphere of social production and wage employment (Zeleza, 1988). This created unequal opportunity structures between female and male employment, with women mainly being involved in selling fruits and vegetables to the urban residents while men performed public transport jobs.

The late entry of women in public transport sector has also been linked to government failure to effectively organize and regulate the sector (Wright, 2018). The notion that the sector is chaotic and disorganized persists thus making it unattractive to women. A legal notice No. 161 issued in October 2003 (RoK, 2003; Chitere and Kibua, 2004) and later revised in 2012 (RoK, 2012), popularly known as the *Michuki rules* (Mwangi, 2014) helped to create order in the sector. The notice required vehicle owners to form and join registered transport savings and credit cooperatives (SACCOs) or management companies in order to operate (Koimur, Kangogo and Nyaoga, 2014), and to improve working conditions for workers (McCormick et al., 2016). Enforcement of these regulations has contributed to increased entry of women in the sector (Wright, 2018) as women prefer working in organized systems (Kamau, 2018).

VALUE CREATION IN PUBLIC TRANSPORT ENTERPRISES

The entry of women in the public transport sector justifies an understanding of how they are using social capital as an enabling resource and an important determinant of exploitation of entrepreneurial opportunities (Yousafzai et al., 2015). Increasingly, women are entering the informal public transport sector as conductors, drivers, callers and investors; thus challenging the private-public domestic thesis that confines women in the private household domain. Women in public transport enterprises undertake their public engagement roles alongside their domestic roles that include taking care of household needs and care-giving beyond the household.

The value creation approach conceptualizes women's work as contributing to value creation at four levels, that is, the individual, business, household and societal level (see Introduction, this volume). This holistic view asserts that all activities of women in the different levels are entrepreneurial and have social benefit although women are rewarded differently. For instance, women in Kenya's informal public transport sector are working alongside with men, are earning an income and interacting with society, while at the same time feeding their households, hence deconstructing popular perceptions of exclusion in public roles, power and citizenship. This in turn is giving the sector a different image and acting as a mirror not only to other women, but also to the larger society. Initial entry in such male-dominated sectors often come with mixed perceptions, in particular when the task involves over-exposure such as running around the stage calling customers to board vehicles and playing the conductor role of collecting money and managing passengers. The women discussed in this study have overcome such challenges, although occasionally there are work-related gender disadvantages that entail for instance loss of employment or having to take leave without pay if they take maternity leave; or loss of pay when they take time off to handle individual and household needs since payment is largely based on daily targets.

The women working in the transport sector have mastered the art of working at different levels. At the individual level, they have built an agency that enables them to make decisions and work at different levels. This has enabled them to push the boundaries of the historical domestic thesis setting to which women were restricted in ideology and practice, and to enter spaces outside the home which were man's domain. This push is changing the understanding of gender spaces, the uses of spaces and meaning attached to them (Kinyanjui, 2014), even though the family remains predominantly as the primary context for the female domain. Women's household work, which is often viewed as valueless, is relevant for family and functioning of society. Increasingly, women in public transport enterprises are acting as breadwinners and co-breadwinners, taking care of families and relatives, complementing household income by feeding families, and taking care of expenses such as school fees, rent and bills.

In respect to the business level, some women have broken the glass ceiling to become investors in the transport industry. Some have also risen from the lower ladder moving from calling customers to becoming investors employing others. They are also creating employment and benefiting from incomes accrued from the businesses. Although data on ownership of public transport vehicles is unavailable, there are women (though few) who own vehicles. However, women prefer in most cases to have their vehicles managed by transport companies or SACCOs and this makes their contribution in public transport enterprises to remain invisible. Studies show that globally few women are involved in (Wright, 2018) and benefit directly from employment in the provision of transport (Allen, 2018). However, women are increasingly penetrating the sector and contributing to value creation. Nevertheless, the value created by women's investment in public transport is largely undocumented as well as their contribution to the economy.

METHODOLOGY

This chapter draws from a four-year (2017–2020) joint research project undertaken in Kenya and Tanzania covering three sectors: transport, construction and trade. The

Table 10.1   Job function and work arrangement by sex

	Sex		Total
	Male	*Female*	**N=208**
	n=198	***n*=10**	
	(95.2%)	*(4.8%)*	
Sub-sector			
PSV *(matatu sector)*	113	10	123 (59.1%)
Motorcycles *(boda boda)*	85	10	85 (40.9%)
Job function			
PSV Driver	65	1	66 (31.7%)
sub-sector Conductor	45	5	50 (24.0%)
Matatu owner	0	1	1 (0.5%)
Other (route official, agent, security)	3	3	6 (2.9%)
Motorbike operator	85	0	85 (40.9%)
Work arrangement			
Paid worker	127	9	136 (65.4%)
Own-account/Self-employed: with employees	11	1	12 (5.8%)
Own-account/Self-employed: without employees	60	0	60 (28.8%)

chapter focuses on an informal public transport workers study, which covered two cities in Kenya, Nairobi and Kisumu. A combination of quantitative and qualitative methods that included a survey, focus group discussions and key informant interviews were used in data gathering, between June and December 2018. The study targeted workers who were directly involved in public transport businesses (PSVs and motorcycles) – own-account operators, micro-enterprise owners with a maximum of two employees, and employed workers. Data collection was undertaken in two stages. In stage one, the study covered 75% of the targeted 200 public transport workers drawn from the general population of workers in the two sites. Information about their work as well as the associations they belonged to was obtained. Associations identified in stage one were listed and contacted to cover the remaining 25% interviews that targeted transport workers who belonged to associations. The idea was to examine whether belonging to an association enhanced workers' access to social protection. Overall, 208 interviews were conducted among 198 men (95.2%) and ten women (4.8%). Most interviews (59.1%) were conducted among workers in the matatu sector and 40.9% among motorcycle riders with the matatu drivers having a higher proportion (31.7%) compared to other workers (Table 10.1). The studied women were involved in the PSV enterprises and these are the focus of this chapter.

Table 10.2 *Nature of work and work arrangement*

Work arrangement (self-employed or a paid worker) versus job type				
Work arrangement	**Nature of work**			**Total**
	Paid worker	Own-account: with employees	Own-account: without employees	
Driver	58	7	1	66 (31.7%)
Conductor	50	0	0	50 (24.0%)
Matatu owner	0	1	0	1 (0.5%)
Motorbike operator	23	4	58	85 (40.9%)
Route official/agent/security	5	0	1	6 (2.9%)
Total	**136**	**12**	**60**	**208**
	(65.4%)	*(5.8%)*	*(28.8%)*	*(100%)*

RESULTS AND DISCUSSIONS: WOMEN IN KENYA'S PUBLIC TRANSPORT ENTERPRISES

The Demographics

Women in the public transport sector are largely young, with an average age of 39 years, which is consistent with other studies (GLI, 2017; 2018). In this study, the youngest was aged 28 years and the oldest 52 years. Eight out of the ten women were married even though other studies show that female public transport workers are largely unmarried (Mwangi, 2014; Wright, 2018). Literature shows that education levels among women in public transport are low compared to men and women lack skills to enhance their job mobility (Wright, 2018). In our study, only three women had post-secondary training. Due to low levels of education, women take up the low-paying precarious jobs mainly as conductors. A key informant noted that, 'literacy levels of drivers and conductors are very low and most of them end up in the sector because they could not be absorbed in any other industry'.

Under-Representation of Women in Kenya's Public Transport Enterprises

This study confirms that women involved in public transport enterprises are few and many are employees mainly occupying low paying unskilled jobs. Five out of ten women worked as conductors and three were involved in PSV operations as a security agent, stage manager or SACCO employee. Only one worked as a driver. Nine women were employed and only one owned a PSV vehicle (Table 10.2), similar to the findings of GLI (2017; 2018).

Weaving through Challenges in the Sector

Women are able to penetrate the sector – progressive elements – in spite of unfavourable conditions in a male dominated sector (rough terrain); they have demonstrated their agency in penetrating the sector. A few women have transcended the unfavourable, chaotic, hostile and poor work conditions that characterize the sector (Nyachieo, 2018; Wright, 2018). A key informant in this study observed that;

> ... we have no female drivers or touts, maybe due to the perception that this is a male industry. In addition, the working environment is not women friendly.

During the FGDs, the struggles that women encountered were constantly reminisced, with some male participants indicating that they make it difficult for women to work in the sector. Turnbull (2013) observed that working conditions and gender stereotyping are the main causes of women's low participation in the transport sector. In general, public transport workers in Kenya work in precarious conditions and often have no formal job contracts (GLI, 2017; 2018). Low and unreliable pay, long working hours and bad working conditions characterize public transport work globally (ITF, 2017; Rizzo, 2017) and presents challenges for women who may have families and young children. Results in this study show that public transport workers have low or no social protection coverage, and there is no appreciation of the unique challenges that women in public transport encounter. An FGD participant in Kisumu noted that:

> Women do not get maternity leave. Maternity is not sickness. Any complication is deemed as bad luck ... the only incentives a member on maternity gets are visits and gifts ... visits are normal, to give gifts. (Transport FGD, 1, Kisumu)

Value Created by Women in Public Transport Enterprises

The primary discussion in this chapter is that women create value by participating in public transport enterprises even though less than 1% own vehicles. Women mainly support the enterprises as workers and unlike the vehicle owners, who are invisible, the workers are visible and occupy public spaces previously not occupied by women. A SACCO manager, while referring to the sector, noted that 'it is the face of the SACCO and the workers that is seen and not of the individual investors (owners)'. Thus, it is important to understand the value that women create not just as vehicle owners but also as workers, and as noted by ILO (2019), the greatest asset for a business is its people.

Value created at individual level

Women in public transport value their work and these jobs are their main occupations. Most had worked in the sector for at least one year. The average number of years that women had worked in their current job was 4.77 and in the transport sector in general 6.6 years. All the women were certain about continuing to work in their current jobs in the months and years ahead (Table 10.3). They perceive their jobs as long-term and desire to continue working in the sector. This shows that once women join the sector, they are likely to continue working there and may seek upward job mobility (GLI, 2018) including owning public service vehicles (Mwangi 2014). This

Table 10.3   Related work issues for women

Work-related issue	Frequency	Statistics
Is this your main occupation?		
Yes	10	100%
When did you start working in your current job?		
Less than 1 year	3	Mean: 4.77 years
1–2 years	2	
2–3 years	1	Median: 2.0 years
3–4 years	0	
4–5 years	1	Minimum: 1 month
5 years	1	
More than 5 years	2	Maximum: 18.5 years
When did you start working in this kind of work?		
Less than 1 year	0	Mean: 6.6 years
1–2 years	1	
2–3 years	2	Median: 4.6 years
3–4 years	1	
4–5 years	1	Minimum: 1.5 years
5 years	1	
More than 5 years	3	Maximum: 18.6 years
How would you rate your chance to hold this job next month?		
Absolute certainty	1	
High	9	
Low	0	

resilience has led to more women joining the sector and it is now common, especially in Nairobi, to see women drivers and conductors thus an aspect of value creation.

Value creation at household level

Women who work in the public transport sector are perceived as daring, or hard-core, and are often described as '*mangaa*', meaning that they are 'hard-headed'. However, the women value the work they do and perceive their jobs as normal and dignified. As noted, it is 'what puts food on the table' and helps to educate their children. Hence, it is through this work that the women are able to create value at the family level.

Value creation at societal level

Even though women in the public transport sector are concentrated in conductor jobs, their presence is helping to change perception about work in the sector. Women are perceived as tolerant, honest, polite and with good customer relations. By offering better services and having better customer relations, the notion of 'rogue and rude' transport workers is changing to one of respectable and decent workers, hence creating value. Women's continued involvement and increased participation in public transport enterprises is changing public perception, not only about women working in the sector, but also about public transport work in general. The few women in the sector are forming alliances and are working with non-governmental organizations (NGOs), transport associations and unions to protect their interests. The areas of concern largely relate to gender issues such as sexual harassment, lack of respect, discrimination and harassment by enforcement officers. NGOs like the Flone Initiative and International Transport Workers' Federation (ITF) trained women and encouraged them to build alliances for empowerment and protection of their workspaces. These activities enhanced women's visibility, performance and their entrance in the male dominated sector.

DISCUSSION: RESILIENCE AGAINST ALL ODDS

Being a female worker in Kenya's public transport sector is challenging and it takes great resilience and persistence for the women to remain in the sector. In most cases, negative perceptions regarding women's entrance in the male dominated transport sector persist (WISE, ca. 2012). For many women, public transport is a means of survival with intention to advance to other jobs (Wright, 2018). Few women own public transport enterprises in Kenya and negative perceptions about women working in the sector persist. They confront multiple challenges, first as public transport workers and second as female workers in the sector. The Kenyan public perceives public transport work with appreciation and contempt. Matatus in Kenya provide public transport services to meet the mobility needs of citizens. However, the workers are perceived as ruthless and chaotic, and their relationship with the public is often hostile; and women are gradually changing these perceptions.

Hanlon (2018) and Wright (2018) attributed the concentration of women in lower-paying jobs to gender segregation. With the number of women often not captured in national databases, it is difficult to appreciate the value that women create in the public transport sector. This notwithstanding, the continued entrance of women in the sector is a value creation process by itself as these women are creating their space and entrenching it within the public transport sector. For a long time, and due to socio-cultural and historical reasons, women have remained outside of the public transport sector or are involved in operations jobs that are limited to the private arena.

Women in the public transport sector work outside the realm of 'women's work' in what could be termed as 'isolated acts' that question the 'gendered character of capital' (Connell, 2018). These women enter in workspaces traditionally regarded as men's jobs (Turnbull, 2013; Sonal et al., 2017) thereby challenging traditional and patriarchal perspectives of women's work. Connell (2018) in the gender hierarchy theory observed that social practice is innovative and creative, and responds to particular situations generated within definite structures of social relations. According to Khayesi and Nafukho (2016), matatu entrepreneurship is a self-organizing sector with a well-established logic of practice. In this regard, it is important to explore how women fit (if at all) within this logic of practice as either enterprise owners or operators. Connell and Wood (2005) in their notion of 'commercialization of human feeling' note that women are expected to conduct themselves in societally defined ways. This is the case in Kenya where public transport work has for many years been considered to be men's work with women who attempt to join the sector being seen as rebels.

CONCLUSIONS

The salient presence of women workers in the transport sector is beginning to change the character of the sector and the way women in public spaces are perceived. Employment in the sector enables women to create value at the individual, family and societal levels. This is changing the societal notions of work in the sector, as being a purview of men with women increasingly taking up jobs and challenging the hegemonic notions. This is driven by the fact that women are incrementally building their agency through alliances and leveraging other opportunities for upward mobility. Apart from earning income for their households, their decision-making roles are improving through participation in associational life and engagement with external actors, including unions, workers' federations and capacity-building NGOs. These external engagements advance their image as role models and impact on other women and society at large, thereby changing preconceived patriarchal conceptions of women's work. This is also increasing women's visibility in the public sphere.

The use of women's agency has potential to change societal norms, attitudes and rules in the male dominated transport sector. Aspects such as sexual harassment, lack of respect and discrimination are being addressed through women's voices in associations and partnerships with external actors. These connections are extending women's networks that are relevant for advancing their position not only in the transport sector but also in other spheres of life. They are able to save, leverage resources and invest in the transport business, and support the survival of public transport businesses as workers. In their households, they are taking care of their families, supplementing household income and changing the patriarchal conception of the female gender.

ACKNOWLEDGEMENTS

This collaboration project was undertaken jointly by three partner universities: University of Nairobi in Kenya (UoN), Roskilde University in Denmark (RU), and Mzumbe University in Tanzania (MU). The research team included Winnie V. Mitullah and Anne Kamau (UoN), Lone Riisgaard and Nina Tom (RU), and Godbertha Kinyondo (MU). We thank the Paschalin Basil for supporting the research process, the research assistants who supported data collection in Nairobi and Kisumu, and the study participants who spared their time to share with us their knowledge and experiences. We extend our appreciation to the Ministry of Foreign Affairs of Denmark (DANIDA) for not only funding the research but also building the capacity of two PhD students – Raphael Indimuli (UoN) and to Aloyce Gervas (MU).

REFERENCES

Allen, H. (2018). *Gender and urban transport: smart and affordable. Approaches for gender responsive urban mobility sustainable transport: A sourcebook for policy-makers in developing cities module 7a.* Deutsche Gesellschaft für Internationale Zusammenarbeit (GIZ) GmbH and Sustainable Urban Transport Project. http://www.sutp.org/en/resources/ publications-by-topic/social-issues-in-transport.html.

Bailey, S. & Duggan, B. (2020, January 28). Nairobi's matatu minibuses are getting a high-tech makeover. *CNN Innovative Africa feature.* https://edition.cnn.com/2020/01/28/ business/data-integrated-kenya-intl/index.html.

Behrens, R., McCormick, D., Orero, R. & Omme, M. (2017). Improving paratransit service: Lessons from inter-city matatu cooperatives in Kenya. *Transport Policy, 53*, 79–88. https:// doi.org/10.1016/j.tranpol.2016.09.003.

Cervero, R. (2000). *Informal transport in the developing world.* UN-HABITAT. https:// books.google.co.ke/books/about/Informal_Transport_in_the_Developing_Wor.html?id= _4z7AI6XuH8C&redir_esc=y.

Chitere, P. & Kibua, T. (2004). Efforts to improve road safety in Kenya: Achievements and limitations of reforms in the *Matatu* industry. *IPAR Policy Brief on the Matatu Industry in Kenya.*

Connell, R. (2018). *The Social Organization of Masculinity.* Part 1: Theories of Masculinity. London: Sage Publications.

Connell, R.W. & Wood, J. (2005). Globalization and business masculinities. *Men and Masculinities, 7*(4), 347–364. DOI: 10.1177/1097184X03260969.

FIDA (2008). *Documenting Human Rights Violations of Sex Workers in Kenya: A study conducted in Nairobi, Kisumu, Busia, Nanyuki, Mombasa and Malindi.* FIDA Kenya.

GLI (2017). Nairobi bus rapid transit labour impact assessment: A preliminary research and baseline study report. Global Labour Institute (GLI), Manchester, UK.

GLI (2018). Nairobi bus rapid transit: Labour impact assessment research report. Global Labour Institute (GLI), Manchester, UK.

Graeff, J. (2013). *The organization, issues and the future role of the matatu industry in Nairobi, Kenya.* https://nairobiplanninginnovations.files.wordpress.com/2013/02/the-organization -issues-and-the-future-role-of-the-matatu-industry-in-nairobi_kenya.pdf.

Hanlon, S. (2018). *Where do women feature in public transport?* TransAdelaide, Australia. https://www.fhwa.dot.gov/ohim/womens/chap34.pdf.

Heinze, R. (2018). Fighting over urban space: Matatu infrastructure and bus stations in Nairobi, 1960–2000. *Africa Today, 65*(2), 3–22. DOI: 10.2979/africatoday.65.2.02.

ILO (2019). *Women in business and management: A global survey of enterprises.* International Labour Office, Bureau for Employers' Activities (ACT/EMP). ISBN: 978-92-2-132137-8 (print) 978-92-2-132138-5 (web pdf).

ITF (2017). *The Power of Informal Transport Workers.* International Transport Workers Federation (ITF), Education booklet. https://www.itfglobal.org/en/reports-publications/ power-informal-transport-workers.

Kamau, A. (2018, November 22–23). Women transport workers: Social protection and labour issues. In Naomi Mwaura (Moderator), *Understanding Women in Transport* [Panel Discussion]. Women in Transport Conference, Nairobi, Kenya. https://eastafricawit conference.files.wordpress.com/2018/12/anne-kamau.pdf.

Kamau, A. (forthcoming). Informal transport worker organizations and social protection provision in Kenya. In Lone Riisgaard, Winnie Mitullah and Nina Torm (Eds), *Social Protection and Informal Workers in Sub-Saharan Africa: Lived Realities and associational experiences from Tanzania and Kenya.* Routledge, Taylor & Francis.

Kamau, A., Kamau, P., Muia, D., Baiya, H. & and Ndung'u, J. (2018). *Bridging entrepreneurial gender gap through social protection among women small scale traders in Kenya.* In S.

Yousafzai, A. Fayolle, A. Lindgreen, C. Henry, S. Saeed and S. Sheikh (Eds.), *Women's Entrepreneurship and the Myth of 'Underperformance'*. Edward Elgar Publishing.

KELIN (2016). *Punitive Laws Affecting Sex Workers*. KELIN.

Kempe, R. (2014). Informal economic activity in Kenya: Benefits and drawbacks. *African Geographic Review*, *33*(1), 67–80. http://dx.doi.org/10.1080/19376812.2013.838687.

Khayesi, M. & Nafukho, F. (2016). *Informal Public Transport in Practice: Matatu Entrepreneurship*. Routledge.

Kinyanjui, M. (2014). *Women and the Informal Economy in Urban Africa: From the Margins to the Centre*. Zed Books.

KIPPRA (2017). Kenya Economic Report 2017: *Sustaining Kenya's economic development by deepening and expanding economic integration in the region*. Kenya Institute for Public Policy Research and Analysis (KIPPRA).

Klopp, J. (2012). Towards a political economy of transportation policy and practice in Nairobi. *Urban Forum*, *23*, 1–21. DOI 10.1007/s12132-011-9116-y.

KNBS (2019a). *Economic Survey 2019*. Kenya National Bureau of Statistics. ISBN: 978-9966-102-08-9.

KNBS (2019b). *Statistical Abstract 2019*. Kenya National Bureau of Statistics. ISBN: 978-9966-102-10-2.

Koimur, I., Kangogo, L. & Nyaoga, R. (2014). Assessment of commuter preferences of 14-seater public service vehicles versus alternative modes of public service transport in Nairobi city. *Journal of Business, Economics & Finance*, *3*(1), 115–132.

MacKellar, L. (2009). Pension systems for the informal sector in Asia: Social protection and labour, *SP Discussion Paper*, no. 0903. Human Development Network, the World Bank, Washington, DC.

Maina, A. (2016). Improving tax compliance in the informal sector: A case for public transport 'Matatus' in Kenya. African Tax Research Network (ATRN), *Working Paper* 03.

McCormick, D., Mitullah, W., Chitere, P., Orero, R. & Ommeh, M. (2016). Matatu business strategies in Nairobi. In Roger Behrens, Dorothy McCormick and David Mfinanga (Eds), *Paratransit in African Cities: Operations, Regulation and Reform*. Routledge, Taylor & Francis, pp. 125–154.

Mukabana, E. (2016). Kenya bus service history. *Kenya Bus Service Management* http://kenyabus.net/history.html.

Mutongi, K. (2017). *Matatu: A History of Popular Transportation in Nairobi*. University of Chicago Press, ISBN 978-0226471396.

Mwangi, S. (2014). *Gender Relations in Public Road Transport in Africa*. MA thesis, Institute of Diplomacy and International Studies, University of Nairobi.

Nyachieo, G. (2015). *Socio-Cultural and Economic Determinants of Boda Motorcycle Transport Safety in Kisumu County, Kenya*. Doctoral Thesis at Kenyatta University. https://ir-library.ku.ac.ke/handle/123456789/14844.

Nyachieo, G. (2018, January). Exploring public road passenger transport in Kenya. *International Association for the History of Transport, Traffic & Mobility – T²M*. https://t2m.org/exploring-public-road-passenger-transport-in-kenya/.

Oira, A. & Makori, M. (2015). Challenges affecting investment in public transport (matatu) industry in Nairobi, Kenya. *Strategic Journal of Business and Change Management*, *2* (64), 521–558.

Oluochi, J. (2018). Analysis of the economic value of the standard gauge railway (SGR) and its contributions for Kenya. *International Journal of Social Science and Humanities Research*, *6*(2), 740–748.

Rizzo, M. (2017). *Taken for a Ride: Grounding Neoliberalism, Precarious Labour, and Public Transport in an African Metropolis*. Oxford University Press.

RoK (2003). *Legal Notice No. 161: The Traffic Act (Cap. 403)*. Kenya Gazette Supplement No. 79, October 3, 2003 (Legislative Supplement No. 50). Republic of Kenya.

RoK (2012). *Laws of Kenya: The Traffic Act Chapter 403*. Revised Edition 2012 (2010). National Council for Law Reporting with the Authority of the Attorney General.

RoK (2018). *Kenya Comprehensive Public Expenditure Review: From Evidence to Policy*. Government of the Republic of Kenya, the National Treasury and Planning.

Salon, D. & Gulyani, S. (2019). Commuting in urban Kenya: Unpacking travel demand in large and small Kenyan cities. *Sustainability Journal, 11*(14), 3823, 1–22. https://doi.org/10.3390/su11143823.

Sonal, S., Kalpana, V., Sonali, V. & Shreya, G. (2017). Women and transport in Indian cities, ITDP and Safetipin, New Delhi.

Spooner, D. & Whelligan. J. (2017). *The Power of Informal Transport Workers: An ITF Education Booklet*. Global Labour Institute, Manchester. https://www.itfglobal.org/media/1691170/informal-transport-workers.pdf.

Turnbull, P. (2013). *Promoting the employment of women in the transport sector – obstacles and policy options*. International Labour Office, Working Paper No. 298.

Williams, C.C. & Kedir, A.M (2018). Explaining cross-country variations in the prevalence of informal sector competitors: Lessons from the World Bank enterprise survey. *International Entrepreneurship and Management Journal, 15*, 677–696. https://doi.org/10.1007/s11365-018-0527-2.

WISE (ca. 2012). *Women Employment in Urban Public Transport Sector*. European Union Social Partners' project WISE (Women Employment in Urban Public Transport Sector). http://www.wise-project.net/downl/executive_summary_eng.pdf.

Wissenbach, U. & Yuan, W. (2017). African politics meets Chinese engineers: The Chinese-built Standard Gauge Railway Project in Kenya and East Africa. *Working Paper No. 2017/13*. China Africa Research Initiative, School of Advanced International Studies, Johns Hopkins University, Washington, DC. http://www.sais-cari.org/publications.

Wright, T. (2018). *The Impact of the Future of Work for Women in Public Transport*. International Transport Workers Federation (ITF) and Friedrich Ebert Stiftung, Women Transportation in the World.

Yousafzai, S., Saeed, S. & Muffatto, M. (2015). Institutional theory and contextual embeddedness of women's entrepreneurial leadership: Evidence from 92 countries. *Journal of Small Business Management, 53*(3), 1–18. DOI: 10.1111/jsbm.12179.

Zeleza, T. (1988). Women and the labour process in Kenya since independence. *Transafrican Journal of History, 17*, 69–107.

PART III

VALUE CREATION AT THE HOUSEHOLD AND FAMILY LEVEL

11. Becoming an entrepreneur? Early identity formation among migrant women nascent entrepreneurs

Sanaa Talha and Gry Agnete Alsos

With increasing immigrant populations in many countries, governments are encouraging immigrants to engage in entrepreneurial activities as a means for increasing their socioeconomic participation in the host country (Ram & Jones, 2008) and thereby contribute to value creation for themselves and for society. Faced with challenges in the job market, many immigrants turn to entrepreneurship to secure income (Bird & Wennberg, 2016; Mawson & Kasem, 2019). Moreover, being an immigrant and an ethnic minority may also be a source of entrepreneurial opportunities, for example, related to knowledge about co-ethnic markets or to supplier or customer networks in their home country (Chreim et al., 2018). There is increasing research interest in understanding the particular situations of immigrant women, emphasizing their challenges and opportunities related to entrepreneurship (Chreim et al., 2018; De Vita et al., 2014; González-González et al., 2011) and acknowledging the double disadvantage of being a woman and being of a national minority (De Vita et al., 2014).

The emerging literature on immigrant women entrepreneurs emphasizes the resources available to them when setting up a new business, their motivations for entering into entrepreneurship and their strategies related to the new business (Chreim et al., 2018; González-González et al., 2011). Recent research has studied the identity work of immigrant women business owners, particularly describing how migrant women business owners manoeuvre between the dominant familial norms and values within migrant communities and the social expectations related to their role as business owners (Essers et al., 2013). The issue of 'becoming an entrepreneur' is also a process of identity construction, where individuals navigate between their current identities, their own motivations and intentions, and the social expectations they experience. This chapter addresses the early process of developing an entrepreneurial identity among immigrant women entrepreneurs. We seek to better understand how immigrant women construct their initial entrepreneurial identities when working towards setting up a business. As identity forms the basis of social action (Fauchart & Gruber, 2011; Hoang & Gimeno, 2010), the identity development of immigrant women entrepreneurs influences their strategies and hence the type and extent of the value created.

Identity is the lens through which individuals view and make sense of the world. The research on entrepreneurial identity seeks to understand if, how and when individuals see themselves as entrepreneurs, corresponding to certain beliefs, meanings and behaviours. Two dominant perspectives have been used to discuss entrepreneurial identity. Building on role identity theory, some studies have viewed starting a new business as a transition into a new role for which entrepreneurs need to adjust their skills and networks and integrate their role as entrepreneurs into their overall self-concept, with different identities corresponding to different roles (Hoang & Gimeno, 2010). Building on social identity theory, other studies have emphasized entrepreneurial behaviour as being shaped in relation to how entrepreneurs perceive themselves relative to others through social interaction (Fauchart & Gruber, 2011). Social identity theory also points to the heterogeneity in entrepreneurial identity, that is, different entrepreneurs creating different entrepreneurial identities, depending on the social interactions and cultural contexts that are important to them. For instance, identity work can be performed simultaneously in multiple cultural contexts (Essers et al., 2013).

The issue of entrepreneurial identity is being increasingly seen less as something one has and more as a process of becoming (Hytti, 2005; Kasperova & Kitching, 2014). The process of identity formation takes place in an interaction between the entrepreneur and her environment. Hence, when an individual begins working towards establishing a new business, thereby engaging in her own transition into entrepreneurship, she will start to make sense of what it means for her to become an entrepreneur based on her social interactions within the communities of which she is part. Drawing from repeated interviews with 14 immigrant women seeking to start a new business, this chapter examines how nascent entrepreneurs navigate the process of identity formation.

IMMIGRANT WOMEN ENTREPRENEURS

Entrepreneurship is generally associated with men (Bruni, Gherardi & Poggio, 2004). Research on entrepreneurship among immigrants and ethnic minorities has also mainly focused on men entrepreneurs. Since the research on women entre-preneurs has seldom considered ethnicity and that on immigrant entrepreneurs has hardly discussed gender (Abbasian & Yazdanfar, 2013; Essers & Benschop, 2007), the research on immigrant women entrepreneurs is still scarce. However, there is evidence indicating that immigrant women are more likely to become entrepreneurs compared to native women (Collins & Low, 2010; Light & Gold, 2000). Women entrepreneurs may face disadvantages related to gender bias among resource pro-viders in networks and entrepreneurial ecosystem (Brana, 2013; Brush et al., 2019; Malmström et al., 2017). Having suffered years of subordination based on gender, female entrepreneurs sometimes perceive and behave in stereotypical manners (Fischlmayr, 2002). The literature indicates that immigrant women face even more obstacles in pursuing entrepreneurship than native women, sometimes referred to as 'the double burden' (De Vita et al., 2014).

Immigration itself creates an identity void, which presumably is filled by association and engagement in the country of settlement (Timotijevic & Breakwell, 2000). The displacement causes individuals to seek new meaning and purpose in life. This, combined with the lack of formal employment opportunities, aids the formation of entrepreneurial intentions among immigrants. The literature on mixed embeddedness emphasizes that ethnicity facilitates entrepreneurship by providing access to ethnic-based resources. While this literature helps in understanding the opportunity structures in the environment of immigrant entrepreneurs, it also tends to underestimate the effect of structures related to class and gender (Valdez, 2016). The intersection of ethnicity and gender influences entrepreneurship in specific ways (Chreim et al., 2018). Women immigrants are often not considered potential entrepreneurs by resource providers, their ethnic communities, their families, or themselves (Abbasian & Yazdanfar, 2013; Chreim et al., 2018; Essers et al., 2013). The boundaries of religious, cultural, and institutional gender models typically lead women immigrants to put their roles as mothers, spouses, daughters, and/or housewives ahead of their role as entrepreneurs (González-González et al., 2011; Robichaud et al., 2015). Immigrant women taking the initiative to start a new venture and become entrepreneurs must navigate the expectations of others and themselves when seeking to develop their entrepreneurial identity.

ENTREPRENEURIAL IDENTITY

Entrepreneurial identity is put forward as a concept to help understand how an individual views herself and is viewed by others as an entrepreneur. Identity is defined as a set of personal and behavioural beliefs and characteristics that form one's personality and connect her to a certain group (Collins, 2000). Furthermore, an individual's identity is related to her social relationships, particularly to her membership in social groups (Fauchart & Gruber, 2011). At any point in time, an individual holds multiple identities, for example, as a mother, wife, chorus member, and entrepreneur. Multiple identities translate into multiple meanings that may be complementary or conflicting.

Entrepreneurial identity can be defined as the set of beliefs, attitudes and mindset of a person that identifies them in an entrepreneurial role (Shepherd & Patzelt, 2018). Becoming an entrepreneur typically requires individuals to transition to a new work role as an entrepreneur and thereby develop an entrepreneurial identity (Hoang & Gimeno, 2010). In this process, entrepreneurial identity is formed and reformed under the influence of surroundings and perceptions about oneself and becomes evident by actions (Farmer et al., 2011). There is a strong discourse on 'self' in the entrepreneurship literature, linking entrepreneurial identity to entrepreneurial intentions, actions and outcomes (Jenkins, 2014). However, identity differs from self, as self consists of the cognitive dimension, that is, perception of oneself, while identity includes the concept of self as well as the internalization of these perceptions on multiple levels and contexts (Zacarés & Iborra, 2015). An individual seeking to become an entrepreneur engages in identity work, and her 'self' evolves and changes, changing her attitudes, beliefs, intentions, willingness to act, and eventually her behaviours (Duening, 2017). Hence, identity work is an important element of the entrepreneurial process.

Entrepreneurial identity is considered to include individual values related to value creation, respect for the market and customer needs, and resilience (Duening, 2017). However, the types of value creation sought and how customers are in focus may differ between entrepreneurs with different entrepreneurial identities (Fauchart & Gruber, 2011). For the purpose of this study, we build on the founder identity framework developed by Fauchart and Gruber (2011). Based on social identity theory, this framework distinguishes between three dimensions of identity: (i) basic social motivation, (ii) basis for self-evaluation, and (iii) frame of reference (cf. Brewer & Gardner, 1996). Basic social motivation refers to the main reason why an individual engages in a new business start-up, the basis for self-evaluation refers to the element that the entrepreneur uses to judge herself, and the frame of reference describes how and in relation to whom the entrepreneur derives self-worth (Sieger et al., 2016). Fauchart and Gruber (2011) identified three different types of entrepreneurial identity, which they named Darwinians, Communitarians, and Missionaries. Darwinians are entrepreneurs who are mainly motivated by their self-interest, evaluate themselves based on their professionalism, and use their competitors as their main frame of reference. In contrast, communitarians' basic motivation is to support and be supported by the community to which they belong, evaluate themselves based on authenticity in this community, and use the community that benefits from the product as their frame of reference. Finally, missionaries are those entrepreneurs who derive motivation by advancing a cause in which they believe, evaluate themselves based on responsible behaviour, and use society as their frame of reference. Later research indicates that these three archetypes (and their hybrids) can be found empirically and that they differ in terms of behaviours as entrepreneurs (Alsos et al., 2016).

We use this framework as an analytical tool when analysing the emergent entrepreneurial identities of immigrant women entrepreneurs. Fauchart and Gruber (2011) developed this framework based on (mainly men) entrepreneurs in the sports-related equipment industry. Hence, our analyses will test the boundaries of these concepts by applying them to a very different group of entrepreneurs. There are many reasons to believe that our sample may differ in terms of entrepreneurial identity construction compared to that of sports-equipment entrepreneurs. First, since our sample consists of all women, conflicting identities related to women's familial roles may influence entrepreneurial identity in different ways (Van Staveren & Odebode, 2007). For example, researchers have pointed out that women's motherhood identity may influence the way in which they conduct entrepreneurship (Leung, 2011). Furthermore, as immigrant women, they shape their entrepreneurial identities at the intersection of gender, ethnicity and entrepreneurship while negotiating with different constituencies (Essers & Benschop, 2007), performing their identity work in multiple cultural contexts (Essers et al., 2013). Consequently, social motivation, self-evaluation and frames of reference may correspond to different stimuli and produce different outcomes.

METHOD

The study aims at forming new insights based on an existing theoretical base and hence is abductive in nature. Such reasoning is appropriate for this study, as it started out by reviewing the existing literature and theories on entrepreneurial identity and with the current understanding of entrepreneurship by immigrant women. Then, we selected the founders identity framework developed by Fauchart and Gruber (2011) as the basis of our identity exploration.

Sample Selection

The study aims to explore entrepreneurial identity development by immigrant women nascent entrepreneurs at the beginning of the entrepreneurial process. We build on 14 real-life cases of immigrant women in the process of becoming entrepreneurs. These cases were identified from two incubators for immigrant entrepreneurs located in Oslo, Norway, both of which focus on immigrant entrepreneurs. Norway provides a rather balanced setting to study immigrant women since the welfare state hosts many immigrants and refugees who are provided with basic living benefits. Additionally, Norway is ranked among the countries with the highest level of gender equality, although there are quite visible gender differences in engagement in entrepreneurial activities (Alsos et al., 2016).

The cases were selected on the basis of the following criteria: the women should (i) be nascent entrepreneurs, that is, in the early stages of seeking to establish a new business, (ii) have an immigrant background, (iii) have lived in Norway for more than two years, and (iv) have completed basic education. Among the 14 women selected, two distinct sets of immigrant profiles were identified; seven out of 14 are first-generation immigrants who have recently arrived in Norway (less than five years ago). These women have come for either job prospects or have joined their partners in Norway. The other set comprises women who have lived in Norway for more than 20 years and now have Norwegian citizenship. They typically moved to the country at a very young age as refugees with their families. Furthermore, the women have varying demographic profiles. Some women in the first group have prior entrepreneurial experience in their own country but are starting fresh in Norway. They have various countries of origin, including five who were born in Somalia and five immigrants from European countries.

Data Collection

A semi-structured interview guide for the collection of empirical data was developed and used as a guideline during the interviews while allowing informants to freely tell their stories. The interview guide was designed on the basis of the relevant theories to be studied, that is, the social identity of the immigrant women, their experiences living in Norway, how and why they thought of starting their own ventures, what they want to achieve in life and with their ventures, their understanding of the role of an entrepreneur, and so on. The mode of data collection was face-to-face interviews and observations. One interview was conducted via telephone. For quality purposes, all except the telephonic interview were recorded. The informants were interviewed at two points seven months apart. During the initial round of interviews, the participants were given a clear understanding of the study and how the data would be used. The interviews lasted between 45 and 60 minutes each.

Data Analysis

An iterative process was applied to analyse the data, which alternated between premises derived from the literature and those arising from the data. The interviews were transcribed manually. We initially made Table 11.1 on the basis of the demographic profiles of the informant. The second phase involved rigorous scrutiny of the transcription to find specific answers related to the interview guide. The data were condensed, and the similarities and differences in responses were noted manually. The standout phrases and responses were highlighted and put in separate files to be coded later to make a data matrix. The coding was done manually by identifying similar responses from the entrepreneurs. They were later categorized and subcategorized based on the founder's identity framework. However, some responses did not correspond to any criteria in the founder's identity framework and hence were separately categorized and coded.

FINDINGS

Based on the responses from the interviewed immigrant women entrepreneurs, the following themes were highlighted: (i) motivations for starting their ventures, (ii) the role of their family in venture creation, (iii) their desired outcomes, (iv) their criteria for success, (v) the challenges they have they faced on the basis of gender and immigrant status, (vi) their experience living in the country of settlement. For the purpose of the current study, the motivations, criteria for success and desired outcomes are the focus. Building on the founders identity framework (Fauchart & Gruber, 2011), we analysed entrepreneurs' identity based on basic social motivation, measure of success, and frame of reference.

Basic Social Motivations

Based on the data collected regarding the inspirations for their ventures, three subcategories were identified in terms of basic social motivation: (i) self-/family interest, (ii) community consciousness, and (iii) social responsibility. The findings are illustrated with representative quotes in Table 11.2.

Table 11.1   Overview of cases

Sr. #	Immigrant Background	Age	Years in Norway	Reason for Migration	Education	Current Occupation	Marital Status	Children
1	Bulgaria	25–30	2	Moved with partner	Master's	Part-time and volunteer work	Partner	0
2	Burundi	25–30	12	Job	Bachelor's in process	Part-time and volunteer work	Partner	0
3	Czech Republic	35–40	5	Moved with partner	Master's	Part-time and volunteer work	Married	1
4	France	30–35	4	Moved with partner	Master's	Working in marketing	Partner	0
5	Indian	30–35	3	Moved with partner	Medical doctor	Housewife	Married	1
6	Indian	35–40	4	Moved with partner	Master's	Part-time and volunteer work	Married	1
7	Macedonia	25–30	2	Job	Master's	Part-time and volunteer work	Single	0
8	Pakistan	30–35	30	Family immigration	Master's	Housewife	Married	3
9	Romania	30–35	5	Job	Master's	Part-time and volunteer work	Partner	0
10	Somalia	25–30	20	Refugee	Bachelor's	Part-time work	Married	2
11	Somalia	25–30	20	Refugee	Bachelor's in process	Freelance photographer	Single	0
12	Somalia	30–35	30	Refugee	Bachelor's in process	Part-time work in various shops	Single	1
13	Somalia	30–35	30	Refugee	Nursing	Nurse	Married	2
14	Somalia	35–40	25	Refugee	Nursing	Social worker	Married	2

(i)   Self-/family interest

Personal, family or peer influenced reasons were among the top motivations for these entrepreneurs, per the data collected. Respondents were quick to respond with 'financial stability' as an obvious motivation for their ventures (Table 11.2, SR.1). Almost all respondents mentioned that in this day and age, financial independence for women is undoubtedly the most important.

The stronger basis of motivation quoted by several respondents was self-/personal growth and development, which meant different things to different women, such as adding to knowledge and skill sets, building competent professional identities and improving the chances of being hired in a larger organization. Some argued that peace of mind and building self-confidence are strong motivators (Table 11.2, SR.1). Others said that having the experience to manage a venture in itself is a valuable personal achievement. In addition, these same respondents explained that it is more important for them to have independence than anything else.

Another frequently quoted motivational factor was the family dynamics aspect. Most of the respondents were mothers and, as such, plainly stated that 'family comes

Table 11.2   *Representative quotes of three types of basic social motivation*

	SR. 1: Self-/Family Interest	SR. 2: Community Consciousness	SR. 3: Social Responsibility
	'I do not want to become a part of the social security system.' (# 14)	*'I am a vegan, and I know how hard it is for us to find something good while on trips.' (# 10)*	*'It is like no justice for people from developing countries; they cannot compete internationally.' (# 14)*
	'Situations change so quickly that you cannot wait for others to help.' (# 8)	*'You can see in the news now that we have different needs; I have some knowledge, and I can help women like me.' (# 1)*	*'The system does not really work; they help them get clean and they leave them on the streets again.' (# 9)*
	'I am focusing on me—who I am and trying to be true to myself.' (# 4)		*'You see people struggle for jobs, but organizations, such as Nav, do not help properly.' (# 2)*
Motivation/ Purpose	*'I did not want to leave my daughter with others... I can work on my own time.' (# 3)*		
	'Right now, I have enough time to work on the venture and go home and give my partner time.... You know, getting a job is the end goal.' (# 6)		
	'I have an IT background, and this is teaching me management, strategy, and finance, all reinforcing my current skills.' (# 5)		
	'I think people will know us through our networks.' (# 8)		

first', and hence, in relation to a small-scale entrepreneurial venture, it seems to be a good fit to manage family responsibilities along with satisfying one's own need to be productive (Table 11.2, SR.1). Freedom to work from home was highly appreciated by a few respondents. However, a stronger motivation was to become a role model for their children.

Some mentioned the importance of social integration and networking via the entrepreneurial venture. Making new friends and acquaintances along with building PR in professional circles was considered important.

(ii)   Community consciousness

Another distinct type of primary motivation was derived from their social consciousness. This meant that the motivation came from serving either their ethnic community or some group with which they associated and identified. For these women, the value lies in helping the less privileged, and they said that serving the community provides a sense of satisfaction and achievement (Table 11.2, SR.2).

Table 11.3   Representative quotes of basis of self-evaluation

	SR.1: Personal Achievement	SR.2: Community Building	SR.3: Social Accountability
	'I always had a need for approval; it is a cultural thing. The success I have achieved, well it was what was missing from self, gave me new confidence.' (# 4)	*'I feel I am privileged to have an education; I feel we have a responsibility to give back.' (# 9)*	*'If I am part of this community, I have a responsibility to act responsibly…you know.' (# 9)*
	'It is the most important thing right now; I need to make it to show myself I can do it. With things going wrong in my life, this is kind of my rock.' *'The people you meet along the way build up the business.' (# 8)*	*'You see women just like yourself, struggling in this country…but you see it more and want to do something.'* *'I have found so many women who appreciate what I am doing, so I am on the right track.' (# 4)*	*'We have to help each other out; we need to build society. If I help even one, I will achieve something.' (# 3)*
Measure of Success	*'Of course this is mine; it is just like my baby. It is very important for my growth, and I have learnt so much in the last 6 months. I have matured.' (# 10)* *'My father treated his daughters better than my brothers; he would be proud of me for this.' (# 2)* *'I do this because I do not want my children to fall in the problems of society. This will give them as well as myself confidence.' (# 3)*	*'Ultimately, the aim is earning money, but if you get to help out a few along the way, what can be better than that?' (# 6)*	*'Make the difference; we change the flawed system for immigrants, and we try to fix it.' (# 2)*

(iii)   Societal responsibility

Taking social consciousness to the next level, some informants were either motivated to serve people or had found a solution to a general problem (Table 11.2, SR.3). Two respondents from refugee backgrounds strongly suggested that the legal systems were somewhat flawed for minority groups and were keen to improve them. One of these women was very critical towards the reintegration programmes for substance abusers. Furthermore, reducing social inequality in the international job market was another motivation.

Measure of Success

Three distinct categories can be observed from the interviews that relate to entrepreneurs' self-assessment: personal achievement, community building and social accountability. These three categories are related to how these entrepreneurs would judge the success of their business when started and what would define them as successful in the efforts they now are initiating. For representative quotes, see Table 11.3.

(i)   Personal achievement

Respondents in this category based their evaluation of success on how it affected them personally. Several mentioned the importance of being self-satisfied and content with their lives. They were more concerned about their own thoughts and feelings than market dynamics (Table 11.3, SR.1). Interestingly, making large amounts of money became a secondary priority for these entrepreneurs in comparison to being content. Individuals more inclined towards their personal growth evaluated their self-worth through their own performance. They make benchmarks for themselves and feel satisfied outclassing their own prior achievements. However, for others, feedback from their family seemed central to their idea of success (Table 11.3, SR.1). One respondent mentioned her close bond with her father and that his opinion was the one she valued most. Another stated that, for her, taking proper care of her children and seeing that they do not fall in the pitfalls of the society is reward enough. Some suggested that the quality and strength of their social networks is also an important evaluator for success.

(ii)   Community building

This group evaluated themselves from a world view perspective, stating that social or collective recognition is a means for strong identity creation (Table 11.3, SR.2). These respondents stated that the feedback from those being served held great importance. Such women were driven by fulfilling community needs with the best alternative social entrepreneurs. Some respondents stated that making money while helping others is the best profession, where one obtains financial benefits along with mental satisfaction.

(iii)   Social accountability

The third evaluation mechanism is the social accountability of the entrepreneur or the venture as a whole. Several respondents mentioned their motivation coming from gaps noticed in the system catering to minority groups, meaning that the overall value for them was to bring about some positive change in society at large (Table 11.3, SR.3).

Frame of Reference

The final aspect studied was the frame of reference, that is, the value benchmark or desired outcome on a personal, community or societal level. Based on the responses, three levels were identified: (i) self-/relational awareness, (ii) collective progression and (iii) system accountability. From the interview data, we saw that hardly any of the women referred to competitors as their benchmark. They used terms such as 'we want to do good in the market' or 'of course I would like to succeed', but they did not refer to their competitors. The findings are illustrated with representative quotes in Table 11.4.

Table 11.4   Representative quotes of frame of reference

	SR.1: Self/Family Awareness	SR.2: Collective Progression	SR.3: System Accountability
	'My daughter is the most important thing in my life right now, so I want to be a role model for her.' (# 1)	*'When you apply everywhere without answers, sooner or later you feel there is something wrong with you since no one calls you back.'* (# 10)	*'When systems are failing people, people have to take a stand; I see the issue, I see the problems, and I can do something about it.'* (# 9)
Frame of Reference	*'Of course, my family. I want to settle here and have a business so my brothers and their children can also have a good life.'* (# 12)	*'With this, I am helping all those, not only immigrants, all who want to feel connected to others; they can be part of activities they like.'* (# 11)	*'I know how difficult it was for us; I want to change how authorities see us. They want to help but they do not understand our problems.'* (# 2)
	'If I am not well, how can I take care of my son or be with my husband? I am doing this for me so I can take care of them.' (# 4)		*'I have lived in many different places and seen so much inequality that it hit me: I want to create a level playing field.'* (# 8)

(i)   Self-/family awareness

Strengthening personal and household levels was most commonly identified as the desired outcome. Some mentioned that financial stability and independence for women is very important, but more were highly concerned about their family's well-being (Table 11.4, SR.1). These participants mentioned self-interest as a motivation for their ventures; however, their desired outcome was rather the well-being of their family, and they referred to their family repeatedly throughout the conversation. Furthermore, self-contentment was another major context for the value perspective.

(ii)   Collective progression

Some women were very keen on making a difference in the lives of the people with whom they identified (Table 11.3, SR.2). A few of the participants are working in a specialized employment agency for other immigrant women. They said that they know what it feels like to be new in a new country and not be able to fit in. These women are more concerned about the people they want to serve.

(iii)   System accountability

Two participants in particular talked repeatedly about the lack of proper procedures and systems for minority groups and that they wished to bring about a change in the system so everyone is treated equally and has equal opportunity in a real sense (Table 11.4, SR.3). Another participant spoke passionately about the international market regulations or the lack thereof. She mentioned the outsourcing services to developing countries and the wage differences and said that she aims to bring the world market to a level playing field, at least for international workers (Table 11.4, SR.3).

Table 11.5   *Types of entrepreneurial identities among immigrant women nascent entrepreneurs*

	Self- and family-focused	Immigrant communitarians	Social missionaries
Basic social motivation	Self-/family interest	Community consciousness	Societal responsibility
Basis for evaluation	Personal achievement	Community building	Social accountability
Frame of reference	Self/family	Immigrant community	System

DISCUSSION

The focus of this study was to investigate the entrepreneurial identity formation of immigrant women in the early stages of setting up business ventures in relation to the founders identity framework. Fauchart and Gruber (2011) presented three distinct founders identities: Darwinians, Communitarians and Missionaries. The three vary in terms of motivations, evaluation and frame of reference. Whereas Darwinians are driven by self-interest and evaluate their success on the basis of competition, communitarians are driven by community support and measure their success on the basis of benefits to the community, and missionaries are concerned with the overall good of society.

The findings of this study suggest that the entrepreneurial identity types of immigrant women only partly correspond to the three defined founders' identities. The findings are based on the motivations, measures of success and desired outcomes relative to the social motivations, self-evaluation and frame of reference in the original framework. The findings are summarized in Table 11.5.

The first type of identity, *self- and family-focused entrepreneurs*, refers to the archetype that has their self- and/or family interest as their main basic motivation; these entrepreneurs seek to evaluate their success based on their personal achievements for themselves and their family and use their self and their family as their frame of reference. At first sight, these can look like Darwinians; however, they behave very differently compared to how Darwinians are described by Fauchart and Gruber (2011). In this case, self-interest was not predominantly linked to money or wealth. Instead, it was linked to personal and mental growth and more evidently to the familial roles of the women. We observed that mothers typically translate their self-interest in terms of how they can improve the standard of living for their family, become role models for their children and/or protect them from the ills of society. The basis for evaluations also deviated from Darwinians. Instead of evaluating themselves on the basis of business competencies, immigrant women entrepreneurs measured their success in terms of family approval and personal growth. They believed that their ventures gave value to their roles as daughters, wives and mothers. Positive reinforcements from the family meant they were successful. Furthermore, they were interested in developing a stronger self. This is particularly important, as we know from the literature that the concept of self is the perception of one's being that stems the identity by internalization (Zacarés & Iborra, 2015). For these women, an increasing self-understanding as entrepreneurs strengthened their confidence as entrepreneurs, a reciprocal cycle of identity and venture formation. The frame of reference also varied for these immigrant women entrepreneurs. Per the original framework, self-interested individuals saw value in relation to their competitors. From the results above, it was again based mostly on the family level, that the desired outcome was the improved quality of life and well-being of their families.

As mentioned above, many of the immigrant women who derived their motivations on self-interest based their success and value on their family's well-being rather than on financial or competitive success. Individuals may struggle with having multiple identities, and not having a balance between these identities may cause problems (Chasserio et al., 2014). Being wives and mothers put them in roles and responsibilities that they did not fully understand or accept. This presented the other side of the spectrum, that is, the motivation stemmed from the imbalance of 'self' and had the desired outcome as personal development. Several women said that they are doing it for their mental health and development so that they can take care of their family eventually.

The second category of entrepreneurial identity we termed as *immigrant communitarians*. Similar to the Communitarians in Fauchart and Gruber's (2011) framework, the motivation of immigrant communitarians lies in the support for and from the community. For the entrepreneurs in this study, the community in focus were a group of immigrants, either their ethnic group or immigrants more broadly. Hence, the findings suggest that immigrant women are highly influenced by their ethnic communities. They identified needs within their ethnic community that they aimed to fulfil. These ethnic communities serve as markets as well as support systems for these women. However, some of these women were relatively new immigrants and not yet very culturally connected. Hence, their ideas were related to the communities of which they were part, such as women who moved with their partners, women with heath issues or the vegan community. Many of those with a community focus had derived their ideas from the gaps and opportunities noted within their ethnic communities. This means that having an immigrant identity played a major role in developing their entrepreneurial identity.

The third type of entrepreneurial identity, *social missionaries*, shares many similarities with missionaries. They are motivated by a societal goal, or a societal responsibility, which typically involves some unfairness or perceived faults in the system, which they have detected, that make people suffer. They evaluate themselves based on social accountability and have some sort of 'system' as their frame of reference.

CONCLUSIONS

This study has analysed the initial entrepreneurial identities of immigrant women entrepreneurs in Norway. The findings reveal three distinct types of entrepreneurial identities that partly, but not fully, overlap with the founder identity framework put forward by Fauchart and Gruber (2011) and adopted by Sieger et al. (2016) and

Alsos et al. (2016). We see these findings as contributing to the literature in three basic ways. First, they add to the understanding of immigrant women entrepreneurs by showing how their individual mixture of social contexts contributes to the development of their entrepreneurial identity. Our study supports the importance of family relations and embeddedness in their ethnic community and/or the broader immigrant community for the entrepreneurial identity developed (Essers et al., 2013). Second, the results contribute to the discussion of entrepreneurial identity by identifying distinct forms of identity formation among a group of entrepreneurs seldom included in the mainstream entrepreneurship research. We thereby shed light on the motivations and identities developed by immigrant women entrepreneurs. Third, we add to the discussion on the value creation of immigrant women entrepreneurs. We point to the influences on identity development as factors with implications for value creation. We also highlight the various types of value that women entrepreneurs aim to create for their families, their communities and the wider society.

BIBLIOGRAPHY

Abbasian, S. & Yazdanfar, D. (2013). Exploring the financing gap between native born women- and immigrant women-owned firms at the start-up stage: Empirical evidence from Swedish data. *International Journal of Gender and Entrepreneurship*, 5(2), 157–173.

Alsos, G.A., Clausen, T.H., Hytti, U. & Solvoll, S. (2016). Entrepreneurs' social identity and the preference of causal and effectual behaviours in start-up processes. *Entrepreneurship & Regional Development*, 28(3–4), 234–258.

Bird, M. & Wennberg, K. (2016). Why family matters: The impact of family resources on immigrant entrepreneurs' exit from entrepreneurship. *Journal of Business Venturing*, 31(6), 687–704.

Brana, S. (2013). Microcredit: An answer to the gender problem in funding? *Small Business Economics*, 40(1), 87–100.

Brewer, M.B. & Gardner, W. (1996). Who is this 'we'? Levels of collective identity and self representations. *Journal of Personality and Social Psychology*, 71(1), 83–93.

Bruni, A., Gherardi, S. & Poggio, B. (2004). Entrepreneur-mentality, gender and the study of women entrepreneurs. *Journal of Organizational Change Management*, 17(3), 256–268.

Brush, C., Edelman, L.F., Manolova, T. & Welter, F. (2019). A gendered look at entrepreneurship ecosystems. *Small Business Economics*, 53(2), 393–408.

Chasserio, S., Pailot, P. & Poroli, C. (2014). When entrepreneurial identity meets multiple social identities. *International Journal of Entrepreneurship Behavior & Research*, 20(2), 128–154.

Chreim, S., Spence, M., Crick, D. & Liao, X. (2018). Review of female immigrant entrepreneurship research: Past findings, gaps and ways forward. *European Management Journal*, 36(2), 210–222.

Collins, J. & Low, A. (2010). Asian female immigrant entrepreneurs in small and medium-sized businesses in Australia. *Entrepreneurship & Regional Development*, 22(1), 97–111.

Collins, J.F. (2000). Biracial Japanese American identity: An evolving process. *Cultural Diversity and Ethnic Minority Psychology*, 6(2), 115–133.

De Vita, L., Mari, M. & Poggesi, S. (2014). Women entrepreneurs in and from developing countries: Evidences from the literature. *European Management Journal*, 32(3), 451–460.

Duening, T.N. (2017). Entrepreneurial identity: Professional virtues moderate attraction and persistance. In T.N. Duening & M.L. Metzger (eds), *Entrepreneurial Identity: The Process of Becoming an Entrepreneur* (pp. 1–30). Edward Elgar Publishing.

Essers, C. & Benschop, Y. (2007). Enterprising identities: Female entrepreneurs of Moroccan or Turkish origin in the Netherlands. *Organization Studies*, 28(1), 49–69.

Essers, C., Doorewaard, H. & Benschop, Y. (2013). Family ties: Migrant female business owners doing identity work on the public–private divide. *Human Relations*, 66(12), 1645–1665.

Farmer, S.M., Yao, X. & Kung-Mcintyre, K. (2011). The behavioral impact of entrepreneur identity aspiration and prior entrepreneurial experience. *Entrepreneurship Theory and Practice*, 35(2), 245–273.

Fauchart, E. & Gruber, M. (2011). Darwinians, Communitarians, and Missionaries: The role of founder identity in entrepreneurship. *Academy of Management Journal*, 54(5), 935–957.

Fischlmayr, I. (2002). Female self-perception as barrier to international careers? *International Journal of Human Resource Management*, 13(5), 773–783.

Foss, L. (2004). Going against the grain…: Construction of entrepreneurial identity through narratives. In D. Hjorth & C. Steyaert (eds), *Narrative and Discursive Approaches in Entrepreneurship* (pp. 80–104). Edward Elgar Publishing.

Giudice, M. (2015). Gender differences in personality and social behavior. In J.D. Wright (ed.), *International Encyclopedia of the Social and Behavioral Sciences* (2nd ed., pp. 750–756). Elsevier.

González-González, J.M., Bretones, F.D., Zarco, V. & Rodríguez, A. (2011). Women, immigration and entrepreneurship in Spain: A confluence of debates in the face of a complex reality. *Women's Studies International Forum*, 34(5), 360–370.

Gunnerud, B. (1997). Gender, place and entrepreneurship. *Entrepreneurship & Regional Development*, 9(3), 259–268.

Hoang, H. & Gimeno, J. (2010). Becoming a founder: How founder role identity affects entrepreneurial transitions and persistence in founding. *Journal of Business Venturing*, 25(1), 41–53.

Hytti, U. (2005). New meanings for entrepreneurs: From risk-taking heroes to safe-seeking professionals. *Journal of Organizational Change Management*, 8(6), 594–611.

Jenkins, R. (2014). *Social Identity* (3rd ed.). Routledge. Retrieved from https://www.yourhomeworksolutions.com/wp-content/uploads/edd/2018/08/social_identity__richard_jenkins.pdf.

Kasperova, E. & Kitching, J. (2014). Embodying entrepreneurial identity. *International Journal of Entrepreneurial Behaviour & Research*, 20(5), 438–452.

Leung, A. (2011). Motherhood and entrepreneurship: Gender role identity as a resource. *International Journal of Gender and Entrepreneurship*, 3(3), 254–264.

Lewis, P. (2013). The search for an authentic entrepreneurial identity: difference and professionalism among women business owners. *Gender, Work and Organization*, 20(3), 252–266.

Light, I. & Gold, S. (2000). *Ethnic Economies*. Academic Press.

Malmström, M., Johansson, J. & Wincent, J. (2017). Gender stereotypes and venture support decisions: How governmental venture capitalists socially construct entrepreneurs' potential. *Entrepreneurship Theory and Practice*, 41(5), 833–860.

Mawson, S. & Kasem, L. (2019). Exploring the entrepreneurial intentions of Syrian refugees in the UK. *International Journal of Entrepreneurial Behavior & Research*, 25(5), 1128–1146.

Ram, M. & Jones, T. (2008). Ethnic-minority businesses in the UK: A review of research and policy developments. *Environment and Planning. Government and Policy*, 26(2), 352–374.

Robichaud, Y., Cachon, J.C. & McGraw, E. (2015). Why are female-owned businesses smaller? An empirical study in Canada and the United States. *Journal of Management Policy and Practice*, 16(1), 62–75.

Shepherd, D.A. & Patzelt, H. (2018). Entrepreneurial identity. In D.A. Shepherd & H. Patzelt (eds), *Entrepreneurial Cognition* (pp. 137–200). Palgrave Macmillan, Cham. https://doi.org/10.1007/978-3-319-71782-1_5.

Sieger, P., Gruber, M., Fauchart, E. & Zellweger, T. (2016). Measuring the social identity of entrepreneurs: Scale development and international validation. *Journal of Business Venturing*, 31(5), 542–572.

Timotijevic, L. & Breakwell, G.M. (2000). Migration and threat to identity. *Journal of Community & Applied Social Psychology*, 10(5), 355–372.

Valdez, I. (2016). Punishment, race, and the organization of US immigration exclusion. *Political Research Quarterly*, 69(4), 640–654.

Van Staveren, I. & Odebode, O. (2007). Gender norms as asymmetric institutions: A case study of Yoruba women in Nigeria. *Journal of Economic Issues*, 41(4), 903–925.

Warren, L. (2004). Negotiating entrepreneurial identity: communities of practice and changing discourses. *The International Journal of Entrepreneurship and Innovation*, 5(1), 25–35.

Zacarés, J.J. & Iborra, A. (2015). Self and identity development during adolescence across cultures. In J.D. Wright (ed.), *International Encyclopedia of the Social & Behavioral Sciences* (pp. 432–438). Elsevier.

12. Migrant women entrepreneurs and value creation: narratives of household and community contribution in the British ethnic economy

Milka Kwiatek and Maria Villares-Varela

INTRODUCTION

This chapter presents the perspectives of migrant women entrepreneurs in the UK in relation to the impact of their ventures on generating a meaningful contribution beyond the economic dividend on the household and community levels. Drawing on four in-depth biographical narratives and a selection of participant-produced photographs, we provide an academic platform to migrant women entrepreneurs to present their experiences of entrepreneurship, social value creation and facilitating the process of forging ties of belonging.[1]

Although women make up almost half of international migrants worldwide (49%) and outnumber male migrants in the global North (UN 2017), scholarly work tends to represent female migrants as dependent on their husbands and fathers and underplay their contributions to the productive and reproductive spheres of both countries of destination and origin (Hondagneu-Sotelo 2003). In addition, the fields of migrant entrepreneurship and gender and enterprise have largely overlooked the role of women in the ethnic economy with core theoretical approaches neglecting gendered social structures that shape both migration and entrepreneurship (Ram et al. 2017).

At the time of writing, the UK is immersed in a post-Brexit referendum climate which has placed immigrants at the core of the debates about belonging, citizenship, deservingness and value. The so-called 'hostile environment' initiated by Theresa May, Home Secretary (2010–2016), expanded the ongoing securitization of migration (Lewis et al. 2017). Whilst academic evidence overwhelmingly points out the financial benefits of immigration (Dustmann and Fratini 2013), in the political rhetoric migrants are generally portrayed as dependant on welfare provision and a threat to social cohesion. The only 'deserving' foreigners in this overwhelmingly negative narrative of immigration are those who bring the 'valuable' skills that the British economy needs. However, the definition of 'valuable' is a contentious term and charged with both gendered (Kofman 2014) and class-based conceptions of contribution. Moreover, in these debates, migrant entrepreneurs and their activities are generally ignored.

We argue that these entrepreneurial undertakings should be revisited under what Zhou (2004) highlighted as the non-economic effects of migrant entrepreneurship.

This author suggested in a pivotal paper in the field that the 'noneconomic effects of ethnic entrepreneurship develop an important idea which is noted in the literature but has not been taken seriously, namely that immigrant enterprise can have social effects that go well beyond the economic success of individual entrepreneurs' (Zhou 2004: 1066). Our analyses depart from Jones, Ram and Villares-Varela's (2019) paper which looks at the contribution of migrant entrepreneurs beyond the economic dividend by bringing the voices of women entrepreneurs into the debate.

The chapter is structured as follows: the first part sketches a brief overview of the conceptualizations of value in migrant women entrepreneurship scholarship. What follows is a synopsis of our implemented methodology and the presentation of our case studies. In the second part, we discuss our findings, exploring in detail the two levels of value creation (household and community) that emerge from our participants' accounts.

REVIEW OF THE LITERATURE: (WOMEN) MIGRANT ENTREPRENEURS AND THE CONCEPTUALIZATION OF VALUE

Hair and beauty salons, child-care provision companies, cafes and the selling of traditional clothing, are amongst the businesses that we have in our imaginaries when thinking of migrant women entrepreneurs. These ventures are generally characterized by being of small size and located in saturated sectors of the economy in what are considered as 'low revenue/low value' activities. Early research in the field has pointed out the 'inadequacies' of women's enterprises, suffering the shortcomings of being simultaneously female- and foreigner-owned. Scholars have highlighted how women are more likely to be underfunded (Abbasian and Yazdanfar 2013) and, although they might have higher levels of education and professional experience than their male counterparts, they are more dependent on co-ethnic custom in the service sector (Baycan et al. 2003; for a review of differences between men and women migrant entrepreneurs in the literature see Villares-Varela et al. 2017). Policies supporting migrant women entrepreneurs have followed suit, by trying to 'fix' their underperformance to be similar to men (Taylor and Marlow 2009: 1).

However, these assumptions imply a very narrow conceptualization of value creation (Jones et al. 2017). Responding to this handbook call (Yousafzai et al. 2018), our chapter addresses the reconceptualization of value by giving voice to UK-based migrant women entrepreneurs. We have discussed elsewhere (Jones et al. 2019) how the growing attention to the contribution that migrants make tends to be slanted towards their financial return. This crucial point was already signalled by Min Zhou (2004) when advocating for studying the impact of migrant entrepreneurs beyond their economic effects by looking at their influence on job creation, cushioning competition with native workers, and setting role models for migrant communities. Drawing on the effects of migrant firms in the West Midlands (UK), we explored how, despite the undercapitalization of most of these businesses, they fulfil a crucial role by providing employment, acting as a vehicle of social incorporation into British society, and catering to neighbourhood needs (Jones et al. 2019). However, these accounts did not explore how migrant women entrepreneurs narrate value creation at household or community levels.

The sub-field of women migrant entrepreneurship has pointed to how the gender-blindness of the field (Phizacklea 1998) concealed patriarchal domination sustaining the ethnic economy. Within these contributions, scholars explored the role of women in the ethnic economy, how women contribute to family businesses, and whether entrepreneurship emerges as a means of empowerment for migrant women (for a review see Villares-Varela et al. 2017). These accounts tend to offer polarized narratives between those perspectives that illustrate women as being exploited by family members in the ethnic economy, or those which show entrepreneurial activities under an over-celebratory light (Jones et al. 2017). The latter perspective is generally aligned with the dominant neoliberal paradigm where becoming a woman entrepreneur materializes as the panacea for liberating migrant women from the entrapments of patriarchal domination, and racialized and xenophobic discrimination. However, the picture is much more complex than this binary diatribe. Recent scholarship has demonstrated how contributing to the family firm can simultaneously conform and resist gender ideologies and power relations within the family (Billore, 2011; Essers and Benschop, 2007; Katila, 2008). Similarly, experiences of entrepreneurship as an empowering endeavour beyond the financial and family contribution might also be shaped by other processes such as class positions (Villares-Varela et al. 2017), or the connections with the countries of origin (Villares-Varela and Essers 2018).

METHODOLOGY, METHODS AND DATA

The data collection and analysis used an interpretivist approach (Guba and Lincoln 1994), to capture the experiences of entrepreneurial activity amongst foreign-born women entrepreneurs in the UK.

We have relied on four in-depth biographical interviews with women entrepreneurs of migrant origin (born abroad). Biographical interviews are particularly well suited to research the lives of migrant women entrepreneurs, especially following calls to study entrepreneurship as a process intertwined with other life-cycle circumstances, such as migration, household formation and labour market trajectories, all of which shape the development of the self (Kontos 2003).

The interviewees were accessed using a mix of formal and informal contacts, as well as connections generated through our interaction with organizations operating in the community. We selected four cases of women entrepreneurs to illustrate the different levels of contribution at the community and family levels. All of our interviews took place in early 2019 and in different locations across the South of England. These interviews were followed by an invitation to produce photo folios (Wang 1999) in the form of up to five images and a follow up photo-elicitation interview (Harper 2002) to discuss and comment on their creative work.

The data collected have been analysed using thematic analysis. Some of the emerging themes that we have touched upon relate to the different levels of contribution (financial returns, sense of self and empowerment, household/family contribution, community/society contribution). In this chapter, we focus on the two levels of household and community contributions through the following selected case studies.

Case Studies

Our selection includes the cases of four women entrepreneurs, Daniela, Mariana, Klaudia and Urszula, all born abroad, business owners, and residing permanently in the UK. We include here brief profiles of the four women to illustrate their migratory, occupational and entrepreneurial trajectories.

Daniela was born in Ecuador and was in her mid-thirties at the time of the interview. In Ecuador, she got an accountancy and finance degree but did not find employment adequate to her qualifications. She arrived in the UK in 2011 after a previous emigration to Spain where she lived from 2001 and re-emigrated due to the effects of the 2008 crisis. The years of residency in Spain enabled her to apply for Spanish citizenship and subsequently to move to London as an EU passport-holder, with her younger sister and her two children. She worked in the hospitality industry as a cleaner. She was mentored by a Peruvian entrepreneur in London who runs a successful cleaning company and, after five years of working for her and learning the trade, she took the step of setting up her own company: 'from my friend A. I learnt almost everything I needed'. Her cleaning company is based in a small location in the South of England where the market was less saturated because 'you don't want to compete in London with hundreds of other companies'. At the time of the interview, she had 12 cleaners working for her full time. Her immediate family in the UK consists of her two children (12 and 14 years old), her younger sister and brother in law.

Mariana was born in Brazil and was in her late thirties at the time of the interview. She arrived in the UK when she was approximately 10 years old to join her mother. Before starting her university degree she decided to go back to Brazil with the idea of teaching English. She narrates that she was not taken seriously as an English teacher due to racialized discrimination in Brazilian society towards Afro-Brazilian communities, 'they wanted the blond/blue eyes experience, so a lot of Australians, Germans, they got the jobs'. Feelings of not belonging nor here nor there are frequent in her narrative: 'in Brazil, they always introduced me as the foreigner, "gringa", whilst at the same time, she explains, 'it was weird, because, even then, I dressed like a Brit'. Her high level of English and competitive soft skills landed her an employment opportunity as a secretary in a flourishing company. After three years of thriving in this occupation and being financially independent, her mother suggested that she should complete a university degree. Mariana felt compelled to do so since she had achieved her goals and the expectation that 'you are nobody [in Brazil] if you don't do a degree'. After graduating she took on different roles in different companies where she achieved high levels of managerial responsibility. Due to blocked labour mobility in her employment trajectory in the UK due to racialized discrimination, she started exploring alternative options. During a six-week stay in Brazil, she attended waxing courses, although 'it was more of a plan B'. After a series of unsuccessful interviews in the UK due to being overqualified, her plan B became her plan A. Since then, she runs a thriving beauty salon of a medium-size located in the south of England.

Urszula comes from Poland and is in her early forties at the time of the interview. Together with her wife Malwina, she co-owns a successful and award-winning English language school. Both women embarked on this family venture in the mid-2010s. At the time of the interview, Urszula had lived in the UK for over fourteen years, having migrated just after Polish accession to the European Union in 2004. Urszula describes her decision to leave Poland as motivated by a complex family situation. Urszula's six-year-old son was seriously ill and required specialist medical treatment, the cost of which was prohibitive and well above the income threshold of an average Polish family. Taking the opportunity of the newly opened labour market in Britain, she set off for the UK, hoping to secure employment that would provide the level of earnings required to cover her son's life-saving healthcare. She recalls: 'within three days, my bags were packed. I said: I am leaving. And so I came over here'. Urszula found a job in a local factory and the remittances that she was sending back to her family paid for her son's specialist medical treatment. The boy's health gradually improved and, within a couple of years, Urszula brought the toddler over to the UK and succeeded in finalizing her divorce. Some time after, Urszula embarked on a romantic relationship with Malwina – a Polish woman whom she had met through some friends. The couple transitioned into entrepreneurship together by setting up consulting services firm for Polish migrants. Within a year, a joint decision was made to pursue Malwina's lifelong ambition of opening a language school. The business has been faring well since. The women married in Britain and their marriage, being of the same sex, is not recognized in conservative Poland. They live with Urszula's son who is currently studying at university. At the time of the interview, Malwina was heavily pregnant with the couple's son. The boy had already been denied Polish citizenship by the Polish right-wing government that is promoting the heteronormative constructions of the family.

Klaudia is a Polish national in her early thirties. At the time of the interview, she had been living in the UK for over a decade. Klaudia holds a degree in modern languages, which she completed back in Poland. Having always been interested in linguistics, she chose the English language to pursue a career as a professional translator:

> This is my dream profession. It is for this that I had studied for. I am doing what I love to and makes me feel fulfilled, so I do not treat this as a job. (Klaudia, translating company owner)

Following her graduation in the mid-2000s, Klaudia left Poland and arrived in the UK. She explains the decision to migrate as motivated primarily by a lifelong desire to experience living in another country, rather than one driven by economic reasons: 'I wanted to leave for abroad. And it was not because my life was difficult in Poland, not at all... And I fell in love with this place'. A year after her arrival to the UK, Klaudia decided to use all of her savings to enrol on a one-year postgraduate law diploma at a British university that would enable her to specialize in the field of legal and business translation. Immediately upon its completion, she launched her own business venture – a translating and interpreting company. To gain knowledge of the local market and establish connections with British firms, Klaudia joined a local chamber of commerce. Her active participation in the events organized by the chamber inspired Klaudia to set-up a business networking group for Polish migrants:

> I joined the local Chamber, attended the meetings and learnt. Then, I thought that it would be a great idea to create something similar for the Poles here. Eventually, I noticed more and more Polish businesses popping up. At first, these were mainly Polish shops and hair-dressing salons, not a huge variety, but you could see that this Polish entrepreneurialism was quickly gaining strength. (Klaudia, translating company owner)

Klaudia has since been running her translating company and is the founder and the leader of a locally operating centre for Polish entrepreneurship, which promotes the development and inter-ethnic cooperation of Polish businesses, fosters connections between migrant entrepreneurs, organizations and the broader British host community.

VALUE CREATION AT THE HOUSEHOLD LEVEL: RE-SITUATING FAMILY, SOLIDARITIES AND RECIPROCITIES

The cases of Daniela, Mariana and Urszula help us to redefine the ways in which we think of households and families when studying migrant entrepreneurs. In these three cases, their family compositions are different from the nuclear family in our social imaginaries of mother, father and children.

For Mariana, her current single life means that her family's reference points are her mother and stepdad who now live abroad, her extended family in Brazil, and a close-knit group of friends in the UK and beyond, which translate into the transnational dimension of business support in both directions. She conveys here how she has developed a business venture with some of her redundancy money which is catering for her sister and brother back in Brazil:

> I put most of my money onto the salon [and the rest] onto the bikini business in Brazil with my sister to buy materials, hire a seamstress and put the deposit on a shop [...] and my brother was going to do the surfboards because he could make surfboards [...] So, that's still open and that's still happening. (Mariana, Brazil, beauty salon)

Her knowledge as an entrepreneur is also supporting her mother who is starting a small venture and she prides herself in the capability to help others transnationally by also relying on other women in the family. The non-financial value of these exchanges is highlighted by Mariana, where she emphasizes the female solidarity transnational networks as the main source of self-realization:

> I think when you're getting to the point where you can help other people... like my mother now, she does artwork, so we're going to open up a little website. So, I'm calling my aunty [in Brazil] to make sure that she can get a logo for her, and I'm going to do my mum's website [...] And it is very much as in rewarding with no money, no money whatsoever. (Mariana, Brazil, beauty salon)

For Daniela, her marriage break-up meant that she had to redefine her family from a traditional nuclear composition to a lone head-of-household model. She explains that 'it's us girls now, only us running everything, making sure all works, there is food on the table, all on us'. In this case, she has been supporting her family in both the country of origin and destination. Her business in the UK supported her estranged husband until he got on his feet back in Ecuador and she regularly supports her mother:

> I support my mum, she is now an old lady [...] and until recently I sent money to my ex-husband, you know, I wanted my children to be proud of their dad. He has a taxi now and makes some money, so I send him only when the children go to visit.

More interestingly, a reciprocal exchange of female solidarity between sisters means that Daniela has supported her sister in her higher education degree in nursing in the UK, in exchange for support with the care provision towards Daniela's children. Hence, the business turnover is aiding the upward mobility trajectory of this female-led family:

> My sister wanted to do a degree here, and it is so expensive. She had some support but still... I said, don't worry, I'll help you, you live with me, don't have to pay rent or anything, but try to get into a programme in [location anonymized] so you can help out with the kids [...] So she is always grateful for my financial support but I always tell her I am the one who ends up with a positive balance. (Daniela, Ecuador, cleaning company)

Productive and reproductive spheres are strongly intertwined in these narratives, and Daniela's chosen photograph seems to depict a similar spirit (Figure 12.1). Her chosen photograph depicts some of her cleaning tools, her notepad with bookings and the lunch she prepared in the morning with her children. We can see on the image that her daughter wrote 'Eres la mama más linda del mundo' [You are the most beautiful mum in the world]. She explains that this makes her day and 'makes all the sacrifices worthwhile'. She conveys that this represents what it means for her to be a business-woman which she cannot disentangle from being a mother 'I guess this is what I am: a cleaner, a manager, my bookings are here, my children are here'.

Figure 12.1   Daniela's photograph, 'mum and business owner'

In a similar vein to Mariana's and Daniela's cases, Urszula's story provides an insightful example of the ways in which migrants themselves deconstruct the traditionalist typologies defining entrepreneurial migrant families. In Urszula's narrative, multiple references to entrepreneurship intersect with the rearticulated ideas about family and femininity. She counterposes her first unsatisfactory marriage and her husband's inertia to her current family dynamics. Urszula's narrative paints a more detailed picture of their female-headed family as defined by the centrality of the business and based on female solidarity, a shared sense of mutual support, responsibilities towards the business and realization of the joint entrepreneurial aspirations. In Urszula's account, entrepreneurialism is conceptualized as a lifestyle:

> I would have great difficulties separating my private life and my business as both blend together into a single entity that is my life… We cannot separate work and home, it does not work like that. We may be having the stormiest debates on the future of the business while peeling potatoes. (Urszula, language school owner)

The photographs produced by Urszula consistently reflect this motif (Figure 12.2). Both images depict the intertwinement of the productive and reproductive spheres. In the one on the left, Urszula captured her baby son sleeping in the pram, against the backdrop of an ongoing classroom refurbishment project, with a chair, roll of wallpaper, mixing bowl and other tools in the background.

The image on the right also includes Urszula's son, whose face and head are mostly concealed behind a pile of print-outs. The baby is resting on a couch, between an empty coffee cup and a pack of baby cotton earbuds, and, is being surrounded by loosely scattered print-outs of a Polish e-book. His arm is placed over the page that reads: 'Jak Rozhulać fan-page' meaning: 'how to develop a fan-page'. Reflecting on her photo folio, Urszula offers the following commentary:

> We wanted to renovate the classrooms how we wanted. That involved taking him along and so he participated in the refurbishment. And we needed to learn how to successfully develop a fan-page to support the business needs, so we turned it into an all-out family learning session. (Urszula, language school owner)

Figure 12.2   *Urszula's photographs: 'entrepreneurship as a lifestyle'*
'intertwinement and inseparability of family and business':
'redecorating the premises as a family' and 'learning new
entrepreneurial skills and developing business knowledge together'

Moreover, entrepreneurialism is projected as a value that both women have been able to harness through the experience of running their venture. It has allowed them to develop as individuals and it has strengthened them as a couple and a family unit. This notion of entrepreneurship, and Urszula's understanding of what being a female entrepreneur entails, are closely tied to her ideas about the prevalence of predefined gender norms. Urszula is deeply critical of patriarchal socio-institutional structures and gendered ideologies that she perceives as detrimental to both men and women. In particular, she decries their destructive impact on the female entrepreneurial spirit by depriving women of being able to develop skills necessary to succeed in business:

> We live in a society which is largely encouraging towards men… the society that demands of women to look lovely and to act within the accepted norms. When a boy misbehaves, he is sweet mischief, but when a small girl does the same, she is told off as unruly. It kills the go-ahead attitude necessary for entrepreneurship. (Urszula, language school owner)

Urszula's narrative provides interesting insights on the ways in which reshaping of traditional family roles and gender expectations is navigated in a migrant female-led entrepreneurial household in Britain where both women are able to live their lives free of societal constraints prevalent in the conservative Polish society.

ENTREPRENEURSHIP AS A FACTOR IN THE PROCESS OF FORGING TIES OF COMMUNITY BELONGING: IDENTITY, RECIPROCITY AND ACKNOWLEDGEMENT OF THE ENTREPRENEURIAL CONTRIBUTION

The development of a sense of community belonging seems to be simultaneously a driver and an outcome of being an entrepreneur. Daniela articulates here that it is because of the business that she is able to engage with the broader British community which was more challenging when in paid employment:

> When you run your company, you have to deal with accountants, the council, the banks, the customers, so I managed to get a better idea of what England is, how people like things done, how to be professional at work. I feel part of the country now more than before […] but also, I help others. (Daniela, Ecuador, cleaning company)

Mariana conveys that the local community of entrepreneurs and friends who are business owners are what supports her business, and that she also supports others. Reciprocity heavily features in these narratives. For example, her photograph 2 represents an add-on activity she has incorporated into her initial business within the same space where she now hosts a hairdressing facility. The satisfaction from her connection with the broader community and engagement in solidarity networks is reflected in this expansion of her business. She explains that she engages in a 'gift and counter-gift' logic in her community of small entrepreneurs, which helps others to grow:

> So, it's basically my surrounding friends. What do you need?' So, A. had a salon, she had four hairdressing chairs, she gave me two instead of me paying £250 on a chair. She goes, 'No, here you go. Pay me when you've got it.' 'How much do you want for them, A?' '£50.' So, I've had help from friends, I had guidance from friends. (Mariana, Brazil, beauty salon)

These achievements based on her engagement with the community are also reflected in her photographic selection. She produced an image of the front space of her business allocated for the hairdresser activity and she proudly explains that:

> This is when I had the shop how I wanted to have it, with the flowers, with everything here ready. This is the point when I said 'I have a salon and it looked amazing' [...] we decorated ourselves, you can see her [the hairdresser] moved here, you can see the basin which was a headache plumbing wise, so I was 'oh wow, it looks like a proper little salon instead of empty shelves'. (Mariana, Brazil, beauty salon)

Figure 12.3   *Mariana's photographs: 'front space' salon, 'recreating home' and 'celebration'*

Trying to recreate 'home' in a transnational space is also part of the images she captured (Figure 12.3). She explains that the plants, colours, and fabrics used in the salon aim to represent Brazil in the UK, a sense of cultural identity and belonging away from home:

> These plants I've been meaning to do and the chair I had it for a year and it wasn't refurbed, and it fits now so nicely with everything else, the cascade of the plants and I wanted to take a picture focusing on that [...] I want to recreate a tropical Brazilian vibe, me, like walking to my little salon you are not going to feel anywhere else than in a tropical place. (Mariana, Brazil, beauty salon)

She has also decided to capture herself laying down on the beauty table, which is the view that her customers have, on the first anniversary of the salon, enjoying her success and a well-deserved celebration drink. She conveys that:

> This was the first year anniversary [...] I was busy all day [...] this was the time I started drinking because I couldn't drink before because I had waxes, facials to do. I was 'let me sit down, and enjoy a drink'. I felt it was an achievement because it was one year, and this was

6.30, and it was the time I could relax […] It is the view customers have, I like it. (Mariana, Brazil, beauty salon)

In Klaudia's case, the desire to establish and develop her translating company, coupled with the initially limited access to intra-ethnic social networks and capital as well as an insufficient number of contacts within the growing Polish business community, had led her to become the founder of the local entrepreneurial community. This 'offshoot project' as she terms it, had found a suitable niche, being aimed primarily at Polish budding and aspiring entrepreneurs. The initial purpose behind creating the group was to facilitate cooperation among Polish enterprises:

I have set up this business community that unites active and entrepreneurial individuals to enable networking and building of new connections. It provides local, primarily Polish entrepreneurs, with new possibilities. (Klaudia, translating company owner)

At its inception, the group operated on an informal basis, meeting at different venues once every month or a couple of months. In less than two years, it grew in numbers, gaining considerable popularity and a recognized standing among Poles. This success prompted Klaudia to formalize the group's membership and turn the community into a type of social enterprise project in its own right. The centre's main goal is to encourage business engagement among Polish migrants and to connect them with local, but also regional or UK-wide institutions and organizations through the active outreach. Klaudia explains:

The community is here to facilitate the establishment of new business contacts, enable development opportunities for their companies and, to simply provide ongoing support in building lasting social relationships. I wanted for people to be able to meet up, talk, learn something new and grow their enterprises. (Klaudia, translating company owner)

The thriving group, which also has an active online and social media presence, prides itself on its primary aim of promoting Polish businesses and providing a platform for broader engagement, co-ethnic solidarity, and support and knowledge exchange. The regular meet-ups and events provide a welcoming and safe space for sharing experiences, and knowledge transfer, and, where other successful Polish entrepreneurs tell their stories – serving as role models, providing the needed mentorship and inspiration to aspiring entrepreneurs in the face of ongoing socio-political uncertainty. The community serves as a type of inter and intra-ethnic exchange centre, promoting cross-cultural entrepreneurial exchange and support in the current climate of hostility towards immigrant groups amplified by the pro-Brexit vote. The strength of connections established by Klaudia and her active engagement had also resulted in a number of cooperative inter-ethnic community-based projects, with entrepreneurs from other minority groups, as well as locally based institutional actors, local authorities, charities and British entrepreneurs.

For example, one of the migrant-led initiatives in which Klaudia's community became involved, was the first-to-date locally held award event, showcasing locally run ethnic businesses and social enterprises. The ceremony featured a large number of Polish entrepreneurs, the aim of which was to counter the negative anti-migrant discourses and to demonstrate the active economic and non-economic input, and value contribution added to the broader community by migrant-run enterprises and organizations.

The selection of four photographs produced by Klaudia (Figure 12.4) features a black-and-white image of the female hands clasping a notepad and a pen in readiness for notetaking at one of Klaudia's business community events (Figure 12.4, the image on the left). During the follow-up photo-elicitation interview, Klaudia explained the symbolic meaning behind the image:

> For me, this photo symbolically depicts the moment of the entrepreneurial knowledge transfer and exchange. When the person absorbs this knowledge and jots it down in a form of a note. We provide the source of such knowledge for entrepreneurs. (Klaudia, translating company owner)

Klaudia's next photograph captures a meeting space for the informal gatherings of the business community (Figure 12.4 the image on the right). The choice of this type of space is not random and reflects Klaudia's intention to ensure that the environment provided a friendly, informal and open setting for every participant to benefit from:

> It is a space where we meet, a space with tables and benches to sit on. We want the space to be informal, and less office-like, as the informality of such places is conducive for socialising, making it easier to network and build relationships. A place where they feel comfortable. So, the setting is of importance here so that everyone is at ease to converse. (Klaudia, translating company owner)

Figure 12.4   Klaudia's photographs: 'notetaking hands at one of the Polish business community events', 'new networking space'

Klaudia's entrepreneurial community gatherings take a lot of planning to ensure that the attendees feel welcome and comfortable. Figure 12.5 depicts a prepared table setting, with a bottle of chilled prosecco, half-filled glass flutes decorated with fresh strawberries, an event schedule, and a set of name badges for the community members. Klaudia decided to include this image to illustrate the welcoming nature of the entrepreneurial community gatherings that had been taking place in the evenings. The time of the day is of significance here, since most Polish migrant entrepreneurs would attend the meetings following a long and busy day, and the events were tailored to provide them with an opportunity to not only learn and network but also to wind down. Klaudia explains:

> I wanted to show that it was taking place in the evening, after work, when everyone was able to relax. And the name badges are a symbol of these networking events. It is to depict what they looked like for us. (Klaudia, translating company owner)

Figure 12.5   Klaudia's photographs: 'a "warm welcome" table set-up with name badges and prosecco'

Klaudia emphasizes what she perceives to be the broader social value of entrepreneurship: its potential to forge positive connections and foster cooperation between communities. She also stresses its ability to contribute to building a positive image of Poles as valuable and hard-working members of society:

> This broader social interaction and cooperation with people translates into how we are being perceived… Unfortunately, for us Poles here… we are not being perceived positively… Neither here, nor in other countries. (Klaudia, translating company owner)

This commitment to promoting a positive perception of Poles in Britain is also being internalized on a personal level, through the discourse of self-responsibilization for fostering a more agreeable image of her co-ethnics. In the face of the ongoing Brexit uncertainty, Klaudia considers it to be particularly pressing to dismantle unfavoura-ble ethnicized stereotypes. She emphasizes her belief in the value of ethnic entrepre-neurship as a means of altering the reified categorizations:

> Through my work... I try to remain active in all circles and at different levels... in order to show our better traits: the friendliness, the openness, the professionalism... in the hope that my own efforts will result in improving the opinion of Poles here (...) Through entrepre-neurship we can show that we are able to achieve more than they thought we could initially, that we contribute to the economy, create workplaces. And this is very desirable. (Klaudia, translating company owner)

In Klaudia's narrative, migrant entrepreneurship, the input it creates and the sense of belonging it fosters, emerge as processual and gradual developments, but ones that merit recognition and deserve increased social visibility and acknowledgement:

> We prove we are entrepreneurial, independent and that we can thrive and manage. We become more involved in social life, we give a lot from ourselves and we are simply an integral part of this country, on different levels and across different communities. (Klaudia, translating company owner)

Migrants' entrepreneurial contribution becomes, in Klaudia's narrative, a route via which societal perceptions of migrants and their social standing might be improved. Furthermore, Klaudia justifies claims to migrants' belonging and recognition in their entrepreneurial engagement and the economic as well as non-monetary value it adds to the broader community.

CONCLUDING REMARKS

The perspectives of migrant women presented in this chapter and the subsequent analysis have demonstrated a need to rethink the 'value' of migrant female entrepre-neurship, both at the household and community levels. The departure point for our discussion was Zhou's (2004) assertion about the non-economic effects of migrant businesses, and the growing attention to the contribution of migrant entrepreneurs more broadly (Jones et al. 2019). By bringing into the debate the voices of migrants themselves, we have shown that women entrepreneurs narrate their contributions beyond the financial dividends in nuanced and variegated ways. This chapter has been co-created by the narrative and visual contributions that our interviewees have volunteered to produce.

Our interviewees emphasize the intersecting nature of the business and private spheres. In addition, we have moved beyond the parochial perspectives of migrant family life as the nuclear patriarchal setting, where migrant women entrepreneurs are seen as either empowered or victimized subjects. Our participants' trajectories illu-minate how the traditionalist and gendered family imaginaries surrounding migrant women entrepreneurs become unsettled and redefined. Entrepreneurship emerges as a process, and becoming an entrepreneur is facilitated through strong bonds of female solidarity networks, mutually shared experiences that are transferred between the businesses and households and even transnationally to sustain the enterprises and families. Providing help to families through non-monetary support, care and the transmission of knowledge, skills and capital are often coupled with a sense of community contribution through female solidarity, mentoring of others and leadership.

A greater sense of community rootedness and affective belonging seems to be simultaneously a driver and an outcome of being an entrepreneur. This is achieved by supporting other women via mentoring, assisting community members, and through various forms of broader micro-level engagement that facilitate the development of entrepreneurial undertakings, inter- and intra-ethnic business networks, and adding to the growth of social capital more broadly. Furthermore, entrepreneurship allows women to gain a degree of community recognition. These achievements are in turn projected as a basis for lodging claims of belonging and a justification for broader societal acknowledgment of migrant entrepreneurial contribution to the British society and economy. Given the current socio-political context and the perpetuation of anti-immigrant imagery, the latter appears to be of significant importance – not solely to migrants themselves, but also to the broader community.

NOTE

1. All names have been anonymized.

REFERENCES

Abbasian, S. and Yazdanfar, D. (2013). Exploring the financing gap between native-born women and immigrant women-owned firms at the start-up stage: Empirical evidence from Swedish data. *International Journal of Gender and Entrepreneurship*, 5(2), 157–173.

Baycan, T., Masurel, E. and Nijkamp, P. (2003). Gender differences in ethnic entrepreneurship, *43rd European Congress – European Regional Science Association*, Jyväskylä, Finland, August 27–30, 2003.

Billore, S. (2011). Female immigrant entrepreneurship: Exploring international entrepreneurship through the status of Indian women entrepreneurs in Japan. *International Journal of Gender and Entrepreneurship*, 3(1), 38–55.

Dustmann, C. and Fratini T. (2013). The fiscal effects of immigration to the UK, *Cream Discussion Papers Series*, CDP No 22/13.

Essers, C. and Benschop, Y. (2007). Enterprising identities: Female entrepreneurs of Moroccan or Turkish origin in the Netherlands. *Organization Studies*, 28(1), 49–69.

Guba, E. G. and Lincoln, Y. S. (1994). Competing paradigms in qualitative research. In: Denzin, N. K. and Lincoln, Y. S. (Eds), *Handbook of Qualitative Research*. London: Sage, 105–117.

Harper, D. (2002). Talking about pictures: A case for photo elicitation. *Visual Studies*, 17(1), 13–26.

Hondagneu-Sotelo, P. (Ed.) (2003). *Gender and US Immigration. Contemporary Trends*, Berkeley, Los Angeles and London: University of California Press.

Jones, T., Ram, M. and Villares-Varela, M. (2017). Injecting reality into the migrant entrepreneurship agenda. In: Essers, C., Dey, P., Tedmanson, D. and Verduyn, K. (Eds), *Critical Perspectives on Entrepreneurship. Challenging dominant discourses on entrepreneurship* (Routledge Rethinking Entrepreneurship Research). Abingdon: Routledge, 125–145.

Jones, T., Ram, M. and Villares-Varela, M. (2019). Diversity, economic development and new migrant entrepreneurs. *Urban Studies*, 56(5), 960–976.

Katila, S. (2008). Negotiating moral orders in Chinese families in Finland: Constructing family, gender and ethnicity in a research situation. *Gender, Work and Organization*, 17(3), 298–310.

Kofman, E. (2014). Towards a gendered evaluation of (highly) skilled immigration policies in Europe. *International Migration*, 52(3), 116–128.

Kontos, M. (2003). Self-employment policies and migrants' entrepreneurship in Germany. *Entrepreneurship & Regional Development*, 15(2), 119–135.

Lewis, H., Waite, L. and Hodkinson, S. (2017). 'Hostile' UK immigration policy and asylum seekers' susceptibility to forced labour. In: Vecchio, F. and Gerard, A. (Eds), *Entrapping Asylum Seekers: Social, Legal and Economic Precariousness*. London: Palgrave Macmillan, 187–215.

Phizacklea, A. (1998). Migration and globalization: A feminist perspective. In: Koser, K. and Lutz, H. (Eds), *New Migration in Europe: Social Constructions and Social Realities*. London: Macmillan Press, 21–29.

Ram, M., Jones, T. and Villares-Varela, M. (2017). Migrant entrepreneurship: Reflections on research and practice. *International Small Business Journal*, 35(1), 3–18.

Taylor, S. and Marlow, S. (2009). Engendering entrepreneurship: Why can't a woman be more like a man? Paper presented at the *26th EURAM Conference*, Liverpool.

UN (2017). International migration report, United Nations, http://www.un.org/en/development/desa/population/migration/publications/migrationreport/docs/MigrationReport2017_Highlights.pdf.

Villares-Varela, M. and Essers, C. (2018). Women in the migrant economy: A positional approach to contextualise gendered transnational trajectories. *Entrepreneurship & Regional Development*, 31(3–4), 213–225.

Villares-Varela, M., Ram, M. and Jones, T. (2017). Female immigrant global entrepreneurship: From invisibility to empowerment? In: Henry, C., Nelson, T. and Lewis, K. V. (Eds), *The Routledge Companion to Global Female Entrepreneurship*. Oxon: Routledge, 342–357.

Wang, C. (1999). Photovoice: A participatory action research strategy applied to women's health. *Journal of Women's Health*, 8(2), 185–192.

Yousafzai, S., Henry, C., Boddington, M., Sheikh, S, and Fayolle, A. (2018). Research handbook of women's entrepreneurship and value creation, *Call for book chapters*, Cheltenham, UK and Northampton, MA, USA: Edward Elgar Publishing.

Zhou, M. (2004). Revisiting ethnic entrepreneurship: Convergencies, controversies, and conceptual advancements 1. *International Migration Review*, 38(3), 1040–1074.

13. Iranian women entrepreneurs: creating household value through entrepreneurship

Vahid Makizadeh, Shumaila Yousafzai, Siavash Aein Jamshid and Marzieh Nasiri

INTRODUCTION

Females' businesses have experienced rapid growth in many countries (Véras, 2015). This trend has resulted in a considerable change in the common responsibilities of females (Khan, 2014). Along with the new research stream, scholarly interest has witnessed impressive development in the field of female entrepreneurship (Ahl, 2006; Hughes et al., 2012; Langevang et al., 2015). By developing this field to capture a more accurate understanding of females' entrepreneurship, the need for new research directions are emphasized (Brush et al., 2009; Hughes et al., 2012; Poggesi et al., 2015). Besides, to further develop the women's entrepreneurship research, the analysis of non-western contexts is also strongly encouraged (Brush and Cooper, 2012; De Vita et al., 2014; Mari et al., 2016).

Entrepreneurship is a complex interplay of multilevel factors (De Bruin et al., 2007) and the entrepreneurship literature has been criticized for individualism (Hughes et al., 2012; Essers at al., 2013). Thus, addressing multiple stakeholders in an entrepreneurial ecosystem (Autio et al., 2014), their needs and impacts and where those effects are felt are necessary (Zahra and Wright, 2015). One of the most critical stakeholders of female entrepreneurship is the household and the family. Only recently, analysis of entrepreneurs' activities within the context of their lives has encouraged a family embeddedness perspective (Aldrich and Cliff, 2003; Jennings and McDougald, 2007; Mari et al., 2016; Foley et al., 2018).

Family as the primary stakeholder is the interferer factor between gender and entrepreneurship (Bruni et al., 2000: 159). This is why in women's experiences, family and work are highly intertwined (Aldrich and Cliff, 2003) and households might have a more profound impact on women than men (Brush et al., 2009). A growing number of female entrepreneurs, though not limited to typical gender-specific roles and venturing into the business, are, however, still responsible for a major family responsibility (Neneh, 2017). Consequently, a deeper study of the reciprocal effect of work and family on females' entrepreneurship and its distinctiveness (Poggesi et al., 2015; Mari et al., 2016) is essential (Neneh, 2017).

In current female entrepreneurship studies, the family has been seen as having a negative effect (Luomala, 2018) while the main focus is on general areas like work–life balance (using psychological- and individual-level concepts) and work–family conflict (with a focus on negative effects on an individual level) (e.g., Parasuraman et al., 1996). However, the research direction has changed to consider the positive effects of the work–family link by introducing the constructs of work–family integration and enhancement (Pitt-Catsouphes and Christensen, 2004). Female entrepreneurship studies, even feminist theorists, have a unidirectional approach and have paid more attention to the impact of family, as a source of financial and non-financial support, on the female owned firms (see Greenhaus and Powell, 2006; Eddleston and Powell, 2012; Welsh et al., 2014; Noguera et al., 2015; Mari et al., 2016; Welsh et al., 2016; Meliou and Edwards, 2018). Nevertheless, the female owned businesses have deep impacts on family, even changing its members' attitudes, values and norms (Greenhaus and Powell, 2006).

Female entrepreneurs have been seen as economically and socially disadvantaged (Véras, 2015). This creates questions about how to understand the success of women entrepreneurship (McGowan et al., 2012). In new theoretical progress, focus on female entrepreneurship successes rather than experienced problems is taken into consideration (James, 2012). In the same way, analyses of female entrepreneurship have shifted from a 'gender as a variable' (GAV) approach (Cromie, 1987) towards a focus on 'gender as an influence' (Marlow, 2002; Henry et al., 2016) and agent of change (e.g., Watson, 2013; Shaw et al., 2017; Baker and Welter, 2018).

A review of previous studies shows that the main focus was on female entrepreneurs' economic performance. This one-sided analysis restricts the contribution of entrepreneurial activity, which is commenced by disadvantages such as being female (Welter and Smallbone, 2011). Entrepreneurs have their viewpoints and perceptions of what success means to them. Thus, entrepreneurial success is a multi-dimensional construct that has various indicators of success (Simpson and Docherty, 2004; Wach et al., 2016). Understanding the subjective measures of success seems to be essential for the development of entrepreneurship practice research (Dyke and Murphy, 2006; Gorgievski et al., 2011; Fisher et al., 2014). Subjective entrepreneurial success shows the criteria used by entrepreneurs, rather than the criteria imposed by researchers. However, female entrepreneurs often make exceptional value far away from purely financial contribution. This kind of value takes multiple forms and occurs at various levels. Hence, if the contribution of entrepreneurs in society and the economy is to be recognized, it needs to be documented (Sheikh et al., 2019). However, researchers should regard different dimensions of value created by female entrepreneurship in different areas like family context. In female entrepreneurship, the family is more than a source of support or merely context. While entrepreneurship emerges from inside the family, entrepreneurship processes affect the family that might be as vital as the multiple results. Hence, an entrepreneurial study should consider the family as context, an enabler, and an outcome. Thus, it can be argued that examining the non-economic impact of female firms on the family can provide a deeper understanding of female entrepreneurship than merely focusing on the economic dimensions.

Our review of the literature has shown that there are two areas in the research on female entrepreneurship that require further study. The first one is the inadequate attention paid to female entrepreneurs as agents for creation of non-economic outcomes. The second one is that a few studies on integrated value created by female entrepreneurs at the household level. As female entrepreneurship is happening at the micro-meso-macro context, this chapter aims to reveal the impact of female entrepreneurship on family and investigate the values that women create at the household level. So, we attempt to answer the following research question: *How do the Iranian female entrepreneurs create the non-economic value in the family and household context?*

We contribute to the field of female entrepreneurship by documenting how female entrepreneurs benefit family through enterprising in the context of Iran with its distinctive socio-cultural characteristics and its specific requirements. Iran is ranked 184 out of 187 countries, near the bottom of the World Bank index of women's equality – Women, Business and the Law Index (WBLI) (World Bank, 2019). Foundational laws and societal norms in Iran are unfavorable for female entrepreneurs and women's entrepreneurship in Iran mainly consists of small and home-based businesses (Modarresi et al., 2016). In addition to being family-oriented female entrepreneurs (Valinejad, 2011), about 16.3% of households in Iran have female heads. Government policies on women's entrepreneurship have also been largely aimed at encouraging small businesses around the family matters. Given these facts, a family is an important area that should be studied in female entrepreneurship in Iran.

Following the above and adopting a woman's perspective on value creation in entrepreneurship, this chapter aims to explore the lived experiences of women entrepreneurs to document the value they create at the household level. In order to answer the research question, a narrative approach for three female entrepreneurs from Bandar Abbas, the capital city of Hormozgan province of Iran has been used.[1]

VALUE CREATION BY FEMALE ENTREPRENEURS

The nature of entrepreneurship is to create value from a situation (Anderson, 1998). Values are inherently subjective since they form individuals' judgments (Hechavarría et al., 2017; Nair and Blomquist, 2018). The process of creating value is a path to create results that form value for the firm, its stakeholders, society, and the environment (Elkington 2004). Value is about creating economic and social benefits (rather than distributing available value) through analyzing economic and social connections (Porter and Kramer, 2011). Because of the multi-dimensional nature of value creation, different goals of value creation – economic, social, and environmental – are compatible (Cohen et al., 2008). Specifically, compared to men, female entrepreneurs show more emphasis on subjective value creation in comparison to economic value creation (Hechavarría et al., 2017).

As well as addressing general issues such as nutrition, poverty relief, health, sustainability, rural development and education (Véras, 2015), in line with a dominant stream in entrepreneurship studies, in the female entrepreneurship research, values have traditionally been measured via objective performance measures like the economic and growth measures (Wright and Stigliani, 2013). Financial results can shed only incomplete light on the traditional motivations of female entrepreneurs (Kantor,

2002) for entering into self-employment. Only recently attention has been paid to consider non-financial outcomes (Harris et al., 2008; Greene and Brush, 2018), including self-stated growth (Jamali, 2009) and social impact (Nicholls, 2009; Zahra and Wright, 2015). Beyond the individual benefits, they show social and environmental value goals (Hechavarría et al., 2017). For many women self-employment fits around their family commitments. That is, the accommodation of family needs in some way motivate the start-up decision and a family orientation drives how the firm is managed, and mediates goals concerning firm performance (Harris et al., 2008). Females have distinct motivations, values, and goals that are connected to the way of defining entrepreneurial success by them. Some of them are discussed in the following paragraphs.

Role-Sharing Strategies

Given the interference of family and business boundaries for female entrepreneurs, they pursue role-sharing strategies that can facilitate the improvement of both family and work roles while reducing conflicts (Tu and Hwang, 2014; Neneh, 2017). Female entrepreneurs through these strategies could more easily share resources between work and family. Work roles benefit from family roles through developmental resources, positive affect, and gains in efficiency derived from involvement in the family. This can lead to better nurture their entrepreneurial performance. In other words, their entrepreneurial activity has multiple and simultaneous positive impacts on work and family domains. This means that female entrepreneurs are more productive than male entrepreneurs, a feature that highlights the importance of female entrepreneurship for society (Giménez and Calabrò, 2018).

Family-Driven Motivations

In addition to economic drivers, females are motivated by family-driven motivations. This need is based on the motivation to be independent to accommodate family care (Foley et al., 2018). In other words, they tend to gain productive dependency through which they are able to collect and redistribute resources in ways that are conducive to valued forms of social reproduction, including the education of their children and the care of their elders (Monteith and Campfield, 2019). The reciprocal relationship between entrepreneurship and family dynamics and well-being confirmed by household focus, acknowledging the impact of entrepreneurship on the lives and livelihoods of all family members, not only those involved with the firm (Jennings and Brush, 2013; Carter et al., 2017).

Ethics of Care

A distinct feature of female entrepreneurs related to values derived from their entrepreneurship is the ethics of care. Ethics of care refers to a decision-making framework that focuses on the needs of others (Flanagan and Jackson, 1987), and the corresponding responsibilities and interactions, where care is implied in the blended value creation framework. Females also define power in terms of taking care of others (Hawk, 2011). Thus, this feature leads them to develop some values such as empathy, sympathy, compassion, holism, loyalty, discernment, love, benevolence, community, and promotion of a civil society more readily than men (Held, 2005). Females' care orientations may drive social value goals (Hechavarría et al., 2017).

Value Sharing Strategy

The strategy of value sharing by female entrepreneurs also has a fundamental difference with males. The findings disclose that more ownership of businesses by females is associated with improved welfare for the family. Enhancing females' control over decision-making in the household can lead to the greater well-being of children, especially girls and the diminishing poverty of future generations. This means that reinforcement of the agency of females could lead to more participation in decision-making (Klugman et al., 2014). According to Allen et al. (2008), the returns to the investment in women are much higher than for men, as shown in data on women in development. Females' economic and non-economic gains are more likely to be shared with members of their societies and families. Besides, women are more likely to work for and buy for the community. Researchers have concluded that females invest more of their income in their households, as opposed to men (Véras, 2015).

FEMALE ENTREPRENEURSHIP IN IRAN

According to the World Bank (2017), Iran is the second-largest economy in the Middle East and North Africa (MENA) region after Saudi Arabia, with an estimated Gross Domestic Product (GDP) in 2016 of $412.2 billion. Women comprise of 49.48% of Iran's population of 83,309,996. After the Islamic Revolution in Iran in 1979, women's involvement in Iran's economy has mostly focused on their role as the foundation of the family institution which put emphasis on child-rearing and being a good wife for their spouse. In Iran's regime, where principles of Sharia law rule, men are considered the breadwinners within their immediate families, while wives or daughters are responsible for the household. In other words, a woman's contribution in the economy is considered unnecessary and secondary to that of a man's, which illuminates why Iran ranked 142 between the 149 participating countries in respect to women's engagement in economic activities in 2018 (WEF, 2018) and ranked 14th in the 15 MENA countries with women entrepreneurship (Ács et al., 2016).

Furthermore, a World Bank study on women entrepreneurship, shows that men in the Middle East have a more negative attitude towards women's employment compared to other Asian men (Chamlou et al., 2008) and in this area, women are involved in only 4% of entrepreneurial activities (Arasti and Bahmani, 2017). Iran, as a developing country in the Middle East, is faced with this issue. While there are no explicit laws to prevent women from starting businesses, women entrepreneurship is heavily restricted by widespread societal norms that do not value their engagement in economic activity (Chamlou et al., 2008). Widespread unfavorable and sexist attitudes towards women entrepreneurs, particularly among men, are just some of the ongoing challenges that women have to deal with in managing their businesses (Simarasl et al., 2019). Iran's development plans do not explicitly refer to Iranian women entrepreneurship or any financial provisions for women's entrepreneurial endeavors, they address women breadwinners as an underprivileged group, the employment of whom should be addressed. According to a report published by the Association of Iranian Women Entrepreneurs (2013), only 11% of Iranian women have jobs and from those who are involved in the job market, only 12% are entrepreneurs; therefore, cases in which women become breadwinners of their families are considered as unfortunate, outside the scope of women's responsibilities, and hurting their primary responsibility of catering to their families. Also, a review of the Human Development Index (HDI) and other gender indices such as Gender Development Index (GDI) and Gender Inequity Index (GII) in the last UN Development Programme (UNDP) report reveals that despite the improvement of these indices, the gender indices for Iran are lower than the MENA region, and the world average. Women in Iran have a lower HDI value than men, relative to the world average. Worldwide, the average HDI value for women (0.705) is 5.49% lower than that for men (0.749) while this figure is about 12.9% for Iran. According to UNDP (2018), much of the gap is due to women's lower income and educational attainment in many countries.

Similarly, the World Bank reports, also the last recent years of the Global Entrepreneurship Monitor annual reports (GEM) note this issue in Iran. It shows that, despite an increase in entrepreneurial activities, Iran has not been successful in providing an appropriate environment to encourage women's entrepreneurial activities, and still, there is much room for improvement. The GEM reports show that, notwithstanding an increase in the ratio of female to male total early-stage entrepreneurship (TEAf/TEAm), in Iran and the MENA region, generally, women are less likely to be established business owners because they are less engaged in early-stage entrepreneurship compared to men. Moreover, based on the data derived from GEM reports, some studies show that a gender gap exists in women's participation in business and is significant in women's entrepreneurial activities in Iran and the MENA region (e.g., Kamal and Daoud, 2018; Sarfaraz et al., 2018).

Of course, today, many changes have taken place in several fields that have entirely changed the foundations of former social life, and these changes have influenced social relationships in new ways. An example of this is the change in the role and participation of women in various areas of society. In recent decades, attention has been paid to the status of women in the social planning and socio-economic development programs of Iran. Besides, women's participation in all fields has been considered as an indicator of social and economic development of the country. Moreover, in the last decade, enrollment of women in institutions of higher education in Iran has outnumbered those of Iranian men, however, surprisingly when women graduate from colleges, they are 33% less likely than man to find employment and their marriage and even childbearing decreases the likelihood of their employment (Salehi-Isfahani, 2008). Nevertheless, this blocked mobility, as mentioned in the Forbes report (Guttman, 2015) may lead women to choose entrepreneurship as a career but existing evidence demonstrates that entrepreneurship is not a leveling field for Iranian women.

It quickly becomes evident that there are numerous obstacles and constraints on the way of business creation by Iranian women. As a consequence, women's entrepreneurship research in Iran has mainly focused on studying the barriers for women-owned businesses (e.g., Mirghafoori et al., 2010), environmental barriers (Javaheri and Ghozati, 2004) and motivational factors (e.g., Gelard, 2007; Arasti and Valinejad, 2011) and how to overcome these barriers (e.g., Modarresi et al., 2016) in this context. However, the results of Arasti (2006) show that despite all this and all the challenges that Iranian women entrepreneurs face, they have the required qualities and skills for being competent entrepreneurs at running their businesses like in other parts of the world. In fact, college education has attenuated the negative beliefs toward female entrepreneurs in the society (Arasti and Akbari Jokar, 2008) and gave women entrepreneurs enough self-confidence to deal with these obstacles (Arasti, 2006). Also, it is expected that in time more women will find themselves becoming entrepreneurs than ever before in Iran (Javadian and Singh, 2012).

Regarding the role of family in women entrepreneurship research, research on a sample of 105 Iranian women entrepreneurs found that spouse and children (for married), and parents (for singles), and relatives as a family formed one part of women entrepreneurs' network (Arasti and Akbari Jokar, 2007). While the Iranian society defines the role of women primarily through family and household responsibilities (Arasti and Bahmani, 2017), they experience greater family–work conflict and it is too difficult for them to be a complete mother, wife, and manager. Therefore, they use special strategies to merge both business and family lives and manage them both effectively and intentionally. Consequently, they try to keep their business small because they know they would have more conflicts if they grow their businesses (Arasti et al., 2012). In an Iranian study, Valinejad (2011) categorized women entrepreneurs based on their motivation in five groups as idealist, successful, forced, social, and flexible entrepreneurs. It is noteworthy, in this category flexible entrepreneurs refers to women who focus on their families and quit their work because of their family responsibilities and less flexibility in work. These women follow entrepreneurship to have more flexibility and work–family balance.

METHODOLOGY

As indicated by Henry, Foss and Ahl (2016), entrepreneurship and gender-related research should approach qualitative methodologies such as biographies, case studies, and discourse analyses more carefully. In line with the constructivist inquiry that utilizes more qualitative methods to study the various aspects of female entrepreneurship (Ahl, 2006), this study adopts a constructionist approach to understand the lived experiences of FE in Iran and their contributions towards value creation at the family level. We adopt a narrative approach as a credible research method in entrepreneurship studies (Larty and Hamilton, 2011), as we need to develop insight about people and explore the unique forms of value that female entrepreneurs create through their business activity.

To examine how female entrepreneurs create value at the family level in the context of Iran, we undertook an exploratory study. For the research sample population, we used a database consisting of female entrepreneurs operating in the province of Hormozgan. Women account for half of the population in Hormozgan. Women's participation rate in economic activities for over eight years (2008–2016) has increased from 8.8% to 16.5%, which is higher than the national average (14.9%) and neighboring provinces. The unemployment rate for women aged 15–24 is 23.5%, which is lower than the national average (PBO, 2016). In an increasing trend, 12.8% of households in Hormozgan have female heads (SCI, 2016), and 79% of them are under the support of social welfare programs. So, empowerment and self-employment of these women via small and home-based businesses are one of the main priorities of the government.

The database was obtained from the Office of Women and Family Affairs in the province of Hormozgan. The sample was chosen from successful female entrepreneurs (those who have launched and managed their business for more than five years) to ensure that they are confident samples. Over a period of three months, we conducted a total of 25 interviews. The businesses operated were generally small, with an average of just over ten workers, including the business owner. Given the small number of female entrepreneurs in the province of Hormozgan, we employed purposive sampling for case selection (Silverman, 2005) in different sectors. However, to find out our answers and present our findings, we draw upon the narrative reports of three women entrepreneurs and explore their value contributions, especially at the family level. Respondents were in three different sectors (construction industry, event planning services, tourism).

To make a comprehensive description of how women create value through their entrepreneurial activity, we conducted face-to-face interviews (April 2018) in the local language of the participant (Persian) and then translated them into English. Each interview lasted between 90 and 120 minutes and was scheduled at the participant's office, keeping in mind their family and work constraints. The interviews were loosely structured to give our respondents the freedom to discuss subjects that they considered pertinent. The structure was provided by the general framework derived from the literature: we encouraged the interview respondents to reflect on specific areas of their entrepreneurial experience such as their personal and family lives, the challenges they experienced in entrepreneurship processes, the non-monetary values created for the family. In this way, we ensured that the interviews contained information relevant to our research objectives but that the interviewees were not overly constrained in their responses by the researchers' perspectives. Participants were asked to narrate about their experiences in their business and their perceptions about how it had impacted their life and family. Interviews were tape-recorded with the consent of the participants. We present our findings based on a thematic analysis of the interviews and present narratives of three entrepreneurs and their life as an entrepreneur and their contribution in value creation at the family level.

NARRATIVE 1   NOOSHIN: THE FEARLESS ENTREPRENEUR

Nooshin, 43 years old, founder of an elevator sales and installation company started her business 17 years ago, is specialized in residential and industrial elevators and offers services including sales, installation, after-sales service, and elevator repairs. Additionally, she also provides support services to some other small firms in this industry. Nooshin has two daughters at the ages of 5 and 7. Nooshin's traits, that is, self-confidence and perfectionism, made her choose the entrepreneurial life for herself. Now, she believes her job is one of the critical parts of her life, something which has created value for herself, her family, and the community.

Among the restrictions of her entrepreneurial environment, she made clear how her hard work kept her concentrated in her business life. Due to doubt of the people in her family towards success as a female entrepreneur, she expressed skepticism ('my mother thought that I would be sent to the jail eventually, or be conned, or end up losing') that she received in the early stages of starting a business. However, she continued her attempts in business and kept herself motivated, only to prove that she is doing some valuable and essential work. In achieving her position as an entrepreneur, she believed that her education in law gave her the ability to get involved in entrepreneurship, satisfy herself and convince people about her business skills. Additionally, it strengthened her belief in acquiring education for other women because she thinks it likely that having an education was a strong indicator that women could make money at any time in their lives, just as she had done. She also desired that her children get highly educated to support themselves if the need arose:

> Although, my family did not put limitations on me, they were really stressed about my success in my business. Having no experience of doing any business like that led me to start my business without the monetary support of my family.

The business was an opportunity for her to believe in her abilities and to show that a woman is able to do more than only the housework. While Nooshin gained experience in business, her confidence also improved when she started to ignore negative comments like ('elevator is a masculine industry; you will not be able to do industrial activities'). Formerly, she would be fearful of the statements of the people in the industrial environment. However, slowly, she overcame her fears and learned to trust in her abilities. Hence, after one year of starting the business, she began receiving acknowledgment for her job from the different companies in her city and others who had heard about her skills in setting up, installation, and elevator repairing. People praised Nooshin for her elevator services and trusted her knowledge and skills.

The story of Nooshin about the experience in business and the way it benefited the different areas of life showed an underlying belief in herself; a feeling of confidence and self-confidence to fight against the odds to attain something in life.

By choosing an industrial field, she took absolute responsibility for her business. According to Nooshin, her firm was her responsibility and nobody had responsibility for supporting her. She also narrated total control over her business decisions.

She said that support from friends and family members is critical for every woman to make her choices and achieve any goal in life. However, for Nooshin, it was her persistence which made her successful in business and personal life. She was not successful as an entrepreneurial woman from the first day of starting the business. She encountered different barriers from the community in the way to creating her business. People did not know that elevator servicing could be a woman's job, so they did not trust her initially, mainly for the reason that she was a woman. To change this point of view, she went to large firms in her city and communicated about her business to people:

> I used to saw [sic] people had to construct their project but they did not call me because they did not believe in my knowledge and skills. I used to go to their projects and speak to them about what I was doing. They would say non-positive things about working women but I showed them that I can provide a high level service for them. I also would offer long term services with a lower cost. And, finally they began to call me and I would go to help them any time they needed my service.

Naturally, there were times when Nooshin faced problems in the business, such as the time she had to go to the courier to deliver and unload the cargo. Due to the deliberate absence of her worker, she had to go personally to unload the cargo. The cargo was very heavy, but she did not want to be dependent on her worker. This caused her to have back pain for many days; however, she did not want her clients to be aware of this.

The business gave her a feeling of achievement in life; it also gave Nooshin the means to support family members, especially her husband. She explained that she could not advise her husband without her business. Nooshin encouraged her husband to run a new business.

Talking about her usage of the income, she claims that the level of welfare has been considerably improved for them. A significant part of Nooshin's income was used as working capital and office costs. She has been able to provide her family with higher standards of living. Additionally, she spent her income on her children, providing their needs like their education and clothing. 'All my earnings – net profit – are spent on my family. The biggest portion is focused on education and the provision of quality food and clothes for my children.'

Beyond the daily expenses of the house, Nooshin could buy some assets from her savings. For instance, some are invested in different sectors, such as property, with her husband's advice. Additionally, she also bought the office. All this was from her income. Her husband, being a landlord, did earn and gave her money for the household expenses, but she supported her daughters and their expenses herself from her business income. Since she started her business when she was single, their financial status has always been in good condition. However, her business has brought other benefits to her family.

She says that after making considerable effort and decreasing the financial risks, resulting in some achievements, the situation changed dramatically, and nowadays, her family considers her as social capital. In other words, they are proud of her, which has been mentioned by her many times during this interview. She states:

> As I progressed, they started to believe that I could manage the work, and I felt that they were proud of me. When they saw my performance and the satisfaction of my customers in the city, they changed their attitude regarding my abilities. For instance, my father has complimented me so many times, and my mother seemed satisfied. Since then, they started to have my back more than before.

She also admits that her job position has had a significant impact on her marriage too, and her mother-in-law has been proud of her since she got married. She says, 'when I married, being an entrepreneur was advantageous to me. What I mean is that my social status was taken into account by my husband's family.'

Nooshin's career has changed her role in family decisions and has promoted risk-taking among her family members. She adds, 'owing to being employed at governmental organizations, there had been a little tendency to take a risk in my family before my accomplishments. However, I have succeeded in persuading them to be risk-takers since then.' A good illustration is my brother, who was reluctant to buy a building since my family members tried to stop him from buying a bigger house, but I could convince him to do so. He bought that house, which was a good catch. These days many relatives opt to consult with me when they want to make a decision, which is because of being self-employed. If I were not working like this, they would not have this trust in me.

Moreover, this business has influenced her relationship with her husband. He is recruited in a governmental organization and met her while doing a project. Nooshin believes that her husband has always supported her and encouraged her entrepreneurial orientation. 'Being a working wife has a great impact on our lives, and he has established a company to be self-employed besides being recruited in a state organization.'

She explicitly mentions that her entrepreneurship orientation and her husband's economic perspective on life were underlying reasons for her marriage. 'I should say that since my husband has some economic mindset, my business might have influenced his decision on getting married to me.' Moreover, she believes that her social status as an entrepreneur has led to fewer problems in her family life since they can find solutions through discussions. 'We have always consulted with each other to make a decision in our married life. He has also entrusted the decisions related to our children to me.'

Nooshin is pleased that she has brought up two self-confident children who are independent. She thinks there is a connection between this and her role as a female entrepreneur:

> My daughter is very young, but whenever she comes to my workplace, and I explain some of the job-related issues to her, she realizes my social status and is fully satisfied with that, which can be obviously felt. I can feel that my role as a working mother has impacted her personality a lot and her self-confidence is enhanced because of this.

She is striving to promote an entrepreneurial mentality and self-assurance in her children:

> The achievements that I have made are of great importance to me. In addition to financial outcomes, they have developed my personality. In other words, they have helped me be more asserted, and I have attempted to instill the confidence and determination into my children as well. If a mother suffers from lack of self-confidence, she cannot convey a sense of confidence to her children. To my mind, this is the most precious asset that I could give them. I have two daughters, and I do not want them to be raised in a manner to wait for a prince charming to give them happiness. Conversely, I would like them to be independent and endeavor to gain what they desire to have.

NARRATIVE 2   FATEMEH: THE FAMILY ORIENTED ENTREPRENEUR

Fatemeh, 41 years old and a mother of a 13-year-old son and 15-year-old daughter, started her business 14 years ago in the Bandar Abbas city, Hormozgan province, South of Iran. After offering wedding design services individually, she established her own firm, and expanded her business, resulting in being one of the largest companies in this industry in Bandar Abbas. Being specialized in event planning services, Fatemeh offered services to her clients, including wedding planning, event planning (onsite event management and event execution), and design services.

She started her business with a small amount of money received through bank loans. The business of Fatemeh resulted in a good amount of income for her, just about 150–200 million (Iranian Rial) per month. She used most of her income to expand her business, and she spent the remaining part of her money on household expenses. This was not essential for her to spend part of her money on the household, but she only wanted to contribute in the expenses of the household. A further point to consider is that she does not have any personal deposits, and all her net income is spent on family issues. 'since the very first day of our married life, all our assets have been shared, even the debit cards'. Furthermore, Fatemeh loves her children to have the best clothes, toys, and stationery. She would always try to make new computer games for her boy from her money.

It was easy for Fatemeh to start the business due to support from her family, who provided the initial conditions for her to start the business. She encountered several difficulties while starting her business. However, Fatemeh overcame them with the passage of time. For example, she explained that her family doubted her success at the beginning, and called her a daydreamer, her husband has supported her to run the business: 'They used to tell me that I fantasized a lot. However, my father was the only one who always believed that I would succeed'. She expressed:

It was hard to balance between family responsibilities and work demands. I remember once I forgot to bring my son out of school, and he stayed there for a long time. Despite family support, it was hard to believe for people that we started this business with organizing weddings and have made such progress in founding a special event planning company and owning a wedding hall. Sometimes influenced by the same atmosphere, surprisingly, my husband, who has got my back since I started thinking that I was daydreaming.

However, Fatemeh believed that if women could serve family and parties, then why couldn't they arrange the events. So, eventually, Fatemeh has been able to change the non-positive perception of people regarding working women in general; Fatemeh was able to prove her abilities and skills as a businesswoman by providing effective services to her clients.

She expressed that her family and her husband's support in taking care of the children was significantly important. Nevertheless, everything has changed since Fatemeh's business represented considerable achievements, and these days, most of her family members are working in her company. She thinks that having such reliable and committed people around is of great benefit to her. After her accomplishments, she claims that the trust and respect toward her have increased substantially, and now she plays a pivotal role in family decisions:

When one succeeds in their career, on the one hand, others start to believe in them and respect them more than before. On the other hand, the entrepreneur feels more responsible for their family. For example, each of my family members might have some expectations of me, which they may not have of others. Apart from that, I feel a greater sense of responsibility to my family.

She contends that her self-confidence, as a successful entrepreneur, has been transferred to her family, especially her sisters, who used to be housewives or employed in governmental organizations.

A further point that she mentions is that she feels closer to her family and her husband because this job has provided more consultation opportunities for them:

A higher degree of closeness between my husband and I has resulted from this business, which was not first believed to do well. Not only is my husband certain about my success now, but he also assists me with taking some responsibilities in this business. My job prevents me from giving regular visits to my family, but since their involvement in my business, I frequently see them at the workplace.

As a result of having family members around, she has more time to spend with her children compared to the past, when she could allocate less time to them. This has brought about more satisfaction for her children. 'A few years ago, my children were somewhat dissatisfied with my career as I could not be a complete mother due to job concerns. But now I can be with them more than before.'

Fatemeh tries to spend most of her income on nurturing her children. She has made an effort to plan every step of her children's lives. Fatemeh is so pleased that her entrepreneurial mindset has led to having children with a higher level of independence and assertiveness. Moreover, her entrepreneurship has resulted in her children's willingness to work and has promoted their forward-looking approach and their sense of responsibility:

> One of the advantages of being an entrepreneur could be having a thirteen-year-old son who is completely independent and is more responsible than his peers. I guess that sons raised by entrepreneurial mothers are unconsciously interested in pursuing a career. For instance, my son, Ilia, takes responsibility of the coffee shop in many events and is willing to make a contribution. If I were a housewife mother, I might not be able to bring up such a self-confident son who is able to plan his future and decide on his education and his career.

Fatemeh states that the relationship with her husband has deepened since she became prosperous. This has brought about a more mutual understanding for them, which is translated into a more peaceful life. Having a smile on her face, Fatemeh says, 'unbelievably, we sometimes do not have any arguments for months, which seems unnatural to us'.

She talked positively about her decisions, involvement, and activities in their house. She stated that her family and other relatives would always ask her idea about different matters. She mentioned that starting this business has given her much respect among her family. Due to being the only woman in the house, Fatemeh had to manage her time between her business and her family. She would make breakfast for the family early in the morning and after that, leave the house for her business work as her husband took care of her 7-month-old daughter. From time to time, when Fatemeh had an appointment in the afternoon, her husband would even make ready meat and vegetables for her to cook later and when she was busy, her husband would even bring food from outside. She appreciated the support received from her family, and she also has an idea that it played a significant role in her success as a businesswoman.

NARRATIVE 3   SARA: SENSITIVE ENTREPRENEUR

Sara, 38 years old, a mother of two children and, started her business thirteen years ago by the establishment of a travel agency in Bandar Abbas. Sara has a 3-year-old son and a 6-year-old daughter. Her agency offers services including ticket sales, tours, hotel reservation, and travel insurance. It was only forty days after her first child's birth. 'At the beginning of my work, I had to bring my baby with me to my office.'

According to Sara, it was easy for her to start the business due to support from her family. However, she encountered some challenges in the initial stages of starting her business, which Sara could overcome over a period of time:

> When I started my business, those around me were doubtful of my decisions. For example, I set up my office outside the area where the other tourist offices were located. They all said that you would not succeed here. But with the passage of time and success, more tourist offices were opened in the area. Despite my hard work, I was a shy person. This feature made some of my friends doubt my success.

This is also a job where social relations are essential. But slowly, she overcame this trait and started believing in her ability to do business.

She believes that her tenacity and her husband's support has contributed to her success as a female entrepreneur in the ambiance that she was sometimes mocked. Sara has been able to improve her family's welfare because of spending her income on family-related issues.

With regard to the impact of her position as a woman entrepreneur on family, she says that the most significant achievement of this job has been her improved self-confidence, which has been instilled into her children and her siblings as well. Her entrepreneurial mindset has contributed to having children who are characterized by more self-confidence and, hence, enhanced communication skills and higher independence.

Sara is really pleased that she has been able to provide her family with a sense of pride, and they consider her social capital. Sara narrated a day when she was invited to her child's school as an entrepreneur mother to give a speech to the students about her job. After that day, her children realized the recognition of an independent entrepreneur mother, and have been proud of this. 'They even ask me when I will give the next speech in their school.' Sara has a similar position in her extended family as her income has provided the opportunity to revive her family's traditional career, which had been farming. This is what her brother had attempted to do, but had not succeeded. 'One of the best moments of my life was when I was able to grow my father's farmland. Since he passed away and is very valuable in our local community.' She believes that if she were not an entrepreneur, she would not be able to revive his family legacy.

She also mentions that her entrepreneurship has boosted self-assurance among her family members to take some entrepreneurial initiatives. She mentioned that starting the business gave her a lot of respect amongst people; Sara was valued for her knowledge and education of the business. She stated that her family would always ask her idea on different issues in the house.

When Sara started her business, almost 70% of her time and energy was devoted to her job. However, owing to the expansion of her business during the last five years, she has had more time to spend with her family and children. Regarding the relationship with her husband, she claims that it has not changed at all since he has always been an open-minded man with a positive attitude toward her. It is worth mentioning that after her success, her husband consults with her more.

FINDINGS

Entrepreneurship provides women with opportunities that may help them to improve their status in their families (e.g., Haugh and Tawler, 2016; Xheneti et al., 2018). Female entrepreneurs aiming to go beyond the success of their businesses and also create values for their family. By analyzing the narratives of Nooshin, Fatemeh, and Sara we identify three values for their family (*value at the household level*). These values can be grouped into the positive intra-family dynamics, positive impact of female income on the family members, and change of attitudes towards females, who may now be perceived as agents of change.

The first research theme concerns positive intra-family dynamics. Although initially, female entrepreneurs through role-sharing strategies use family resources such as their husband's support for business development, this can lead to more participation of family members in their businesses. This family cooperation is the outcome of female entrepreneurial activity and is also expressed through 'closed relationship and more intimacy among family members'. Evidence suggests that involvement of family members in female's businesses may have a positive impact on the 'increased their risk-taking and entrepreneurial intent'. As is evident from Nooshin and Fatemeh's accounts, they act as role models and their entrepreneurial activity significantly contributes to their family members' intentions to being entrepreneurial. Moreover, female entrepreneurs try to create opportunities in the form of business for household members. We also find evidence for personal growth of household members. The literature streams on female entrepreneurship have investigated their personal growth (e.g., Korsgaard and Anderson, 2011; Véras, 2015; Sheikh et al., 2019), but there is paucity of research on how female entrepreneurship could influence personal growth of their family members. Each of the women tells the story that their entrepreneurial journey had given their children a strong level of self-confidence. They believe that if they did not have entrepreneurial activity and were just housekeepers, their children's confidence would not be at this level. The impact of a mother's entrepreneurship was about the 'independence and sense of responsibility of the children'. The children that have an entrepreneurial mother show more independence and find themselves responsible in their personal life.

The second research theme shows the positive impact of an increased female income on the family members, provided the income is yielded within it. Our findings suggest that distinct features of female entrepreneurs such as family-driven motivations and value-sharing strategies (Allen et al., 2008; Klugman et al., 2014) cause them to invest more of their income in the household. All interviewees stated that they spend a significant part of their revenue on the educational and pedagogical needs of their children. The interference between entrepreneurship and family well-being acknowledges the impact of female entrepreneurship on the lives and livelihoods of all family members. The narratives suggest that a higher income supported education and household expenses, improved the living standards of the house and resulted in better overall well-being of the family. Our analysis shows that their value-sharing strategies at the household level are integrated and multi-dimensional. Findings show that widespread distribution of business profits at the family level has a compensatory nature. This means that in order to compensate for their shortcomings (in their own opinion) in family roles, they are trying hard to share benefits gained with family members. The findings also indicate that females' value creation cycle at the family level has a reverting nature. Entrepreneurs studied at first had different levels of family support; something that initially caused and continued to support their success in their entrepreneurship activities. In the next stages, and after the success of female entrepreneurs, they also return a significant proportion of created value based on a generous pattern to the family. These impacts could be seen in better standards of living and enhancement in the overall well-being of the household members (Jennings and Brush, 2013; Ribes-Giner et al., 2019).

Moreover, we also find evidence of a change in the attitudes towards women after starting their entrepreneurial careers. In this regard, scholars have discussed the spillover effects of work on family (Greenhaus and Powell, 2006), including the love and respect received by the family because of participation in paid work (Hammer et al., 2002), improvement in women's status, increased recognition and respect for work, and sharing of domestic responsibilities. The narratives herein reflect that women are valued for their knowledge and business acumen and thus are respected more by family members and spouses. It also results in changes in gender role attitudes wherein domestic responsibilities are shared by the husband and the wife, thus enabling women to give time to their businesses.

This finding shows that ethics of care and enacting a supportive role for all family members (e.g., Flanagan and Jackson, 1987; Hechavarría et al., 2017) in females represents an opportunity to enhance desired family values such as respect, love, and empathy.

TAKING FORWARD: TOWARD A VALUE APPROACH TO FEMALE ENTREPRENEURSHIP

In contrast to the theoretical approach that has introduced females as disadvantaged entrepreneurs, females' entrepreneurship is the source of value creation at various levels. Created value is not merely of economic nature and includes non-economic dimensions. Dimensions that express the distinctive characteristics and priorities of female entrepreneurs.

In this study, along with the growing trend of attention to entrepreneurship research, in order to provide a more detailed picture of the female entrepreneurship in a developing country, we looked at the created value by them at the family level. The context that within it many female entrepreneurs focus on their families. For this purpose, we've gone beyond the current abstract assumptions such as the linking or interaction of entrepreneurship and family, and studied the value created by female entrepreneurs at the family level in its multiple dimensions. In this contribution, we highlighted subjective values associated with the lived experiences of female entrepreneurship in Bandar Abbas. Such substantial, family values are ascertained in the family domain.

The research indicates that beyond the perception of family as a problem (Luomala, 2018), supporter (Monteith and Campfield, 2019) or context (Baker and Welter, 2018), family utilizes value created by female entrepreneurs; outcomes that have a positive impact on the spouse, children and other family members. These outcomes improve the position of female entrepreneurs from support-seeking entrepreneurs to the agents of value creation. Change that goes beyond common stereotypes and informs gender not as a limitation force, indeed as a factor in changing and improving the quality of family life. It can be expected that this impact is not limited to the family level and includes other levels such as social and business. So, we need to know more on how female entrepreneurship creates subjective values on other levels and also in different institutional contexts. While we have identified some values at the family level, despite the multi-dimensionality of those, future research is needed into in-depth measurements of dimensions in large-scale studies.

To conclude, we believe that subjective values of female entrepreneurship will be a relevant area for the future research, given the recent change in females' business status around the world. Through our research, we open a debate on intertwined notion of family and work. Previous research has mainly considered individual values and has also paid more attention to the impact of family on entrepreneurial activities. We hope that our discussion will stimulate future research on subjective values of female entrepreneurship.

NOTE

1.   All names have been anonymized.

REFERENCES

Ács, Z.J., Szerb, L., & Autio, E. (2016). *Global Entrepreneurship and Development Index 2015*. Cham: Springer.

Ahl, H. (2006). Why research on women entrepreneurs needs new directions. *Entrepreneurship Theory and Practice*, 30(5), 595–621.

Aldrich, H.E., & Cliff, J.E. (2003). The pervasive effects of family on entrepreneurship: Toward a family embeddedness perspective. *Journal of Business Venturing*, 18(5), 573–596.

Allen, I., Elaine, E., Amanda; L, Nan, D, Monica, G., & Global Entrepreneurship Research Association (2008). *Global Entrepreneurship Monitor (GEM): 2007 Report on Women and Entrepreneurship*. GERA; Babson College; The Center of Women's Leadership at Babson College.

Anderson, A.R. (1998). Cultivating the Garden of Eden: Environmental entrepreneuring. *Journal of Organizational Change Management*, 11(2), 135–144.

Arasti, Z. (2006). Iranian women entrepreneurs: The effective socio-cultural structures of business start-up, *Pajohesh Zanan*, 4(2), 93–119 (in Persian).

Arasti, Z., & Akbari Jokar, M.R. (2007). The Iranian women entrepreneurs' networks and business start-up. *Women's Studies (motaleat-i zanan)*, 4(3), 5–22 (in Persian).

Arasti, Z., & Akbari Jokar, M.R. (2008). A research on characteristics of Iranian educated women entrepreneurs businesses and their problems in starting their business up. *Daneshvar Shahed University*, 32(5), 37–46 (in Persian).

Arasti, Z., & Bahmani, N. (2017). Women's entrepreneurship in Iran. In S. Rezaei, L.-P. Dana, & V. Ramadani (Eds.), *Iranian Entrepreneurship* (pp. 109–137). Cham: Springer.

Arasti, Z., Rezayee, S.O., Zarei, B., & Panahi, S.M.S. (2012). A qualitative study on environmental factors affecting Iranian women entrepreneurs' growth orientation. *Journal of Management and Strategy*, 3(2), 39.

Arasti, Z., & Valinejad, M. (2011). Type of entrepreneurs incentives among Iranian women. *Women's Studies* (motaleat-E- zanan), 5(3), 99–125 (in Persian).

Association of Iranian Women Entrepreneurs. (2013). Interactions between family management and business of women entrepreneurs. In *Association of Iranian Women Entrepreneurs Magazine*, Tehran, Iran: DCAI (in Persian).

Autio, E., Kenney, M., Mustar, P., Siegel, D., & Wright, M. (2014). Entrepreneurial innovation: The importance of context. *Research Policy*, 43(7), 1097–1108.

Baker, T., & Welter, F. (2018). Contextual entrepreneurship: An interdisciplinary perspective. *Foundations and Trends in Entrepreneurship*, 14(4), 357–426.

Bruni, A., Gherardi, S., & Poggio, B. (2000). *All'ombra della maschilità: storie di imprese e di genere*. Milano: Guerini e Associati.

Brush, C.G., & Cooper, S.Y. (2012). Female entrepreneurship and economic development: An international perspective. *Entrepreneurship & Regional Development*, 24(1–2), 1–6.

Brush, C.G., De Bruin, A., & Welter, F. (2009). A gender-aware framework for women's entrepreneurship. *International Journal of Gender and Entrepreneurship*, 1(1), 8–24.

Carter, S., Kuhl, A., Marlow, S., & Mwaura, S. (2017). Households as a site of entrepreneurial activity. *Foundations and Trends® in Entrepreneurship*, 13(2), 81–190.

Chamlou, N., Klapper, L., & Muzi, S. (2008). *The Environment for Women's Entrepreneurship in the Middle East and North Africa*. Washington, DC: The World Bank.

Cohen, B., Smith, B., & Mitchell, R. (2008). Toward a sustainable conceptualization of dependent variables in entrepreneurship research. *Business Strategy and the Environment*, 17(2), 107–119.

Cromie, S. (1987). Motivations of aspiring male and female entrepreneurs. *Journal of Organizational Behavior*, 8(3), 251–261.

De Bruin, A., Brush, C.G., & Welter, F. (2007). Advancing a framework for coherent research on women's entrepreneurship. *Entrepreneurship Theory and Practice*, 31(3), 323–339.

De Vita, L., Mari, M., & Poggesi, S. (2014). Women entrepreneurs in and from developing countries: Evidences from the literature. *European Management Journal*, 32(3), 451–460.

Dyke, L.S., & Murphy, S.A. (2006). How we define success: A qualitative study of what matters most to women and men. *Sex Roles*, 55(5–6), 357–371.

Eddleston, K.A., & Powell, G.N. (2012). Nurturing entrepreneurs' work–family balance: A gendered perspective. *Entrepreneurship Theory and Practice*, 36(3), 513–541.

Elkington, J. (2004). Enter the triple bottom line. *The Triple Bottom Line: Does It All Add Up*, 11(12), 1–16.

Essers, C., Doorewaard, H., & Benschop, Y. (2013). Family ties: Migrant female business owners doing identity work on the public–private divide. *Human Relations*, 66(12), 1645–1665.

Flanagan, O., & Jackson, K. (1987). Justice, care, and gender: The Kohlberg-Gilligan debate revisited. *Ethics*, 97(3), 622–637.

Fisher, R., Maritz, A., & Lobo, A. (2014). Evaluating entrepreneurs' perception of success: Development of a measurement scale. *International Journal of Entrepreneurial Behavior & Research*, 20(5), 478–492.

Foley, M., Baird, M., Cooper, R., & Williamson, S. (2018). Is independence really an opportunity? The experience of entrepreneur-mothers. *Journal of Small Business and Enterprise Development*, 25(2), 313–329.

Gelard, P. (2007). Productivity Iranian women entrepreneurs. *Journal of Commerce*, 12(46), 179–209 (in Persian).

Giménez, D., & Calabrò, A. (2018). The salient role of institutions in women's entrepreneurship: A critical review and agenda for future research. *International Entrepreneurship and Management Journal*, 14(4), 857–882.

Gorgievski, M.J., Ascalon, M.E., & Stephan, U. (2011). Small business owners' success criteria: A values approach to personal differences. *Journal of Small Business Management*, 49(2), 207–232.

Greene, P.G., & Brush, C.G. (Eds.) (2018). *A Research Agenda for Women and Entrepreneurship*. Cheltenham, UK and Northampton, MA, USA: Edward Elgar Publishing. https://doi.org/10.4337/9781785365379.

Greenhaus, J.H., & Powell, G.N. (2006). When work and family are allies: A theory of work–family enrichment. *Academy of Management Review*, 31(1), 72–92.

Guttman, A. (2015). *Set to take over tech: 70% of Iran's science and engineering students are women*, www.forbes.com/sites/amyguttman/2015/12/09/set-to-take-over-tech-70-of-iransscience-and-engineering-students-are-women/#c18f70565870 (accessed 10 June 2016).

Hammer, L.B., Colton, C.L., Caubet, S.L., & Brockwood, K.J. (2002). The unbalanced life: Work and family conflict. In: Thomas, J., & Herson, M. (eds) *Handbook of Mental Health in the Workplace* (pp. 83–102). Thousand Oaks: Sage.

Harris, C., Morrison, R., Ho, M., & Lewis, K. (2008). Mumpreneurs: Mothers in the business of babies. Proceedings from the Australia and New Zealand Academy of Management Conference, Auckland, New Zealand (December).

Haugh, H.M., & Tawler, A. (2016). Linking social entrepreneurship and social change: The mediating role of empowerment. *Journal of Business Research*, 133, 643–658.

Hawk, T.F. (2011). An ethic of care: A relational ethic for the relational characteristics of organizations. In M. Hamington & M. Sander-Staudt (Eds.), *Applying Care Ethics to Business* (pp. 3–34). Dordrecht, the Netherlands: Springer.

Hechavarría, D.M., Terjesen, S.A., Ingram, A.E., Renko, M., Justo, R., & Elam, A. (2017). Taking care of business: The impact of culture and gender on entrepreneurs' blended value creation goals. *Small Business Economics*, 48(1), 225–257.

Held, V. (2005). *The Ethics of Care: Personal, Political, and Global*. Oxford: Oxford University Press.

Henry, C., Foss, L., & Ahl, H. (2016). Gender and entrepreneurship research: A review of methodological approaches. *International Small Business Journal*, 34(3), 217–241.

Hughes, K.D., Jennings, J.E., Brush, C., Carter, S., & Welter, F. (2012). Extending women's entrepreneurship research in new directions. *Entrepreneurship Theory and Practice*, 36(3), 429–442.

Jamali, D. (2009). Constraints and opportunities facing women entrepreneurs in developing countries: A relational perspective. *Gender in Management: An International Journal*, 24(4), 232–251.

James, A.E. (2012). Conceptualizing 'woman' as an entrepreneurial advantage: A reflexive approach. In: Hughes, K.D., & Jennings, J.E (eds), *Global Women's Entrepreneurship Research: Diverse Settings, Questions and Approaches* (pp. 226–240). Cheltenham, UK and Northampton, MA, USA: Edward Elgar Publishing.

Javadian, G., & Singh, R.P. (2012). Examining successful Iranian women entrepreneurs: An exploratory study. *Gender in Management: An International Journal*, 27(3), 148–164.

Javaheri, F., & Ghozati, S. (2004). Barriers of women entrepreneurship: The study of influence of sexual injustice on women entrepreneurship in Iran. *Journal of Iran Sociology*, 5(2), 161–178.

Jennings, J.E., & Brush, C.G. (2013). Research on women entrepreneurs: Challenges to (and from) the broader entrepreneurship literature? *The Academy of Management Annals*, 7(1), 663–715.

Jennings, J.E., & McDougald, M.S. (2007). Work–family interface experiences and coping strategies: Implications for entrepreneurship research and practice. *Academy of Management Review*, 32(3), 747–760.

Kamal, S., & Daoud, Y. (2018). Explaining the gender gap in entrepreneurial propensity. In N. Faghih & M. R. Zali (Eds.), *Entrepreneurship Ecosystem in the Middle East and North Africa (MENA)* (pp. 327–350). Cham: Springer.

Kantor, P. (2002). Gender, microenterprise success and cultural context: The case of south Asia. *Entrepreneurship Theory and Practice*, 26(4), 131–143.

Khan, N. (2014). Family to work conflict among working mothers in UAE. *European Scientific Journal*, 10(20), 205–216.

Klugman, J., Hanmer, L., Twigg, S., Hasan, T., McCleary-Sills, J., & Santamaria, J. (2014). *Voice and Agency: Empowering Women and Girls for Shared Prosperity*. Washington, DC: The World Bank.

Korsgaard, S., & Anderson, A.R. (2011). Enacting entrepreneurship as social value creation. *International Small Business Journal*, 20(10), 1–17.

Langevang, T., Gough, K.V., Yankson, P.W., Owusu, G., & Osei, R. (2015). Bounded entrepreneurial vitality: The mixed embeddedness of female entrepreneurship. *Economic Geography*, 91(4), 449–473.

Larty, J., & Hamilton, E. (2011). Structural approaches to narrative analysis in entrepreneurship research: Exemplars from two researchers. *International Small Business Journal*, 29(3), 220–237.

Luomala, K. (2018). *Mumpreneurs?, everyday complexities in the realm of time, money, business and motherhood*. Ph.D. thesis, University of Turku, Turku School of Economics.

Mari, M., Poggesi, S., & De Vita, L. (2016). Family embeddedness and business performance: Evidences from women-owned firms. *Management Decision*, 54(2), 476–500.

Marlow, S. (2002). Self-employed women: A part of or apart from feminist theory? *International Journal of Entrepreneurship and Innovation*, 2(2), 83–91.

McGowan, P., Redeker, C.L., Cooper, S.Y. & Greenan, K. (2012). Female entrepreneurship and the management of business and domestic roles: Motivations, expectations and realities. *Entrepreneurship & Regional Development*, 24, 53–72.

Meliou, E., & Edwards, T. (2018). Relational practices and reflexivity: exploring the responses of women entrepreneurs to changing household dynamics. *International Small Business Journal*, 36(2), 149–168.

Mirghafoori, H., Tooranloo, H., & Taheridemneh, M. (2010). Investigating the barriers of women's entrepreneurship in Iran society. *Journal of Management Transformation*, 2(1), 47–64.

Modarresi, M., Arasti, Z., Talebi, K., & Farasatkhah, M. (2016). Women's entrepreneurship in Iran: How are women owning and managing home-based businesses motivated to grow? *International Journal of Gender and Entrepreneurship*, 8(4), 446–470.

Monteith, W., & Campfield, L. (2019). Business as family, family as business: Female entrepreneurship in Kampala. Uganda. *Geoforum*, 101, 111–121.

Nair, S., & Blomquist, T. (2018). The temporal dimensions of business incubation: A value-creation perspective. *The International Journal of Entrepreneurship and Innovation*, 10.1177/1465750318817970.

Neneh, B.N. (2017). Family support and performance of women-owned enterprises: The mediating effect of family-to-work enrichment. *The Journal of Entrepreneurship*, 26(2), 196–219.

Nicholls, A. (2009). We do good things, don't we?: Blended value accounting in social entrepreneurship. *Accounting, Organizations and Society*, 34(6–7), 755–769.

Noguera, M., Alvarez, C., Merigo, J.M., & Urbano, D. (2015). Determinants of female entrepreneurship in Spain: An institutional approach. *Computational and Mathematical Organization Theory*, 21(4), 341–355.

Parasuraman, S., Purohit, Y.S., Godshalk, V.S., & Beutell, N.J. (1996). Work and family variables, entrepreneurship career success, and psychological wellbeing. *Journal of Vocational Behavior*, 48(3), 275–300.

PBO (2016). Plan and budget organization. https://hormozgan.mporg.ir/FileSystem/View/File .aspx (accessed 10 November 2019).

Pitt-Catsouphes, M., & Christensen, K. (2004). Unmasking the taken for granted. *Community, Work & Family*, 7(2), 123–142.

Poggesi, S., Mari, M., & De Vita, L. (2015). What's new in female entrepreneurship research? Answers from the literature. *International Entrepreneurship and Management Journal*, 12(3), 735–764.

Porter, M.E., & Kramer, M.R. (2011). Creating shared value: How to fix capitalism and unleash a new wave of growth?, *Harvard Business Review*, January–February, 2–17.

Ribes-Giner, G., Moya-Clemente, I., Cervelló-Royo, R., Perello-Marin, M.R. (2019). Domestic economic and social conditions empowering female entrepreneurship. *Journal of Business Research*. https://doi.org/10.1016/j.jbusres.2017.12.005.

Salehi-Isfahani, D. (2008). Are Iranian women overeducated? *Brookings Institution Newsletter*. https://www.brookings.edu/opinions/are-iranian-women-overeducated (accessed 8 March 2008).

Sarfaraz, L., Mian, S.A., Karadeniz, E.E., Zali, M.R., & Qureshi, M.S. (2018). Female entrepreneurship, internationalization, and trade liberalization in Iran, Pakistan, and Turkey. In N. Faghih & M.R. Zali (Eds.), *Entrepreneurship Ecosystem in the Middle East and North Africa (MENA)* (pp. 677–690). Cham: Springer.

SCI (2016). Statistical Centre of Iran. https://www.amar.org.ir (accessed 10 November 2019).

Shaw, E., Wilson, J., & Pret, T. (2017). The process of embedding a small firm in its industrial context. *International Small Business Journal*, 35(3), 219–243.

Sheikh, S., Yousafzai, S., Sist, F., Ar, A.A., & Saeed, S. (2019). Value creation through women's entrepreneurship, in Yousafzai, S., Fayolle, A., Lindgreen, A., Henry, C., Saeed, S., & Sheikh, S. (Eds.), *Women Entrepreneurs and the Myth of 'Underperformance': A New Look at Women's Entrepreneurship Research* (pp. 20–33). Cheltenham, UK and Northampton, MA, USA: Edward Elgar Publishing.

Silverman, D. (2005). *Doing Qualitative Research: A Practical Handbook*. London: Sage.

Simarasl, N., Pandey, S., & Mathias, B.D. (2019). A study of network blockages and effective entrepreneurial strategies, Academy of Management Conference, Boston, MA, USA.

Simpson, M., & Docherty, A.J. (2004). E-commerce adoption support and advice for UK SMEs. *Journal of Small Business and Enterprise Development*, 11(3), 315–328.

Tu, C., & Hwang, S. (2014). Innovation and success in micro-enterprises: The role of family and environments. *International Proceedings of Economics Development and Research (IPEDR)*, 70(17), 86–89.

UNDP (United Nations Development Programme) (2018). National Human Development Report 2018: Planning the Opportunities for a Youthful Population, Human Development Report Office, UNDP, New York.

Valinejad, M. (2011). *Identify the impact of incentives to Iranian women entrepreneurs grow their businesses*. Master thesis, University of Tehran (in Persian).

Véras, E.Z. (2015). Female entrepreneurship: from women's empowerment to shared value creation. *International Journal of Management Science and Business Administration*, 1(3) 50–63.

Wach, D., Stephan, U., & Gorgievski, M. (2016). More than money: Developing an integrative multi-factorial measure of entrepreneurial success. *International Small Business Journal*, 34(8), 1098–1121.

Watson, T.J. (2013). Entrepreneurship in action: Bringing together the individual, organizational and institutional dimensions of entrepreneurial action. *Entrepreneurship & Regional Development*, 25(5–6), 404–422.

WEF (2018). The global gender gap report (database), http://www3.weforum.org (accessed 5 September 2018).

Welsh, D.H.B., Kim, G., Memili, E., & Kaciak, E. (2014). The influence of family moral support and personal problems on firm performance: The case of Korean female entrepreneurs. *Journal of Developmental Entrepreneurship*, 19(3), 1–17.

Welsh, D.H.B., Memili, E., & Kaciak, E. (2016). An empirical analysis of the impact of family moral support on Turkish women entrepreneurs. *Journal of Innovation & Knowledge*, 1(1), 3–12.

Welter, F., & Smallbone, D. (2011). Institutional perspectives on entrepreneurial behavior in challenging environments. *Journal of Small Business Management*, 49(1), 107–125.

World Bank (2017). World Bank Annual Report 2017, World Bank, Washington, DC.

World Bank (2019). Women, Business, and the Law 2019: A Decade of Reform. February, Info Dev, World Bank, Washington, DC.

Wright, M., & Stigliani, I. (2013). Entrepreneurship and growth. *International Small Business Journal*, 31(1), 3–22.

Xheneti, M., Karki., S.T., & Madden, A. (2018). Negotiating business and family demands within a patriarchal society – the case of women entrepreneurs in the Nepalese context. *Entrepreneurship & Regional Development*, DOI:10.1080/08985626.2018.1551792.

Zahra, S.A., & Wright, M. (2015). Understanding the social role of entrepreneurship. *Journal of Management Studies*, 53(4), 610–629.

PART IV

VALUE CREATION AT THE SOCIETAL LEVEL

14. Saudi Arabian women entrepreneurs: agents of change and value creators

Hayfaa Tlaiss

Previous entrepreneurship studies have primarily been preoccupied with explaining value creation and entrepreneurial success through focusing on monetary/objective measures, such as increased profitability and sales (Kirkwood, 2016), business survival, continuity (Gorgievski et al., 2011) and growth (Fisher et al., 2014). Despite the importance of these indicators or measures, recent studies argue that an exclusive focus on financial performance and monetary/objective performance indicators does not fully capture notions of value creation (Zahra et al., 2009). To that effect, several studies revealed that entrepreneurs conceptualise their entrepreneurial success using subjective conceptualisations, such as achieving personal fulfilment and work–life balance (Jayawarna et al., 2011) and through value creation in terms of achieving socially desirable and responsible outcomes (Fisher et al., 2014) and having a positive impact on the wider community (Angel et al., 2018).

Furthermore, while women's entrepreneurship has been the focus of ever-increasing research attention and studies, empirical studies of Arab women entrepreneurs have two main shortcomings. First, there is limited understanding of how Arab women entrepreneurs perceive their own success given the preoccupation of previous studies with the barriers and challenges faced in the context of their conservative, masculine and patriarchal societal culture (Al-Ahmadi, 2011; Al-Asfour et al., 2017). Second, the geographic focus of the currently available studies has been skewed towards specific countries, with the majority focused on United Arab Emirates (Tlaiss, 2015) and Lebanon (Tlaiss, 2019; Tlaiss and Kauser, 2019), with minimal studies, other than that by McAdam et al. (2018) looking at other Arab countries and encompassing Saudi Arabia. Third, when Saudi Arabian women's entrepreneurship is researched, the majority of previous studies have been descriptive in nature and mostly focused on identifying the characteristics of the Saudi women entrepreneurs (e.g., Zamberi Ahmad, 2011a, 2011b), with scant research focusing on gender and socio-cultural values (e.g., McAdam et al., 2018).

To attend to this research gap, this chapter aims to investigate how Saudi Arabian women entrepreneurs celebrate their success and create value through their entrepreneurship. In doing so, I recognise gender as a dynamic, social performance whose articulations change across time and context (Butler, 1993). Through conducting in-depth interviews, I try to give the women entrepreneurs a voice and contextualise the findings within the societal, cultural and gender structures of Saudi Arabia. Accordingly, I move away from research interested in identifying the "general laws of entrepreneurship which might transcend context" (Hjorth et al., 2008, p. 81 in

Zahra, 2007) and try to better understand the unique experience of Arab women's entrepreneurship. To better understand this uniqueness and grasp the interplay between the intertwined societal, cultural and gendered multi-layered context of Saudi Arabia and the interactions between agency and these factors in value creation, I also capitalise on intersectionality theories (Calás et al., 2009).

This chapter proceeds as follows. I commence by providing an overview of the key constructs of entrepreneurial success and the major shortcomings in the literature. Then I discuss the methodology used. Next, I lay out the findings and discuss them within relevant literature. I conclude by highlighting the major contributions of this chapter and by offering suggestions for future studies.

LITERATURE REVIEW

Entrepreneurial outcomes and success have been mostly studied in reference to the performance and the success of a business activity (Tlaiss, 2019). Hence, the focus has been on performance indicators concentrated on objective monetary/financial conceptualisations, such as business survival and continuity, increased profitability and business growth (Fisher et al., 2014), as well as income and wealth creation (Kirkwood, 2016). Despite the importance of these indicators for evaluating entrepreneurial activities, such an exclusive focus ignores both an entrepreneur's personal motivations for starting their own businesses (Gorgievski et al., 2011) and social impact (Zahra et al., 2009). This focus on financial indicators also disadvantages entrepreneurial activities created by women and minorities and the value that these entrepreneurs create at various levels of the economy and society (Welter, 2011).

In this regard, recent studies suggest that entrepreneurs establish their businesses and conceptualise their entrepreneurial success through non-monetary, subjective indicators, such as having high customer satisfaction (Wach et al., 2016) or being socially responsible (Jayawarna et al., 2011). Accordingly, the logic of narrowing entrepreneurial activities to strictly monetary terms is called into question. For example, while entrepreneurs in Columbia conceptualised their entrepreneurial outcomes and success through monetary and non-monetary criteria (Angel et al., 2018), those in the Netherlands perceived their personal satisfaction as more important than wealth (Gorgievski et al., 2011).

The shortcomings are also related to the lack of attention paid to how women entrepreneurs experience value creation and entrepreneurial success, particularly amongst those in the Arab world. To further explain, the male entrepreneur is often promoted as the ideal entrepreneur and this problematises the feminine (Ahl and Marlow, 2012). Furthermore, women-owned businesses are often labelled as underperforming despite studies demonstrating that women-owned firms perform slightly better than those owned by men (Marlow and McAdam, 2013). However, our knowledge of how women entrepreneurs experience their own entrepreneurial success and value creation is scant as previous studies have primarily focused on understanding men's experiences (Fisher et al., 2014; Angel et al., 2018). Furthermore, despite the unchallenged importance of contextual factors in entrepreneurial actions (Yousufazi et al., 2015), previous studies have predominantly been conducted in Western contexts (Tlaiss, 2019), with minimal attention attributed to the multiple realms of value that result from women's entrepreneurship in different contexts. This is particularly true and relevant in the context of Arab women entrepreneurs (Tlaiss and Kauser, 2019) and especially for women in Saudi Arabia (McAdam et al., 2018).

To further explain, the Kingdom of Saudi Arabia is the birthplace of Islam and is home to the two holy cities of Mecca and Medina. Accordingly, the socio-cultural environment is highly traditional, patriarchal and conservative; women are thus expected to be caregivers and men are expected to be breadwinners. Business life is also strongly entrenched in patriarchal cultural values and is heavily influenced by a conservative religious society (Tlaiss and Elamin, 2016). This ultimately creates a very challenging environment for women wishing to create their own businesses and careers outside their homes. Any reference to the culture of Saudi Arabia is incomplete without reference to Islam. Although Islam grants women the right to education, employment and entrepreneurship (Tlaiss, 2015), the religious scholars in Saudi adhere to the strictest interpretation of Islam, thus prioritising the roles of women as mothers and wives (Al-Asfour et al., 2017). These scholars further fuel the masculine culture and patriarchy in Saudi by emphasising the conservative, traditional interpretations of verses in the Quran that result in restricting women's mobility and freedom and limiting their interaction with men in public (Al-Asfour et al., 2017). Collectively, these factors create a constraining environment for women wishing to pursue organisational careers or entrepreneurial ventures.

In an attempt to reduce international criticism, the Kingdom of Saudi Arabia pursued several initiatives to improve the overall status of women in the country. These initiatives included campaigns to encourage the education of females and their participation in the labour force. Consequently, Saudi females account for more than 50% of Saudi university graduates (Central Department of Statistics and Information, 2014), with the gender gap in education having closed by more than 90% (World Economic Forum, 2012). The number of women employed in the private sector has tripled since 2011, to reach a total of 180,000 by the end of 2012 (Ministry of Labor, 2013). In 2016, the Crown Prince Mohamed Bin Salman Al Saud launched Vision 2030, which is a blueprint of the government's plan for the future of Saudi Arabia. The Vision aims at reducing the country's dependency on oil, promoting the diversity of its economy and further developing several public service sectors, such as health, recreation and tourism. One of the most notable goals of Vision 2030 is increasing women's economic participation from 22% to 30% and advancing their careers (Vision 2030, 2018). These objectives have been accompanied by several long-anticipated reforms, including the removal of the ban on women driving, efforts to eliminate the gender-pay gap and allowing women to start their own businesses and to join the army. It is therefore within this context – a country attempting to bridge traditional and conservative towards development and economic advancement – that this current study seeks to explore women's entrepreneurship and value creation activities in Saudi Arabia.

METHODOLOGY

To achieve my objectives, I adopted a social constructionist perspective (Zahra and Wright, 2011). Accordingly, gender is explored as a situated practice that entrepreneurs perform (Butler, 1993) and construct differently across contexts and cultures (Ahl, 2006). Given that gender is discursively constructed at the interconnections of various social markers, including societal values and cultural norms, I also lean on intersectionality theory (Calás et al., 2009) to capture these intersections.

As per the suggestion of Tlaiss and Kauser (2019), the term *entrepreneur* was operationalised as an individual who owned and managed a business and was self-employed. Purposeful sampling (Neergaard, 2007) through capitalising on network and reference-based sampling was used. Therefore, my personal connections were used to identify entrepreneurs interested in participating in the study and once interviewed, the participants were asked to point towards other key informants (Neergaard, 2007).

Face-to-face, semi-structured interviews were conducted and the interviewees were promised complete anonymity throughout the process (accordingly, the names in the findings section have been changed). The interviews were tape recorded and lasted between 60 and 120 minutes. The interviews were directly transcribed and coded using thematic analysis. The interviewees were asked to talk about how they conceptualise their entrepreneurial success. Given that some of the interviews were conducted in Arabic or a mix of Arabic and English, the manuscripts were translated and back-translated by the researcher and an independent bilingual researcher familiar with the area of research (Tlaiss, 2019; Tlaiss and Kauser, 2019).

The resulting sample consisted of five Saudi women entrepreneurs. All the interviewees had a tertiary educational degree and were married with at least two children. The women were between 40 and 57 years of age. All businesses operated in the services sector and included a beauty spa and a hair salon, a chain of restaurants, an educational institute, a chain of pharmacies, and a medical laboratory. These business operations ranged in longevity from 7 to 15 years and employed between 9 and 60 people.

The interviews were analysed thematically using template analysis (Tlaiss, 2019). Through thematic analysis, I focused on determining the coherence of the data collected and the extent to which it deepened our understanding of the value creation process of Saudi women entrepreneurs (Patton, 1990). To analyse the data, an initial code book was established based on a literature review and guided by the interview questions (Miles and Huberman, 1994). Then, after every interview, I read the interview manuscripts and coded them. The analysis was initially conducted on each interviewee and then systematically compared across interviewees to facilitate theoretical generalisation. Furthermore, I compared the initial code book to the emerging themes in order to identify convergent themes (Miles and Huberman, 1994). Accordingly, the initial code book was modified to include the emerging themes and a final coding template was reached (Strauss and Corbin, 1990).

FINDINGS AND DISCUSSION

Acknowledging Entrepreneurial Success Through Islamic Feminism and a Patriarchal Society

The Saudi women entrepreneurs, similar to their Lebanese counterparts (Tlaiss, 2019), reported experiencing entrepreneurial success. The interviewees celebrated their entrepreneurial experiences and choice of career against a backdrop of socio-cultural barriers. In other words, the Saudi women spoke about their difficult journey in entrepreneurship and about the masculinity of their society and how it extended to entrepreneurship, which was perceived to be a male's domain. This was clear in what Maha said:

> Of course, I feel successful…being an entrepreneur in Riyadh is not a woman's job and yet I opened my own business.

Accordingly, the women in this Saudi Arabian study confirmed the findings of previous studies elsewhere in the Arab world (Tlaiss and Kauser, 2019) regarding the heavy gendering of the entrepreneurial domain. They also stressed the negative influence of socio-cultural values on their entrepreneurship as well as attempts by male counterparts to put them out of business:

> Saudi society is very conservative and traditional so according to them, my place was in the house looking after my children and not having a chain of pharmacies (Danah)

Meanwhile, Leen stated:

> Things were not as easy several years ago when I decided to open my laboratories…the men in the business tried to drive me bankrupt.

These findings confirm the conservative status of Saudi Arabian society and the emphasis it attributes to traditional gender roles as well as the confinement of women to roles within their homes as mothers and homemakers (Tlaiss and Elamin, 2016; Al-Asfour et al., 2017).

All the entrepreneurs in this study demonstrated a high level of agency and a great determination to make their businesses survive and succeed as per Aljohara's comments:

> I was not willing to give up…I am very stubborn and I was determined to make it happen and it did.

The women also demonstrated agency in developing an in-depth knowledge of Islamic teachings regarding gender equality and using these teachings to assert their career choice as entrepreneurs and to silence their critics. In other words, when criticised by their families or society for their entrepreneurship, the Saudi women entrepreneurs used quotes from the Quran and Hadeeth to highlight the equal worth between men and women in Islam as well as the right of women to seek education and leadership positions if they wish to. To that effect, Danah stated:

> Allah created men and women as equals...it is very clear in the Quranic verse 'He that works evil will not be requited but by the like thereof: and he that works a righteous deed – whether man or woman – and is a Believer – such will enter the Garden (of Bliss): Therein will they have abundance without measure.' (40th Quranic verse of Surat Ghafir (The Forgiver))

The women also spoke about their right to work, as granted by Islam, and described their religion as supportive of their work outside their homes, their entrepreneurship and making money. They also focused on the freedom and equality that Islam grants women to claim their right to start and run their own business. This is clear in what Leen stated:

> Islam is not a limitation at all...on the contrary, there are several examples in Islamic history of strong women who were successful businesswomen, including the wife of the Prophet (PBUH).

Accordingly, along with Tlaiss (2015) and McAdam et al. (2018), we demonstrate how Saudi women capitalised on a feminist interpretation of Islam to overcome societal barriers and to create their own businesses.

Nevertheless, all of the interviewees highlighted the change that is taking place in Saudi society. They particularly spoke about the growing attention being paid to women's entrepreneurship through a number of government entities providing funding and support, such as Munshaat. This is clear in the following excerpt:

> The new generation of females are very lucky...this is the best time to be a woman in Saudi...the government is providing its full support and encouraging women to create their own business. (Alanoud)

The interviewees also expressed their support to the changes in social expectations from women. Aljohara stated, 'Things are changing quickly in Saudi Arabia...no one today expects women to stay at home...People today are getting used to seeing women as medical doctors, lawyers, and business owners.' The Saudi women also spoke about the changes in national rules that support women, such as allowing women to drive and the positive effect of Vision 2030 on increasing the number of women in the workforce. Maha said; 'Vision 2030 has been instrumental for helping women...today, businesses are looking for women to hire...you see Saudi women working as cashiers and in restaurants and in hotels which is great...you see them drive to work.'

Value Creation at the Societal Level

When asked to conceptualise their entrepreneurial success, the Saudi women attributed special attention to their contribution to society through value creation. Accordingly, our findings support the claims of Welter (2011) regarding the importance of value creation as a measure of entrepreneurial success. Nevertheless, we extend this argument by providing empirical evidence of how value creation takes place within the context of Arab Muslim women. In other words, all the interviewees were cognisant of the importance of their businesses to both their local economy and society. These women have created value at the societal level through creating their own businesses and growing them and more importantly through providing employment for young Saudi women. The interviewees also spoke about how their businesses are instrumental in developing their economies and in employment creation. This is clear in Alanoud's statement:

> My entrepreneurial success is very clear through my contribution to the local economy... the majority of my employees are women...I give them employment and thus improve their overall standards of living.

The Saudi women in this study also celebrated their entrepreneurial success and value creation through their current status as role models. To further explain, after several years of being entrepreneurs and based on their experience and achievements, our interviewees are being celebrated today as role models. Universities and semi-governmental entities invite these interviewees to be motivational speakers in the hopes of inspiring young women who are interested in creating their own businesses. This is illustrated in the following excerpts:

> I was a guest speaker in a very prestigious university and I spoke to young undergraduate female students about my business and what it takes to be an entrepreneur. (Aljohara)
> I sit on the board of several committees in governmental and semi-governmental entities whereby my feedback is solicited on how to make Saudi a better place for women's businesses. (Maha)

Hence, we argue that these women created value at the societal level through being role models for young women and change agents for more societal change. We also demonstrate how these women create value through their social impact, particularly through having a positive impact on Saudi society. These findings are thus aligned with those of Angel et al. (2018) and Zahra et al. (2009).

All the women entrepreneurs in this study spoke about their role as mentors. One spoke about meeting with young Saudi women who are interested in creating their own business and providing them with advice:

> I, along with other Saudi women entrepreneurs, created this online community whereby young Saudi women who are interested in starting their own business can contact me and I provide them with the advice they need. (Leen)

The interviewees also spoke about helping young Saudi women interested in starting their own business by connecting them with venture capitalists as well as providing them with advice on how to start a business.

This is value creation at the societal level and is evident in Alanoud's words:

> I often meet with young Saudi women who are interested in creating their own business. If I find their idea feasible and has potential, I refer them to the bank that I work with and put in a good word for them so they can get the loan they need to get started.

Accordingly, we demonstrate how Saudi women entrepreneurs experience their entrepreneurial success through being mentors to young women and thus being socially responsible. By encouraging young women to be entrepreneurs, these women are contributing to societal change. The women are supporting a movement away from traditional norms and attitudes that limit women's suitability to domestic chores and pushing boundaries towards women embracing entrepreneurial ambitions and intentions.

CONCLUSIONS AND SUGGESTIONS FOR FUTURE STUDIES

In this chapter, I examined how women entrepreneurs experience and conceptualise entrepreneurial success and how they create value. Saudi Arabia is a conservative, patriarchal country that is undergoing fundamental ideological, societal, cultural, economic and political change and is the empirical setting of this study. Accordingly, the empirical findings demonstrate how entrepreneurial success is a subjective concept within which entrepreneurs have their own understanding and conceptualisations of what success means to them. Saudi women entrepreneurs assessed their entrepreneurial success from within broader perspectives, whereby they factored in their conceptualisations of value creation at the societal level. In addition, the women in this study portrayed personal agency and capitalised on a feminist perspective to Islamic teachings in order to construct their own entrepreneurship within a conservative, masculine context rather than accepting patriarchal interpretations. The women negotiated their entrepreneurial choices and navigated through Islam and patriarchal societal structures and constraints.

Through the provisions of these findings, I make three key contributions. First, I contribute to research on entrepreneurial success and value creation by demonstrating how Saudi women experience their entrepreneurial success through their ability to create value for others at their societal level. This finding provides evidence of how women entrepreneurs create value through being role models, mentors and employment-providers. We respond to previous scholarly calls (Fisher et al., 2014; Angel et al., 2018) and focus on how women entrepreneurs experience entrepreneurial success. These findings are also critical as they provide novel information on value creation and challenges compared to previous studies that limit the conceptualisations of entrepreneurial success to financial/non-financial perspectives (Gorgievski et al., 2011; Fisher et al., 2014; Kirkwood, 2016; Angel et al., 2018). Second, I contribute to research on women's entrepreneurship outside European and North American contexts. This study provides evidence of the importance of contextual factors in improving our understanding of the experiences of women entrepreneurs around the world (Yousufazi et al., 2015; Tlaiss and Kauser, 2019). Third, I contribute to a growing stream of research that focuses on Arab women's agency. The findings of this study are new as the majority of what is currently available focuses on the agency of women in countries such as Lebanon (Tlaiss, 2019; Tlaiss and Kauser, 2019) and United Arab Emirates (Tlaiss, 2015). This study also demonstrates how Saudi women entrepreneurs use their agency to adopt an Islamic feminist perspective in order to overcome societal barriers and navigate their entrepreneurship through a patriarchal culture.

My examination of the entrepreneurial success of Saudi women entrepreneurs, particularly in terms of value creation, results in a number of suggestions for future research. First, future studies could explore whether Saudi women create value at an organisational or individual level. Second, cross-country research throughout the Arab world is really needed to better understand how patriarchy and Islam are reflected in women's entrepreneurship. Third, it would be also very interesting to see future studies dig deeper into enhancing our understanding of whether and how the objective/subjective, financial/non-financial dichotomy of entrepreneurial success, which is commonly used in Western contexts, unfolds in the context of the Arab world, particularly in Saudi Arabia. It would be particularly useful to explore gender differences in the conceptualisations of entrepreneurial success in the context of both male and female Arab entrepreneurs.

REFERENCES

Ahl, H. (2006). Why research on women entrepreneurs needs new directions. *Entrepreneurship Theory and Practice. 30* (5), 595–621.

Ahl, H., and Marlow, S. (2012). Exploring the dynamics of gender, feminism and entrepreneurship: Advancing debate to escape a dead end? *Organization. 19* (5), 543–562.

Al-Ahmadi, H. (2011). Challenges facing women leaders in Saudi Arabia. *Human Resource Development International. 14* (2), 149–166.

Al-Asfour, A., Tlaiss, H.A., Khan, S.A., and Rajasekar, J. (2017). Saudi women's work challenges and barriers to career advancement. *Career Development International. 22*(2), 184–199.

Angel, P., Jenkins, A., and Stephens, A. (2018). Understanding entrepreneurial success: A phenomenographic approach. *International Small Business Journal. 36* (6), 611–636.

Butler, J. (1993). Critically queer. *GLQ: A Journal of Lesbian and Gay Studies. 1*(1), 17–32.

Calás, M.B., Smircich, L., and Bourne, K.A. (2009). Extending the boundaries: Reframing 'entrepreneurship as social change' through feminist perspectives. *Academy of Management Review. 34* (3), 552–569.

Central Department of Statistics and Information (2014). *The Kingdom of Saudi Arabia.* http://www.cdsi.gov.sa/ [23 August 2014].

Fisher, R., Maritz, A., and Lobo, A. (2014). Evaluating entrepreneurs' perception of success: Development of a measurement scale. *International Journal of Entrepreneurial Behavior & Research.* **20** (5), 478–492.

Gorgievski, M.J., Ascalon, M.E., and Stephan, U. (2011). Small business owners' success criteria, a values approach to personal differences. *Journal of Small Business Management.* **49** (2), 207–232.

Jayawarna, D., Jones, O., and Macpherson, A. (2011). New business creation and regional development: Enhancing resource acquisition in areas of social deprivation. *Entrepreneurship & Regional Development.* **23** (9–10), 735–761.

Kirkwood, J.J. (2016). How women and men business owners perceive success. *International Journal of Entrepreneurial Behavior & Research.* **22** (5), 594–615.

Marlow, S., and McAdam, M. (2013). Gender and entrepreneurship: Advancing debate and challenging myths; exploring the mystery of the under-performing female entrepreneur. *International Journal of Entrepreneurial Behavior & Research.* **19** (1), 114–124.

McAdam, M., Crowley, C., and Harrison, H. (2018). To boldly go where no [man] has gone before: Institutional voids and the development of women's digital entrepreneurship. *Technological Forecasting & Social Change.* 1–11. DOI: 10.1016/j.techfore.2018.07.051.

Miles, M.B., and Huberman, A.M. (1994). *Qualitative Data Analysis: An Expanded Sourcebook* (2nd ed.). Thousand Oaks, CA: Sage.

Ministry of Labor (2013). *The Annual Statistical Report.* Ministry of Labour, Government of the Kingdom of Saudi Arabia.

Neergaard, H. (2007). Sampling in entrepreneurial settings. In: H. Neergaard and J. Ulhøi (eds), *Handbook of Qualitative Research Methods in Entrepreneurship.* Cheltenham, UK and Northampton, MA, USA: Edward Elgar Publishing, pp. 253–278.

Patton, M. (1990). *Qualitative Evaluation and Research Methods* (2nd ed.). Newbury Park: Sage.

Strauss, A., and Corbin, J. (1990). *Basics of Qualitative Research: Grounded Theory Procedures and Techniques.* Newbury Park, CA: Sage.

Tlaiss, H. (2015). Entrepreneurial motivations of women: Evidence from the United Arab Emirates. *International Small Business Journal.* **33** (5), 562–581.

Tlaiss, H. (2019). Contextualizing the career success of Arab women entrepreneurs. *Entrepreneurship & Regional Development.* **31** (3–4), 226–241.

Tlaiss, H.A., and Elamin, A. (2016). Human resource management in Saudi Arabia. In P. Budhwar and M. Mellahi (eds), *Handbook of Human Resource Management in the Middle East.* Cheltenham, UK and Northampton, MA, USA: Edward Elgar Publishing, pp. 141–160.

Tlaiss, H., and Kauser, S. (2019). Entrepreneurial leadership, patriarchy, and gender in the Arab world: Lebanon in focus. *Journal of Small Business Management.* **57** (2), 517–537.

Vision 2030 (2018). Vision 2030. http://vision2030.gov.sa/en [20 April 2018].

Wach, D., Stephan, U., and Gorgievski, M. (2016). More than money: Developing an integrative multi-factorial measure of entrepreneurial success. *International Small Business Journal.* **34** (8), 1098–1121.

Welter, F. (2011). Contextualizing entrepreneurship: Conceptual challenges and ways forward. *Entrepreneurship Theory and Practice.* **35** (1), 165–184.

World Economic Forum (2012). *The Global Gender Gap Report.* World Economic Forum, Switzerland.

Yousufazi, S.Y., Saeed, S., and Muffatto, M. (2015). Institutional theory and contextual embeddedness of women's entrepreneurial leadership: Evidence from 92 countries. *Journal of Small Business Management.* **53** (3), 587–604.

Zahra, S.A. (2007). Contextualizing theory building in entrepreneurship research. *Journal of Business Venturing.* **22** (3), 443–452.

Zahra, S.A., Gedajlovic, E., Neubaum, D.O., and Shulman, J.M. (2009). A typology of social entrepreneurs: Motives, search processes and ethical challenges. *Journal of Business Venturing. 24* (5), 219–232.

Zahra, S.A., and Wright, M. (2011). Entrepreneurship's next act. *The Academy of Management Perspectives. 25* (4), 67–83.

Zamberi Ahmad, S. (2011a). Businesswomen in the Kingdom of Saudi Arabia: characteristic, growth patterns and progression in a regional context. *Equality, Diversity and Inclusion: An International Journal. 30* (7), 610–614.

Zamberi Ahmad, S. (2011b). Evidence of the characteristics of women entrepreneurs in the Kingdom of Saudi Arabia: An empirical investigation. *International Journal of Gender and Entrepreneurship. 3* (2), 123–143.

15. Exploring societal value creation through women's informal entrepreneurial activities in Nepal – a narrative approach[1]

Mirela Xheneti and Shova Thapa Karki

INTRODUCTION

Women's economic participation including through entrepreneurship has been often linked to economic growth, poverty reduction and social development (Kabeer, 2005; Bruton et al., 2013). Women have been found to reinvest a higher percentage of their earnings on household well-being (e.g. education, nutrition and childcare) than men (Nichter and Goldmark, 2009), producing positive ripple effects onto the next generations and wider communities (ILO, 2016). Women's increased income also supports them in renegotiating their social relations at home, through gained independence and increased power in household decision-making (Kabeer, 2005; Xheneti et al., 2019).

Despite the understanding that women's entrepreneurial activities fulfil more than a simple economic function, accounts that explore in full how women balance management values such as profit seeking or business growth with more traditional values such as family, community and social norms and customs remain limited and not part of the mainstream entrepreneurship literature. When the literature discusses social value creation this is very much related to social entrepreneurship (Wilson and Post, 2013). Taking these issues into consideration, the aim of this chapter is to explore how women participating in informal entrepreneurship in a developing context create value through nurturing social relations in their communities. Our starting point in this chapter is that women's entrepreneurial activities in the informal economy reflect to a large extent the economic and socio-cultural characteristics of their context with diverse implications for societal value creation.

Empirically, we draw on data collected through semi-structured interviews with 90 women entrepreneurs involved in informal entrepreneurial activities in three cities in Nepal.[2] Our analysis of this dataset for the purposes of different studies (Thapa Karki and Xheneti, 2018; Xheneti and Thapa Karki, 2018; Xheneti et al., 2019) has led to a very good familiarity with the data and as importantly, the ways in which these women talk, amongst other things, about social value creation through their informal entrepreneurial activities. As a result, in this chapter, we have selected the narratives of three women entrepreneurs – one in each of the cities investigated – to illustrate in full how normative and social institutions, as well as women entrepreneurs' social positions guide their decisions in relation to value creation through their informal entrepreneurial activities. The narratives of women entrepreneurs in the informal economy capture three main ways through which they create value at the societal level – changing perceptions about women's work; supporting other women in the community either directly through employment or through other forms of social interaction; and finally, acting as role models in their communities.

Our intention in this chapter is not to provide generalised accounts but rather to show the richness of life experiences and value creation through women's entrepreneurial activities in the informal economy. By doing so, this chapter aims to contribute to debates about the non-economic value of entrepreneurship (Korsgaard and Anderson, 2011; Welter and Xheneti, 2015) emphasising the role of context in shaping women's choices. The chapter is structured as follows: In Section 1 we provide a broad discussion of what value means in the entrepreneurship literature, emphasising the contribution of women entrepreneurship literature in highlighting values other than economic. We continue with a more focused review of how value in the informal economy is being created by women at multiple levels of analysis. Next, we discuss our methods followed by the presentations and analysis of three narratives of women entrepreneurs in Nepal. The chapter concludes with some avenues for future research in the topic.

ENTREPRENEURSHIP AND SOCIAL VALUE CREATION

There has been widespread interest in social value creation in many different disciplines, entrepreneurship included. In the entrepreneurship field, most discussions of value creation have centred on the economic value created through the establishment of new ventures and job creation, all contributing factors to economic growth, increased competitiveness and wealth generation (Audretsch et al., 2006). Acs et al. (2013), for example, equate productive entrepreneurship with social value creation taking Baumol's (1990) typology of productive, unproductive and destructive as a starting point. Others have started to look at alternative value dimensions of entrepreneurship: entrepreneurship is seen as a solution to poverty (Bruton et al., 2013), a mean towards sustainable development (Surie and Ashley, 2008; Hall et al., 2010), and a solution to societal problems (Zahra et al., 2009). However, Korsgaard and Anderson (2011) argue that value creation and social outcomes are not the pursuit of social enterprises alone. Forms of entrepreneurship, such as 'everyday entrepreneurship' (Welter et al., 2017) and entrepreneurial activities run by marginalised groups (Baker and Welter, 2017) also contribute to social value creation. Given that entrepreneurial behaviour is socially embedded, the type of opportunities individuals pursue are very much enabled and constrained by their context (Thornton et al., 2011; Welter and Xheneti, 2015). As such, value is created when individuals, households or even whole communities nurture family and social relations through their engagement in different entrepreneurial activities (Welter and Xheneti, 2015: 256). Hence, prioritising the measurable economic value only neglects the subjective, temporal and contextual nature of value creation (Kantor, 2005; Welter and Xheneti, 2015).

In this regard, research on women entrepreneurship has been quite influential in highlighting social value creation. By providing evidence on the diverse motives, goals and outcomes of women entrepreneurship (Jennings and Brush, 2013), this literature has challenged the under-performance hypothesis and female deficits in running businesses (Marlow and Swail, 2014). Additionally, the women entrepreneurship literature by conceptualising entrepreneurship as social change (Calas et al., 2009) and emancipation (Rindova et al., 2009) has heightened concern for non-economic contributions of women entrepreneurship. As gender reproduces socio-economic differences (Marlow, 2002; Rouse et al., 2013), it is important to attend to its constructed nature within particular socio-cultural contexts and life circumstances, if we are to understand what value entrepreneurship creates. We bring this discussion further to the case of informal entrepreneurial activities run by women in developing contexts and patriarchal societies.

THE VALUE OF WOMEN'S INFORMAL ENTREPRENEURIAL ACTIVITIES IN DEVELOPING CONTEXTS

There is no better area of study than the intersection of the informal economy and gender to appreciate the ways in which individuals create multiple forms of value at different contexts and points in time. The informal economy contributes around 40–60% of developing countries' GDPs (Vanek et al., 2014) and provides more than 60% of total employment in non-agricultural employment (ILO, 2014). Its subsistence nature, characterised by necessity-based entrepreneurship, low growth propensity, and lack of recognition by the state (Perry et al., 2007) make it 'not worth studying' (Jennings and Brush, 2013). However, research has consistently shown that the informal economy provides alternative means to livelihoods and reduces poverty (Gough et al., 2003; Langevang et al., 2012), offers a creative and transitional space to test capability (Adom and Williams, 2012), and is a vehicle for social mobility amongst the urban poor (Timilsina, 2011). The informal economy creates social and economic value for the poor by also narrowing the gap between provider and the customer through close interaction within communities (Viswanathan et al., 2014).

In the context of women entrepreneurship, existing literature has highlighted the role of women entrepreneurship in value creation at multiple levels (Mayoux, 2003). For instance, at the individual level, economic independence (Kabeer, 2005), renegotiation of social relations, increased decision-making power (Xheneti et al., 2019), and enhanced agency for personal growth, life aspirations, and improved well-being (Thapa Karki and Xheneti, 2018) have been associated with entrepreneurship in the informal economy. This not only contributes to improvement in self-confidence and life satisfaction but also in self-belief regarding personal capacity and ability to negotiate business and family demands, as well as dignity and respect (Xheneti et al., 2019).

At the household level, women contribute immensely through higher investment on household well-being, including children's education and nutrition bringing rippled effects to future generations (Kantor, 2005; Nichter and Goldmark, 2009). Women's monetary contribution to the household also improves their household status, changing attitudes towards them, gaining support for business development, and greater control over business and profit (Xheneti et al., 2019). This is particularly important in patriarchal societies where women hold a subordinate position to their male counterparts (Aderinto, 2001).

At the business level, improved confidence, independence and greater entre-preneurial experience allows women to access networks beyond family and close relatives facilitating business growth and expansion (Kantor, 2005). Reliance on close networks is often limited to the close family and neighbourhood (Mehra, 1997) while a good source of finance and support can limit their potential to access to wider networks, and in turn hindering venture growth (Meagher, 2013). Access to wider networks supports women entrepreneurs in building their social capital and in the process creating value for their business, their networks, and their wider communi-ties. Women's 'community-mindedness' (De Vita et al., 2014) explains their time investment in developing and nurturing social relationships (Grant, 2013).

Beyond the individual, household and business levels, women entrepreneurs also add value to the wider society through communal empowerment, social interaction, and transferring positive outcomes to the wider society (Welter and Xheneti, 2015; Thapa Karki and Xheneti, 2018). As shown by Al-Dajani and Marlow (2013), displaced home-based women entrepreneurs in Jordan used the traditional crafts to create a legitimate niche to connect, share their skills with women outside their com-munity and conserve their heritage. Operating in a highly constrained environment, women used their skills to create a market for their products, and involved other women in income generation activities, facilitating communal as well as economic empowerment. These women not only help in improving attitudes towards other women but can also become role models for the next generation or other women entrepreneurs by improving their self-belief and confidence on their ability to become an entrepreneur (Mayoux, 1998; Markussen and Røed, 2017).

Overall, entrepreneurship enables women to challenge the socio-cultural norms, fight for their rights, gain voice and visibility, thus affecting their lives and those of other women, girls and disadvantaged groups (Zahra and Wright, 2015). Thus, women entrepreneurship contributes to social value creation at multiple levels. How this value creation, however, is negotiated and translated in particular socio-cultural contexts would further improve our understanding both of the nature of the value created and its subjective, temporal and contextual nature. We discuss these issues further by focusing on the case of a developing country such as Nepal.

METHODOLOGY

Study Context – The Patriarchal Nepalese Society

With a population of 25 million people and traditionally a largely agricultural indus-trial base, Nepal is ranked in 105th place in the 'Doing Business Index' among 189 countries (World Bank, 2016), and in 145th place in the Human Development Index (UNDP, 2015). A large proportion (96%) of the economically active population in Nepal is employed in the informal sector (Suwal and Pant, 2009). The extensive informal economy in Nepal is often attributed to a number of reasons including the ten-year long Maoist conflict, labour migration, weak private sector development and socio-economic changes (Sharma and Donini, 2012). The conflict positively impacted women self-employment rates due to the displacement of men and the need to maintain household livelihoods during the war (Menon and Rodgers, 2015).

The number of women employed in the informal economy (77.5%) is much higher than men (70%) (Suwal and Pant, 2009). In fact, Nepal has the highest female labour participation rate (80%) among other South Asian countries such as Bangladesh (36%), Sri Lanka (32.9%), India (27.2%) and Pakistan (24.4%) (ILO Nepal, 2014). Despite this high participation in economic activities fuelled by years of economic hardship and large institutional change, Nepal continues to be a stratified society with unequal power relations, caste-based stratification, and socially prescribed roles, behaviour and expectations for men and women (ILO, 2005). Gender-based constraints in particular highly influence the nature and scope of women's entrepre-neurial activities and, as we have shown through various studies, the value generated by women's work.

Method

Data for this chapter was collected as part of a project whose main goal was to understand women's transitions to the formal economy by acknowledging their diverse experiences in the informal economy in Nepal. The original project focused on three different cities, each with a variety of economic activities and structural relationships, including Kathmandu, the capital city, Biratnagar, the second largest city, and Pokhara, the tourism capital. A stratified sampling strategy was chosen for the selection of women entrepreneurs on the basis of diverse enterprise dynamics as indicated in the National Labour Force Survey (NLFS, 2008) and a variety of locations exhibiting diverse economic activities. Our data comes from interviews conducted in early 2015. In each study site, we conducted 30 interviews; a total of 90 interviews for the whole project.

Various other studies we have conducted based on this dataset (Thapa Karki and Xheneti, 2018; Xheneti et al., 2019) made visible the rich descriptions of women's journeys from gaining support for their activities to generating value at multiple levels such as individual, household and social level. For this chapter, we focused on interviews where women talked about value creation at the community/societal level.

By doing so, we identified a number of subthemes such as acting as 'role models', changing perceptions about women's work in the community and challenging gender roles, and supporting other women and the local community more broadly. In order to illustrate these subthemes and the intersections between them we use the narratives of three women in the three study regions. Not only are these three narratives richer but they also capture different market dynamics and social relationships in these regions highlighting contextual differences in women entrepreneurship and value creation. We also need to emphasise that while we rely on the voices of women in our study to capture societal value creation, it is also our interpretation of their stories that is visible in presenting these accounts.

SOCIAL VALUE CREATION OF WOMEN'S ENTREPRENEURSHIP – THREE NARRATIVES

In this section, we discuss the narratives of Maya from Kathmandu, Neelam from Pokhara and Shruti from Biratnagar. There are a number of similarities in their life stories especially in relation to rationales for setting up their businesses and the gender constraints they had faced during the course of their lives. What clearly emerges from these narratives is that the gender order influences to a large extent the actions they take and their responses to their families and communities. However, there are also some variations between the three that point out how women's agency is to a large extent enabled and constrained by their life circumstances and the socio-cultural context.

CHANGING PERCEPTIONS ABOUT WOMEN'S WORK

NARRATIVE 1   MAYA FROM KATHMANDU

Maya's journey into starting up a business tells a story of resilience and courage. Having been subjected to a very difficult marriage characterised by constant financial struggles, abuse and lack of support from an alcoholic husband, Maya decided to learn how to knit, first by seeing how her neighbour did it and afterwards participating in a number of trainings. Maya saw knitting as the only skill she could utilise in order to provide for her family. Gaining experience over 13 years by working to order for various different suppliers, she finally felt confident enough to start her own business. As she states in her interview: 'As I became more experienced and started to create new designs, I then started my own business.' At the beginning her operations were quite small. She brought wool from suppliers in a small bag, did the knitting and took the products back. Gradually, Maya started to engage other women in the community. She bought the wool, distributed it to her employees to make the items required for one of her main business partners in Thamel (big tourist market in Kathmandu), who exports these items abroad. Women are paid according to piece rate. Maya gets orders for 400–500 pieces a week for which she is given 15–30 days to complete the work involving many of the women in her community. Currently Maya has almost 60 women working for her. Understanding the expectations in the Nepalese society for women to take care of household duties and childcare, Maya involves mainly housewives for which this line of work would not compromise their family responsibilities. Similarly, Maya involved women who own shops and can do some knitting while waiting to serve customers. This not only shows that many of these shops are in saturated markets; hence, the demand for products is low but also the resourcefulness of women in these communities who try to make the most of the time they have available by earning extra income. By involving so many women, Maya has become known in the community. Everybody knows her although not necessarily by her name. She is known as the *knitter*. Despite employing many women, Maya talks about the lack of interest towards knitting as it is not a job that pays very well. She states that: 'the neighbours are happy with me because I have given them the opportunity to earn some money in their free time by knitting. I think I have brought some change to their lives, although it is not a lot but something is better than nothing.' Maya also talks about the difficulties of running a business being a woman. She says: 'If there was a man in my place, he would not have faced the problems I did. Nobody would question a man if he comes late but there will be lots of questions for a woman.' Maya recalls the negative attitudes of her husband and her neighbours towards her for meeting with her suppliers until late in the evening. Like many other women starting their own businesses in the informal sector, Maya was also subjected to negative attitudes about the value of her work. Her family and neighbours often showed a lack of confidence in her abilities often laughing at the kind of work she does and its significance; her husband equating it with a waste of time. With her perseverance, however, Maya managed to change the hostile attitudes towards her by showing them that her business could provide a regular income and support the family and children: 'Everybody thinks I have earned my living with this waste of time.'

Maya's story is reminiscent of the struggles that many women face in patriarchal societies to gain access to work and have their work valued by their families and communities. On the one hand, Maya's story shows what much of the literature on the informal economy suggests when it comes to women's choices. They choose informality for lack of other options due to their domestic roles or reproductive objectives related to sustaining their household or educating children (Neves and Du Toit, 2012). Similarly, the skill Maya chose to focus on – knitting – is also congruous with gender stereotypes whereby women's work is being seen to be an extension of their domestic identities (Ntseane, 2004; Fongchingong, 2005). This is further illustrated by how most women that work for her do this type of job by not compromising their household roles or household dynamics whereby men are seen as the breadwinners.

On the other hand, there is also a temporal dimension to Maya's story that shows how informal work allowed her to take control of her life at a time when she was heavily dependent on an alcoholic and abusive husband. Maya's work gave her the confidence to walk away from her dysfunctional marriage and create a new family. It also gave her the confidence to start and expand her business. As the story unfolds, we see Maya progressing in her line of business as she gained more experience and started challenging the gender biased norms in her community. A wide body of literature suggests that in many patriarchal societies women's work is perceived as less important than that of men (Franck and Olsson, 2014). Hence, Maya had to persevere with her work to show to both her husband and her community that she could achieve something with her work. There are multiple values Maya has created with her work, from personal development, increased business acumen and household contribution to community development. However, what Maya's story really tells is that women can step outside the boundaries of their homes and lead the change by challenging gender stereotypes in relation to what women can do and what they can achieve through their work.

A STORY OF WOMEN SUPPORTING OTHER WOMEN

NARRATIVE 2   NEELAM FROM POKHARA

Neelam has been working in tailoring for almost 18 years. Her involvement in this line of business activity clearly illustrates how women support and encourage each other in their communities. Neelam was married at an early age (20 years old) and lived in a large extended family as per the Hindu tradition. Living with in-laws, Neelam felt like she was under constant supervision with no decision-making power, especially in relation to participation in paid work, other than farming. With the passing away of her father-in-law and the division of land amongst all sons, the joint family separated into individual households. This gave Neelam the courage to do something with her life and support the family as her husband did not have a job. She was highly influenced by two other women in her network who acted as role models for her. Her sister-in-law, who was educated and worked as a teacher, advised Neelam to gain tailoring skills. Similarly, Neelam received advice from one of the local women leaders (Tusha, herself a tailor) who also suggested training to become a tailor as a good way for Neelam to be economically active. Neelam combined household work with training, all while she was pregnant with her fourth child. While she received permission to participate in training, she did not get much help from her family: 'They didn't give me a penny. I asked my father for money to cover the training fees. I struggled a lot during training. I used old bed sheets and saris. I never forgot what I learned. I learned with great difficulty.' Tusha also helped her to access opportunities for work –

teaching tailoring to others. For Neelam, Tusha is: 'the main pathfinder in my life'. Training other women gave Neelam the confidence she needed to start her own business. Once her daughter was born, Neelam opened her first tailoring shop using Tusha's old sewing machine. Due to caste-based discrimination in Nepal, Neelam faced difficulties in early days as people in her neighbourhood did not consider tailoring to be a reputable job for women from a higher caste like hers. This forced Neelam to find a partner to share responsibilities and face these social challenges. Her business partnership was successful for some time and Neelam credits her business partner for teaching her how to keep basic accounts of the shop, recalling how she would sell clothes often at cost price. However, the partnership broke when her partner got married and decided not to work anymore, suggesting that marriage and family life are often not compatible with paid work for women, particularly when they marry into a well-off family. While tailoring to order, she also started training other women in her shop and provided training materials to those who do training for the Village Development Committee. All these activities gave Neelam a great sense of satisfaction seeing how her work could benefit the livelihoods of other women. Neelam's goal is to help others earn and also save money. She is also very understanding of the difficulties with money many of her customers face, finding excuses for them not collecting the ordered clothes from the shop. Being a business owner for many years has also helped Neelam become active in many organisations run by women (like mothers' groups) that support women's income generation activities and local infrastructure developments. Neelam is proud of all her achievements. She recalls how her husband did not initially believe in her but once she became successful, he was happy. She also feels accomplished when Tusha uses her name as an exemplary entrepreneur which makes Neelam very popular with trainees. Neelam's main message to other women is: 'a women can do business even when the time is not favourable. The main thing is courage.'

Neelam's story has a number of parallels with Maya's story especially in relation to rationales for starting a business, changing attitudes towards their work or the satisfaction that women gain from becoming independent and worthy contributors to the family's livelihood. Neelam's story, however, points out some other dynamics that are more common in smaller cities where large extended families live together. Neelam only managed to break away from the home boundaries after the extended household dissolved. As importantly, Neelam's story points out how life circumstances and particular critical incidents in one's life open up a whole range of opportunities and explain to a large extent women's extent to agency. Neelam's encounter with Tusha, the local woman leader, shows how women can support each other through increasing their confidence and access to wider networks (Sheikh et al., 2018). Neelam's business partner supported her in improving her business skills and enhancing her ability to run the business successfully. As Neelam built her social capital through Tusha's support and active involvement in various organisations in the city, she was able to create multiple levels of value – for her business, networks, and the wider community.

Neelam's 'community-mindedness' (De Vita et al., 2014) is also evident in the way she interacts with both her trainees and her customers, highlighting her empathetic attitude towards the struggles that many women face with income and livelihoods in small and poor communities. Neelam's story really illustrates that profit is not the main objective women running business in the informal economy have. Instead, many of them invest their time in establishing and developing social relations in their communities (Grant, 2013). These social interactions not only lead to knowledge exchange which proves essential for Neelam herself and the women she now supports but they also slowly change the ways entrepreneurial activities are regarded by the local community (Gianetti and Simonov, 2004).

BEING A ROLE MODEL IN THE COMMUNITY

NARRATIVE 3   SHRUTI FROM BIRATNAGAR

Shruti and her family migrated to Biratnagar from a remote village. Shruti worked in a jute mill for three years, getting an award as a reliable worker. Shruti and her husband, however, had to think of alternative ways to make their living. Initially, they opened a cosmetic store, which ran for 11 years, but did not provide enough money to support their family. In the last four years, they diversified into garlands for wedding ceremonies: 'We started with the amount of five thousand rupees.[3] We made two garlands to test the market. When they sold immediately, we started to make more and of different designs.' Shruti emphasises hard work and perseverance as the qualities that supported their success in this new line of business: 'We bring raw materials at seven in the morning. Others can't labour like us… Others also do this business, but they can't make quality garlands. Quality of grass is very important, and it is difficult to collect green grass, it is a very hard and concentrated work. The customers come to me because of the quality of our materials.' The success from the garland business allowed them to build the house and due to the quality of their product they have become well known in Biratnagar. 'Everybody in Biratnagar knows our shop… They call me the sister who makes garlands of beads, flowers and grass…We are an example of entrepreneurship in Biratnagar.' Differently from other women in this context, Shruti and her family have identified a market that is not as saturated as other markets where most women develop their business activities. Shruti has also close relationships with her customers who support her in various ways, including internationalisation, with one customer selling her product in America. With many Nepalese living abroad, she is now targeting Australia. Business growth enabled Shruti to develop contacts with other suppliers for making garlands, employ local residents and support them to start their own shops after gaining some experience. Shruti has trained twenty employees so far. She believes that depending on others is not a good thing. This is the reason she would like to transfer this skill to other women so they can be independent. Shruti's success has attracted the attention of the town. So rare are these examples of successful entrepreneurship that many local residents suggest the local television should broadcast about it. However, despite the potential of this business Shruti has no big plans: 'I am satisfied with this business. In the future, I want to extend the shop by adding more varieties of garlands and wedding items…I have no big dream.'

Shruti's story is also one of livelihood struggle especially following migration to the city where the social networks to rely upon are almost non-existent and they need to be developed from scratch. Migration stories often suggest a different set of family dynamics especially when both partners need to work together towards sustaining their livelihood in the big city. In this respect, Shruti's story, differently from the other two, does not focus on efforts to challenge hostile family attitudes towards her work. Being separated from her close networks due to migration, Shruti has been able to engage in many activities without any scrutiny from family members. This suggests that the context of women's agency is very important in understanding the patterns of their entrepreneurship.

As importantly, Shruti's story is a clear illustration of a successful entrepreneur or role model who has captured the imagination and popular discourse of the local community perhaps helping others to see how Shruti's reality can be close to their reach too (Radu and Loué, 2008). As importantly, Shruti represents a credible role model given her transition from migrant to someone that has achieved business success. The way the local community has reacted towards Shruti's experience suggests the potential she has to act as a role model in this community. Not surprisingly, most literature suggests that people react better to individuals who are similar to them either through community relationships by living close to each other, or similar along different dimensions such as age, gender, background and so on (Radu and Loué, 2008). Shruti, like the other two stories presented in this chapter, also considers her position crucial in supporting other women to do something with their lives and be independent, thus, creating value at the societal level.

OUTLOOK – THE SOCIETAL VALUE OF WOMEN'S ENTREPRENEURSHIP

The social value created through women's entrepreneurship has been the subject of increasing research in the entrepreneurship literature. Challenging the focus on the economic function of entrepreneurial activity, this research agenda has aimed to make visible the multiple levels of value that are created through women's entrepreneurship which are equally, if not more, important than their business longevity and performance. Our chapter took these discussions as a starting point and aimed to further explore how women participating in informal entrepreneurship in a developing country context create value through nurturing social relations in their communities. We relied upon the narratives of three informal women entrepreneurs in three different cities in Nepal.

This helped us explore the different ways in which value at the societal level is created, highlighting their life circumstances and the economic and socio-cultural characteristics of their contexts. More specifically, our stories allowed us to see how women create value at the societal level through challenging attitudes towards women's work, supporting other women in the community directly through employment or indirectly through involvement in support organisations, and finally, through being a role model in the community. By focusing on a narrative approach, we were able to make visible the processes through which these different societal value outcomes were achieved. A processual view of value creation allows to understand how women's agency develops over time together with the constraints and enablers of this agency. Our stories clearly demonstrated that despite similar motives for engaging in the informal economy, these three women faced slightly different challenges, of a personal, family or migratory nature, in doing entrepreneurship. They also had access to different forms of support for their activities.

Taken together, the findings of this chapter make a number of contributions to the literature: First, we respond to calls for exploring value outcomes other than economic ones amongst marginalised groups of entrepreneurs. Our focus on societal value creation of women in the informal economy is quite unique in this respect, challenging the survivalist or limited choice factors that are mainly associated with this type of entrepreneurship. Second, our narrative approach offers a more subjective and dynamic view of value creation over time by also highlighting the value spillovers from one level of value creation to another. Finally, our chapter strongly suggests that future studies that aim to explore the value creation through entrepreneurship need to take into account women's life circumstances, the socio-cultural characteristics of their contexts and most importantly, their temporal dimensions.

NOTES

1. *Acknowledgement*: The empirical data collection was supported by the Centre for Economic Policy Research and the Department for International Development, UK within their Private Sector Development Scheme, Exploratory Research Grant No 2533. We thank the three Research Assistants, who supported the data collection process in Nepal.
2. All names have been anonymised.
3. £1 = Rs 130.

REFERENCES

Acs, Z. J., Boardman, M. C. and McNeely, C. L. (2013). The social value of productive entrepreneurship. *Small Business Economics*, 40(3), 785–796.

Aderinto, A. A. (2001). Patriarchy and culture: The position of women in a rural Yoruba community, Nigeria. *The Anthropologist*, 3(4), 225–230.

Adom, K. and Williams, C. C. (2012). Evaluating the motives of informal entrepreneurs in Koforidua, Ghana. *Journal of Developmental Entrepreneurship*, 17(1), 1250005.

Al-Dajani, H. and Marlow, S. (2013). Empowerment and entrepreneurship: A theoretical framework. *International Journal of Entrepreneurial Behaviour and Research*, 19(5), 503–524.

Audretsch, D. B., Keilbach, M. C. and Lehmann, E. E. (2006). *Entrepreneurship and Economic Growth*. New York: Oxford University Press.

Baker, T. and Welter, F. (2017). Come on out of the ghetto, please! Building the future of entrepreneurship research. *International Journal of Entrepreneurial Behavior & Research*, 23(2), 170–184.

Baumol, W. (1990). Entrepreneurship: Productive, unproductive and destructive. *Journal of Political Economy*, 98(5), 893–921.

Bruton, G. D., Ketchen, D. J. and Ireland, R. D. (2013). Entrepreneurship as a solution to poverty. *Journal of Business Venturing*, 28(6), 683–689.

Calas, M. B., Smircich, L. and Bourne, K. A. (2009). Extending the boundaries: Reframing 'entrepreneurship as social change' through feminist perspectives. *Academy of Management Review*, 34(3), 552–569.

De Vita, L., Mari, M. and Poggesi, S. (2014). Women entrepreneurs in and from developing countries: Evidence from the literature. *European Management Journal*, 32(3), 451–460.

Fonchingong, C. C. (2005). Negotiating livelihoods beyond Beijing: The burden of women food vendors in the informal economy of Limbe, Cameroon. *International Social Science Journal*, 57, 243–253.

Franck, A. K. and Olsson, J. (2014). Missing women? The under-recording and under-reporting of women's work in Malaysia. *International Labour Review*, 153, 209–221.

Gianetti, M. and Simonov, A. (2004). On the determinants of entrepreneurial activity: Social norms, economic environment and individual characteristics. *Swedish Economic Policy Review*, 11, 44.

Gough, K. V., Tipple, A. G. and Napier, M. (2003). Making a living in African cities: The role of home-based enterprises in Accra and Pretoria. *International Planning Studies*, 8 (4), 253–278.

Grant, R. (2013). Gendered spaces of informal entrepreneurship in Soweto, South Africa. *Urban Geography*, 34(1), 86–108.

Hall, J. K., Daneke, G. A. and Lenox, M. J. (2010). Sustainable development and entrepreneurship: Past contributions and future directions. *Journal of Business Venturing*, 25(5), 439–448.

ILO (2005). *A Report on Micro and Small Enterprise Policy Review in Nepal 2003*. Kathmandu: International Labour Office, International Labour Organization.

ILO (2014). *Transitioning from the Informal to the Formal Economy Report V(1)*. International Labour Conference, 103rd Session. Geneva, International Labour Organization.

ILO (2016). Women's entrepreneurship development – the ILO approach to women's entrepreneurship development – sustainable enterprises, www.ilo.org/wcmsp5/groups/public/—ed_emp/—emp_ent/—ifp_seed/documents/publication/wcms_175471.pdf.

ILO Nepal (2014). *Nepal Labour Market Update*. International Labour Organization, Country Office for Nepal. November.

Jennings, J. E. and Brush, C. G. (2013). Research on women entrepreneurs: Challenges to (and from) the broader entrepreneurship literature? *The Academy of Management Annals*, 7, 663–715.

Kabeer, N. (2005). Gender equality and women's empowerment: A critical analysis of the third millennium development goal. *Gender and Development*, 13(1), 13–24.

Kantor, P. (2005). Determinants of women's microenterprise success in Ahmedabad, India: Empowerment and economics. *Feminist Economics*, 11(3), 63–83.

Korsgaard, S. and Anderson, A. R. (2011). Enacting entrepreneurship as social value creation. *International Small Business Journal*, 29(2), 135–151.

Langevang, T., Namatovu, R. and Dawa, S. (2012). Beyond necessity and opportunity entre-preneurship: Motivations and aspirations of young entrepreneurs in Uganda. *International Developing Planning Review*, 34(4), 439–459.

Latu, I. M., Schmid Mast, A., Lammers, J. and Bombari, D. (2013). Successful female leaders empower women's behaviour in leadership tasks. *Journal of Experimental Social Psychology*, 49(3), 444–448.

Markussen, S. and Røed, K. (2017). The gender gap in entrepreneurship: The role of peer effects. *Journal of Economic Behaviour & Organization*, 134, 356–373.

Marlow, S. (2002). Women and self-employment: a part of or apart from theoretical construct? *International Journal of Entrepreneurship and Innovation*, 3, 83–91.

Marlow, S. and Swail, J. (2014). Gender, risk and finance: Why can't a woman be more like a man? *Entrepreneurship & Regional Development*, 26, 80–96.

Mayoux, L. (1998). Women's empowerment and micro-finance programmes: Strategies for increasing impact. *Development in Practice*, 8(2), 235–241.

Mayoux, L. (2003). From marginalisation to empowerment: Towards a new approach in small enterprise development. Paper presented to SDC Employment and Income Division Workshop 'Small Enterprise Development and Empowerment'. Study Centre Gerzensee, Switzerland.

Meagher, K. (2013). Unlocking the informal economy: A literature review on linkages between formal and informal economies in developing countries. Manchester: WIEGO.

Mehra, R. (1997). Women, empowerment, and economic development. *Annals of the American Academy of Political and Social Science*, 554, 136–149.

Menon, N. and Rodgers, Y. M. (2015). War and women's work: Evidence from the conflict in Nepal. *Journal of Conflict Resolution*, 59(1), 51–73.

Neves, D. and Du Toit, A. (2012). Money and sociality in South Africa's informal economy. *Africa*, 82, 131–149.

Nichter, S. and Goldmark, L. (2009). Small firm growth in developing countries. *World Development*, 37(9), 1453–1464.

NLFS (2008), Report on the Nepal labour force survey: Statistical report, Central Bureau of Statistics, National Planning Commission Secretariat, Government of Nepal, Kathmandu, July.

Ntseane, P. (2004). Being a female entrepreneur in Botswana: Cultures, values, strategies for success. *Gender and Development*, 12, 37–43.

Perry, G. E., Maloney, W. F., Arias, O. S., Fajnzylber, P., Mason, A. D. and Saavedra-Chanduvi, J. (2007). *Informality: Exit and Exclusion*. Washington, DC: The World Bank.

Radu, M. and Loué, C. (2008). Motivational impact of role models as moderated by 'ideal' vs. 'ought to self-guides' identifications. *Journal of Enterprising Culture*, 16(4), 441–465.

Rindova, V., Barry, D. and Ketchen, D. J. (2009). Entrepreneuring as emancipa-tion. *AMR*, 34, 477–491, https://doi.org/10.5465/amr.2009.40632647

Rouse, J., Treanor, L. and Fleck, E. (2013). The gendering of entrepreneurship: theoretical and empirical insights. *International Journal of Entrepreneurial Behaviour & Research*, 19, 452–459.

Sharma, J. R. and Donini, A. (2012). *From Subjects to Citizens? Labour Mobility and Social Transformation in Rural Nepal*, Medford, Feinstein International Centre, Tufts University.

Sheikh, S., Yousafzai, S., Sist, F., Akdeniz, A. R. and Saeed, S. (2018). Value creation through women's entrepreneurship. In Yousafzai, S., Fayolle, A., Lindgreen, A., Henry, C., Saeed, S. and Sheikh, S. (eds), *Women Entrepreneurs and the Myth of 'Underperformance': A New Look at Women's Entrepreneurship Research*. Cheltenham, UK and Northampton, MA, USA: Edward Elgar, pp. 20–30.

Surie, G. and Ashley, A. (2008). Integrating pragmatism and ethics in entrepreneurial leadership for sustainable value creation. *Journal of Business Ethics*, 81(1), 235–246. https://doi .org/10.1007/s10551-007-9491-4

Suwal, R. and Pant, B. (2009). Measuring informal sector economic activities in Nepal. Paper presented on the Special IARIW – SAIM Conference on 'Measuring the Informal Economy in Developing Countries'. 23–26 September 2009, Kathmandu, Nepal.

Thapa Karki, S. and Xheneti, M. (2018). Formalizing women entrepreneurs in Kathmandu, Nepal: Pathway towards empowerment? *International Journal of Sociology and Social Policy*, 38(7–8), 526–541.

Thornton, P. H., Ribeiro-Soriano, D. and Urbano, D. (2011). Socio-cultural factors and entrepreneurial activity: An overview. *International Small Business Journal*, 29(2), 105–118.

Timilsina, K. P. (2011). An urban informal economy: Livelihood opportunity to poor challenges for urban governance. *Global Journal of Human Social Science*, 11(2), 25–31.

UNDP (2015). *Human Development Report 2015: Overview. Work for Human Development*. United Nations Development Programme.

Vanek, J., Chen, M. A., Carre, F., Heintz, J. and Hussmanns, R. (2014). Statistics on the informal economy: Definitions, regional estimates & challenges. *WIEGO Working Papers*.

Viswanathan, M., Echambadi, R., Venugopal, S. and Sridharan, S. (2014). Subsistence entrepreneurship, value creation, and community exchange systems: A social capital explanation. *Journal of Macromarketing*, 34(2), 213–226.

Welter, F., Baker, T., Audretsch, D. B. and Gartner, W. B. (2017). Everyday entrepreneurship: A call for entrepreneurship research to embrace entrepreneurial diversity. *Entrepreneurship Theory and Practice*, 41(3), 311–321.

Welter, F. and Xheneti, M. (2015). Value for whom? Exploring the value of informal entrepreneurial activities in post-socialist contexts. In McElwee, G. and Smith, R. (eds), *Exploring Criminal and Illegal Enterprise: New Perspectives on Research*. Bingley: Emerald Publishing Group, pp. 253–275.

Wilson, F. and Post, J. (2013). Business models for people, planet (& profits): Exploring the phenomenon of social business, a market-based approach to social value creation. *Small Business Economics*, 40, 715–737.

World Bank (2016). *Doing Business 2016: Measuring Regulatory Quality and Efficiency: Economy Profile*. Nepal: World Bank.

Xheneti, M. and Thapa Karki, S. (2018). Gender embeddedness in patriarchal contexts undergoing institutional change: Evidence from Nepal. In Yousafzai, S., Lindgreen, A., Saeed, S., Henry, C. and Fayolle, A. (eds), *Contextual Embeddedness of Women's Entrepreneurship: Going beyond the Gender-neutral Approach*. New York: Routledge, Chapter 8.

Xheneti, M., Thapa Karki, S. and Madden, A. (2019). Negotiating business and family demands within a patriarchal society – the case of women entrepreneurs in the Nepalese context. *Entrepreneurship and Regional Development*, 31(3–4), 259–278.

Zahra, S., Gedajlovic, E., Neubaum, D. O. and Shulman, J. M. (2009). A typology of social entrepreneurs: Motives, search processes and ethical challenges. *Journal of Business Venturing*, 24(8), 519–532.

Zahra, S. A. and Wright, M. (2015). Understanding the social role of entrepreneurship. *Journal of Management Studies*, 53(4), 610–629.

16. Women entrepreneurs as agents of change in the Americas: redefining the bottom line

Ruta Aidis

INTRODUCTION

Increasingly, research shows that entrepreneurship is not a gender-neutral phenomenon (Jennings and Brush, 2013:681) Studies indicate that women have higher care orientations (e.g. Calhoun, 2012) and are more likely to start social entrepreneurship than men (Hechavarria et al., 2012). Women entrepreneurs are found to be more likely than their male counterparts to emphasize non-monetary motivations such as social and environmental issues (Braun, 2010; Brush, 1992; Buttner and Moore, 1997). New research is applying a holistic approach to identifying the significant non-financial value that is created by women entrepreneurs (e.g. Welter, 2011) often focusing on solo female entrepreneurs (Sheikh et al., 2018). The blended value approach, also referred to as the 'triple bottom line' is a useful framework for better understanding how organizations create benefits on multiple levels, particularly in terms of economic, social and environmental value (Cohen et al., 2008).

Anecdotal evidence has long supported the notion that women entrepreneurs tend to hire women employees. Two recent surveys provide further support for this claim. The US-based 2018 State of Women's Entrepreneurship survey found that women founders were disproportionately likely to hire other women (Weisul, 2018). Among firms engaged in international trade, women-led enterprises have significantly higher shares of women employees (OECD/WTO, 2017). But it is still rare for small and medium-sized enterprise (SME) surveys to record or count the gender of employees.

Through exploring the business practices of six female entrepreneurs, this chapter contributes to the emerging stream of research utilizing a blended value approach. These six women entrepreneurs are all SME owners but operate in diverse sectors, in different institutional environments and country contexts located in North and Central America. In addition to their day-to-day business operations, each female entrepreneur provides added support to women as employees. One group of women entrepreneurs supports their female employees working in their companies directly, while the other group supports women employees indirectly, providing products and services targeting their needs as women workers.

Taken individually, the practices these women SME owners incorporate as part of their business operations are likely to have a small overall effect. However, if these practices were adopted more widely, the effect would be considerable. In many countries, SMEs constitute the main employers and exert a large impact on women's livelihoods as employees.

We address this knowledge gap by exploring the added value created by women entrepreneurs for their employees. We apply the model proposed by Sheikh et al. (2018) that is based on solo women entrepreneurs. This model illustrates the additional value created by women entrepreneurs but we include two additional value levels that are relevant for women entrepreneurs that employ other women and women entrepreneurs who create added value by addressing the unmet needs of working women.

This chapter is structured into eight sections. The next section contains a literature review that presents the main issues and dispels common notions and expectations with regards to gender, blended value, ethics and employer entrepreneurs. The methodology used for the case studies is presented in section three. Section four includes three case studies of women entrepreneurs who help women workers by addressing their unmet needs and section five presents three case studies of women entrepreneurs who help their women employees. A discussion is provided in section seven and this chapter ends with conclusions and recommendations in section eight.

LITERATURE REVIEW

Value Creation, SMEs and Women's Entrepreneurship

Traditionally in entrepreneurship research, the value being created by the enterprise was limited to economic value (Zahra and Wright, 2016:611) that contributed to economic growth (Audretsch et al., 2006; Baumol, 1986). Economic gains such as job creation, innovation and revenue were emphasized while other issues such as social values in entrepreneurship were relegated to a conceptual black box, almost a residual (Korsgaard and Anderson, 2011:135). Though the evaluation of entrepreneurial activity in economic terms is important, it often results in a one-sided analysis in which entrepreneurship is evaluated and appraised solely in monetary terms, without reference to its social impact (Zahra et al., 2009). Indeed, entrepreneurship processes have social outcomes that may be just as important as economic ones (Korsgaard and Anderson, 2011:136).

The development and growth of social enterprises focused first and foremost on social impact and not profits led to an increased acknowledgement that entrepreneurs could be socially responsible while being profitable (Zahra and Wright, 2016:614). However, when the discussion of non-monetary value creation in entrepreneurship is restricted to social entrepreneurs, this excludes the full scope of value created by all entrepreneurs, not just social entrepreneurs (Sheikh et al., 2018:20). As one of the world's most celebrated male entrepreneurs, Sir Richard Branson notes, this is far from the truth: 'I truly believe that if you take care of your employees, they will take care of your business' (Branson, 2015).

Blended value is a relatively new conceptual framework used in entrepreneurship research, that highlights a broader range of value generated through entrepreneurship. Specifically, blended value acknowledges the creation of financial, social and environmental value through entrepreneurship that benefits society and entrepreneurs (Nicholls, 2009). This framework suggests natural tradeoffs and complementarities among these three dimensions of value occur as part of entrepreneurial endeavors. The blended value concept can be applied to independent entrepreneurs and established companies alike (Zahra and Wright, 2016:621).

The shift to refocus entrepreneurial research on 'everyday entrepreneurship' is another important development that eschews theoretically privileging a narrow special case of entrepreneurship as the distinctive domain of entrepreneurship scholarship (Welter et al., 2016:7). Instead this approach underscores that entrepreneurship research should be a tool for shaping social and economic equity, construed to include not only issues of structural inequality but also empowerment and emancipation more broadly (Rindova et al., 2009).

When it comes to business value creation and its impact on employees, the mass media and popular business journals tend to emphasize the role played by large corporations. For example, in the US, annual lists compiled by business magazines rank the 'Top 10 best employers for women' and the '75 best large workplaces for women' (Forbes, 2018; Fortune, 2019). In this regard, large corporations have an advantage: greater visibility, more staff and resources as well as human resource and corporate social responsibility departments that can be mobilized to address the needs of their female employees well beyond the scope of SMEs.

In contrast, SMEs tend to be resource-constrained especially in terms of time, effort, and access to information. SMEs also tend to have fewer resources to amplify the visibility of their achievements. As a result, it is often incorrectly assumed that corporate policies and practices are likely to wield greater influence on workers. When in reality, in many countries, it is the masses of SMEs that far outnumber corporations and constitute the main private sector employers. In the US, over 80 percent of private sector employees were employed by SMEs in 2016[1] and in Latin America, SMEs generate more than half of all employment, and one fourth of GDP (CAF, 2016; United States Census Bureau, 2019). In other words, taken collectively, internal SME policies and practices exert a significant impact on the global working population.

In order to lay the foundation for understanding possible gendered differences in value creation, we adopt the gendered perspective of the moral theory of the ethics of care and justice first introduced by Gilligan (1982) and applied by Hechavarria et al. (2017). This theoretical approach differentiates between two basic ethical value systems: justice, which is strongly linked with men, and care, which is strongly linked with women.

The ethics of justice places a premium on individual autonomous choice and equality. Variations of this theory encompass notions of balancing rights and responsibilities and a masculine-oriented value system prioritizing fairness, rights and obligations (French and Weis, 2000:125). In contrast, the ethics of care, a feminine oriented value system, focuses on the interconnectedness among the parties involved and nurturing behavior (Flanagan and Jackson, 1987). Research indicates that women are more likely to place greater priorities on social and environmental value creation goals over economic goals (Jaffee and Hyde, 2000).

In a large quantitative study based on Global Entrepreneurship Monitor (GEM) data from 48 countries, Hechavarria et al. (2017) found support for a gendered difference between the ethics of care vs. the ethics of justice orientation for entrepreneurs. Specifically, they found that women entrepreneurs, regardless of country context, were more likely to be positively correlated with social goals and negatively correlated with economic goals than male entrepreneurs. With one important caveat: In post materialistic environments (i.e. national societies that emphasize autonomy, self-expression and well-being) both men and women entrepreneurs are more likely to report social and environment goals over economic goals than entrepreneurs in materialistic societies. In other words, the global tendencies indicated that women entrepreneurs are more likely to prioritize social goals (related to care activities) vs. purely economic goals, while only under certain conditions, such as when economic conditions improve and as individuals become more prosperous, men entrepreneurs also aspire to social goals.

Through qualitative studies, authors such as Sheikh et al. (2018) explore the specific meaning of success and performance for each woman entrepreneur. They posit that 'each woman has her own story and offers her own unique value to add to her entrepreneurial environment' and identify four main levels of value creation:

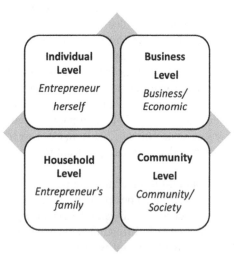

Note: The value level is shown in bold and the beneficiary who accrues the value is shown in italics.
Source: Adapted from Sheikh et al. (2018:21).

Figure 16.1 *Levels of value creation in women's entrepreneurship*

The individual value level, the business value level, their family/household level and society/community value level (ibid.). These four value levels and the corresponding beneficiaries that accrue the value are shown in Figure 16.1.

METHODOLOGY

Whenever possible, interviewees were initially identified through purposeful sampling utilizing personal networks and connections (Neergaard, 2007). In other instances, potential interview candidates were identified through online searches or using the snowball sampling method. Once located, the qualitative data collected for these case studies resulted from open-ended phone-based or face-to-face interviews conducted by the author. Additional published materials or follow-up emails were utilized to supplement the original interview content. The interviews took place in 2018 in the context of two separately funded projects: Four of the women entrepreneurs were interviewed as part of Healthy Women, Healthy Economies project in Asia Pacific Economic Cooperation (APEC) economies.[2] Two additional women entrepreneurs were identified as part of gender assessments funded by the United States Agency for International Development (USAID).[3]

The transcribed interviews were content-analysed to identify categories and themes. An analysis was then conducted through a within and cross-case approach which is the most appropriate technique for exploring relationships among different cases (Eisenhardt and Graebner, 2007).

Identifying Case Study Candidates

In general, the prevailing discourse regarding women's entrepreneurship tends to focus on the experiences of female entrepreneurs themselves with less attention paid to the experiences of women entrepreneurs as employers. The focus on solo women entrepreneurs is understandable given the large percentage of solo women entrepreneurs and relatively small percentage of female entrepreneurs with employees.

It proved difficult to convey a broader concept of value added as it relates to women entrepreneurs who are employers. More often than not, it was assumed that the interview would focus on the personal characteristics, challenges and successes of the women entrepreneur herself rather than the benefits she provides to her female employees. It became clear that though the concept of 'addressing the needs of women as employees' or 'providing additional benefits for women as employees beyond what is legally required' is gaining visibility as a 'concept' within large corporations focused on gender diversity, it is still an under-researched area for SMEs.

The characteristics of the six women entrepreneurs interviewed and their businesses are presented in Table 16.1. The six interviews were classified into two broad categories: First, women entrepreneurs who help women workers by addressing unmet needs and second, women entrepreneurs who help their women employees.

Table 16.1   Six case study characteristics

Entrepreneur Enterprise (Country)	Sector	Value added	Benefiting women employees	Process of finding the entrepreneur
1. Terri Piasecki Charm and Hammer (USA)	Retail Ecommerce	Safety	External as customers	Internet search
2. Ana Lucia Cepeda Bolsa Rosa (Mexico)	Ecommerce	Flex-time work	External as customers	2017 Cartier Women's Initiative Awards Finalist
3. Sarah Miller and Amanda Teelini[1] PRT app (USA)	Internet technologies application	Parenting	External as customers	Internet search
4. Jennifer Higgins MC Global[2] (Canada)	Internet technologies	Maternity/ Healthcare	Internal as employees	Snowball method
5. Sofia Moya de Pena Vanguardia Group (Honduras)	Recycling and manufacturing	Sexual Harassment	Internal as employees	Snowball method
6. Maria Pacheco Wakami (Guatemala)	Retail Ecommerce	Quality of Life	Internal as employees	Snowball method

Notes:
[1]   The names of the entrepreneurs and app name have been anonymized.
[2]   The name of the entrepreneur and business name have been anonymized.

In all six cases, supporting and advocating for women as employees is a central theme in their 'for profit' business operations. Figure 16.2 shows the four main value added areas addressed: Health and safety issues (MC Global and Vanguardia), Sex appropriate safety gear (Charm and Hammer), Working mothers (Bolsa Rosa and PRT app) and Quality of Life (Wakami).

During the interviews, it became clear that the women entrepreneurs' commitment to add value for women is manifested through their business operations. In the following two sections, we present the case studies utilizing this perspective.

WOMEN ENTREPRENEURS HELPING WOMEN AS WORKERS

In this section, we present three case studies of women entrepreneurs who started businesses to address an unmet need of women workers. The first business, Charm and Hammer, addresses the needs for sex appropriate safety gear. The second and third businesses presented, Bolsa Rosa and PRT app, address the needs of working

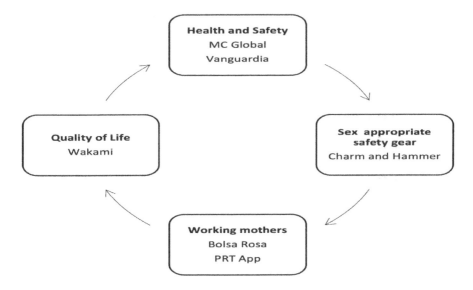

Figure 16.2   Illustration of the main need met for women employees

mothers. Bolsa Rosa increases opportunities for women to work flex-time and PRT app supports women and their partners in balancing parenting responsibilities with full-time employment positions and careers.

Added Value: Providing safety

In the past, safety equipment for sectors such as construction and mining was made to fit an average man's physical dimensions. As women started working on construction jobs, large manufacturing companies began manufacturing unisex versions of safety clothing and gear that could also be used by women. While unisex safety gear is appropriate for some situations, women also require correctly sized and fitted clothing and equipment especially for hazardous settings.

Terri Piasecki – Charm and Hammer (USA)

After spending more than 20 years working in the male-dominated US construction industry, Terri Piasecki was promoted to safety manager at an environmental construction company. In this position, Terri noticed that local professional protective equipment (PPE) distributors only stocked products that met the needs of male workers. As a result, women working at construction jobs had a much harder time accessing equipment that fit properly and could fully protect them if needed.

This was a serious issue: PPE for men or unisex styles do not always fit women's build and dimension. Women are not just smaller-sized men, their body configurations and proportions are different. Terri noticed that while large corporations could set aside the resources to identify and purchase the right size and fit of safety gear for their women employees, this process is often perceived as too time-consuming and costly for SMEs. More often than not, SMEs provide unisex PPE for women, even if they do not provide the best fit.

In many countries, such as the US, safety needs of women are not effectively enforced through the national regulatory environment. Terri decided to improve this situation by starting her own business to address the specific needs of women construction workers.

In 2003, Terri started Charm and Hammer, a women-owned business selling PPE for women working in construction. Over the years, Charm and Hammer continued to expand its inventory and it currently stocks the largest variety of professional grade safety gear designed and sized specifically for women in the US. Through its online sales, it has also become a major distributor of all types of professional grade safety gear for women worldwide.

Sadly, Terri still finds the lack of information and awareness a major impediment for companies to stocking appropriate PPE for women. In some cases, employers do not allow women to procure their own safety equipment. As Terri notes, "I'll have women place an order, only to have it canceled later that day or the next day because their supervisor won't allow them to purchase or provide their own safety equipment."

In other cases, women themselves will put up with PPE that does not fit (often bought in bulk online). These women workers do not want to be viewed as a 'picky' or require gear that needs to be special ordered at a considerable cost (since it is purchased in smaller quantities).

Added Value: Meeting the Needs for Flex-Time Employment and Supporting Working Parents

It is often difficult for women workers to combine traditional working hours with the demands of motherhood. In many cases, employers consider childbearing and childrearing a working mother's personal responsibility that should be managed outside of working hours. Due to the lack of flexible options in the workforce, a substantial proportion of mothers withdraw from employment after childbirth.

A 2014 study in the US found that 67 percent of women who were not working by choice would be likely to go back to work if they were offered flexible hours (KFF, 2014). In the UK, flexible work arrangements are linked to higher feelings of balance and job satisfaction, as well as a higher likelihood of being promoted (Wichert, 2014).

In the following case studies, we present two women entrepreneurs that built successful businesses by addressing the unmet needs of 'working mothers' through offering flex-time employment and employer funded parenting support.

Ana Lucia Cepeda – Bolsa Rosa (Mexico)

Ana Lucia Cepeda started her online business, Bolsa Rosa (Pink Bag) in 2014, after witnessing the large numbers of educated women forced to leave their jobs in Mexico. After investigating the cause, Ana realized that even though Mexican labor laws allow for part-time and flex-time work, most companies only offered traditional full-time employment options. As a result, women were leaving their jobs because companies were unwilling to offer flexible working arrangements to support work/ life balance for mothers.

Through her business, Ana Lucia was able to remove three impediments critical for women to continue working after motherhood. First, she raised awareness of the business case for adopting flex-time work arrangements in both the private and public sector and second, she connected these new job opportunities with mothers seeking permanent but flex-time positions. Third, Ana worked with businesses to shift internal company culture from evaluating work performance to the hours spent working at the office to focusing on achieved results and deliverables regardless of it, the work was conducted in the office or at home in the evening. Initially, most of Bolsa Rosa's clientele were SMEs since human resources policies at most larger companies in Mexico were not yet equipped to accommodate permanent, flex-time workers.

In 2019, Bolsa Rosa expanded its operations to include a novel online certification program. The program, popular among human resource managers and independent consultants, teaches proven methods for transforming a traditional work culture to include flex-time and remote work options.

PRT App – Sarah Miller and Amanda Teelini (USA)

The PRT app, co-founded by Sarah Miller and Amanda Teelini in 2016, is an innovative new approach to addressing the needs of working parents. PRT provides comprehensive prenatal and postpartum care services via its app to its clients by connecting them to vetted experts, ranging from lactation consultants and parenting therapists to preparing for adoption. In addition, parents can schedule consultations that take place in-person or online with specialists that can be accessed via 24/7 text messaging. PRT is currently operating in 35 countries.

In practice, the PRT app helps working parents navigate challenges such as: What are my options for sleep training the baby, so that I can get sleep too?; How do I pump at work?; How should I talk to my manager about my transition back to work?; or, I am an LGBTQ parent. How do I prepare for the baby?

For employers, PRT provides tailor-made programs and coverage that can accommodate the needs of both large companies and SMEs since each company can choose the number of employees covered as well as the number of sessions available per employee.

Companies of all sizes have experienced direct and indirect benefits from providing the PRT app to their employees. Some have found that the app results in healthcare savings as well as attraction and retention of female employees. One company was even able to maintain close to a 100 percent return-to-work rate for parents who took parental leave when using the PRT app. Indirect benefits of the PRT app include increased active engagement of working fathers in parenting and an increased sensitivity in the workplace towards the needs of working parents.

An unexpected consequence of providing the PRT app to employees has been a workplace 'baby boom effect': a sudden increase in employee pregnancies. Anecdotal evidence indicates that the app seems to foster a sense of security and support for millennials in navigating the challenges of work life and parenthood.[4]

WOMEN ENTREPRENEURS ADDING VALUE FOR THEIR FEMALE EMPLOYEES

In this section, the case studies of three women entrepreneurs illustrate the diverse strategies that can be incorporated to add value for female employees. The first female entrepreneur in this section, Jennifer, provides additional health benefits to her female employees at MC Global. In the second business described, Sofia commits to protecting her female employees in the male dominated waste management and recycling sector from sexual harassment. The third female entrepreneur, Maria, provides a holistic approach to improving the overall quality of life for her employees.

Added Value: Female Employee Health, Safety and Well-Being

Though global data is lacking, a national US survey company identified a consistent trend of greater numbers of women delaying medical care (McCarthy, 2017). A study by the US Commonwealth Foundation found that women require more healthcare services and pay higher out-of-pocket medical costs during their reproductive years than men do. Women's more frequent healthcare needs and higher cost potentially help explain why women are more likely to postpone needed medical care (ibid.).

Sexual harassment in the workplace is a worldwide phenomenon (IFC, 2016). Studies indicate that the more employees perceive that sexual harassment is tolerated in the workplace, the higher the incidence of sexual harassment is likely to be and correspondingly, the lower job satisfaction is likely to be (Estrada, 2011:423). Gender composition of employees is also an influencing factor: The greater the proportion of men in the workplace or in a specific job role, the more likely women are harassed (Willness et al., 2007).

A commonly held belief is that sexual harassment is not an issue for SMEs. However according to a 2016 Manta poll of 594 US small business owners, 67 percent of employers have no anti-harassment policies or training in place. At the same time, 41 percent of respondents reported that sexual harassment policies were unnecessary given their small workforce (Aidis and Rubin, 2018). In many countries, small businesses are legally exempt from adopting formal sexual harassment policies. Even if SMEs adopt a formal sexual harassment policy, employees may not know how or where to submit a complaint or what resources are available because many small businesses do not have a dedicated human resources department.

Jennifer Higgins – MC Global (Canada)

Located in Canada, MC Global founded by Jennifer Higgins is one of the few companies in the tech sector to be both led and co-founded by a woman engineer. The added value MC Global offers to female employees is a gender-balanced workplace in the traditionally male dominated tech sector and providing female employees additional maternity and health benefits.

As a small tech business, MC Global has intentionally created a female-friendly work culture by ensuring a gender-balanced workplace and by offering additional maternity and medical benefits for their female employees. As Jennifer notes, "Our 50/50 male/female employee ratio is unusual for the tech sector and required deliberate interventions to achieve given the shortage of female candidates."

Jennifer noticed that young women seek employers that offer additional medical benefits and when these additional benefits are offered, they are also more likely to take advantage of these benefits including pharmaceuticals, specialists, semi-private hospital rooms, physical therapy and life insurance. Though the Canadian government provides basic healthcare coverage for all its citizens, additional maternity and medical benefits can act as an important differentiator for attracting female talent especially in a highly competitive industry like the tech sector. According to Jennifer, providing these additional benefits is a win–win situation: By attracting a gender balanced team and supporting their health and well-being.

Sofia Moya de Pena – Vanguardia (Honduras)

Sofia Moya de Pena's business Vanguardia in Honduras shares some similarities with Jennifer's business MC Global in Canada. Both were started in male dominated sectors and both committed to developing a gender balanced work environment.

Like most recycling businesses in Honduras, Vanguardia is family-owned. However Vanguardia is different in several key ways: Sofia's mother started Vanguardia 30 years ago with a staff of only nine employees. Over the years, business operations and staff grew and now Vanguardia employs more than 330 individuals. Vanguardia is a model for gender equality in the traditionally male-dominated recycling and manufacturing sector. For example, Vanguardia's general manager, Sofia Moya de Pena and the majority of company managers are women. According to Sofia, women are not given preferential treatment; they are hired based on qualifications just like men. However, the company culture is based on the principles of gender equality that women and men should have an equal voice in company meetings and decision-making. This results in high numbers of women candidates for employment vacancies. Vanguardia's reputation for being fair to women and family-friendly has also contributed to higher retention rates and the participation of women at all levels and in all aspects of the company – both management and industrial.

Central to Vanguardia's ethos is their commitment to inclusive business, practices, gender equality and a workplace free of sexual harassment. During their induction process, new employees are shown a slide presentation that illustrates Vanguardia's zero tolerance for sexual harassment. New employees and existing employees are also informed that sexual harassment needs to be reported and disciplinary measures including dismissal will be taken.

Added Value: Improving Employee Quality of Life

The final case study is guided by both a 'profit-oriented inclusive business' perspective and a social-oriented 'smart investment' methodology. In practice this means that both increasing the income of women workers and improving their personal and family's quality of life are given equal importance. Every Wakami initiative begins with women drawing a picture of their individual and collective dreams for the future. This drawing creates a roadmap for their goals.

Maria Pacheco – Wakami (Guatemala)

Wakami was established in 2006 by Maria Pacheco in order to address the needs of rural women for sustainable livelihoods for themselves and their families. The novel Wakami model created by Maria incorporates both a profit-oriented inclusive business perspective with a social-oriented 'smart investment' methodology. Each has separate yet aligned goals: the inclusive business model strives to increase income for rural women and their families, while the smart investment approach focuses on improving the quality of life of these women and their families. In practice, the smart investment methodology provides a platform for women to access products and services and allows rural families to invest their income strategically in order to improve their homes and their children's education and nutrition.

Wakami's business model mandates that in every participating rural community, one local woman must become a businessowner and hire local women to produce traditionally inspired jewelry and accessories. In return, Wakami trains the women and purchases the finished accessories from the local businesswoman who pays the women for their work. In that way, a local business eco-system is formed: the local businesswoman learns to check quality control and develops financial and business management skills while a larger group of local women learn the skills for making high quality accessories that can be sold on global markets. In terms of its performance, Wakami measures its achievements based on both financial and social benefits. For example, in 2016, Wakami incubated 20 rural businesses with more than 530 producers participating in the value chain, and 96 percent of the participants were women. In the past five years, Wakami headquarters has experienced a growth of 550 percent in sales of its products in over 20 countries.

More recently, Wakami expanded its production to include clothing and handbags that are made using traditional methods such as weaving with foot and backstrap looms and using natural dyes. In addition to their online sales, Wakami has increased its sales outlets in Guatemala and expanded to selling products in Costa Rica and El Salvador. Wakami is also diversifying to include travel tours for individuals interested in visiting and interacting with Wakami's women producers located in rural villages.

DISCUSSION

All six female entrepreneurs presented exemplify a blended value approach highlighting a broader range of value creation through entrepreneurship beyond economic gains. All show that added value for women (as employees and workers) can be compatible with successful business development.

The case studies also provided some support for the theory of ethics (Gilligan, 1982) and specifically the female-oriented value system of the ethics of care that focuses on the interconnectedness among parties involved and nurturing behavior. The four levels of value creation introduced by Sheikh et al. (2018) were a useful starting point for analysis but proved limiting when applied to women entrepreneurs as employers. Since the vast majority of women-owned businesses do not have employees, this fundamental distinction is easy to overlook. Based on our analysis, two additional levels of value creation were noted: value creation for women employees and value creation for women workers as clients.

Though the sample size is small, the six case studies presented in this chapter challenge several widespread assumptions regarding SMEs abilities for added value creation. Often it is assumed that SMEs operating in wealthy, developed countries are more capable of providing added value than those operating in less developed countries. A study of 48 countries found that entrepreneurs in post-materialistic countries are more likely to emphasize social and environmental benefits of their companies than simply economic gains (Hechavarria et al., 2017). The case studies presented in this chapter operate in both developed and developing country contexts in North and Central America.

Similarly, it is often assumed that providing added value in the form of benefits for female employees is costly. As the case of Ana, founder of Bolsa Rosa demonstrates, both the business and women workers can benefit. Finally, the assumption that SME benefits for women employees can only occur in traditionally female sectors is also challenged. The six case studies presented in this chapter operate in diverse sectors, including male-dominated sectors such as the tech sector, manufacturing and recycling.

CONCLUSIONS AND RECOMMENDATIONS

The issues addressed in each of the six case studies of women entrepreneurs operating in the Americas varied, ranging from specific safety needs for women workers and supporting working mothers reentering the workforce to providing an inclusive business model that focuses on 'quality of life' and gender equity in male dominated sectors. Yet an overarching commonality in these case studies is the commitment to providing added value as part of their everyday business operations. They are all examples of a blended values approach to entrepreneurship and their added value activities are related to the ethics of care, a nurturing behavior towards other women, which supports the notion of a female oriented value system introduced by Gilligan (1982).

Though this study was limited in scope to a qualitative study of a small initial sample of women entrepreneurs in the Americas, several practical and research oriented recommendations are provided below.

At the practical level, it would be useful for targeted surveys of SMEs to be conducted in order to better understand the prevalence of additional value and benefits for women at the enterprise level and capture any gendered differences found between male-led and female-led enterprises. These activities could be initiated by local and national governments in cooperation with existing SME business organizations.

Working together with the media, governments could also increase awareness and visibility of the instrumental role SMEs play in providing additional value to women workers as a strategy to incentivize additional SMEs to adopt similar practices. At the global level, international, governmental and non-governmental organizations should work together to fund mixed methods research (combining qualitative and quantitative approaches) of SMEs (both women and men owned) to better understand the prevalence and variations of strategies and initiatives to provide added value and benefits for female (and male) employees and customers.

Further research is also needed. The six case studies presented in this chapter provide only a glimpse into an area that deserves further systematic research in order to develop a better understanding of the size, scope and variations of approaches that already exist in the SME sector. Researchers should disaggregate data on benefits offered to female (and male) employees based on business size.

Finally, the development of specific terminology that clearly communicates the 'added value' created by entrepreneurs for women as workers would allow greater opportunities for theory building, hypothesis testing and comparative studies.

NOTES

1. In the United States SMEs are defined as companies with less than 500 employees. Employer firms with fewer than 500 workers employed 46.8 percent of private sector payrolls in 2016. Employer firms with fewer than 100 workers employed 33.4 percent (United States Census Bureau, 2019).
2. For more information see APEC's Healthy Women, Healthy Economy website: https://www.apec.org/healthywomen. For the project report see Aidis and Rubin (2018).
3. For the Wakami case study from Guatemala, see Aidis (2018); for the Vanguardia case study from Honduras, see Aidis and Khaled (2019).
4. Based on an interview with one of PRT app's client companies.

REFERENCES

Aidis, R. (2018). *Women's Entrepreneurship Diagnostic – Guatemala*, USAID Report, https://bit.ly/338L4F4

Aidis, R. and Khaled, D. (2019). *Women's Economic Empowerment and Equality (WE3) Technical Assistance Municipal Waste Management and Recycling WE3 Gender Analysis*, USAID Report, doi: 10.13140/RG.2.2.34571.64808

Aidis, R. and Rubin, C. (2018). APEC Healthy Women, Healthy Economies Guidebook on SMEs, Report prepared for USAID and APEC (Asia Pacific Economic Cooperation), https://www.researchgate.net/publication/336617443_APEC_Healthy_Women_Healthy_Economies_A_Guidebook_for_SMEs

Audretsch, D. B., Keilbach, M. C. and Lehmann, E. E. (2006). *Entrepreneurship and Economic Growth*. New York, NY: Oxford University Press.

Baumol, W. J. (1986). Entrepreneurship: Productive, unproductive, and destructive. *Journal of Business Venturing*. 11, 3–22.

Branson, R. (2015). Tweet, April 15, 2015, Twitter, https://twitter.com/richardbranson/status/588361313501458432?lang=en

Braun, P. (2010). Going green: Women entrepreneurs and the environment. *International Journal of Gender and Entrepreneurship*. 2(3), 245–259.

Brush, C. (1992). Research on women business owners: Past trends, a new perspective and future directions. *Entrepreneurship Theory and Practice*. 16(4), 5–31.

Buttner, E. H. and Moore, D. P. (1997). Women's organisational exodus to entrepreneurship: Self-reported motivations and correlates with success. *Journal of Small Business Management Review*. 34(3), 552–569.

CAF Development Bank of Latin America (2016). Latin America: In search of more competitive SME's, June 13, 2016, https://www.caf.com/en/currently/news/2016/06/latin-america-in-search-of-more-competitive-sme/

Calhoun, C. (2012). *Contemporary Sociological Theory*. Chichester, UK: Wiley.

Cohen, B., Smith, B. and Mitchell, R. (2008). Toward a sustainable conceptualization of dependent variables in entrepreneurship research. *Business Strategy and the Environment*. 17(2), 107–119.

Eisenhardt, K. M. and Graebner, M. E. (2007). Theory building from case: Opportunities and challenges. *Academy of Management Journal*. 50(1), 25–32.

Estrada, A. X. (2011). Evaluating a brief scale measuring psychological climate for sexual harassment. *Military Psychology*. 23(4), 410–432.

Flanagan, O. and Jackson, K. (1987). Justice, care, and gender: The Kohlberg–Gilligan debate revisited. *Ethics*. 97(3), 622–637.

Forbes (2018). America's best employers for women, 2018. https://www.forbes.com/pictures/5b4664f2a7ea4341970e4629/americas-best-employers-f/#5129e32d6e94

Fortune (2019). 75 best large workplaces for women. http://fortune.com/best-workplaces-for-women/

French, W. and Weis, A. (2000). An ethics of care or an ethics of justice. *Journal of Business Ethics*. 27, 125–136. https://doi.org/10.1023/A:1006466520477

Gilligan, C. (1982). *In a Different Voice*. Cambridge, MA: Harvard University Press.

Hechavarria, D., Ingram, A., Justo, R. and Terjesen, S. (2012). Are women more likely to pursue social and environmental entrepreneurship? Chapter 7 in Hughes, K. and Jennings, J. E. (eds), *Global Women's Entrepreneurship Research: Diverse Settings, Questions and Approaches*. Cheltenham, UK and Northampton, MA, USA: Edward Elgar Publishing, 135–151.

Hechavarria, D., Terjesen, S., Ingram, A., Renko, M., Justo, R. and Elam, A. (2017). Taking care of business: The impact of culture and gender on entrepreneurs' blended value creation goals. *Small Business Economics*. 48, 225–257.

International Finance Corporation (IFC) (2016). *SheWorks Knowledge Report: Putting Gender Smart Commitments into Practice*. Report. http://edge-cert.org/wp-content/uploads/2017/11/SheWorksFinalReport.pdf

Jaffee, S. and Hyde, J. (2000). Gender differences in moral orientation: A meta-analysis. *Psychological Bulletin*. 126(5), 703.

Jennings, J. E. and Brush, C. G. (2013). Research on women entrepreneurs: challenges to (and from) the broader entrepreneurship literature? *The Academy of Management Annals*, 7, 663–715.

Kaiser Family Foundation/New York Times/CBS News (KFF) (2014). Non-employed poll, December 2014. http://files.kff.org/attachment/kaiser-family-foundation-new-york-times-cbs-news-non-employed-poll-topline

Korsgarrd, S. and Anderson, A. R. (2011). Enacting Entrepreneurship as social value creation. *International Small Business Journal*. 29(1), 135–151. https://doi.org/10.1177/0266242610391936

McCarthy, J. (2017). U.S. women more likely than men to put off medical treatment. *Gallup Polls*, December 7, 2017. https://news.gallup.com/poll/223277/women-likely-men-put-off-medical-treatment.aspx

Neergaard, H. (2007). Sampling in entrepreneurial settings. Chapter 10 in Neergaard, H. and Uhloi, J. P. (eds), *Handbook of Qualitative Research Methodology in Entrepreneurship*. Cheltenham, UK and Northampton, MA, USA: Edward Elgar Publishing, 253–278.

Nicholls, A. (2009). We do good things, don't we? Blended value accounting in social entrepreneurship. *Accounting, Organisations and Society*. 34, 755–769.

Organisation for Economic Co-operation and Development (OECD) (2017). *OECD Employment Outlook*. Report. https://www.oecd-ilibrary.org/employment/oecd-employment-outlook-2017_empl_outlook-2017-en

OECD and World Trade Organization (WTO) (2017). Closing the small-business and gender gap to make trade more inclusive, Chapter 8 in *Aid For Trade At A Glance 2017: Promoting Trade, Inclusiveness and Connectivity for Sustainable Development*. Report. OECD. 219–241. https://www.wto.org/english/res_e/booksp_e/aid4trade17_chap8_e.pdf

Rindova, V., Barry, D. and Ketchen, D. J. (2009). Entrepreneurship as emancipation. *Academy of Management Review*. 34(3), 477–491.

Sheikh, S., Yousafzai, S., Sist, F., Akdeniz, A. R. and Saeed, S. (2018). Value creation through women's entrepreneurship, Chapter 2 in Yousafzai, S., Fayolle, A., Lindgreen, C., Henry, C., Saeed, S. and Sheikh, S. (eds), *Women's Entrepreneurship and the Myth of Underperformance: A New Look at Women's Entrepreneurship*. Cheltenham, UK and Northampton, MA, USA: Edward Elgar Publishing, 20–33.

United States Census Bureau (2019). *Annual Survey of Entrepreneurs*. https://www.census.gov/programs-surveys/ase/data/tables.html

Weisul, K. (2018). Report: Female entrepreneurs much more likely to employ women. *Inc. magazine online*. December 20, 2018. https://www.inc.com/kimberly-weisul/these-entrepreneurs-hired-very-few-men.html

Welter, F. (2011). Contextualizing entrepreneurship: Conceptual challenges and ways forward. *Entrepreneurship, Theory and Practice*, 35(1), 165–184.

Welter, F., Baker, T., Audretsch, D. and Gartner, W. (2016). Everyday entrepreneurship: A call for entrepreneurship research to embrace entrepreneurial diversity. *Entrepreneurship: Theory and Practice*. September, 2016, doi: 10.1111/etap.12258/full

Wichert, I. (2014). How flexible working is good for you – and for your career. *The Guardian*, April 24, 2014. https://www.theguardian.com/women-in-leadership/2014/apr/24/flexible-working-career-progression-work-life-balance

Willness, C. R., Piers, S. and Kibeom, L. (2007). A meta-analysis of the antecedents and consequences of workplace sexual harassment. *Personnel Psychology*, 60(1), 127–162.

Zahra, S., Gedajlovic, E., Neubaum, D. O. and Shulman, J. M. (2009). A typology of social entrepreneurs: Motives, search processes and ethical challenges. *Journal of Business Venturing*, 24, 519–532, doi:10.1016/j.jbusvent.2008.04.007.

Zahra, S. and Wright, M. (2016). Understanding the social role of entrepreneurship. *Journal of Management Studies*, 53(4), 610–629, doi: 10.1111/joms.12149

17. Women entrepreneurs creating value in a democratic South Africa – emerging beyond the informal sector

Ethné Swartz, Caren Scheepers and Frances Amatucci

INTRODUCTION

Value creation at the societal level is critical in South Africa given the legacy of apartheid, a legalized system of separation and racial discrimination. Twenty-six years after the end of apartheid in 1994, South Africa remains a highly unequal society in terms of wealth distribution,[1] with the poor comprising 55% of the population; unemployment remains high among formerly disadvantaged groups, especially the country's youth (World Bank, 2019). Social value creation through job creation and economic inclusion is critical to safeguard democracy.

We use frameworks by Zahra and Wright (2016) and Welter (2011) to discuss how women entrepreneurs create social value. These authors contributed to theory development around creating social value through entrepreneurship, augmenting our understanding of phenomena through elucidating context. South Africa is an emerging economy wrestling with a "middle income economy trap" (World Bank, 2019); we show how women entrepreneurs in our case studies create value by filling institutional voids, created by apartheid, in education, property rights, investment and job creation. We consider how women entrepreneurs contribute to value creation in this unique context and in turn, how this context enables women entrepreneurs to create value (Smallbone & Welter, 2009).

Value creation at the social level is especially important in South Africa where human agency and political action resulted in one of the most progressive constitutions globally. We investigate how women ensured that property and individual rights for women were enshrined in law, removing barriers to entrepreneurship. South Africa's political and historical contextual dimensions reveal factors that impact economic and legal outcomes (Swartz & Amatucci, 2018). Our research is therefore positioned within and aligned to Welter's (2011) and the entrepreneurship contextualization framework by Baker and Welter (2018).

Our research question is, "How have women entrepreneurs in South Africa created value at the level of society?" A secondary question is: "How does the South African political and historical context influence this value creation?" We use a qualitative case study research approach to ground the theoretical narrative and pay homage to the women transforming sectors such as education, investment, edu-tainment and digital services.

The first section of our chapter reviews relevant literature on value creation. The next section discusses the South African context before we present our methodology. We then present case studies to ground our argument that social value is created as an outcome of entrepreneurial agency (Friedman, 2016; Smallbone & Welter, 2009) especially when entrepreneurs *choose* to create social value, while creating economic wealth. We conclude with a discussion of implications for future research and policy.

LITERATURE REVIEW – VALUE CREATION, CONTEXT AND ENTREPRENEURSHIP

We offer an overview of recent debates on value creation and contextualizing entrepreneurship, followed by a more focused discussion on the part women played in South Africa's political history to set the scene for our cases. This "scene setting" elucidates the path-dependent nature of development in South Africa (Friedman, 2016).

Scholarship has moved from a focus on traditional financial value to entrepreneurial activities that include social value or social wealth. Nicholls (2009) introduced the concept of 'blended value' which incorporates financial, social and environmental value. Korsgaard and Anderson (2011) argue that entrepreneurship is as much a social as an economic endeavor. For instance, Welter and Xheneti (2015) examine types of value creation generated from the informal entrepreneurial activities in post-Socialist contexts; entrepreneurs generated economic and social value at the individual, community and society levels, and in the short run and long run. Our research on post-apartheid South Africa builds on these studies of major societal transformation by exploring how women entrepreneurs create social and economic value. Given the far-reaching change that had been required to end apartheid, South Africa was an ideal context for the current study on the role of human agency of women entrepreneurs.

Slavova's (2019, p.9) contributions on value creation in South Africa's energy industry, used the model of shared value (Porter & Kramer, 2011) suggesting that value is *relational* and consists of "… benefits (e.g., financial income, social inclusion, environmental impact) relative to costs (e.g., time and resources required) shared between the entrepreneurs and those affected by their ventures".

This reframing of "value creation" to include social and environmental considerations in the role that women entrepreneurs play has been neglected. This neglect is particularly problematic in emerging markets where participation rates for women in entrepreneurial activities, in both formal and informal sectors, are increasing faster than the general population, resulting in significant impacts on societal, economic and political landscapes.

Many scholars emphasize the importance of context in determining social value (Aslund & Backstrom, 2015; Welter & Xheneti, 2015; Zahra & Wright, 2016). The contextualization perspective has gained support in entrepreneurship also (Jones & Wadhwani, 2006; Ucbasaran, Westhead, & Wright, 2001; Welter, 2011; Welter, Baker, & Wirsching, 2018; Zahra, 2007). Welter (2011) identifies four dimensions of context as business, social, spatial and institutional – *where* entrepreneurship happens. There are many examples of both top-down (theories of context) and bottom-up context effects on entrepreneurship in post-Soviet countries (Smallbone & Welter, 2009). Through reciprocity, external context influences entrepreneurship, and in turn, entrepreneurship influences the external context. Furthermore, the temporal and historical (*when*) are also critical (Welter et al., 2018). We define temporal to include images taken at different times either discretely (snapshots) or continuously.

Kolk, Rivera-Santos and Rufin (2018) note the importance of context for researchers who focus on Africa, with scholars selecting either context-bound or context-specific frameworks. Our study is context-specific and adopts the contextualization framework to illuminate South Africa's political transformation and impact on entrepreneurship. The contextual approach reveals the path-dependent nature of entrepreneurial choice (Jones & Wadhwani, 2006). Friedman (2015) shows how change trajectories in South Africa are marked by significant societal advances while retaining elements that previously sustained social relations, connections, and other factors from the apartheid system. Given these conditions, the framework of Zahra and Wright (2016) helps to deconstruct how entrepreneurs create social value, using five pillars which enhance positive outcomes and minimize negative outcomes associated with entrepreneurship:

1. Support of societal efforts to improve quality of life, human progress and human existence.
2. Strategies to counter dysfunctional outcomes of entrepreneurship – governance abuses, environmental degradation and abuses through technology use.
3. Redefining the scope of entrepreneurship to include the informal sector.
4. Entrepreneurship as a social multiplier to accelerate new venture creation.
5. Adopting blended value frameworks, including financial, social and environmental outcomes.

We utilized these pillars to analyse four cases of women entrepreneurs in South Africa. Our last two sections offer our findings and discuss implications. As explained, we intended to explore the interaction between the agency of women entrepreneurs within the complex South African reality, paying attention to the historical and political dimensions of context. Guillén (2014) cites a 2010 World Bank report that argues that equal rights under the law results in a greater percentage of businesses owned or managed by women. Our next section provides important historical and legal background on the condition of women and the agency of a coalition of South African women that has proven critical to securing property rights for women in the country.

SOUTH AFRICAN WOMEN – POLITICAL AGENCY FOR HUMAN PROGRESS

Legal and property rights are important social value creation pathways. In this section we discuss how South African women claimed these rights. We illustrate the struggles involved in achieving outcomes in line with the first pillar of the Zahra and Wright (2016) framework. Without this historical context about the efforts of political activists acting as *entrepreneurs*, the cases in this chapter would lack meaning (Wadhwani, Kirsch, Welter, Gartner and Jones, 2020, p.11): "… entrepreneurial actors have extensive agency … opportunities are *created*[2] as entrepreneurs act upon context."

Social value creation in South Africa thus begins with women (women activists and a mass movement of women) shaping the writing of the South African constitution to ensure individual rights for *women*. Women earned the legal and property rights so critical to the legal and institutional environment for business. The gains of these women activists demonstrate the *social value* that flows from their struggle – women entrepreneurs enjoy the same legal rights as men in areas identified by the World Bank (2019) as leading indicators for entrepreneurship: (1) Does the law prohibit discrimination in access to credit based on gender? (2) Can a woman sign a contract in the same way as a man? (3) Can a woman register a company in the same way as a man? (4) Can a woman open a bank account in the same way as a man?

Indeed, outcomes for home and land ownership in South Africa show gains in gender parity across the country and all racial and socio-economic groups (Statistics South Africa, 2014). Decisions by the Constitutional Court demonstrate the importance of legal rights that women have won (Cowan, 2007) and the agency noted by Friedman (2015). South African women occupy a tenuous position in a patriarchal society marked by high levels of violence and political resistance. The Apartheid State was a product of British and Dutch colonialism, with an economy dominated by British capital. Afrikaners and indigenous South Africans were excluded from control of most economic sectors; black Africans were denied legal and property rights, becoming the primary source of cheap labor (O'Meara, 1996). This legacy prevails in the mixed legal system that has evolved, consisting of Roman-Dutch, English common law and, for traditional communities, customary law (Oxford University, 2019).

These processes were highly gendered – the colonial powers and the Afrikaner Nationalist movement restricted women to the home, best expressed in the Afrikaner Nationalist phrase, "Vrou en Moeder" (this phrase translates into "Wife and Mother"). This prescribed the role that white South African women came to adopt. Afrikaner women contributed to demands for the vote for women but acquiesced to White Nationalists and abandoned a racially inclusive alliance (Vincent, 1999). Ultimately white women supported suffrage for women based on race (Meintjes, 1996). Resistance to apartheid would become the kiln that burnished women's leadership in politics and society and awaken their agency.

During the transition to democracy (1994–1996) an inclusive coalition pushed for the protection of women's rights to be included in the South African Constitution. Women organized to form institutions where none had previously existed and so ensure equity through the constitution. Khanna and Palepu (1997) argue that emerging markets suffer from institutional voids and the formation of a Women's National Coalition (WNC) to ensure protections for women presents an excellent example of such a void being filled. The WNC pushed for women to participate and for the new Constitution to consider women's emancipatory concerns (Cowan, 2007; Meintjes, 1996). Parliament adopted, in 1994, *A Women's Charter for Effective Equality*, enshrining women's rights in the new constitution.

Individual rights ensured that women would have legal rights to hold property, open bank accounts, or own a company. These are rights fundamental to entrepreneurship and restricted under African customary law which treats women as minors. Thus, without access to the Constitutional Court, African women are subject to customary law which is valid only if deemed not to conflict with the values and provisions of the South African Constitution (Oxford University, 2019).

Political activists united with the WNC and pressured the (mostly) male ANC members at the negotiating table (McLeod, Johnson, Meintjes, Brown, & Oosterveld, 2014, pp.355–356):

> ... to take on board what women wanted and needed, and perhaps more importantly, to include more women in the negotiating teams.

Women leaders created a Women's Legal Center (WLC) to ensure their hard-won (justiciable) rights would be implemented and enforced (Cowan, 2007). The Constitutional Court has upheld property rights and land tenure for women. In 2004, the WLC won two important cases. In the first, the Court declared primogeniture unconstitutional (primogeniture is the practice, in custom and law, of the eldest son automatically inheriting family assets); in the second case, the Court accorded women married under Muslim rites the same entitlements to property enjoyed by women married under common law.

Establishing property rights and land tenure rights for women therefore set precedents in enabling the conditions for (legal) ownership of assets that determine economic independence and wealth creation through entrepreneurship.

WOMEN'S ENTREPRENEURSHIP IN SOUTH AFRICA: PATHWAYS AND CHALLENGES

Having shown how women pushed institutional level change, we now consider women entrepreneurs and, in line with the focus of this volume, *"How do they do it?"*. In emerging economies new firms are critical for economic inclusion, alleviating poverty and reducing unemployment (World Bank, 2019). This is pertinent in South Africa with its high unemployment rates (Herrington, Kew, & Mwanga, 2017), estimated at 26–27%, and 53% for youth (World Bank, 2019), Women's entrepreneurship is critical for economic advancement particularly given data that attitudes towards entrepreneurship in South Africa have become more positive (Herrington et al., 2017).

Another positive indicator is that women's labor force participation has increased, estimated by the World Bank to be 41.61% in 1990, rising to 47.92% in 2017 (The Global Economy, 2019) and to 43.8% in 2018 (Statistics South Africa, 2017). Women's labor force participation rose by 38% for the period 1993 and 2008 (Leibbrandt, Woolard, McEwen, & Koep, 2010), due to improving educational attainment, rising numbers of households headed by women, and because of the effect of the HIV crisis on households. Greater labor force participation is paralleled by an increasing rate of entrepreneurship among women in South Africa, though still lagging rates for men overall (Herrington et al., 2017). The South African government estimates that for the period 2001–2006, women constituted 40% of entrepreneurs and that Black women participated at a rate of 50% for all women, largely driven by the government policy of Black Economic Empowerment (BEE).

Overcoming Barriers

Barriers to women's entrepreneurship in South Africa span the gamut of the GEM Entrepreneurial Factor Conditions (EFC) framework.[3] The typical woman entrepreneur is a black South African who is either self-employed or runs a micro-business, operating in the informal or service sector (Statistics South Africa, 2017; Department of Trade and Industry, IFC, & Finmark Trust, 2006). Women lack financial and other resources because their economic progress (Statistics South Africa, 2017) has been slow. Despite greater labor market participation and accounting for 43.8%[4] of the workforce, women are still more likely to be unemployed than men, work in domestic service, work in the informal sector as traders (47.6% of the informal sector), or do unpaid (considered "non-market") work. These roles are in community, social and personal services dependent on social and government grants, supplemented by remittances. Women-owned firms skew smaller than their male-owned counterparts (SBP Alert, 2013) but more black women are migrating from street vending towards franchising, furniture manufacturing, printing and travel services, or property development. Concomitant with these shifts, barriers increase because of an intersection of race, class and gender (Scott et al., 2012).

Entrepreneurs need access to professional services but continued residential segregation (Friedman, 2015) and inertia on the part of professional service providers render access difficult. Banks and other services are scant in townships that remain home to the formerly disadvantaged. Finance for women entrepreneurs lacks appropriate banking products, is unaffordable, with collateral requirements that prevent women from accessing business loans (DTI et al., 2006). Access to finance is therefore an important barrier to entrepreneurship (Sage Foundation South Africa, 2017; Scott et al., 2012). The International Finance Corporation of the World Bank, in the Department of Trade and Industry South Africa report (2005), observed both supply and demand barriers, with only 36% of black women reporting access to banking facilities. Financial literacy, lack of financial confidence and lack of awareness of financing sources were additional obstacles (Chinomona, 2015; Derera, Chitakunye, & O'Neill, 2014).

Societal and cultural norms significantly impact women entrepreneurs. Women entrepreneurs find it harder to raise business finance (DTI et al., 2006). Government research further suggests a lower level of entrepreneurial activity in South Africa, relative to other countries, because women do not believe they have the skills to start a business (DTI, 2005). This lack of self-efficacy is deepened by a cultural barrier of a negative perception of entrepreneurship as a viable career option (Sage Foundation South Africa, 2017). The Sage Foundation specifically highlights the need for role models – this is true for all South Africa's neighboring economies as well (Lebakeng, 2008). Women entrepreneurs are often driven from survivalist intentions (Lebakeng, 2008), while a dearth of women entrepreneurs who start opportunity-focused companies reinforces the limited aperture that shapes the entrepreneurial visions of younger women and youth.

The importance of education and training in entrepreneurship is therefore evident. These include school and university programs as well as those provided by the private sector. Irene (2016) found a pattern of women giving up entrepreneurship and taking up paid employment when they encountered difficulties. However, they repeatedly returned to entrepreneurship, leading them to become de facto serial entrepreneurs. Inferences can also be made from the findings on the inability of South African women SMME[5] operators to sustain their businesses. Bureaucratic systems and taxes are important barriers to women entrepreneurs. The growth of SMEs would benefit from less and more targeted government regulation (SBP Alert, 2013).

RESEARCH METHODOLOGY

Our epistemological position is that a constructionist perspective is most appropriate when conducting research on women entrepreneurs (Ahl, 2006). Constructionism holds that gender cannot be divorced from social context and is created by the perceiver; gender is socially constructed and shaped by social forces. Following Henry, Foss and Ahl (2016), we selected a qualitative case study methodology as a valuable research design to adopt. Our sample consisted of women entrepreneurs who were growing their ventures as we wished to focus beyond the informal sector. In line with the focus of this volume, we wished to establish how and why these created value and their understanding of value.

We conducted a literature review on women's entrepreneurship in South Africa (highlights from this review are in the previous section), which informed our semi-structured interview schedule. Our interview schedule included questions on the interviewees' background, entrepreneurial vision, funding of their businesses, the start-up phase, the evolution of the business, scaling and exiting, where appropriate. We used a non-probability, purposeful sampling method, and recruited respondents

Table 17.1   *Sample characteristics*

Entrepreneur	Company Characteristics and Social Value Contribution
Louisa Mojela, WIPHOLD	Investment fund established with funding raised in townships. WIPHOLD NGO Investment Trust has redistributed proceeds to thousands of beneficiaries. Invests in projects in poor communities and targets women entrepreneurs.
Dr. Judy Dlamini, Mbekani Group	Holding group with investments distributed across property, facilities management, education and educational technology. Employs 150 staff members.
Aisha Pandor, SweepSouth.com	Digital platform connecting 8,000 domestic workers with employment opportunities. Employs 40 staff.
Megan Kruger, Shine Group and ICT	Shine Group is a property and talent management agency in fashion and entertainment, employing 13 people. ICT is a PBO that educates disadvantaged youth for jobs in hospitality and employs 6 staff.

through a snow-balling strategy, recruiting entrepreneurs through university networks and posts on LinkedIn groups. Two of the authors conducted and transcribed the interviews in the Gauteng region of South Africa during the first half of 2019. We analyzed the data by developing themes as we read and coded the interview transcripts. This was an iterative process as we reviewed the interview transcripts. Additionally, we triangulated interview data by sourcing information from companies' websites, media articles and press releases. Our research consisted of a larger pool of interviews,[6] drawing respondents from food retailing, investment management and impact investment, ed-tech, Artificial Intelligence (AI) logistics, food and hospitality education, insure-tech, digital domestic services, spirits production, digital transformation consulting and cyber security.

Given our focus on the social value that women entrepreneurs create, we selected four cases that address our research question.

FINDINGS

Table 17.1 summarizes information about the four cases that ground our analysis. Of note is the variety of sectors in which these women operate and the number of jobs they have created. The short case studies provide evidence of how women entrepreneurs purposefully use their companies to contribute to social value while minimizing the social costs associated with apartheid's legacy. The short cases are the active constructions by these entrepreneurs as they interpreted why they started their companies and the value that they believe they create in South Africa. These accounts are malleable and an interpretation of their past acts (Wadhwani et al., 2020). Nonetheless, given the neglect of such *context-specific* accounts of building businesses, these stories are important and we reflect in the next section on what we can learn about value creation in South Africa.

Case #1: Women's Investment Portfolio Holdings (WIPHOLD)

In 1994, four black women set up WIPHOLD with R500,000 seed capital, listing the investment fund on the Johannesburg Stock Exchange (JSE) in 1997 (DTI, 2005). Louisa Mojela and Gloria Serobe, two of the original founders, remained at the helm of the company. WIPHOLD was the first women-led investment company to list on the JSE[7] and raised R500 million from their listing. Their uniqueness lies in their active participation in the organizations in which they invest. WIPHOLD was the BEE partner of Old Mutual Group from 2004 to 2014. WIPHOLD raises local and international financing, through its large capital and asset base. As BEE partners WIPHOLD had performance agreements with Old Mutual, which provided regular income for working capital requirements.

WIPHOLD was made possible first by the initial seed capital of R500,000 in 1994, raised from ordinary black women in townships. Second, government creates the environment for business to trade in an open market, influencing the effectiveness of the financial services system. The financial system is dependent on a foundation of impeccable ethics, to create the context for fair deals, which are transparent and perceived as legitimate in a democratic South Africa. WIPHOLD would not have been able to raise the R500 million in shares at their listing in 1997 without anti-apartheid reforms.

New constitutional and legislative frameworks in South Africa highlight gender equality and encourage empowerment through the Broad-Based Black Economic Empowerment Act (BBBEE or BEE for short) which promotes an increase in the extent to which black women own and manage existing and new enterprises. This framework enabled WIPHOLD to collaborate with Old Mutual as a BEE partner.

WIPHOLD invested capital wisely, choosing to invest their competence as well as their capital. We highlight this aspect as it represents the social wealth dividend for companies in which WIPHOLD invests. For example, they offer training in financial skills and transformation, as well as financial services to these companies. We propose that this characteristic of the women-led investment companies makes a huge difference to their financial investments and allows their investments to grow exponentially. This illustrates the multiplier effect when social investment escalates the return on financial investments.

In 2003 WIPHOLD created a second trust, the WIPHOLD NGO Trust, which has an 18.7% shareholding in WIPHOLD. Over R80 million has been distributed to the over 200,000 beneficiaries of this Trust. The WIPHOLD Investment Trust has a 15% shareholding in WIPHOLD. R144 million has been distributed to the 1,400 direct beneficiaries of this Trust and R346 million to 18,000 indirect beneficiaries (DTI, 2005).

Women entrepreneurs who receive WIPHOLD investments endeavor to grow their businesses and the guidance in financial services from WIPHOLD multiplies their effort. This growth is a manifestation of social wealth, since these women entrepreneurs have an influence of empowerment in their own families and communities, which in turn creates more opportunity for entrepreneurship.

Case #2: Dr. Judith Dlamini – Founder and CEO, Mbekani Group

"We need positive African stories to build a positive mind-set in the African child"
(Dlamini, quoted in Dugmore, 2019).

Dr. Nobuhle Judith Dlamini is the Chancellor[8] of Wits University in Johannesburg, South Africa. Her achievements are myriad. She obtained a medical degree, advanced degrees in business, investment management, and created the Mbekani Group in 1996 as a holding company for investments and operations in property, facilities management, fashion, tourism and surgical equipment. Mbekani Group employs over 150 staff members.

Dlamini relates that when she grew up, "…it was a crime to have my complexion. Yet I was raised by parents who encouraged me to pursue my education and who told me I could be anything I chose to be" (Dugmore, 2019). Her parents refused to be broken by the apartheid system and their resilience and entrepreneurial spirit supported Dlamini's success. She enjoys the support of her husband, Sizwe Nxasana, whom she met at school. Sizwe was one of the first black accountants in South Africa.

Dlamini and her husband formalized their philanthropy in 2009, through a Public Benefit Organization (PBO) called Mkhiwa Trust. Mkhiwa is a Nxasana clan name. Mkhiwa focuses on three main areas: health, education and rural development. Both their children, Sifiso and Nkanyezi became involved in these initiatives. In 2016 Dlamini founded the Sifiso Learning Group, named for her deceased son. The group includes Future Nation Schools (FNS), Sifiso Publishers, Sifiso Education Properties and Sifiso EdTech. The group promotes gender equality from the youngest age in their three preschools and two high schools in Gauteng. Dlamini emphasizes that Africans have to celebrate their African-ness and intellectual contributions to the world.

Dlamini's book, *Equal but Different* is based on life story interviews from 14 women from diverse backgrounds, all of whom have risen to top leadership positions (Dlamini, 2017). The book explores the intersection of race, gender and social class and its effect on women leaders' career progression. Her most recent book, *The Other Story* (Dlamini, 2019), features African achievers, testimony to her quest in sharing positive African stories.

Case # 3: Aisha Pandor: Founder of SweepSouth.com – the South African Uber for Domestic Services

Over one million domestic workers in South Africa service the needs of households (Statistics South Africa, 2017). This workforce is mostly black and female, comprising some of the most under-appreciated and vulnerable in society. South Africa has an oversupply of low-skilled labor, a legacy of the apartheid context which prevented the masses of black people from accessing quality education.

Aisha Pandor, the co-founder of SweepSouth.com, a digital platform for domestic workers, spotted an opportunity for digital intermediation in the domestic service industry which suffers from inefficiencies in supply and demand. Pandor and her husband and co-founder, Alen Ribic, drew on the Uber model in which drivers are connected to riders via an online platform. Pandor set out to restore dignity to women whose only option was domestic work. Pandor's case portrays the pursuit of societal change at the cognitive institutional realm as workers at SweepSouth.com are called "SweepStars" instead of the derogatory terms used to describe their roles. Additionally, women earn a living wage.

Pandor holds a Ph.D. in Human Genetics from the University of Cape Town (UCT) and describes herself as impatient to create societal impact. This desire led her to leave a lucrative corporate consulting career to found SweepSouth. Pandor and Ribic founded SweepSouth in 2013 after resigning from their full-time corporate roles, cashing in their pensions and using proceeds from their house and car sales as seed funding for the business. By 2018, the online platform had grown to connect 8,000 previously unemployed domestic workers with clients looking for home cleaning services. By 2019 SweepSouth employed 40 staff in two regional offices.

Ribic developed the company's new media technology to supply online, on-demand home and business cleaning services. The app-based platform connects clients with reliable, diligently vetted cleaning staff at affordable rates. Eighty-three percent of the SweepStars are breadwinners, most of them single mothers with at least four dependents. Only 22% of these women had a pension plan or any form of savings. SweepSouth.com negotiated free life insurance coverage (to the value of R400,000 and disability coverage of R200,000) for their SweepStars.

SweepSouth encourages their SweepStars to apply a micro-entrepreneurial model where they upsell services so clients book more hours. SweepSouth Whatsapp groups for SweepStars build community, enabling women to share tips with one another. SweepSouth uses this platform to inspire and share ideas, creating community and differentiating their service from traditional placement agencies.

In October 2014 the company won the SiMODiSA StartupSA conference "Get-Up Start-Up" award which included partial sponsorship for a trip to Silicon Valley (Coetzee, 2014). Vinny Lingham of Newtown Partners, became SweepSouth's first investor and the company has raised additional venture funding. SweepSouth provides opportunities for thousands of women; however, in 2019 there were 80,000 unemployed domestic workers who had applied to join the platform as a SweepStar and SweepSouth will have to scale to meet this demand.

Case # 4: Megan Kruger: Founder and CEO of Shine Group

Megan Kruger exemplifies how "market feminism" (Scott, 2006) can create social gains by creating opportunity for the disadvantaged. Kruger is founder, CEO and co-owner of the Shine Group, and a founding partner of a production company, Aarushi (Pty) Ltd. Kruger also serves on the board of Infinity Culinary Training (ICT) in Cape Town, as the company's head of Business Affairs. ICT is a registered Public Benefit Organization (PBO), funded with donations from the USA and South

Africa. In September 2019, after 10 years of operation, ICT graduated its 500th student.

"Transform, Educate and Add Value" is Kruger's motto, inspired by growing up poor in a suburb east of Johannesburg and her dream of becoming a teacher. She dropped out of the University of the Witwatersrand to become an international fashion model. In 1984 Kruger opened an agency in Johannesburg, followed by a partnership with an investor, and the establishment of the agency, Network Models. The height of the apartheid era was a challenging time to start a business and by 1994 Network Models was insolvent as South Africa suffered from the isolation of a global business boycott of the country.

Moving to Cape Town, Kruger's fashion and beauty industry network helped her land contracts to train models and start a new partnership, 2M-Power. When that partnership ended in 2001, Kruger purchased G3 Models and Head Models, the seeds for the Shine Group. In 2010 Shine Group bought a 46,000 sq foot building in Gauteng, to create an event and film studio complex. Kruger was about to form a partnership with a film school and add value to society by enabling young people to access space to create films. Her vision was that young people could use the space to create films and share their experience of their corner of South Africa!

Financial sustainability steered Shine Group to reconsider operating as a purely social venture. Having taken on debt to purchase the studio building, Kruger had to prioritize how to monetize the studios, renting the space to a black producer who collaborates with SABC-TV1, 2 and 3. Shine Studios have enjoyed great success with two series. *Daily Thetha* is an interactive show that addresses burning problems that South African youth face. The second show, *The Big Debate*, embraces controversial issues, including legal reform and urban land rights. Shine Group also generates income from renting the space for events, launches, and entertainment engagements. By 2019, Shine Group employed 13 employees in Johannesburg.

The Shine Group continues to focus on social value creation but have to operate profitably. Two state-owned companies create great uncertainty for all companies. Eskom, the South African power generation company, is a monopoly. Regular power outages and high electricity prices have impacted income at Shine Group. There are also limited distribution opportunities for television content in South Africa. SABC-TV1 has been inconsistent in honoring commercial agreements, again impacting Shine Group's revenues. Kruger (2019) admits that while she is values-driven, enterprises need revenues and profits to create social value:

> Value comes from people and from doing things with and for others. Financial success is different and also important. You want to be able to pay employees, you want to have a nice warm place to live and eat.

In 2010 Kruger co-founded ICT that trains disadvantaged students for free to become chefs and place them in the food industry. ICT employs three teachers, all ICT graduates, as well as three administrators. Kruger serves on the board as Director of Business Affairs and helps to fundraise. The Woolworths Group hosts ICT in Cape

Town. Kruger's vision is for all ICT graduates to live with dignity and build careers, or enabling them to study abroad.

DISCUSSION

We now turn to discuss HOW the women entrepreneurs in our cases create social value. Given the social gains achieved by the WNC, we believe the Zahra and Wright (2016) framework overlooks value creation through women's political agency. The case of South Africa shows the need for a sixth pillar to reflect the contribution to constitutional change, and we would categorize this as entrepreneurs helping to *reframe legal and constitutional rights to close gender gaps.* In this sense, entrepreneurship would be focused on the creative combination and recombination of resources and structures as those who seek change envision opportunity. Following Schumpeter (1947) such a definition would include individuals and organizations (including political organizations) as performing an entrepreneurial function. We discussed in an earlier section how this occurred in South Africa and how critical this was to ensure women had legal rights to protect the gains of their entrepreneurial activities.

Social wealth creation occurs when entrepreneurship connects to other societal efforts aimed at improving the quality of life, achieving progress, and enriching human existence, in line with Zahra and Wright's (2016) first pillar. The case studies in this chapter demonstrate that these women entrepreneurs perceived success not only in terms of financial metrics but also social elements such as providing educational opportunity (Mbekani group), creating jobs (SweepSouth) and providing financial education to communities previously excluded from the formal economy (WIPHOLD; Shine Group). This theme recurs throughout the cases in this chapter.

With regards to the second pillar of Zahra and Wright (2016) on countering the negative effects of entrepreneurship, several of the women entrepreneurs were instrumental in countering the negative effect of inequality with regards to access to financial services (WIPHOLD and SweepSouth) and education (Mbekani Group and Shine Group). Our cases suggest that the pillars of Zahra and Wright (2016) are actually interdependent. The second pillar as mentioned above, is linked to the emphasis on the informal sector, as the third pillar. For example, access to finance (WIPHOLD and SweepSouth) offers opportunities for the informal sector to scale their businesses and facilitate development of new ventures in rural areas, as the fourth pillar indicates.

Assumptions about economic roles are redefined by successful women entrepreneurs (SBP, 2013) and in this way they contribute to societal level change. Women-led Black Economic Empowerment (BEE) investment groups such as WIPHOLD connect entrepreneurial activities to other societal efforts to improve the quality of life of their beneficiaries. Women entrepreneurs contribute at the societal level by being employers: it is estimated that women comprise 23% of South African employers (SBP, 2013).

The fifth pillar of Zahra and Wright (2016) involves "... pursuing blended value at the organizational level by ... balancing the creation of financial, social and environmental wealth". In this regard, women-led BEE investment groups such as WIPHOLD play an important role in redressing the wrongs of apartheid through a redistribution of financial wealth. The WIPHOLD case therefore show women as pioneers in addressing the voids of offering investment vehicles that included women investors, disrupting cultural and social norms.

The emergence of women-owned companies with the potential to scale due to exploiting digital platforms is an exciting development. SweepSouth.com exemplifies transformative change for sectors dogged by the same inefficiencies that Aisha Pandor identified in South Africa's domestic cleaning industry. As Africa embraces the Fourth Industrial Revolution, South African women will increasingly play a role in making life better for themselves, their families, and society.

CONCLUSION

How do women entrepreneurs in South Africa create value at the societal level and how does the South African context influence this value creation? In answering these research questions, we used Zahra and Wright's (2016) "five pillars" to systematically evaluate the social value created by the women entrepreneurs, while the tenets of contextualization (Welter, 2011) enabled us to show HOW women entrepreneurs have created social value. These frameworks led us to consider contributions in the legal sphere – South African women ensured the Constitution contained individual and property rights for women, cementing gains in home and land ownership in perpetuity. Individual and property rights are justiciable, and fundamental. We suggest that the Zahra and Wright (2016) framework should incorporate political movements or actors as a means of social value creation, especially in contexts where institutional gaps exist. We suggest that this would augment the value creation literature, addressing fundamental structural change in societies. In line with Wadhwani et al. (2020, p.10) we believe this missing element would enable researchers to address how "... entrepreneurial action shapes change."

Our illustrative cases ground our discussion of how women entrepreneurs contribute to social and blended wealth creation by creating new institutional forms. Women seized on regulatory system changes to build investment and financing vehicles for financial inclusion, especially for rural and agricultural business owners. Women entrepreneurs have influenced the normative system by providing new role models and setting new gender role expectations through scaling and growing companies.

Similarly, at the cognitive level, women entrepreneurs are filling voids in education, investment finance, edu-tainment and real estate. Dr. Dlamini is of particular note in creating "shared value" (Porter & Kramer, 2011). Beyond financial and social value, Dr. Dlamini's focus on the psychological needs of the "African child" and Megan Kruger's empathy for youth and solving the root causes of poverty are important perspectives about how societies create social wealth. We believe this mindset is vital to how "shared value" is perceived in countries undergoing fundamental transformations.

Our literature review offers a deeper understanding of the human agency contribution of women. Our study contributed to a heightened awareness of women's role in democratic change in South Africa. Using our case study analyses we demonstrated how South Africa's political and historical context created the environment for the emergence of these women-founded enterprises that contribute to a multiplier effect of social value creation. The contribution of some of these women entrepreneurs in our sample was more indirect, such as investment in education (Shine and Mbekani Groups) and other more direct investments, through offering employment and financial means (SweepSouth and WIPHOLD).

Government and policy makers should note the important role of women entrepreneurs, and offer encouragement and recognition for their efforts, and where appropriate, funding to assist in scaling their services.

NOTES

1.   South Africa has a Gini coefficient of .63.
2.   Our emphasis to indicate women's agency.
3.   The 2014 EFCs are: finance, government policy, bureaucracy and taxation, government programs, entrepreneurial education and training, R&D transfer, infrastructure, internal markets, and social and cultural norms (https://www.gemconsortium.org/wiki/1142).
4.   Women make up 55.1% of the South African population in 2018 (Statistics South Africa, 2017).
5.   SMME is defined as Small, Micro and Medium Enterprises.
6.   Interviews were conducted with 13 respondents in three urban locations. That data is currently being analyzed using NVivo.
7.   The company chose to delist from the JSE in 2003 because of the short-termism of investors.
8.   Chancellor of a university is a ceremonial role, while the vice-chancellor is the academic head.

REFERENCES

Ahl, H. (2006). Why research on women entrepreneurs needs new directions. *Entrepreneurship: Theory and Practice*, 30(5), 595–621. https://doi.org/10.1111/j.1540-6520.2006.00138.x

Aslund, A., & Backstrom, I. (2015). Creation of value to society: A process map of the societal entrepreneurship area. *Total Quality Management and Business Excellence*, 26(3–4), 385–399.

Baker, T., & Welter, F. (2018). Contextual entrepreneurship: An interdisciplinary perspective, *Foundations of Entrepreneurship*, 14(4), 357–426.

Chinomona, E. (2015). Women in action: Challenges facing women entrepreneurs in Gauteng Province in South Africa. *International Business & Economics Research Journal*, 14(6), 835–850.

Coetzee, J. (2014). SweepSouth sweeps up award at SiMODiSA Startup SA, *Venture Burn*, October 13, 2014 accessed October 23, 2018, http://ventureburn.com/2014/10/sweepsouth-sweeps-award-simodisa-startup-south-africa/.

Cowan, R. (2007). Women's representation on the courts in the Republic of South Africa, accessed February 12, 2019, https://digitalcommons.law.umaryland.edu/cgi/viewcontent.cgi?article=1017&context=wle_papers.

Department of Trade and Industry (DTI) (2005). South African women entrepreneurs: A burgeoning force in our economy. A special report. Government of South Africa, Pretoria.

Department of Trade and Industry, IFC and Finmark Trust (2006). Access to finance for women entrepreneurs in South Africa: Challenges and opportunities. Department of Trade and Industry (DTI), National Government South Africa, Pretoria.

Derera, A., Chitakunye, P., & O'Neill, C. (2014). The impact of gender on start-up capital: A case of women entrepreneurs in South Africa. *The Journal of Entrepreneurship*, 23(1), 95–114.

Dlamini, J. (2017). *Equal but Different: Women Leaders' Life Stories*. Sandton: Sifiso Publishers.

Dlamini, J. (2019). Interview with authors. April 16, 2019. Johannesburg.

Dlamini, J. (2019). *The Other Story: A Fireside Chat with African Achievers*. Sandton: Sifiso Publishers.

Dugmore, H. (2019). What drives Judy Dlamini's success. *Mail & Guardian*, January 4, 2019, accessed March 23, 2019, https://mg.co.za/article/2019-01-04-00-judy-dlamini-is-a-success-story.

Friedman, S. (2015). The Janus face of the past: Preserving and resisting South African path dependence. In Mangcu, X. (ed.), *The Colour of Our Future: Does Race Matter in Post-Apartheid South Africa?* Johannesburg, SA: Wits University Press, 45–63.

Friedman, S. (2016). Enabling agency: The Constitutional Court and social policy. *Transformation*, 91(1), 19–39.

Guillén, M. (2014). The world of women entrepreneurs. In Guillén, M. (ed.), *Women Entrepreneurs: Inspiring Stories from Emerging Economies and Developing Countries*. New York: Routledge, 1–8.

Henry, C., Foss, L., & Ahl, H. (2016). Gender and entrepreneurship research: A review of methodological approaches. *International Small Business Journal*, 34(3), 217–241.

Herrington, M., & Kelley, D. (2012). *Global Entrepreneurship Monitor African Entrepreneurship: Sub-Saharan African Regional Report*. Accessed September 18, 2021, https://www.babson.edu/Academics/centers/blank-center/global-research/gem/Documents/GEM%202012%20Africa%20Report.pdf

Herrington, M., Kew, J., & Mwanga, A. (2017). *Global Entrepreneurship South African Report 2016/2017: Can Small Business Survive in South Africa?* University of Cape Town.

Irene, B. N. O. (2016). Women entrepreneurs: A cross-cultural study of the impact of the commitment competency on the success of female-owned SMMEs in South Africa. *International Journal of Sciences: Basic and Applied Research*, 27(2), 70–83.

Jones, G. & Wadhwani, R. D. (2006). Schumpter's plea: Rediscovering history and relevance in the study of entrepreneurship. *Harvard Business School Working Paper*. 06-036. Accessed January 2019, http://www.hbs.edu/research/pdf/06-036.pdf.

Khanna, T., & Palepu, K. G. (1997). Why focused strategies may be wrong for emerging markets. *Harvard Business Review*, 75(4), 41–51.

Kolk, A., Rivera-Santos, M., & Rufin, C. R. (2018). Multinationals, international business and poverty: A cross-disciplinary research overview and conceptual framework. *Journal of International Business Policy*, 1(1), https://ssrn.com/abstract=3164324.

Korsgaard, S., & Anderson, A. R. (2011). Enacting entrepreneurship as social value creation. *International Small Business Journal*, 20(10), 1–17.

Kruger, M. (2019). Interview with authors. April 6, 2019. Johannesburg.

Lebakeng, M. (2008). An exploration of women entrepreneurship in Lesotho. Unpublished MBA thesis, Wits Business School, Johannesburg.

Leibbrandt, M., Woolard, I., McEwen, H., & Koep, C. (2010). Better employment to reduce inequality further in South Africa in tackling inequalities in Brazil, India, China and South Africa: The role of labour market and social policies. Paris: *OECD Publishing*, 209–262.

McLeod, L., Johnson, R., Meintjes, S., Brown, A., & Oosterveld, V. (2014). Gendering processes of institutional design: Activists at the negotiating table. *International Feminist Journal of Politics*, 16(2), 354–369. DOI: 10.1080/14616742.2014.918777.

Meintjes, S. (1996). The women's struggle for equality during South Africa's transition to democracy. *Transformation Critical Perspectives on Southern Africa*, 30, 47–64.

Nicholls, A. (2009). We do good things, don't we? Blended value accounting in social entrepreneurship. *Accounting, Organization and Society*, 34(6), 755–769.

O'Meara, D. (1996). *Forty Lost Years: The Apartheid State and the Politics of the National Party 1948–1994*. Johannesburg: Ravan Press/Ohio University Press.

Oxford University (2019). *Oxford University Bodleian Library Guides: South African Law: Legal System*. Accessed February 12, 2019, https://ox.libguides.com/c.php?g=422906&p=2888047.

Pandor, A. (2018). Interview with authors. September 26, 2018. Cape Town.

Porter, M., & Kramer, M. (2011). Creating shared value. *Harvard Business Review*, 89(1–2), 62–77.

Sage Foundation South Africa (2017). *The Hidden Factors: Fostering Female Entrepreneurship: The Report*. www.sage.comm/za.

SBP Alert (2013). Understanding women entrepreneurs in South Africa. *Alert SBP Business Environment Specialists. Issue Paper 3*, Accessed April 25, 2019, http://www.sbp.org.za/uploads/media/SBP_Alert_-Understanding_Women_Entrepreneurs_in_SA.pdf.

Scott, L. (2006). Market feminism: The case for a paradigm shift. *Advertising and Society Review*, 7(2), January.

Scott, L., Dolan, C., Johnstone-Louise, M., Sugden, K., & Wu, M. (2012). Enterprise and inequality: A study of Avon in South Africa. *Entrepreneurship Theory and Practice*, May, 543–568.

Schumpeter, J. A. (1947). The creative response in economic history. *Journal of Economic History*, 7(2), 149–159.

Slavova, M. (2019). Shared value through energy entrepreneurship in South Africa. *GIBS Working Papers Showcase on Green Entrepreneurship in South Africa*, February 19, 2019. Accessed February 22, 2019, https://www.gibs.co.za/about-us/centres/entrepreneurship-development-academy/Documents/GIBS_Working_Papers_Showcase_on_Green_Entrepreneurship_SA_V2%5b1%5d.pdf.

Smallbone, D., & Welter, F. (2009). *Entrepreneurship and Small Business Development in Post-Socialist Economies*. London: Routledge

Statistics South Africa (2014). Gender Series I: Economic Empowerment, 2001–2014. *Statistics South Africa*, Report No 03-10-14. Accessed March 11, 2020, http://www.statssa.gov.za/publications/Report-03-10-04/Report-03-10-042014.pdf.

Statistics South Africa (2017). Gender Series IV: Economic Empowerment 2001–2017. *Statistics South Africa*, Report No 03-10-17. Accessed April 5, 2019, http://www.statssa.gov.za/?page_id=1854&PPN=03-10-17.

Swartz, E., & Amatucci, F. (2018). Framing second generation gender bias: Implications for women's entrepreneurship, *Journal of Developmental Entrepreneurship*, 23(1), 1850009. https://doi.org/10.1142/S1084946718500097.

The Global Economy (2019). South Africa: Female labor force participation. Accessed February 23, 2019, https://www.theglobaleconomy.com/South-Africa/Female_labor_force_participation/.

Ucbasaran, D., Westhead, P., & Wright, M. (2001). The focus of entrepreneurial research: Contextual and process issues. *Entrepreneurship Theory & Practice*, 25(4), 57–80.

Vincent, L. (1999). A cake of soap: The Volksmoeder ideology and Afrikaner women's campaign for the vote. *The International Journal of African Historical Studies*, 32(1), 1–17. Accessed November 1, 2019, https://www.jstor.org/stable/220803.

Wadhwani, D., Kirsch, D., Welter, F., Gartner, W., & Jones, G. (2020). Context, time, and change: Historical approaches to entrepreneurship research. *Strategic Entrepreneurship Journal*, 14(1), 1–17.

Welter, F. (2011). Contextualizing entrepreneurship: Conceptual challenges and ways forward. *Entrepreneurship Theory & Practice*, 35(1), 165–184.

Welter, F., Baker, T, & Wirsching, K. (2018). Three waves and counting: The building tide of contextualization in entrepreneurship research. *Small Business Economics*, 52(2), 319–330. https://doi.org/10.1007/s11187-018-0094-5.

Welter, F., & Xheneti, M. (2015). Value for whom? Exploring the value of informal entrepreneurial activities in post-socialist contexts. Exploring criminal and illegal enterprise. *New Perspectives on Research, Policy and Practice*, 5, 253–275.

World Bank (2019). Unemployment, total (% of total labor force)(modeled ILO estimate) – South Africa. Accessed September 20, 2019, https://data.worldbank.org/indicator/SL.UEM .TOTL.ZS?locations=ZA.

Zahra, S. A. (2007). Contextualizing theory building in entrepreneurship research. *Journal of Business Venturing*, 22(3), 443–452.

Zahra, S. A., & Wright, M. (2016). Understanding the social role of entrepreneurship. *Journal of Management Studies*, 53(4), 610–629.

18. Indian transgender women creating social value through social entrepreneurship

Roshni Narendran

INTRODUCTION

This chapter focuses on transgender women entrepreneurs and the impact of their entrepreneurial ventures on the creation of social value for the transgender community. Drawing on media interviews and publicly available narratives of the journey of two transgender women entrepreneurs, the chapter makes a unique contribution to the female entrepreneurship scholarship by foregrounding the discourse on gender non-conforming individuals in entrepreneurship.

For more than three decades, studies on women's entrepreneurship have focused on cisgender heterosexual male and female entrepreneurs who act within narrowly gendered spaces (Al-Dajani et al., 2015; Marlow & Martinez Dy, 2018). Thus, the call by mainstream scholars for equality between men and women in entrepreneurial spaces has focused on the conventional binary of the two genders at the expense of others. Others are considered to be an 'out-group' of gender identities, such as gay, lesbian, transgender person, asexual, intersex, and queer – all of which are quite often excluded from mainstream visibility in discussions of gender and entrepreneurship (Marlow et al., 2018). Transgender employees report being publicly revealed as a transgender person, being deliberately threatened, and being emotionally and physically abused (Schilt & Connell, 2007; Budge et al., 2010). Such discriminatory behaviour leads to exclusion from mainstream employment and exclusion from family and friends, which causes stress, anxiety, depression, substance abuse and suicide. For this reason, there is a need to provide avenues for transgender women in the community to gain access to the opportunities enjoyed by the binary sexes. The entrepreneurs discussed in this chapter have the expertise and resources to address this social need (Zahra et al., 2009).

The call for chapters that proposed this volume opened the debate on unconventional value outcomes for women in multiple contexts. Therefore, I use the concept of value creation to analyse the journey of two transgender women entrepreneurs. Sheikh et al. (2018) discuss four levels of value creation for women entrepreneurs: individual level, business level, household level and social level. In this chapter, I focus mostly on social value creation, especially in the context of transgender women entrepreneurs. The turmoil experienced by transgender women turns their journey of gender transformation into one of social value creation. This chapter reviews critically the process of how two prominent transgender women entrepreneurs in South India – make-up artist, Renju Renjimar, and activist, writer and filmmaker, Kalki Subramanian – create value for the transgender community. These women entrepreneurs were chosen because of their prominence and their entrepreneurial ventures which generate income for members of the transgender community.

To map the social value created by these two transgender women entrepreneurs, this chapter is organized as follows: First, the relevant literature on social value is discussed. Second, the method used to collect data is discussed, followed by analysis and discussion of the data. Finally, the chapter concludes by highlighting how further scholarship on entrepreneurship is needed to pursue the topic of transgender persons and other gender non-conforming individuals in entrepreneurship.

LITERATURE REVIEW

In the past, scholars have associated entrepreneurship with economic development (Schumpeter, 1934), profit (Cole, 1959), and growth (Carland et al., 1984). Such studies explored the connection between entrepreneurship and the economic well-being of a business. They focused on creating value in terms of value for customers and subsequently wealth for owners (Hitt & Ireland, 2005). Many studies in entrepreneurship focused on *economic* wealth creation rather than *social* value creation.

Social value creation is associated with social activities – in this case, the term *social* refers to a complex phenomenon which is difficult to identify the activities and projects that are considered to be creating value (Nicholls & Cho, 2008; Choi & Majumdar, 2014). Social value creation is about resolving social problems through avenues such as generating income for socially disadvantaged groups or delivering medical assistance to poverty-stricken communities (Dees, 2007). Social value creation in fact involves 'virtuous behavior (Sullivan Mort et al., 2003, p. 82), altruistic objectives (Tan et al., 2005), and the promotion of a social purpose' (Choi & Majumdar, 2014, p. 367). Choi and Majumdar (2014) consider that social value is a prerequisite for social entrepreneurship.

Social Entrepreneurship – Creating Social Value

From among the three types of social entrepreneur discussed by Zahra et al. (2009), I expand on the social bricoleur. Social bricoleurs 'perceive and act upon opportunities to address a local social need they are motivated and have the expertise and resources to address' (Zahra et al., 2009, p. 523). Social bricoleurs help to mitigate serious local social problems (Zahra et al., 2009). Transgender women entrepreneurs (social bricoleurs) create social value by mitigating the social castigation and abuse encountered by the transgender community. Zahra et al. (2009, p. 524) discuss the knowledge required to identify, frame and evaluate a potential opportunity. In this chapter, I argue that social entrepreneurs gain the knowledge required to address the social problem through their personal experience.

Value generation is how social entrepreneurs convert their abilities and organizational resources to realize value within society (Hlady-Rispal and Servantie, 2018). Value generation can encompass organizational resources such as finance and skills of the individuals to generate value. In the case of transgender women entrepreneurs, they create businesses in spite of the various political, legal, institutional, economic, cultural, and religious challenges. Entrepreneurs who have been victims of childhood trauma will be aware of the imbalance in the social system when it comes to the creation of value for stakeholders (Barendsen & Gardner, 2004; Verstraete & Jouiso n-Laffitte, 2011) because they are aware of 'what is valuable' and where value resides (Lepak et al., 2007, p. 181). The challenges faced are similar to women entrepreneurs (see Sheikh et al., 2018, p. 23), but are in fact more severe owing to the lack of social acceptance of their gender identity. The existing institutions and incentives may not be able to cope with new complexities (Auerswald, 2009). Similarly, society has embraced the socially constructed roles of a man and woman (Butler, 2004), when an individual embraces a gender identity outside the set of established social boundaries, there arises a different set of relationship dynamics between the society and the individual. Transgender women entrepreneurs are able to understand the dynamics within the society to generate value. In the case of transgender women entrepreneurs, previous experience equips them to be aware of the problems encountered by their community, and this facilitates their interaction with the networks within the transgender community to generate value. After identifying the social problem, they focus on value sharing.

Value sharing is the transfer of value from the social enterprise to the wider community or ecosystem (Hlady-Rispal & Servantie, 2018). In the case of the transgender community, transgender women entrepreneurs who have experienced exclusion from society create a social enterprise with the expectation that this will create value for others in the community who have suffered physical and emotional abuse, exclusion from education, or exclusion from family and society (Badgett, 2014). The social enterprise acts as the architect for the advantages it provides to the society (Porter & Kramer, 2011). The distribution of value helps build a network of relations with external stakeholders (Demil & Lecocq, 2010; Zott et al., 2011; Amit & Zott, 2015). Social enterprise may enhance human capabilities, increase freedom or build level of trust (Auerswald, 2009). Having gone through the process of gender transition and the negative experience of detraction from society, transgender individuals imagine a goal of creating social value for other transgender individuals – in this case, creating a social enterprise to share value with other members of the community. In such a context, transgender women entrepreneurs interact with other transgender individuals in the broader society to achieve the goal of providing them with opportunities equal to those of other members of the society.

METHODOLOGY

The Context

India is one of the most populated countries in the world, with a population of 1.339 billion (World Bank, 2019). As per the 2011 census, 487,803 transgender individuals live in India (Census India, 2011). There could also be more transgender persons who are hesitant to reveal their gender identity in fear of being dismissed, threatened or subject to abusive social attitudes (Ozturk, 2011; Ahmed et al., 2014). Unlike those in many other countries, transgender individuals in India have a complicated history. Hindu mythology includes, for example, the story of a male god's transformation into a goddess, and one of the prominent deities in South India (Ayyappan) was considered to be the son of two male gods (Agoramoorthy & Hsu, 2015). Thus, social acceptance of gender diversity and even of gender fluidity has been evident to some extent. Owing to their mythological significance, some transgender communities in India are considered to have the power to curse or bless people and this prominence has prompted some people to invite transgender individuals to weddings and other auspicious ceremonies for their blessings (Monro, 2010). However, attitudes towards transgender individuals in India started to change when the British introduced the Indian Penal Code in 1860, declaring homosexuality a crime (Agoramoorthy & Hsu, 2015); hence many transgender individuals were arrested and abused by the police. Since then, transgender individuals have been subjected to discrimination and violence (Elischberger et al., 2018).

Those in the transgender community who have revealed their gender identity have been subjected to abuse and castigated by their families (Badgett, 2014). The exclusion of transgender women from mainstream employment opportunities has made starting a business a suitable option for transgender women entrepreneurs. However, India's overall rank on the World Bank's Ease of Doing Business Index is only 77 out of 190 (Doing Business, 2019), indicating the difficulty of starting a business in India regardless of gender identity. Antony and Johny (2017) describe how discrimination endured by members of the transgender community prevents many from meeting their basic needs owing to the social stigmatization and discrimination that denies them jobs in the mainstream. Some transgender individuals have undertaken commercial sex work to meet their basic needs (Antony & Johny, 2017), thus raising many social problems within the transgender community that need to be addressed. In this chapter, I discuss how two transgender individuals have striven to solve the problems faced by members of their community.

Sample and Analysis

This chapter focuses on two prominent South Indian transgender woman entrepreneurs running businesses. The data were obtained from Indian newspaper articles and from media interviews that have reported on the make-up artist, Renju Renjimar, and the entrepreneur, activist, writer and filmmaker, Kalki Subramanian. Renjimar and

Table 18.1   Data used for the study

Author/Publication	Year	Source title	Source
Conway	2019	*My story, by Kalki – Sahodari Foundation.*	http://ai.eecs.umich.edu/people/conway/TSsuccesses/Kalki/Kalki.html.
Nair/Deccan Chronicle	2018	*The idea of independence*	https://www.deccanchronicle.com/lifestyle/viral-and-trending/150818/the-idea-of-independence.html
DNA India	2019	*Liberty, equality, identity: Giving wings to the transgender community in India*	https://www.dnaindia.com/lifestyle/report-liberty-equality-identity-giving-wings-to-the-transgender-community-in-india-2174903
India Today	2019	*8 Indian transgender people who were the firsts in their fields*	https://www.indiatoday.in/education-today/gk-current-affairs/story/list-of-transgenders-firsts-who-made-it-big-in-their-fields-1276415-2018-07-03.
Jose Talk	2019	*Breaking the barriers to success | Renju Renjimar | Josh Talks Malayalam*	https://www.youtube.com/watch?v=z46FgUKVsvQ.
Metro Malayalam	2018	*Let's get talking with Metro Malayalam | Episode 8 | Interview with Renju Renjimar.*	https://www.youtube.com/watch?v=KYg-7Rkhrek
News Glitz	2019	*Kalki Subramaniam on being an artist for helping other transgenders | An interview with Transgender.*	https://www.youtube.com/watch?v=Gym9qwraESM
Ted Talk	2018	*Breaking binaries, establishing identity | Kalki Subramaniam | TEDxDumas*	https://www.youtube.com/watch?v=_j1NzEGMNdo
The India Observer	2017	*Why Kalki Subramaniam got a standing ovation at Harvard India Conference.*	https://theindiaobserver.com/kalki-subramaniam-standing-ovation-harvard/
Times of India	2018	*Travails of the trans community*	https://timesofindia.indiatimes.com/city/kochi/travails-of-the-transcommunity/articleshow/65881559.cms
The Hindu	2018	*Being Revathi*	https://www.thehindu.com/entertainment/theatre/in-a-mono-act-a-revathi-gives-a-moving-account-on-what-it-means-to-be-a-transgender/article23559497.ece
The Hindu	2019	*When transgender people tell their pain through art…*	https://www.thehindu.com/entertainment/art/angry-indian-goddesses/article26664585.ece
Kannadasan/The HinduBechu/The New Indian Express	2018	*First-of-its-kind skilling programme for transgenders kept alive by participants' enthusiasm at Kochi's St Teresa's College.*	http://www.newindianexpress.com/cities/kochi/2018/feb/15/first-of-its-kind-skilling-programme-for-transgenders-kept-alive-by-participants-enthusiasm-at-koch-1773742.html
The New Indian Express	2017	*The Aphrodite touch – Renju Renjimar most sought after make-up artist*	https://www.newindianexpress.com/cities/kochi/2017/jan/11/the-aphrodite-touch--renju-renjimar-most-sought-after-make-up-artist-1558299.html

Author/Publication	Year	Source title	Source
The New Indian Express	2018	*Transgender persons to sizzle the ramp at 'Queen of Dhwayah' beauty pageant.*	http://www.newindianexpress.com/cities/ kochi/2018/jun/17/transgender-persons -to-sizzle-the-ramp-at-queen-of-dhwayah -beauty-pageant-1829230.html
The New Indian Express	2018	*TGs get a beauty spot.*	http://www.newindianexpress.com/cities/ kochi/2018/nov/19/tgs-get-a-beauty-spot -1900429.html
Yourstory.com	2019	*I am happy and liberal than most 'born women' I have seen – Kalki Subramaniam.*	https://yourstory.com/2015/05/kalki -subramaniam/
Youth India	2019	*Documentary on Kalki Subramaniam: A transgender, Super woman.*	https://www.youtube.com/watch?v= CDxwbCYQ3rc.

Subramanian are the founders of two prominent not-for-profit organizations: Renjimar is the co-founder of Dhwayah and Subramanian founded the Sahodari Foundation. Data were drawn from two sources. First, publicly available interviews help to elucidate their journeys as prominent transgender women entrepreneurs who are agents of social change. Second, news articles on Dhwayah and the Sahodari Foundation were selected that referred specifically to social value creation. The source of the data is given in Table 18.1.

Data Analysis

Gender manifests as an identity through which people recognize themselves and others (West & Zimmerman, 1987; Risman, 2004). The case of transgender individuals is one in which they decide to accept an identity contrary to that through which broader society identifies them. The LGBT community receives scant attention in entrepreneurship scholarship. Therefore, I chose not to use quantitative analysis, which is generally criticized in gender studies for using gender as a mere binary variable (Stevenson 1990; Allen & Truman, 1993). To understand the values of an individual's interpretation of their life and gain visibility as an orator of their experience (Bracke & Puig de la Bellacasa, 2004; Golombisky, 2006), qualitative analysis is more suitable. Very little is known about the role of transgender women entrepreneurs in creating social value, and deeper insight into the phenomenon is warranted. Thus, the case for a qualitative research design is strong. This chapter draws on Renju Renjimar's and Kalki Subramanian's narrations of their respective journeys as women entrepreneurs, and also draws on newspaper articles reporting how they have created social value. The data are related to the key themes within the literature. First, I coded data that relates to: (i) how the transgender women identified themselves as the sex opposite from that to which they were assigned at birth; (ii) problems/trauma faced by transgender women as they embraced the sex opposite from that to which they were assigned at birth; and (iii) the creation of new venture. Second, the data were further coded to identify key theoretical concepts such as value generation and value creation.

FINDINGS AND DISCUSSION

Kalki Subramanian – the Journey from Value Creation from the Individual Level to Social Value Creation

The past experiences of transgender women entrepreneurs locate them as a source of motivation for the creation of social value. Kalki Subramanian grew up in Tamil Nadu, India (Conway, 2019). Kalki was from a middle-class Indian family (Conway, 2019). Her father was generous and helped the poor community (Conway, 2019). Since Kalki was 10 years old, she wanted to be a girl, 'and wearing skirts and frocks excited me beyond anything else' (Conway, 2019, para 4). Kalki states that:

> It was the most difficult period of my life. I was in school, as an effeminate confused boy student. (Yourstory.com, 2015, para. 6)

Kalki made friends with a transgender woman (*The India Observer*, 2017; Ted Talk, 2018). One friend, who made her livelihood through sex work, was kidnapped and raped (*The India Observer*, 2017; Ted Talk, 2018). Witnessing the emotional and physical trauma her friend underwent, Kalki realized the discrimination faced by the transgender community in India (Ted Talk, 2018):

> So that was when my first anger arose against the injustice being done to the transgender population. I have witnessed it, and since then, in so many instances of my life I have seen so many, especially the young people, commit suicide, being murdered, being raped. (The India Observer, 2017, para 2)

Kalki's experience shows the initial stages of value generation. As a social bricoleur, Kalki perceived and acted upon the opportunity to address a serious social problem. This helped to build a social enterprise to provide the means to help the transgender community in India.

Kalki told *The Better India* news outlet (Aranha, 2018) that:

> Isolation made me stronger. As I was alone, the only recourse left to me was to lose myself in studies. Coming from a family of highly educated people, academics came naturally to me. It is education that has helped me to become who I am. (Aranha, 2018, para 6)

This statement resonates with how Kalki has striven to create value for herself. Entrepreneurs create value for themselves through enhanced agency and enriched personal growth and development (Sheikh et al., 2018). Kalki used enhanced agency over her life choices to embrace her gender identity against mainstream society's wishes and used her academic excellence to start the Sahodari Foundation. Kalki's educational background helped her to write magazine articles and poems to sell to the masses (Aranha, 2018; Youth India, 2019).

Value sharing

In addition to creating value at the individual level, through awareness and knowledge of various issues faced by the transgender community, Kalki was able to create opportunities for others. As hers is a social entrepreneurial venture, value creation at the business and community levels overlap. Many of the business-level activities of the Sahodari Foundation are associated with educating the society about the equal rights of transgender individuals. They share the problems faced by the transgender community through art. The Sahodari Foundation in association with Coimbatore One organized a one-act play featuring Revathi, a transgender woman who shares an account of the discrimination and abuse she faced due to her gender non-conforming identity (*The Hindu*, 2018). Similarly, the Sahodari Foundation organized an activity where transgender women could share their stories through painting (*The Hindu*, 2019). An exhibition of participants' paintings, called 'Shut up', shared the abuse received from the public and even from the authorities for being a transgender person (Kannadasan, 2019). In these ways, the transgender individuals utilize their art to send a message to the community regarding their discrimination.

In addition to the support provided for the transgender community through art, the Sahodari Foundation also has a Facebook site, 'Jobs for Trans', that promotes jobs for transgender individuals (DNA India, 2019). The dominant social mission of providing equal rights and equality to the transgender community has enabled the Sahodari Foundation to focus on the social value they have been generating within Indian society.

In an effort to provide equality for the transgender community in India, the Sahodari Foundation joined with transgender activists to meet with the most influential politicians in the country, paving the way for the creation of the Transgender Welfare Board in South India, the implementation of college admission reserved for transgender women, and a government panel of doctors to help transgender individuals attain sex reassignment surgery (Conway, 2019). In this way, the foundation has provided value to its community.

Based on local knowledge, Kalki was able to share social value with the transgender community.

Renju Renjimar – the Journey from Value Creation from the Individual Level to Community Level

Realization of gender transformation

Renju Renjimar had a different journey to gender identification. Renjimar was aware of her gender identity since she was very young child (Metro Malayalam, 2018). In her interview, Renju explained that her family did not express any dislike of her choice of gender identity. Renju's family accepted her. The profession she chose was to be a beautician on the sets of motion pictures. At the beginning of her career, she encountered problems in her journey to becoming a popular make-up artist:

There were moments I broke down on film sets. But I stood strong and braved all the hatred. If some random light-boy smirks at me now, I will definitely give him a piece of my mind. But mostly I try to reason with people. There are some extremely talented people among our community, but they are denied a platform to prove their skill. (*The New Indian Express*, 2017, para 2)

Renju mentioned the harassment she faced from society (see Jose Talk, 2019). Eventually she gained recognition in the film industry and became a prominent make-up artist for actresses in South India. Realizing that many transgender women are castigated by their families, Renjimar, like Kalki, also acted on the opportunity to address a serious social problem where members of the transgender community are abandoned by their family. The mothers insist their children embrace their socially assigned gender and sex, which is considered exploiting motherhood into a business, that is, the discrimination within the family acts as the starting point for discrimination against the transgender community (Metro Malayalam, 2018).

It is the personal experience that is a significant motivator for entrepreneurs to be change agents and to find new means of social value creation (Jose Talk, 2019). Renju faced discrimination from mainstream society and listened to the experiences of other transgender individuals in Kerala, South India. Renju and others from the transgender community started a not-for-profit arts organization called Dhwayah (Metro Malayalam, 2018) which aims to create social value within mainstream society by giving transgender individuals more confidence to be active in the mainstream.

Value sharing

The transgender community has been excluded from social and cultural participation (Chakrapani, 2010). Being excluded from their families in particular, they have little opportunity to continue their education and fail to find jobs in the mainstream (Chakrapani, 2010). Dhwayah realized the set of social norms and rules that hinders transgender individuals from gaining mainstream employment and education. To address this gap within the ecosystem, the organization arranged communicative English development courses for transgender individuals (Bechu, 2018). Dhwayah founded a school of drama and organized a beauty pageant among other developments. In an effort to create social value for transgender women, they brought many prominent actors, politicians, and other cultural figures to participate in Dhwayah's beauty pageant (*The New Indian Express*, 2018). The efforts of Dhwayah's beauty pageant organizers were such that:

[The] 'Queen of Dhwayah' could well prove a game changer in society's perception of the [transgender] community and indeed can help erase the stigma attached to them. Also, the pageant will provide them with an avenue to showcase and develop their [transgender community] artistic talents. (*The New Indian Express*, 2018, para 3)

Through such efforts, Dhwayah provides transgender individuals in the community the chance to recover from stigmatization and attain recognition from the society. Shyama Prabha, the Dhwayah pageant winner in 2017, now works for the Social Justice Department of the Government of the State of Kerala (*The New Indian Express*, 2018). Thus, the social value that accompanied community recognition stimulated social change. Recently, Dhwayah started the Dhwaya Beauty Academy, with the aim of providing transgender people with vocational education by teaching them the art of makeup (*The New Indian Express*, 2018b). This shows Dhwayah's efforts to stay focused in creating social value among the transgender community in Kerala by spreading awareness. Fourteen transgender women and one transgender man performed a drama sponsored by Dhwayah called *Parayan Maranna Kathakal* (Narration of Forgotten Stories) in 2018 to convey their struggles in the community (*Times of India*, 2018).

CONCLUSION

In spite of the bullying they have endured in their lives, transgender women entrepreneurs have created enterprises in South India. Kalki's passion for art and writing helped her to create the Sahodari Foundation, through which she was able to create value by providing platforms to fight against discrimination. Similarly, Renju Renjimar's endurance through many challenges to become a successful make-up artist led her to create value for transgender individuals by providing a platform for them to showcase their talent, fight against discrimination, and develop skill sets, all of which help to bring the transgender community into the mainstream. Indian society's discriminatory attitude toward gender transformation has helped transgender women entrepreneurs to develop goals through which they could create social value. Future studies should look beyond the cisgender heteronormative (i.e. the male–female sexual binary) by giving equal importance to entrepreneurs of other gender identities.

Based on the findings, I make two major contributions. First, entrepreneurship research has long been dominated by men, and a heterosexual, cisgender man has long been a metonym for the typical entrepreneur (Marlow & Martinez Dy, 2018; Marlow et al., 2018). This chapter addresses this shortcoming in the literature by going beyond the socially accepted binary sexes to focus on transgender women entrepreneurs who have become social bricoleurs working to solve problems within their community. The second contribution of this chapter is to expand the focus beyond the barriers of entrepreneurship. Members of the transgender community face many problems; however, it is important to understand how such barriers contribute to their resilience and the creation of social value for other members of the community. This is one of the few works within the scholarship on female entrepreneurship that moves beyond the mainstream studies of male and female entrepreneurs.

REFERENCES

Agoramoorthy, G. & Hsu, M. J. (2015). Living on the societal edge: India's transgender realities. *Journal of Religion and Health, 54*(4), 1451–1459.

Ahmed, U., Yasin, G. & Umair, A. (2014). Factors affecting the social exclusion of eunuchs (hijras) in Pakistan. *Mediterranean Journal of Social Sciences, 5*(23), DOI: 10.5901/mjss.2014.v5n23p2277.

Al-Dajani, H., Carter, S., Shaw, E. & Marlow, S. (2015). Entrepreneurship among the displaced and dispossessed: Exploring the limits of emancipatory entrepreneuring. *British Journal of Management, 26*(4), 713–730.

Allen, S. & Truman, C. (1993). Women and men entrepreneurs: Life strategies, business strategies. In S. Allen & C. Truman (Eds), *Women in business: perspectives on women entrepreneurs* (pp. 1–13). Routledge.

Amit, R. & Zott, C. (2015). Crafting business architecture: The antecedents of business model design. *Strategic Entrepreneurship Journal, 9*(4), 331–350.

Antony, P. & Johny, J. C. (2017). Social work intervention for the empowerment of transgender community in Kerala, India. *Journal of Social Work Education and Practice, 2*(2), 1–9.

Aranha, J. (2018). *From Ostracised Teen to Trans Icon: The Incredibly Inspiring Journey of Kalki!* https://www.thebetterindia.com/149605/kalki-subramaniam-transgender-sahodari -foundation/.

Auerswald, P. E. (2009). Entrepreneurship and social value. *Stanford Social Innovation Review, 7*(2), 50–55.

Badgett, M. V. (2014). *The economic cost of stigma and the exclusion of LGBT people: A case study of India.* http://crossasia-repository.ub.uni-heidelberg.de/3693/1/Cost%20of %20Stigma%20LGBT%20India.pdf.

Barendsen, L. & Gardner, H. (2004). Is the social entrepreneur a new type of leader? *Leader To Leader, 34*, 43–50.

Bechu, S. (2018). *First-of-its-kind skilling programme for transgenders kept alive by participants' enthusiasm at Kochi's St Teresa's College.* http://www.newindianexpress.com/cities/kochi/2018/feb/15/first-of-its-kind-skilling-programme-for-transgenders-kept-alive -by-participants-enthusiasm-at-koch-1773742.html.

Bracke, S. & Puig de La Bellacasa, M. (2004). Building standpoints. The feminist standpoint theory reader: Intellectual and political controversies. In. S. G. Harding (Ed.), *The feminist standpoint theory reader: Intellectual and political controversies* (pp. 309–316). Psychology Press.

Budge, S. L., Tebbe, E. N. & Howard, K. A. (2010). The work experiences of transgender individuals: Negotiating the transition and career decision-making processes. *Journal of Counseling Psychology, 57*(4), 377.

Butler, J. (2004). *Undoing gender.* Psychology Press.

Carland, J. W., Hoy. F., Boulton, W. R. & Carland. J. C. (1984). Differentiating entrepreneurs from small business owners: A conceptualization. *Academy of Management Review, 9*(2), 354–359.

Census India (2011). *Transgender in India.* https://www.census2011.co.in/transgender.php

Chakrapani, V. (2010). *Hijras/transgender women in India: HIV, human rights and social exclusion.* https://archive.nyu.edu/jspui/bitstream/2451/33612/2/hijras_transgender_in _india.pdf.

Choi, N. & Majumdar, S. (2014). Social entrepreneurship as an essentially contested concept: Opening a new avenue for systematic future research. *Journal of business venturing, 29*(3), 363–376.

Cole, A. H. (1959). *Business enterprise in its social setting.* Harvard University Press.

Conway, L. (2019). *My story, by Kalki-Sahodari Foundation.* http://ai.eecs.umich.edu/people/conway/TSsuccesses/Kalki/Kalki.html.

Dees, J. G. (2007). Taking social entrepreneurship seriously. *Society*, *44*(3), 24–31.

Demil, B. & Lecocq, X. (2010). Business model evolution: in search of dynamic consistency. *Long Range Planning*, *43*(2–3), 227–246.

DNA India (2019). *Liberty, equality, identity: Giving wings to the transgender community in India*. https://www.dnaindia.com/lifestyle/report-liberty-equality-identity-giving-wings-to-the-transgender-community-in-india-2174903.

Doing Business (2019). *Ease of doing business score*. https://www.doingbusiness.org/en/rankings.

Elischberger, H. B., Glazier, J. J., Hill, E. D. & Verduzco-Baker, L. (2018). Attitudes toward and beliefs about transgender youth: A cross-cultural comparison between the United States and India. *Sex Roles*, *78*(1–2), 142–160.

Golombisky, K. (2006). Gendering the interview: Feminist reflections on gender as performance in research. *Women's Studies in Communication*, *29*(2), 165–192.

Hitt, M. A. & Ireland, R. D. (2005). *The Blackwell encyclopedia of management: Entrepreneurship*. Blackwell.

Hlady-Rispal, M. & Servantie, V. (2018). Deconstructing the way in which value is created in the context of social entrepreneurship. *International Journal of Management Reviews*, *20*(1), 62–80.

India Today (2019). *8 Indian transgender people who were the firsts in their fields*. https://www.indiatoday.in/education-today/gk-current-affairs/story/list-of-transgenders-firsts-who-made-it-big-in-their-fields-1276415-2018-07-03.

Jose Talk (2019). *Breaking the barriers to success | Renju Renjimar | Josh Talks Malayalam*. https://www.youtube.com/watch?v=z46FgUKVsvQ.

Kannadasan, A. (2019). *When transgender people tell their pain through art…* https://www.thehindu.com/entertainment/art/angry-indian-goddesses/article26664585.ece

Lepak, D. P., Smith, K. G. & Taylor, M. S. (2007). Value creation and value capture: A multi-level perspective. *Academy of Management Review*, *32*(1), 180–194.

Marlow, S. & Martinez Dy, A. (2018). Annual review article: Is it time to rethink the gender agenda in entrepreneurship research?. *International Small Business Journal*, *36*(1), 3–22.

Marlow, S., Greene, F. J. & Coad, A. (2018). Advancing gendered analyses of entrepreneurship: A critical exploration of entrepreneurial activity among gay men and lesbian women. *British Journal of Management*, *29*(1), 118–135.

Metro Malayalam (2018). *Let's get talking with Metro Malayalam | Episode 8 | Interview with Renju Renjimar*. https://www.youtube.com/watch?v=KYg-7Rkhrek.

Monro, S. (2010). Towards a sociology of gender diversity: The Indian and UK cases. In S. Hines & T. Sanger (Eds.), *Transgender identities* (pp. 242–258). Academic Press.

Nair, V. (2018). *The idea of independence*. https://www.deccanchronicle.com/lifestyle/viral-and-trending/150818/the-idea-of-independence.html.

News Glitz (2019). *Kalki Subramaniam on being an artist for helping other transgenders | An interview with Transgender*. https://www.youtube.com/watch?v=Gym9qwraESM

Nicholls, A. & Cho, A. H. (2008). Social entrepreneurship: the structuration of a field. In A. Nicholls (Ed.), *Social entrepreneurship: new models of sustainable change* (pp. 99–118). Oxford University Press.

Ozturk, M. B. (2011). Sexual orientation discrimination: Exploring the experiences of lesbian, gay, and bisexual employees in Turkey. *Human Relations*, *64*, 1099–1118.

Porter, M. & Kramer, M. R. (2011). *Creating shared value: How to reinvent capitalism – and unleash a wave of innovation and growth*. http://ressources.aunege.fr/nuxeo/site/esupversions/c9c186ba-f7d5-4ebe-bd74-d375387f45e8/res/res.pdf.

Risman, B. J. (2004). Gender as a social structure: Theory wrestling with activism. *Gender & Society*, *18*(4), 429–450.

Schilt, K. & Connell, C. (2007). Do workplace gender transitions make gender trouble? *Gender, Work & Organization*, *14*(6), 596–618.

Schumpeter, J. (1934). *The theory of economic development: An inquiry into profits, capital, interest, and the business cycle.* Harvard University Press.

Sheikh, S., Yousafzai, S., Sist, F., Ar, A. A. & Saeed, S. (2018). Value creation through women's entrepreneurship. In S. Yousafzai, A. Fayolle, A. Lindgreen, C. Henry, S. Saeed & S. Sheikh (Eds.), *Women entrepreneurs and the myth of 'underperformance': a new look at women's entrepreneurship research* (pp. 20–33). Edward Elgar Publishing.

Stevenson, L. (1990). Some methodological problems associated with researching women entrepreneurs. *Journal of Business Ethics, 9*(4–5), 439–446.

Sullivan Mort, G., Weerawardena, J. & Carnegie, K. (2003). Social entrepreneurship: Towards conceptualisation. *International Journal of Nonprofit and Voluntary Sector Marketing, 8*(1), 76–88.

Tan, W., Williams, J. & Tan, T. (2005). Defining the 'social' in 'social entrepreneurship': Altruism and entrepreneurship. *International Entrepreneurship and Management Journal, 1*(3), 353–365.

Ted Talk (2018). *Breaking binaries, establishing identity | Kalki Subramaniam | TEDxDumas.* https://www.youtube.com/watch?v=_j1NzEGMNdo.

The Hindu (2018). *Being Revathi.* https://www.thehindu.com/entertainment/theatre/in-a-mono-act-a-revathi-gives-a-moving-account-on-what-it-means-to-be-a-transgender/article23559497.ece.

The Hindu (2019). *When transgender people tell their pain through art...* https://www.thehindu.com/entertainment/art/angry-indian-goddesses/article26664585.ece.

The India Observer (2017). *Why Kalki Subramaniam got a standing ovation at Harvard India Conference.* https://theindiaobserver.com/kalki-subramaniam-standing-ovation-harvard/.

The New Indian Express (2017), *The Aphrodite touch – Renju Renjimar most sought after make-up artist.* https://www.newindianexpress.com/cities/kochi/2017/jan/11/the-aphrodite-touch---renju-renjimar-most-sought-after-make-up-artist-1558299.html.

The New Indian Express (2018). *Transgender persons to sizzle the ramp at 'Queen of Dhwayah' beauty pageant.* The New Indian Express. http://www.newindianexpress.com/cities/kochi/2018/jun/17/transgender-persons-to-sizzle-the-ramp-at-queen-of-dhwayah-beauty-pageant-1829230.html.

The New Indian Express (2018b). *TGs get a beauty spot.* The New Indian Express. http://www.newindianexpress.com/cities/kochi/2018/nov/19/tgs-get-a-beauty-spot-1900429.html.

Times of India (2018). *Travails of the trans community.* https://timesofindia.indiatimes.com/city/kochi/travails-of-the-trans community/articleshow/65881559.cms.

Verstraete, T. & Jouison-Laffitte, E. (2011). A conventionalist theory of the business model in the context of business creation for understanding organizational impetus. *Management International/International Management/Gestiòn Internacional, 15*(2), 109–124.

West, C. & Zimmerman, D.H. (1987). Doing gender. *Gender & Society, 1*(2), 125–151.

World Bank (2019). *Population.* https://data.worldbank.org/indicator/SP.POP.TOTL.

Yourstory.com (2015). *I am happy and liberal than most 'born women' I have seen – Kalki Subramaniam.* https://yourstory.com/2015/05/kalki-subramaniam/.

Youth India (2019). *Documentary on Kalki Subramaniam: A transgender, super woman.* https://www.youtube.com/watch?v=CDxwbCYQ3rc.

Zahra, S. A., Gedajlovic, E., Neubaum, D. O. & Shulman, J. M. (2009). A typology of social entrepreneurs: Motives, search processes and ethical challenges. *Journal of Business Venturing, 24*(5), 519–532.

Zott, C., Amit, R. & Massa, L. (2011). The business model: Recent developments and future research. *Journal of Management, 37*(4), 1019–1042.

19. Generation Y females in Ireland: an insight into this new entrepreneurial potential for value creation

Angela Hamouda, Kate Johnston and Rebecca Nevins

INTRODUCTION

From the 1980s onwards economists and policy makers alike promoted the vital role of entrepreneurship as a driver of economic growth and employment. According to Wennekers and Thurik (1999), a shift towards supply side economics at this time, an era characterized by stagflation and high unemployment, led economists to re-evaluate the role of small firms, entrepreneurship and economic output. In support of this economic value perspective, numerous studies documented a direct positive link between entrepreneurship, innovation, job creation and economic output (Holmes and Schmitz, 1990; Hisrich and Peters, 1998; Shane, 2003; Acs, 2006; Van Praag and Versloot, 2007).

To fully explain and understand the link between entrepreneurial activity and economic growth and job creation, scholars sought to examine more closely the motivations driving entrepreneurs to succeed. The standard economic model of entrepreneurship assumes entrepreneurs were motivated by self-interest and profit motive. While this was the dominant theory (Knight, 1921; Schumpter, 1934; Hitt et al., 2012), researchers such as Johnson (1990), Collins et al. (2004) and Baum et al. (2012), began to suggest that the standard value creation model of entrepreneurship was inconclusive.

The emergence of female entrepreneurship as a separate research area in the 1980s (Hisrich and O'Brien, 1981, 1982; Scott, 1986), further challenged the traditional value creation model typically accepted by scholars. As noted by Meyer (2018), much of the early literature on entrepreneurship was male focused. The emergence of research into female entrepreneurship, as a separate but related discipline, suggested that unlike many of their male counterparts, female entrepreneurs did not view entrepreneurship solely as an economic endeavor. Rather the motivation behind entrepreneurship was intertwined with personal, social and in some cases, wider community goals (Buttner and Moore, 1997; Robinson, 2001; Marlow and Carter, 2004; Carter et al., 2007). Acknowledging this research, Bird and Brush (2002), for example, concurred that the evidence indicates clear differences in the way that female businesses are started and managed, compared to their male counterparts. Jennings and Brush (2013) documented that female entrepreneurs bring with them their own value system and as such do not conform to the traditional value creation model championed by the traditional theorists. Moreover, important differences in the motivations of male and female entrepreneurs observed that women are more motivated to pursue entrepreneurial goals that have wider social impact (Marlow and McAdam, 2013).

The rise of the Millennial generation has further reignited the debate on the traditional value creation model of entrepreneurship. From the extant research, the evidence suggests that this generation is unlike previous generations in terms of their value system and motivations. Research suggests that millennial entrepreneurs, often referred to as 'millennipreneurs' (BNP Wealth Management, 2017) have a different value system (Myers, 2010) and as such represent a potential new force in the entrepreneurial landscape. Research indicates that millennials have a strong growth mindset (Lloyd et al., 2013), are more likely to be risk takers (Koloba, 2017), seek autonomy and greater work–life balance (Myers, 2010; Twenge et al., 2010; Weyland, 2011) and thrive on challenges and creativity and expect responsibility earlier in their careers (Severt et al., 2009) than previous generations. In many respects, parallels can be drawn with the environmental movement and social movement of the 1960s and early 1970s.

How these characteristics and motivations impact on their entrepreneurial endeavors, is now emerging as an area of research (Vadera, 2020). For a small country such as Ireland, where entrepreneurship has been at the forefront of economic and social development and where millennials will be the largest generational cohort on the planet by 2025 (Deloitte, 2017), understanding their motivations and aspirations for entrepreneurship and how support agencies should respond, is now a growing area of concern.

To address this research gap, the aim of this study is to explore how this new Generation – Gen Y female entrepreneurs are redefining entrepreneurship in Ireland, in particular to explore their motivations and characteristics and the barriers and challenges they experience. It is envisaged that this new wave of entrepreneurs are challenging our typical view of entrepreneurs and in turn are calling into question the supports needed to encourage growth among this cohort. A number of specific objectives are of particular importance:

1. To investigate the characteristics and motivations of millennial female entrepreneurs.
2. To identify how these motivations influence their entrepreneurial value system and aspirations.
3. To explore how relevant enterprise support organizations perceive this cohort and the extent to which current policy supports these millennial entrepreneurs.

VALUE CREATION AND ENTREPRENEURSHIP

Academics and policy makers have long recognized the value creation potential from entrepreneurship. As early as Schumpter (1934) and Knight (1921) and more recently Hitt et al. (2012), entrepreneurship has become central to value creation and is viewed as a core driver of economic wealth. Particularly noteworthy is the pioneering work of Drucker (1984) who viewed entrepreneurship as an economic force of change. As noted by Fayolle (2007), the role of entrepreneurship in economic success, innovation and new product development, for the most part, remained the central theme of any discussion on entrepreneurship and value creation.

Throughout the last three decades, the value creation model of entrepreneurship beyond the standard economic development model has gained considerable momentum. Initial work of authors such as Alvarez and Barney (2007) and Trivedi and Stokols (2011) were among the first to address the wider personal and social value outputs of entrepreneurship. According to this viewpoint, while value creation is at the heart of entrepreneurship, value creation should not be limited to economic and financial wealth. For example, Stokes and Wilson (2010) conclude that the value creation output of entrepreneurship can take the form of personal growth, personal wealth, family, security and social impact. Furthermore, work by Johnson (1990); Collins et al. (2004) and Baum et al. (2012), conducted that the standard value creation model of entrepreneurship was inconclusive. Similarly, Berrone, Cruz, Gomez-Melia and Larraza-Kintana (2010) defined value in terms of the socio-emotional and personal motivational model.

Viewing entrepreneurship and value creation through this wider social lens began to challenge our understanding and discussion of what motivates entrepreneurship beyond purely economic gain. This was further strengthened by the emergence of research into female entrepreneurship, which played a key role, challenging the standard economic value creation model of entrepreneurship. This research recognizes that female business owners, irrespective of the size, type or scope of their business, are motivated and have a different value system than their male counterparts (Carter and Allen, 1997; Bird and Brush, 2002; Brush, 2006; Hechavarria et al., 2016). A point in case is the work of Jennings and Brush (2013), who argue that female entrepreneurs do not view their businesses as separate economic entities but rather as endeavors entwined with other aspects of their lives, particularly their family relationships and responsibilities.

Female entrepreneurs are motivated by different strategies including; collaborations, work–life balance and diversity strategies, which are often in contrast to the typical male strategies (Kropf et al., 2003). Similarly, research shows that women might be more motivated to pursue entrepreneurial goals that have social impact (Marlow and McAdam, 2013). Moreover, a recent study confirms that women often pursue business opportunities to satisfy social needs, rather than focusing on traditional business outcomes such as growth or profit (Solesvik et al., 2019). Similarly, they bring a different perspective, often, seeing themselves as 'change agents' who create value through entrepreneurship (Yousafza et al., 2018). Furthermore, it has been highlighted that females are often unconsciously more socially responsible than males in their enterprises, and the internal climate and satisfaction of employees and customers are at least equally important for them as achieving profitability goals (Owen et al., 2013).

Taken together, this research suggests that female entrepreneurs have a uniquely different motivational model underlying their entrepreneurial endeavors. As such the traditional economic value model has been redefined and extended over recent years, viewing entrepreneurship as a driving force in social good, improving quality of life, solving deep rooted societal problems and in building human capacity (Kistruck et al., 2011). It is also worth noting that in this context, entrepreneurship has opened many opportunities for educators, policy makers and governmental bodies (Tariq et al., 2016).

THE RISE OF GEN Y – MILLENNIAL GENERATION

Much has been written on the emergence of Gen Y. Defined as those born between 1980 and 2000 also known as millennials, E-generation or Echo Boomers, mil-lennipreneurs, this distinct group is now a growing topic of debate (BNP Wealth Management, 2017; Liu et al., 2019). According to the recent Deloitte Survey (2017) within the next five years, by 2025, millennials will account for 75% of the workforce worldwide and in some sectors, they now account for two-thirds of the workforce.

The rise of millennials as a distinct group, has led to a growing number of studies examining the motivations and aspirations of this cohort. A review of the existing literature reveals some interesting evidence on the unique mindset and motivations that is distinctly different to previous generations. Table 19.1 summarizes some of the existing research to date.

In reviewing these studies, the research suggests that millennials convey many of the characteristics and motivations typically associated with entrepreneurs. According to Loubier (2017), Gen Y female entrepreneurs are natural 'problem solvers', have more 'grit' and a strong willingness to manage stress and balance stress. As noted by Fenn (2009), author *of Upstarts!: How Gen Y Entrepreneurs are Rocking the World of Business and 8 Ways You Can Profit from Their Success*, they tend to be highly collaborative and utilize their networks, relationships and reputation to propel their business forward.

However, as noted by Parkinson (2017) for example, they are often viewed as a disruptive force; representing a new breed of entrepreneurs who have an entirely different motivation and value system than the generations before them. Research suggests millennials are more motivated to benefit the environment and the greater good than previous generations (D'Andria and Gabarret, 2017). Rather than focusing on profit, they are driven to create a better world and have a more positive social impact on others than their parents' generation and are willing to pay a premium for sustainable offerings (Nielsen, 2015). This is further supported by research from BNP Paribas Global Entrepreneur Report (BNP Wealth Management, 2017) which found that Gen Y have a pronounced personal drive to make a difference and be different. What this research collectively indicates, is that their motivation towards

Table 19.1   The entrepreneurial mindset of Gen Y

Characteristics of Gen Y	Implications for Entrepreneurship and Value Creation
Freedom – to express themselves and freedom to choose their own path.	Having ***autonomy*** to make their choice of when and where to work is critical (Weyland, 2011) and they have a costs-benefits approach to work. They value autonomy, leisure and work–life balance (Twenge et al., 2010) and see work as less central to their lives when compared with Baby Boomers and Generation X (Macky et al., 2008). Greater concern with free and personal time (D'Andria and Gabarret, 2017).
Customization – they feel the need to customize everything, including their jobs.	They are more creative and innovative when at work; therefore being in an innovative and creative environment is important to them (Bansal, 2017). Furthermore, the need to feel valued and be ***influential in their workplace*** is also high on their agenda and for this they need a boss who respects their views, is willing to listen to them, and is flexible in accepting their opinions (Beck and Wade, 2004).
Scrutiny – as they learn early on to be skeptical and critical about what they see and read in the media.	A fundamental difference noted in the literature is that Generation Y has **little trust in the government** and the status quo and feels that the government is unable to protect them (Weinbaum et al., 2016).
Integrity – they are honest and transparent.	As noted by D'Andria and Gabarret (2017), they have a ***strong environment and societal focus***. Having an impact on society is a core part of what defines this group. They prefer to work for a company with good Corporate Social Responsibility (Aguirre et al., 2001) and place significant importance on having meaning to their work (Hurst and Good, 2009).
Collaboration – they collaborate well with their friends and with their co-workers. They are inclined to use collaboration tools like I.M., Facebook both at work and in their personal life.	As noted by Naim and Lenka (2017) focusing on value creation of social media and collaboration as a fundamental part of their motivation.
Speed and Immediacy – as they require immediacy in response to projects.	Making an important impact ***immediately*** on projects they are involved with and are looking for immediate gratification and an opportunity to excel (Spiro, 2006), and the demand for instant everything (Behrens, 2009; Cahill and Sedrak, 2012).
Innovation and Risk Takers	Koloba (2017) noted that students of this Gen Y consider themselves as innovative, risk takers and independent.

value creation is focused towards a greater need for freedom and work–life balance and with a clear emphasis on sustainability, social and environmental impact.

While numerous studies cite them as technologically savvy (Pountain and Robins, 2000), the use of technology has also provided a negative value in the millennial generation because they now expect to have instant everything (Behrens, 2009; Cahill and Sedrak, 2012). With internet speed providing instant access to any answer, this generation now expects to have instant answers and instant feedback. Moreover, research also suggests that they can be perceived as difficult and challenging to deal with. For example, some common complaints from Baby Boomers are that they can be difficult to interact with and exude a sense of entitlement (Deal et al., 2010), are more demanding than their more elder and experienced counterparts (Levenson,

2010). Furthermore, they have become known as the '*Look at Me*' generation, being considered too confident and concerned with their own interests, they have also been perceived to be impatient, lacking in work ethic, self-important, disloyal and often to gain important positions in large projects soon after being hired (Myers and Sadaghiani, 2010).

MILLENNIALS IN IRELAND

In the context of Ireland, a country that typically has amongst the highest birth rates,[1] Gen Y represents a large cohort within the Irish economic system. Moreover, entrepreneurship remains one of the most important components of Ireland's business ecosystem (Fitzsimons and O'Gorman, 2017). Over the first 30 years, successive government investment in education and skills development has produced 'a quality workforce – a nation of people armed with relevant knowledge, entrepreneurial agility and analytical skills' (Department of Education and Skills, 2016).[2] Currently, Ireland has one of the most educated workforces in the world (Eurostat, 2019). Recent research from the Deloitte Millennial Survey (2017): findings from Ireland, suggest that Gen Y will be the largest generational cohort, accounting for 75% of the workforce in the next five years. Hence, in order to maintain Ireland's economic growth, understanding and adapting and responding to this new generation will be vital.

Given the potential economic and social impact of this cohort, an interesting question arises as to what are the motivational and value systems of this generation and how is this impacting on our traditional view of entrepreneurship? For example, given that the millennium motivations and values extend beyond the traditional profit motive, to include a greater focus on social and environmental responsibility, how is this new generation challenging or disrupting our understanding of entrepreneurship? Moreover, how should support agencies react to support this generation? These questions are fundamental to our understanding of what it will mean to be an entrepreneur in the 21st century and how best we adapt and support this new cohort of entrepreneurs.

METHODOLOGY

The overall objective of the study was to explore a new generation of female entrepreneurs – Gen Y. An exploratory research approach was used to identify and investigate new insights suggested by the results of the study. An exploratory study is a valuable means of 'what is happening; to seek new insights; to ask questions and to assess phenomenon in a new light' (Robson, 2002, p.59). For the study, the focus is on female entrepreneurs of Gen Y in Ireland and the research aims to contribute to the limited literature in the space. The objective of the research is to first establish the motivations, characteristics, barriers and challenges facing this cohort and also to explore their experience of accessing enterprise supports. Additionally, the perceptions of enterprise support representatives of this cohort will be explored and whether or not the current enterprise support policies are meeting the needs of this target group.

Surveys were used to collect data from a sample of Gen Y female entrepreneurs in Ireland. A survey provides an efficient tool for collecting background, quantifiable data from a specific sample, as well as gathering qualitative information from respondents in the form of experiences and views (Saunders et al., 2016). The surveys were anonymous and were distributed through representatives in regional enterprise support agencies who acted as gatekeepers. Additionally, the survey was also posted on social media which was live for three weeks. The final number of responses was 92. The final survey consisted of 19 questions and was designed to establish a business profile, their characteristics and motivations, their experience of enterprise supports and the challenges they face.

Structured interviews were held with representatives of enterprise support agencies to gain an insight into their perceptions of this new generation of female entrepreneurs and whether or not current enterprise supports are suitable for the target group. Bryman (2016) illustrates that the structured interview means that each respondent receives the same interview stimulus as any other. Interviews were carried out face-to-face and via telephone, depending on the availability and location of the interviewee. The advantages of interviews as illustrated by Cameron and Price (2009) are that they are flexible; there is a degree of interactivity, they present a richness of information, networking opportunities and illustrative quotes to record. Three interviews were carried out with enterprise support representatives, one with a large enterprise support organization and two were with smaller run support entities. The interviews were recorded and lasted between 30–60 minutes.

SURVEY FINDINGS

As outlined in Table 19.2, of the 92 responses, the majority, 57% (53) are aged between 31 and 36 years and highly educated to degree (64%) and Master's level (22%). The businesses are young with 59% (48) less than two years old, and 90% operating for profit businesses. The sample was drawn from a broad range of sectors, the largest sector being services (beautician, hairdresser, personal trainer) 26% (23), followed by professional services 25% (23), administration 19% (17) and information and communications 13% (12).

The Characteristics of Gen Y Female Entrepreneurs in Ireland

These Gen Y female entrepreneurs convey core entrepreneurial traits of being open-minded, creative and have a strong need for independence. This concurs with research which suggests that this generation shows clear traits associated with entrepreneurship (Bansal, 2017; Koloba, 2017). Interestingly, the desire to make an impact

Table 19.2   *Sample composition (n=89)*

AGE		Education		Age of Business	
18–24 yrs	9	Below Degree Level	10	0–2 yrs	48
25–30 yrs	30	Degree	59	2–3 yrs	16
31–36 yrs	53	Post-Degree	23	3+ yrs	22
INDUSTRY					
Services beautician, hairdresser, personal trainer	23	Information and Communications/ Technology	12		
Professional services	23	Health and Social work	10		
Administration	17	Other	4		

Table 19.3   *Perceived Characteristics of Gen Y Female Entrepreneurs (n=75)*

Characteristic	1	2	3	4	5
Open mindedness	0%	1%(1)	8%(4)	24%( )	63%(47)
Charismatic	0%(0)	9%(7)	32%(25)	36%(27)	21%(16)
Shy	23%(17)	21%(16)	29%(22)	24%(18)	3%(2)
Creative	0%(0)	7%(5)	21%(16)	32%(24)	40%(30)
Empathetic	3%(2)	11%(8)	12%(9)	25%(19)	49%(37)
Risk Taking	1%(1)	12%(9)	35%(26)	39%(29)	13%(10)
Independent	0%(0)	1%(1)	7%(5)	39%(29)	53%(40)
Impulsive	7%(31)	31%(23)	23%(17)	24%(18)	16%(12)
Technologically Savvy	1%(1)	3%(2)	20%(15)	17%(13)	12%(9)

Note: Using the Likert scale, respondents were given a list of statements about how they would describe themselves and were asked to indicate the degree to which each statement does or does not describe them according to the scale as follows: (1) Does not describe me at all (2) Does not describe me enough (3) Neutral (4) Describes me moderately (5) Describes me very well.

on the world (46%) and wanting to have a social impact (36%) are also key motivators for the group which has already been highlighted that millennials have a strong environmental and societal focus (D'Andria and Gabarret, 2017). Furthermore, this concurs with research into female entrepreneurship, which suggests that unlike many of their male counterparts, female entrepreneurs did not view entrepreneurship solely as an economic endeavor, but their motivation was intertwined with personal, social and in some cases wider community goals (Buttner and Moore, 1997; Robinson, 2001; Marlow and Carter, 2004; Carter et al., 2007). The majority of respondents also recognize what studies have consistently shown (Pountain and Robins, 2000) that these entrepreneurs are tech savvy (44%) and strongly agree that they are more tech savvy (49%).

Table 19.4   Top 8 Motivations of Gen Y Female Entrepreneurs (n=75)

Motivational Factor	1	2	3	4	5	Rank
Freedom/Flexibility	1%(1)	3%(2)	8%(6)	9%(7)	79%(59)	1
To Be my own Boss	1%(1)	1%(1)	12%(9)	15%(11)	71%(53)	2
Opportunity to Make Money	3%(2)	5%(2)	11%(8)	33%(25)	48%(36)	3
To Challenge Myself	7%(5)	8%(6)	15%(11)	21%(16)	49%(37)	4
Identified an Opportunity	3%(2)	5%(4)	23%(17)	20%(15)	49%(37)	5
To Make an Impact	13%(10)	11%(8)	12%(9)	20%(15)	44%(33)	6
To Support my Family	11%(8)	13%(10)	15%(11)	21%(16)	40%(30)	7
Having a Social Impact	15%(11)	13%(10)	17%(13)	19%(14)	36%(27)	8

Note: Using the Likert scale, respondents were given a list of statements about how they would describe themselves and were asked to indicate the degree to which each statement does or does not describe them according to the scale as follows: (1) Does not describe me at all (2) Does not describe me enough (3) Neutral (4) Describes me moderately (5) Describes me very well.

The Changing Value Creation Motivations of Gen Y

Current research suggests that Gen Y have moved towards a more comprehensive value creation model of entrepreneurship (Tapscott, 2000; Aguirre et al., 2001; D'Andria and Gabarret, 2017). To investigate this further, the group was asked to rank in order of importance financial and non-financial motivations in their decision to become an entrepreneur.

From Table 19.3, it is clear that this group is more interested in autonomy, and the flexibility and freedom that entrepreneurship offers, as opposed to the traditional perspective driven by money. Freedom and the opportunity to be their own boss were ranked as the top two motivators. Money is still important but ranked 3rd by the entrepreneurs.

Interestingly, value creation in terms of making an impact, supporting their family and having a social impact were all ranked within the top eight motivators. Nearly two thirds of the entrepreneurs ranked 'making an impact' and 'support for my family' as important motivators. This lends further support to the notion that Gen Y female entrepreneurs place considerable importance on the personal and social value impact in their consideration of entrepreneurship as a viable career option.

Challenges

The research has long recognized the challenges facing female entrepreneurs (Brush, 1997; Carter, 2000; Carter et al., 2001; Marlow, 2002; Brush et al., 2004; Brush, 2006). This study indicates (as outlined in Table 19.3) that Gen Y female entrepreneurs face challenges in the area of accessing finance and supports. Respondents highlighted the most significant challenges were generating an income for themselves (55%) and financing their business (58%). Despite their drivers and motivations, access to finance and funding is still a major challenge facing Gen Y female entrepreneurs.

*Table 19.5   Top 5 Challenges Experienced by Gen Y Female Entrepreneurs
(n=75)*

Challenges	1	2	3	4	5	Rank
Financing my Business	12%(8)	12%(8)	18%(12)	25%(17)	33%(22)	1
Generating an Income for Myself	12%(8)	3%(2)	30%(20)	21%(14)	34%(23)	2
Pressure to Succeed/Fear of Failure	16%(11)	13%(9)	28%(19)	22%(15)	19%(13)	3
My Credibility as a Business Owner	15%(10)	19%(13)	36%(24)	18%(12)	12%(8)	4
Start-up Education and Training	33%(22)	19%(10)	19%(13)	15%(10)	13%(9)	5

Note: The Likert scale where respondents had to rate challenges on a scale of one to five with one
not being a challenge at all and five being a significant challenge.

Fear of failure and pressure to succeed were identified by 41% of the respondents
as a major challenge. This was ranked 3 in terms of overall challenges. This could
be a cultural-specific issue as recent research suggests that fear of failure is deterring
entrepreneurs in Ireland (*Irish Times*, 2014). Other related challenges ranked in the
top six were not being seen as credible, and access to start-up training and education.
While Ireland is amongst the best in Europe in terms of offering a suite of start your
own business programs for entrepreneurs, this finding indicates that the current training and education programs offered may not be meeting the needs of this new cohort.
This raises the question of a possible disconnect between demand (entrepreneurs'
needs) and supply (current training provision).

Gen Y does not feel pressured to conform to normality, nor was gender considered a challenge (73%). Furthermore, they did not experience pressure from family
and friends (67%), nor did they feel any pressure to conform; nor was age a barrier
(74%). Interestingly, work–life balance does not feature as a significant challenge for
this group. This explanatory research suggests that Gen Y female entrepreneurs are
different from their previous generations in terms of confidence and mindset.

Accessing Enterprise Supports

There is no doubt that entrepreneurship support for female entrepreneurs has been
a strong feature of the Irish enterprise development landscape in the last number of
years. In every major town and city in Ireland, SYOB programs, and those specifically designed for female entrepreneurs have been a consistent feature. What is surprising from the current research is that two-thirds (76%) of the Generation Y Female
entrepreneurs did not access any supports in the start-up or development of their
business. Given the proliferation of female enterprise in Ireland, this is surprising.
The question is *why is this generation of entrepreneurs not being reached*?

INTERVIEW FINDINGS

In-depth interviews were held with three representatives from different enterprise support organizations.[3] The interviewees were made to carry out the interviews over the telephone. Agencies were identified through a search of the relevant organizations' websites and contacted via e-mail and follow-up telephone call where arrangements were made. The in-depth nature of the interviews meant that interviews were conducted over the space of five days, with in some cases, follow-up telephone calls. The interviews were analysed using thematic analysis where the researcher identified themes and patterns of meanings across a dataset. This approach is widely used in qualitative research, especially to analyze interviews (Judger, 2016). Thematic analysis is a method used for identifying, analyzing, and reporting patterns (themes) within the data (Clarke and Braun, 2013). The findings are presented under the themes of their perception of Gen Y female entrepreneurs.

A New Generation of Female Entrepreneurs

The representatives from enterprise support agencies in Ireland have witnessed a surge in Generation Y entrepreneurs in the last few years in the relevant geographic areas. Some interesting themes emerged from these initial interviews.

Theme 1: Skillset and Characteristics: A central theme discussed by all support agencies was the viewpoint that Gen Y is highly educated and technologically savvy. This concurs with research from Pountain and Robins (2000). Unfortunately, it is suggested that the use of technology has a negative impact. According to the representatives:

> '… they are often bombarded with the next thing…' 'background noise as in, social media platforms and information coming at them from every angle…' 'It is hard for them to focus on something and see it through, there are so many different distractions.'

The representatives also suggest that as a result they can often lack focus and are more concerned with speed and an instant response rather than having to work to achieve results. Prior research highlights that because they now expect to have instant everything (Behrens, 2009; Cahill and Sedrak, 2012) with internet speed providing instant access to any answer, this generation now expects to have instant answers and instant feedback.

Theme 2: Motivations and Attitudes: An interesting theme to arise from the interviews is the emerging differences in motivations and attitudes of Gen Y towards entrepreneurship. All the support representatives concurred with the view that their motivations of entrepreneurship are more individualistic in nature. As one representative noted that, 'When Generation Y is looking for a career and jobs, they are not asking what I can do for the job or business, they are asking what the job can do for me.' This view would certainly concur with prior research from Twenge et al. (2010), Weyland (2011) and D'Andria and Gabarret (2017) regarding the need for autonomy and research which suggests that they seek immediate gratification and an opportunity to excel (Spiro, 2006). The attitude to risk was an important theme also discussed by the representatives and would suggest they have a different attitude to risk than their predecessors. Statements such as:

...There is a sense of false confidence, they do not feel afraid, which is a great thing too.

What is interesting is that prior research by Wilson, Kickul, and Marlino (2007) into the risk attitudes of male and female entrepreneurs typically found that female entrepreneurs are often less confident or willing to engage in risky business ventures, which affects their entrepreneurial intentions. The initial findings from this research suggests that Gen Y female entrepreneurs may not have the same attitude to risk aversion as previous generations of female entrepreneurs.

Theme 3: Perceptions and Challenges working with this new Cohort: Perhaps one of the strongest themes to emerge from the discussions was the view that Gen Y female entrepreneurs are viewed in a negative way by support representatives. Statements such as '…. they do not assume responsibility and pass responsibility like you would pass a book.' 'They also live in the moment a lot…. and need a little bit more direction; they feel that they know more than they know.' 'You get the best out of them when you micro-manage them…'

These statements would appear to suggest that Gen Y female entrepreneurs are seen more as a challenge rather than an opportunity. Certainly, prior research has alluded to the challenges with working with these entrepreneurs, ranging from difficulties around a sense of entitlement (Deal et al., 2010), viewed as more demanding than previous generations (Levenson, 2010), with a strong focus on their own interests (Myers and Sadaghiani, 2010). This research is in line with this viewpoint.

DISCUSSION AND CONCLUSIONS

The study has sought to explore the characteristics and value creation motivations of a new generation of female entrepreneurs in Ireland – Gen Y. Ireland as a small open economy has long championed entrepreneurship as a means of economic development and more recently a driver of social change, through promotion of female entrepreneurship. Consecutive governments have developed policies and a national strategy on entrepreneurship which have played a key role in Ireland's success. Ireland now has one in thirteen women who will start a business at some stage in their careers.

By 2025, it is estimated that 75% of the workforce will be within the millennial generations (Deloitte, 2017). However, research within this chapter has identified that this generation has a different mindset, motivations and value system than previous generations (Fenn, 2009; Loubier, 2017; Parkinson, 2017). How this generation is shaping our typical view of entrepreneurship is an important issue. Evidence from this initial study, involving both surveys of Gen Y female entrepreneurs and interviews with support agencies working in this space suggest that this group have a value system that is different from the traditional model. The research suggests they are more interested in autonomy and maintaining their independence and making a social impact rather than driven by money and financial gain. Interviews with support agencies also concur with this viewpoint and further support the view that Gen Y female entrepreneurs have a value system and motivation towards personal and social value creation in their consideration of entrepreneurship as a viable career option.

However, the research also suggests that understanding and working with Gen Y female entrepreneurs is challenging. Their attitudes to risk and return are different; they are typically less risk averse, but require more immediacy in terms of feedback and results. There is also some evidence to support the view that they can convey a false sense of confidence and have quite an individualistic approach to business opportunity.

In terms of future research, this study would suggest a number of new avenues for further research. First, the authors recognize that this is a preliminary study into what is clearly an important and growing area of research. An important question is how are the motivations and values and attitudes of Gen Y female entrepreneurs impacting on our understanding of what it means to be an entrepreneur? Given their value system, how is this impacting in terms of the type of businesses they are drawn to, particularly in the social enterprise sector? Does Gen Y represent a new brand of entrepreneur within the entrepreneurial landscape? Second, to what extent can the results reported in this study be generalized to their male counterparts? Are we seeing a move away from the traditional economic masculine model of entrepreneurship towards a more balanced approach which is inclusive of social responsibility? Finally, the challenges raised by this initial research by support agencies in working with this cohort presents some concern where the perception of Gen Y female entrepreneurs has been somewhat negative. They are viewed as having a false sense of confidence and a reluctance to engage in traditional supports and training. At some level, this would indicate a '*disconnect*' between support agencies and this generational group.

Ultimately, the role of support agencies is to create a favorable entrepreneurial ecosystem to promote and support entrepreneurial engagement. Gen Y potentially represents an untapped source of economic growth which is vital for future economic growth and sustainability. Therefore, it is vital to understand how we can better align supports and training to this generation and reflect the business environment in which they typically operate.

NOTES

1.   Ireland typically has a very young population with the highest proportion in the EU under 15 years old.

2.   Ireland now ranks as the 7th most entrepreneurial country in the world. The most recent GEM report illustrates that eleven out of every one hundred people are active entrepreneurs and business owners, underlining the dramatic growth in entrepreneurial activity in Ireland each year following the recession (Fitzsimons and O'Gorman, 2017).
3.   Including Enterprise Ireland, Local Enterprise Office and a Regional Women's Business Network.

REFERENCES

Acs Z.J. (2006). 'How is Entrepreneurship Good for Economic Growth?' *Innovations*, 1(1), pp. 97–107.

Aguirre, J.L., Brena, R. and Cantu-Ortiz, F.J. (2001). 'Multiagent-Based Knowledge Networks', *Expert Systems Applications*, 20(1), pp. 65–75.

Alvarez, S.A. and Barney, J.B. (2007). 'Discovery and Creation: Alternative Theories of Entrepreneurial Action', *Strategic Entrepreneurship Journal*, 1, pp.1–2.

Bansal, N. (2017). 'Motivation & Attitude of Generation Y in India: An Exploratory Study', *The Indian Journal of Industrial Relations*, 53(1), 102–114.

Baum, R.J., Frese, M. and Baron, R. (2012). *The Psychology of Entrepreneurship*. Brighton: Psychology Press.

Beck, J.C. and Wade, M. (2004). 'Got Game: How the Gamer Generation Is Reshaping Business Forever'. http:// www.citeulike.org/group/1820/article/ 1000730 [Accessed 10 10 2021].

Behrens, W. (2009). 'Managing Millennials. Marketing Health Services', *Worldwide Hospitality and Tourism Themes*, 29(1), pp. 19–21.

Berrone, P., Cruz, C., Gomez-Mejia, L.R. and Larraza-Kintana, M. (2010). 'Socio Emotional Wealth and Corporate Responses to Institutional Pressures: Do Family-Controlled Firms Pollute Less?' *Administrative Science Quarterly*, 55(1), pp. 82–113.

Bird, B. and Brush, C. (2002). 'A Gendered Perspective on Organisational Creation', *Entrepreneurship Theory and Practice*, 26(3), pp. 41–65.

BNP Wealth Management (2017). 2017 Paribas Global Entrepreneur Report. 'Understanding the Pursuit of Success Among 21st Century Elite Entrepreneurs', https://group.bnpparibas/uploads/file/2017_bnpp_entrepreneur_report_final_sd.pdf [Accessed 10 11 2021].

Brush, C.G. (1997) 'Women-Owned Businesses: Obstacles and Opportunities', *Journal of Developmental Entrepreneurship*, 2(1), pp. 1–24.

Brush, C. (2006). 'Women Entrepreneurs: A Research Overview.' In M. Casson, B. Yeung, A. Basu and N. Wadeson (Eds.), *The Oxford Handbook of Entrepreneurship* (pp. 611–628). Oxford: Oxford University Press.

Brush, C.G., Carter, N., Gatewood, E., Greene, P. and Hart, M. (2004). 'Women in the Venture Capital Industry: Trends in Participation and Influence.' Presented at the 2nd Diana International Conference, Stockholm, May 28–30, 2004.

Bryman, A. (2016). *Social Research Methods*. 5th edition. Oxford. Oxford University Press.

Buttner, H.E. and Moore, D.P. (1997). 'Women's Organizational Exodus to Entrepreneurship: Self-Reported Motivations and Correlates with Success', *Journal of Small Business Management*, 35(1), pp. 34–46.

Cahill, T.F. and Sedrak, M. (2012). 'Leading a Multigenerational Workforce: Strategies for Attracting and Retaining Millennials', *Frontiers of Health Services Management*, 29(1), pp. 3–15.

Cameron, S. and Price, D. (2009). 'Business Research Methods: A Practical Approach', UK Higher Education Business Management, London: CIPD, p. 121.

Carter, N. and Allen, K. (1997). 'Size-Determinants of Women-Owned Businesses: Choices or Barriers to Resources', *Entrepreneurship and Regional Development*, 9(3), pp. 211–220.

Carter, S. (2000). 'Improving the Numbers and Performance of Women-owned Businesses: Some Implications for Training and Advisory Services', *Education and Training*, 42(4/5), pp. 326–333.

Carter, S., Anderson, S. and Shaw, E. (2001). 'Women's Business Ownership: A Review of the Academic, Popular and Internet Literature' Sheffield: Small Business Service.

Carter, S., Shaw, E., Lam, W. and Wilson, F. (2007). 'Gender, Entrepreneurship, and Bank Lending: The Criteria and Processes Used by Bank Loan Officers in Assessing Applications', *Entrepreneurship Theory and Practice*, 31(3).

Clarke, V. and Braun, V. (2013). 'Teaching Thematic Analysis: Overcoming Challenges and Developing Strategies for Effective Learning', *The Psychologist*, 26(2), pp. 120–123.

Collins, C.J., Hanges, P. and Locke, E.A. (2004). 'The Relationship of Achievement Motivation to Entrepreneurial Behavior: A Meta-Analysis', *Human Performance*, 17(1), pp. 95–117.

D'Andria, A. and Gabarret, I. (2017). *Building 21st Century Entrepreneurship*. London: John Wiley & Sons.

Deal, J., Altman, D. and Rogelberg, S. (2010). 'Millennials at Work: What We Know and What We Need to Do (if Anything)', *Journal of Business & Psychology*, 25(2), pp. 191–199.

Deloitte (2017). '2017 Millennials Survey: Apprehensive Millennials: Seeking Stability and Opportunities in an Uncertain World'. https://www2.deloitte.com/ie/en/pages/about-deloitte/articles/2017_millennials_survey.html [Accessed 24 11 2017].

Department of Education and Skills (2016). 'Irish National Skills Strategy, 2025', Dublin: Irish Government.

Drucker, P. (1984). 'Our Entrepreneurial Economy', *The Harvard Business Review*, 1984 issue.

Fayolle, A. (2007). *Entrepreneurship and Value New Creation: The Dynamic of New Entrepreneurial Process*. Cambridge: Cambridge University Press.

Fenn, D. (2009). *Upstarts!: How Gen Y Entrepreneurs are Rocking the World of Business and 8 Ways You can Profit from their Success*. New York: McGraw-Hill.

Fitzsimons, P. and O'Gorman, C. (2017). Global Entrepreneurship Monitor Report (2017). A Survey of Entrepreneurship in Ireland.

Hechavarria, D.M., Terjesen, S.A., Ingram, A.E., Renko, M., Justo, R. and Elam, A. (2016). 'Taking Care of Business: The Impact of Culture and Gender on Entrepreneurs' Blended Value Creation Goals', *Small Business Economics*, 48(1), pp. 225–257.

Hisrich, R.D. and O'Brien, M. (1981). 'The Woman Entrepreneur from a Business and Sociological Perspective.' In K.H. Vesper (Ed.), *Frontiers of Entrepreneurial Research* (pp. 21–39). Boston, MA: Babson College.

Hisrich, R.D. and O'Brien, M. (1982). 'The Woman Entrepreneur as a Reflection of the Type of B Business.' In K.H. Vesper (Ed.), *Frontiers of Entrepreneurial Research* (pp. 54–67). Boston, MA: Babson College.

Hisrich, R.D. and Peters, M.P. (1998). *Entrepreneurship* (4th ed). New York: McGraw-Hill.

Hitt, M.A., Ireland, R.D., Sirmon, D.G. and Trahms, C.A. (2012). 'Strategic Entrepreneurship: Creating Value for Individuals, Organisations and Society'. *SSRN Electronic Journal*, 25(2).

Holmes, T.J. and Schmitz, J.A. (1990). 'A Theory of Entrepreneurship and its Application to the Study of Business Transfers', *Journal of Political Economy*, 98, pp. 265–294.

Hurst, J.L. and Good, L.K. (2009). 'Generation Y and Career Choice: The Impact of Retail Career Perceptions, Expectations and Entitlement Perceptions', *Career Development International*, 14(6), pp. 570–593. [Accessed 05 03 2018].

Irish Times (2014). 'Fear of Failure is Deterring Entrepreneurs: A Second Chance Programme Could Help Remove Stigma and Empower those Starting Businesses', August 5, 2014.

Jennings, J.E. and Brush, C. (2013). 'Research on Women Entrepreneurs: Challenges to (and from) the Broader Entrepreneurship Literature', *The Academy of Management*, 7(1), pp. 663–715.

Johnson, B.R. (1990). 'Towards a Multi-Dimensional Model of Entrepreneurship – the Case of Achievement Motivation and the Entrepreneur', *Entrepreneurship Theory and Practice*, 14(3), pp. 39–54.

Judger, N. (2016). 'The Thematic Analysis of Interview Data: An Approach Used to Examine the Influence of the Market on Curricular Provision in Mongolian Higher Education Institutions'. University of Leeds. Paper.

Kistruck, G., Webb, J.W., Sutter, C.J. and Ireland, R.D. (2011). 'Micro Franchising in Base-of-the Pyramid Markets: Institutional Challenges and Adaptations to the Franchise Model', *Entrepreneurship Theory and Practice*, 3(11), pp. 503–531.

Koloba, H.A. (2017). 'Is Entrepreneurial Orientation a Predictor of Entrepreneurial Activity? Gender Comparisons among Generation Y Students in South Africa', *Journal of Gender & Behaviour*, 15(1), pp. 8265–8283.

Knight, F.A. (1921). *Risk, Uncertainty and Profit*. New York: Harper & Row, 1965, Google Scholar.

Kropf, M.B., Moore, M., Galinsky, E., Salmond, K., Bond, J.T. and Harrington, B. (2003). 'Leaders in a Global Economy: Study of Executive Women and Men. Executive Summary.' www.catalystwomen.org.

Levenson, A. (2010). 'Millennials and the World of Work: An Economist's Perspective', *Journal of Business & Psychology*, 25(2), pp. 257–264.

Liu, J., Zhu, Y. Serapio, M. and Cavusgil,. S.T. (2019). 'The New Generation of Millennial Entrepreneur: A Review and Call for Research', *International Business Review*, 28(5).

Lloyd, T., Shaffer, M.L., Stetter, C., Widome, M.D., Repke, J., Weitekamp, M.R. and Paul, I.M. (2013). 'Health Knowledge among the Millennial Generation', *Journal of Public Health Research*, 2, pp. 38–46.

Loubier, A. (2017). 'Why Female Millennipreneurs Succeed in Business', Forbes, May 22, 2017. https://www.forbes.com/sites/andrealoubier/2017/05/22/why-female-millenni preneurs-succeed-in-business/#3e13eb4033d3 [Accessed 10 10 2021].

Macky, K., Gardner, D., Forsyth, S., Dries, N., Pepermans, R. and De Kerpel, E. (2008). 'Exploring Four Generations' Beliefs about Career: Is "Satisfied" the New "Successful"?' *Journal of Managerial Psychology*, 23(8), pp. 907–928.

Marlow, S. (2002). 'Women and Self-Employment: a Part of or Apart from Theoretical Construct?' *International Journal of Entrepreneurship and Innovation*, 3(2), pp. 83–93.

Marlow, S. and Carter, S. (2004), 'Accounting for Change: Professional Status, Gender Disadvantage and Self Employment', *Women in Management Review*, 19(1), pp. 5–17.

Marlow, S. and McAdam, M. (2013). 'Gender and Entrepreneurship: Advancing Debate and Challenging Myths; Exploring the Mystery of the Under-performing Female Entrepreneur', *International Journal of Entrepreneurial Behavior and Research*, 19(1), pp. 114–124.

Meyer, N. (2018). 'Research on Female Entrepreneurship: Are we Doing Enough?' *Polish Journal of Management Studies*, 17(2), pp. 158–169.

Myers, D. (2010). *Social Psychology*. New York: McGraw-Hill Higher Education.

Myers, K. and Sadaghiani, K. (2010). 'Millennials in the Workplace: A Communication Perspective on Millennials' Organizational Relationships and Performance', *Journal of Business and Psychology*, 25(2), pp. 225–238.

Naim, M.F. and Lenka, U. (2017). 'The Impact of Social Media and Collaboration on Gen Y Employees' Engagement', *International Journal of Development Issues*, 16(3), pp. 289–299.

Nielsen (2015). 'Green Generation: Millennials say Sustainability is a Shopping Priority'. Nielsen.com. https://www.nielsen.com/eu/en/insights/article/2015/green-generation-mill ennials-say-sustainability-is-a-shopping-priority/ [Accessed 10 10 2021].

Owen, R., Bessant, J. and Heintz, M. (2013). *Responsible Innovation: Managing the Responsible Emergence of Science and Innovation in Society.* Chichester: Wiley.

Parkinson, S. (2017). HSBC 'Essence of Enterprise', p. 3. HSBC Private Banking.

Pountain, D. and Robins, D. (2000). *Cool Rules: Anatomy of an Attitude.* London: Reaktion Books.

Robinson, S. (2001). 'An Examination of Entrepreneurial Motives and their Influence on the Way Rural Women Small Business Owners Manage their Employees', *Journal of Developmental Entrepreneurship*, 6(2), pp. 151–167.

Robson, C. (2002). *Real World Research: A Resource for Social Scientists and Practitioner Researchers.* Oxford: Blackwell.

Saunders, M., Lewis, P. and Thornhill, A. (2016). *Research Methods for Business Students* (7th ed.). Edinburgh: Pearson.

Schumpter, D.A. (1934). *The Theory of Economic Development: An Enquiry into Profits, Capital, Credits, Interest and the Business Cycle.* Piscataway: Transaction Publishers.

Scott, C.E. (1986). 'Why More Women are Becoming Entrepreneurs', *Journal of Small Business Management*, 24(4), pp. 37–44.

Severt, D., Randall, S.U. and Curtis, C.R. (2009). 'Employee Motivation and Organizational Commitment: A Comparison of Tipped and Nontipped Restaurant Employees', *International Journal of Hospitality and Tourism Administration*, 10(3), pp. 253–269.

Shane, S. (2003). *A General Theory of Entrepreneurship: The Individual Opportunity. Nexus.* Cheltenham, UK and Northampton, MA, USA: Edward Elgar Publishing.

Solesvik, M., Iakovleva, T. and Trifilova, A. (2019). 'Motivations of Female Entrepreneurs: A Cross-national Study', *Journal of Small Business and Enterprise Development*, 26(5), pp. 684–705.

Spiro, C. (2006). 'Generation Y in the Workplace', *Defense AT&L*, 16, p. 19.

Stokes, D. and Wilson, N.C. (2010). 'Entrepreneurship and Marketing Education, Time for the Road Less Travelled?' *International Journal of Entrepreneurship and Innovation Management*, 11(1), pp. 95–108.

Tapscott, D. (2009). *Grown Up Digital. How the Net Generation is Changing Your World.* New York: McGraw-Hill.

Tariq, M.Y., Junaid, M. and Shah, S. (2016). 'Entrepreneurship and Value Creation Curriculum at Macro, Meso and Micro Level', *NICE Research Journal.* ISSN: 2119-4282. March 2016.

Trivedi, C. and Stokols, D. (2011). 'Social Enterprises and Corporate Enterprises: Fundamental Differences and Defining Features', *The Journal of Entrepreneurship*, 20(1), pp. 1–32.

Twenge, J.M., Campbell, S.M., Hoffman, B.J. and Lance, C.E. (2010). 'Generational Differences in Work Values: Leisure and Intrinsic Values Decreasing', *Journal of Management*, 36(5), pp. 1117–1142.

Vadera, S. (2020). 'A Study on the Growth of Millennial Entrepreneurs in India'. Paper Presented at the European Conference on Innovation and Entrepreneurship, Aveiro, Portugal.

Van Praag, C.M. and Versloot, P.H. (2007). 'What is the Value of Entrepreneurship? A Review of Recent Research', *Small Business Economics*, 29(4), pp. 351–382.

Weinbaum, C., Girven, R.S. and Oberholtzer, J. (2016). *The Millennial Generation: Implications for the Intelligence and Policy Communities.* Santa Monica, CA: Rand Corporation.

Wennekers, S. and Thurik, R. (1999). 'Linking Entrepreneurship and Economic Growth', *Small Business and Economics*, 13(1), pp. 27–55.

Weyland, A. (2011). 'Engagement and Talent Management of Gen Y', *Industrial and Commercial Training*, 43(7), pp. 439–445.

Wilson, F., Kickul, J. and Marlino, D. (2007). 'Gender, Entrepreneurial Self-Efficacy and Entrepreneurial Career Intentions: Implications for Entrepreneurship Education', *Entrepreneurship Theory and Practice*, 31(3), pp. 387–406.

Yousafza, S., Fayolle, A., Lindgreen, A., Henry, C., Saeed, S. and Sheikh, S. (2018). *Women Entrepreneurs and the Myth of Underperformance: A New Look at Women's Entrepreneurship Research*. Cheltenham, UK and Northampton, MA, USA: Edward Elgar Publishing.

20. Radically overperforming women entrepreneurs in Mexico City: Alimentos Para Todos as a high impact social innovation case
Hans Lundberg

INTRODUCTION

Women entrepreneurship is, to a minor extent, associated with big size, grand scale and massive scope (e.g. OECD, 2004; Morris et al., 2006; McGowan et al., 2012; Welter, 2019). In this chapter, I contribute to this gap in literature on women entrepreneurship via a case study about the high societal impact of women entrepreneurs in the food bank *Alimento Para Todos* (APT) in Mexico City. Overall, this case revolves around a distinct contextual capacity to combine massive scope with authentic relations (henceforth, the 'hybrid capacity' of APT). To explore this hybrid capacity, the empirical purpose of this chapter is to narrate and analyze a case study of APT with a focus on its (mostly) women entrepreneurs in key positions, while the theoretical purpose is to challenge the 'underperformance hypothesis' of women entrepreneurs (Yousafzai et al., 2018a, 2018b). These purposes are guided by the research question: 'how do the entrepreneurs in APT create social value in constrained environments?' To introduce in more detail what is meant by 'distinct contextual capacity', a few words about the context in this case: Greater Mexico City is one of about ten metacities in the world. A 'metacity' is a "massive conurbation of more than 20 million people" (United Nations, 2006:8), not to be confused with 'megacity' (cities with more than 10 million people, of which there are almost 40 in the world). The population in *Mexico City proper* is (2015) just below 9 million people (Instituto Nacional de Estadística y Geografía, 2019), while *Greater Mexico City* is estimated to have a population on about 21.7 million people (MacroTrends, 2019). A metacity is:

> a heterogeneous, dynamic urban region composed of multiple dense centers, intervening suburbs, embedded green spaces, and diffuse boundaries between traditional cities, suburbs, and exurbs. Metacities are characterized as patch dynamic systems, in which neighborhoods, districts, boundaries, and the exchanges among patches change over time. Governance in metacities is polycentric, that is, shared among different jurisdictions and with formal and informal social institutions. The metacity is a conceptual framework for understanding socio-ecological relationships and adaptive processes across different, specific neighborhood situation. It is a way of understanding any city as a patchy "system of systems." (BES Urban Lexicon, 2012, pp. 1–2)

The complexities such a context generates are endless and constantly in flux, so to systematically and over time 'get something of value done' therein poses specific challenges and requires skills and competencies that are difficult to relate to for persons not having lived or worked regularly in a metacity. An extended description of the case context is therefore provided below, in order to facilitate a deepened understanding of quite an extreme context.

VALUE CREATION THROUGH ENTREPRENEURSHIP

When the concept of value began to be conceived as something else other than economic value, an early body of literature focused on distinguishing non-monetary forms of value from economic value (e.g. Korsgaard & Anderson, 2011; Dietz & Porter, 2012; Acs et al., 2013; Welter & Xheneti, 2015; Zahra & Wright, 2016; Jones et al., 2017). Once distinctions were made, combinatory value approaches came about quite logically, commonly referred to as blended value approaches (e.g. Nicholls, 2009; Hechavarría et al., 2016). Once these two approaches (distinguishing-a-from-b-approaches and blending-a-with-b-approaches) were around, the time had come for deepening our understanding of these two main approaches. Applied to the field of women entrepreneurship, one line of research therefore focuses on the *various types* of non-monetary value creation women entrepreneurs bring about (Korsgaard & Anderson, 2011; Welter & Xheneti, 2015; Jones et al., 2017), for instance widened empowerment, agency and space for decision-making and thereby increased individual well-being (Al-Dajani & Marlow, 2013; Gries & Naudé, 2011), improving the sense of personal fulfilment and work–life balance (Jayawarna et al., 2011), achieving socially desirable and responsible outcomes (Fisher et al., 2014), having a positive impact on the wider community (Angel et al., 2018) and nurturing and improving family relations and social relations (Kantor, 2005; Welter & Xheneti, 2015). Another line of research focuses on *different levels* of value creation (both monetary and non-monetary value) that women entrepreneurs bring about, for instance Sheikh et al. (2018) and their focus on value creation on four analytical levels (individual level, business level, family/household level, society/community level).

This study departs from both of these latter lines of research (various types of non-monetary value creation by women entrepreneurs combined with a focus on society/community level) but also adds another approach, a critical one. This study relies upon the critical review of SVC done by Sinkovics et al. (2015). They argue there are major problems with too broad and vague definitions of SVC, such as "something of value for society" (Dietz & Porter, 2012), "the enactment of entrepreneurship" as enough to be seen as SVC (Korsgaard & Anderson, 2011) or framing the economic value entrepreneurs produce as (also) SVC by highlighting the very general notion that productive entrepreneruship also has social components (Acs et al., 2013). Such broad definitions are useless if the aim is to operationalize SVC in a distinct way. Instead, Sinkovics et al. (2015, p. 341) "propose to reconceptualise the idea of social value creation as social constraint alleviation," where 'social constraints' "are defined as the limitations of a system that keep it from attaining its goal," where 'system' refer to systems consisting of people (i.e. a specific social stratum) and where 'social constraint alleviation' is based on the distinction between organizations that bypass or exploit a social constraint and organizations that absorb it. This distinction is fundamental, as, they argue, organizations "that design their business models in such a way that their day-to-day operations absorb a social constraint [...] achieve a significant development impact on the communities in which they are embedded" (Sinkovics et al., 2015, p. 341). Their second main argument is that it is not enough to consider only the internal system of an organization and its stakeholders; equally needed to be able to measure, estimate, analyze and compare SVC is to include a second system on societal level. They therefore link SVC to human rights, more specifically to what Wettstein (2012) coins as socio-economic human rights, and thereby create a two-system view on SVC (see Figure 20.1).

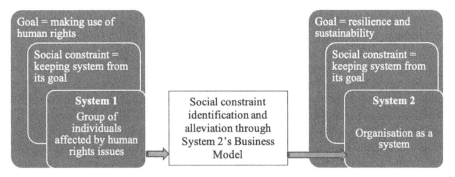

Source: Sinkovics et al. (2015), p. 356.

Figure 20.1   A two-system view of social value creation

In sum, this narrower definition of SVC and the two-system view of SVC offered by Sinkovics et al. (2015) facilitates operationalization of the SVC construct, differentiating between organizations targeting *symptomatic problems* and those targeting *root causes* and make more systematic analyses possible, as their framework is founded in a systematic literature review and constructive critique of existing conceptualizations of SVC and results in a systematic suggestion built on people-oriented system theory.

APT, being a social entrepreneurship (SE) case focusing on SVC is in one sense a mainstream case, as SVC is commonly discussed in relation to SE (Wilson & Post, 2013). In another sense, the APT case provides a more critical perspective to SE and SVC research, in that it departs from a more critically oriented model (Sinkovics et al., 2015), it focuses on data from an under-represented geographical context (Mexico) and it provides a high-impact-and-massive-scope women entrepreneurship case which contrasts with the low- and mid-impact cases more common in the fields of SE, SVC and women entrepreneurship.

METHODOLOGY

This case study was carried out by following Flyvbjerg's approach to case studies (2006), combined with a model for narrative analysis (Kim, 2016) that forefronts the lived experiences of case actors. Originating in Polkinghorne (1995), and refined by Mishler (1995), Kim (2016) developed this model for narrative analysis further via emphasizing the 'told' over the 'telling' where the researcher's central task is "to establish a balance between the two kinds of temporal order. The *telling* means the researcher's narrating, and the *told* means the data that are told by the participant" (Kim, 2016, pp. 199–200). Field studies were done December 2018–May 2019, where 14 persons were interviewed (semi-structured interviews of 80–90 minutes each (except two shorter interviews of 25 minutes) with seven women entrepreneurs, one male entrepreneur, two community leaders, two Centro de Abastos coordinators, one Walmart route operator and one Walmart employee). Additionally, three major processes were shadowed and documented; donor rounds in Centro de Abastos (two rounds), operator routes to major donor companies (one Walmart route) and field observation of 'a normal day in the life of APT' (three full days of observing and documenting the unfolding intensity of events in the two main APT warehouses). Connected to my field study was also the making of a documentary film, which led to two additional visits to APT for film purposes, which in turn further informed the field study. Finally, APT also generously shared much secondary data.

CASE INTRODUCTION

The societal need in Mexico for the work of food banks such as APT is very high. Over 50% of the population in Mexico lives in structural poverty (2013), of which 37.1% are classified as non-indigent poor (persons whose lack of resources forces them to live below a publicly agreed minimum standard) and 14.2% as indigents (a person lacking all/most basic resources for normal life) (United Nations, 2014).

The societal need for the work of food banks globally is very high. At one end of the problem, there is enough food "produced in the world to feed everyone, yet one in nine people globally go hungry," which amounts to 820–870 million people (The Global FoodBanking Network, 2018, p. 5). At the other end of the problem is "one-third of food produced for human consumption worldwide wasted or lost," which "amounts to roughly USD 990 billion worldwide and produces the equivalent of 3.3 billion tons of greenhouse gases" (The Global FoodBanking Network, 2018, p. 6). Individual countries (e.g. France, Denmark, Italy) and multi-lateral political organizations (e.g. initiatives to pass "an EU-wide proposal to end food waste" in all EU-member countries; McCarthy, 2016) are political examples on what also creates

Source: Photo by Lundberg, H., December 6, 2018.

Figure 20.2   Overview of APT main warehouse

big business opportunities: "Tackling food wastage can be a $2.5 trillion market opportunity for businesses" (Gilchrist, 2019).

CASE CONTEXT

The *massive scope* dimension introduced earlier that is the regulating, inhibiting and enervating but also enabling, allowing and energizing structural and discursive dimension affecting all aspects of life in this context, is in this case made up of the following four key actors/contexts: *Alimento Para Todos*, *Iztapalapa*, *Central de Abasto* and *Walmart de México y Centroamérica*:

1. ***Alimento Para Todos* (APT)**, founded in 1994, is "the largest independent food bank of Mexico […] [that] collect unused food and basic goods still suitable for human consumption, in order to give them to people living in poverty" (Alimento Para Todos, 2019).

2. APT is located in ***Iztapalapa***, a crime-ridden and socio-economically marginalized borough, and the most populous (about 2 million people) of the 16 boroughs of Mexico City proper.

3. Merchants operating at ***Central de Abasto*** (**CdeA**), located in ***Iztapalapa***, are ***the first major type of donor to APT***. Central de Abasto is the "most important commercial establishment in Mexico and the largest of its kind in the world. The market handles over 30,000 tons of merchandise daily, representing 80% of the consumption [of Greater Mexico City] [...], generates 70,000 jobs directly and attends to more than 300,000 people per day" (Wikipedia). To be at Central de Abasto from early morning (03:30-ish) to noon, when the febrile main activities take place, is a majestic human experience difficult to do justice to in textual format. That said, it is no walk in the park, especially not for the merchants operating here. It is a crime-ridden area with major problems such as robbery, violent kidnapping episodes (merchants often have private security) and prostitution (including prostitution of minors), and significant problems with underage workers and small-scale drug trafficking. As often, when arriving as an outsider but in company with contextually trusted and known persons (representatives of APT), one is treated with warmth, curiosity and generosity. Hard contexts are not only hard; they tend to generate amounts of love, care and humanity on par with the levels and layers of hardness.

4. ***Walmart de México y Centroamérica*** (**Walmex**) is **the second major type of donor to APT** (representing the category 'big companies' in this case). Walmart Inc., of which Walmex is a division, is "the world's largest company by revenue – over US$500 billion, according to Fortune Global 500 list in 2018 – as well as the largest private employer in the world with 2.2 million employees" (Wikipedia). Walmex is the largest division of Walmart Inc. outside USA: "As of January 31, 2019, Walmart operated 2,442 retail outlets in Mexico [...]. As of 2012, the company was Mexico's largest private sector employer with 209,000 employees. Approximately one-fifth of Walmart stores in the world are in Mexico" (Wikipedia).

The *authentic relations* dimension also discussed in the introduction is a core value for APT, internally as well as in interactions with many and very different stakeholders, and is here illustrated in more detail via five quotes/examples:

Example 1:

We went to a community in Mexico City, very poor. Sometimes we think that because it is in the city, we won't find poverty; however, that community is located in a hill and it is very cold. When I entered the first room, I asked the children why they liked so much to go to school, because they said they loved to. Usually children don't like to go to school, so I was wondering why. And everyone shouted that it was because in school they did eat. My efforts, meetings and discussions with the team, every conflict we have had, all bad days; it translates to one thing, that these children were able to eat. (*Anabel Díaz*, Head of Funding & Institutional Development, APT)

Example 1 illustrates that authentic relations generate clear-cut links between efforts made and meaning perceived, which helps people get their priorities right (right-for-them).

Example 2:

Each year, in October, a campaign takes place, in which the young men of the national military service go door-to-door to gather basic food. One of the objectives of this campaign is to motivate and contribute to create a donation culture in the Mexican population, which is really needed. And a curious fact, is that every year we find that the people that have less or the people that know what it is to suffer food shortage, are the ones that are more supportive. If we would do a study in all the donation centers we will find that the municipalities that give more are those with more shortcomings. (*Mónica Lozano*, Head of Administration, APT)

Example 2 illustrates that authentic relations generate such proximities to contextual realities, that lived experiential insights do away with discursively circulated fake "knowledge," in this case the general perception that it is people that are better off that donate more.

Example 3:

The Global Food Banking Network has been organizing these international events for ten years now. The purpose is to share good practice in combatting food waste and hunger. It has been interesting to see how they solve this in, for instance, countries with limited resources, like in Africa. In Africa they really have low levels of food waste, but on the other hand they have a lot of hunger. It is inspiring to see how food banks there do their job and how they do it well. (*Mariana Jiménez Cárdenas*, Head of Institutional Relations, APT)

Example 3 illustrates that authentic relations tend to strip away layers of secrecy, tactics and opacity common in many other forms of organizational exchange, and thereby direct focus to what matters.

Example 4:

We are a non-profit organization that aim to work as a Fortune 500 company. We have to leave aside everything that does not add value. To build a team that is used to win is difficult. It breaks with Mexican mentality in general as we are in a context not used "to win." I therefore hire on attitude. More specifically, capacity to lead, adapt and having a willingness to fight. (*Bernardo Landeros*, CEO, APT)

Example 4 illustrates that authentic relations and strict business mentality are not mutually exclusive; on the contrary, internal clarity on the latter frees energy and resources to be spent on the former.

Example 5:

Is Central de Abasto part of your life?
Yes, it is much of my life.
A final word expressing your feeling for Central de Abasto?
Love, because we are in charge of giving happiness, you may say, to the families.
Simply love?
Yes, love.
(*Yazmín Vázquez*, Coordinator at CdeA, APT; her voice on lines 2, 4 and 6).

Example 5 illustrates that authentic relations are... well, authentic; we sense them when we experience them, we know how it feels when the phenomena inter-subjectively is generated between us, but their in-depth truth-values are difficult to express in "plain text," which is why this section is written from the perspective of the respondents (the 'told'; Kim, 2016, pp. 199–200).

FINDINGS

APT is dealing with food that irregularly is dismissed by commercial actors, while humans are hungry in re-occurring and predictable patterns. The operational logic of APT is thereby characterized by a high capacity to synchronize seemingly incompatible rhythms, flows, logics and actors. APT excels in managing a vast variety of human food in major volumes with extraordinary accuracy under intense time pressure; a logistical and managerial excellence accentuated by the individual persistence and organizational resilience to do so systematically 365 days per year, year in, year out. APT combines these "hard factors" with a value- and purpose-driven organizational culture emphasizing close, warm and authentic relations. Immediately, when entering APT's main warehouse, this "hard/soft-combo" is communicated with omnipresent clarity (see Figure 20.2). Now, having staged the case, and focusing on trying to evoke emotional interest in the case, I turn to the more analytical presentation of the case findings, based on the announced model (Sinkovics et al., 2015).

Social Outcomes on Societal Level

One hundred and four APT employees (2019) operate a network of about 2,200 donors that annually donate about 1,200 tons of food (mainly) and non-food items (supplementary), which is dignified (unpacked, cleaned up, sorted, reorganized, repackaged) by 11,300 volunteers and turned into 1.9 million "food kits" per year that provide food (and non-food items) to over 65,000 people per week in five states of Mexico, every day of any year (APT Annual Report 2017; APT Development Model Report, 2018; various interviews). This is the central social outcome that APT generates. Another important social outcome is the positive influence on societal norms and attitudes towards women that APT generates. The importance of this outcome and its contribution to mend the tormented social glue and social fabric of Mexico, combined with the fact that this outcome is generated by an organization led 90% by women entrepreneurs, cannot be overstated in a Mexico infamous for extreme levels of machoista, inequality, femicide and domestic violence against women.

System 1 Related Aspects of APT Success ('Group of Individuals Affected by Human Rights Issues')

Having food to eat is part of the economic, social and cultural rights, which in turn are part of several broader instruments for human rights (Center for Economic and Social Rights, 2019) and also being the SDG goal 2, 'Zero Hunger' (United Nations, 2019). Within the lens of the two-system view of SVC above (Sinkovics et al., 2015), is APT targeting *symptomatic problems*, not *root causes*. This focus is very deliberate for APT (see details below, on the strict focus on *simplicity* of APT's business model). In essence: APT consists of a group of individuals (104 employees and 11,300 volunteers) passionately dedicated to contribute to mitigate the problems with food waste in Mexico that another group of individuals (over 65,000 beneficiaries) is suffering from (hunger, shortage of food, not enough nutritious food). As the focus in this chapter is on APT, not beneficiaries, the findings from now on are organized as "A day in the life of APT" written in first person voices of APT individuals. The findings will follow APT's organizational chart (see Figure 20.3) and its operational logic, in which operations take absolute center stage while management, public rela-

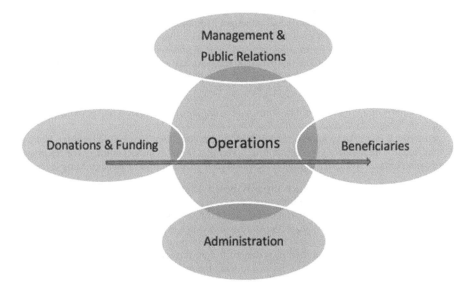

Source: APT Development Model Report, 2018, p. 37; re-worked by author to foreground operations.

Figure 20.3 *Organizational chart and operational logic (the arrow) of APT*

tions and administration is essential for supporting the smooth execution of APT's complex and intensive operations.

First Major Type of Donor to APT: Central de Abasto Merchants ('Donations & Funding')

At 4:30am, I start my commuting from my house. It takes me about 2.5 hours to get to work, depending on the traffic. I arrive to APT, check in and I arrive to the CdeA at 8:30am at the latest. I start my work by asking each donor if there are products for me to pick up. I go hall by hall, and booth by booth. This is the lettuce area. Then is the "epazote," then the carrots, then the coriander and then is a red booth in which they deal with very diverse products. I finish my shift at 4pm. And then I commute back to my house. I love my job. (*Guadalupe Aguilar Dávila*, Coordinator at CdeA, APT)

For me CdeA is magnificent, gigantic and alive night and day. It is magnificent because it is a gigantic area in which you can find everything. (*Yazmín Vázquez*, Coordinator at CdeA, APT)

Second Major Type of Donor to APT: Big Companies ('Donations & Funding')

I wake up at 6am, have breakfast, and then pick up the van. I quickly review the van, that the tires are fine, and every 15 days I check the oil. Then, I start my route. Every store takes 45 minutes to 2 hours. I like to interact with people, talk to them. Many times, when we are scanning the products, we have time to chat. I have tried to do it like that always. My parents taught me to be nice and polite to everyone, and since I've been working here I have done it with the people of the stores as well as with my colleagues. Then it develops more. I was always taught to be polite and nice with people and I try to do it as I was taught. I am also patient, trustworthy, reliable and punctual. I lift about a ton in average per day. Now, at my age [41 years], I get tired. I have been here for 23 years. Fifteen years ago, I didn't get tired. I arrived to my house, changed and went to play football. I daily played football. I fell asleep without a problem and woke up the next day at 5–6am, without any problem. (*Valentín Juárez*, Operator and Responsible for 1 of 18 Walmart Routes with 6 Walmart Stores on his Route, APT)

It would be good if there would be some way to donate dairy products and perishable products, the meats, the cheese, and all these things that is very sad to dispose, to have to soap up and throw it away, knowing that it could benefit someone else. That would be great. But we can't do it. The moment you scan it, it tells you that is not a product suitable for donation. (*Roxana Ordaz*, Walmart Employee, Responsible for Donations at a Bodega Aurrerá Store)

This is my first job ever! When my new boss told me what the job was about, I was shocked. Why? Because I am a little girl, I am 22 years and I was to lead only men; amazing men, that are my friends, my partners, that I like, I love, each one of them. My boys are on the street all day, in the traffic, in the stores, sometimes they don't eat in order to do their work. This, because if they don't arrive to a store in time, they can say "no, you're late, come back tomorrow," and then they don't fill their daily quota and feel bad. I repeat, it was difficult for me. First thing I did was to learn the names of all my boys. Then, knowing their routes, knowing the first store, the last store, etc., knowing what they like. This is my main method, to go with them on their routes, at least once per week. It is very important to meet each other. I am used to responsibility since young age and is a very honest person, and like to say things face-to-face. I am very open and extrovert, I am a singer, and I love to interact with people. So, I think this colour my interaction with people, I can talk about literally anything with anyone. I also have good education from my raising up and from the best university in Mexico. (*Esmeralda Castro*, Head of 18 Walmart Routes & Their Operators, APT)

I arrived to this institution as part of my social service seven years ago, and I stayed. My area, the fund procurement area is fundamental, as it is the basis for all benefits to our beneficiaries. It is also important to analyse it from donors' perspective. APT is increasingly not only food bank, but transcending to be a strategic ally to be inserted in the value chain of companies. One of my main motivations to work here is to know that I work to improve my country, contributing to society, reducing negative impact on environment and having the certainty that APT rewards talent for committed people and that you can have a career development as in any company. (*Anabel Díaz*, Head of Funding & Institutional Development, APT)

The Heart and Soul of APT ('Operations')

I have been working for seven years in APT. What I like most of my work is the daily operations, scheduling and attending the pickups, to be in the warehouse, organize and to attend the beneficiaries. It is very dynamic and I like very much to work here, that's why I've been here for so long. At 5–5:30am, the first driver sends their location to let us know that he has arrived and is ready to start his route. At 7am, it may happen that a driver is missing and then I have to decide who can be sent in his place so that the donation won't be lost. The most tiresome hours in operations is around 8am, when we have to move all the transport units and to prepare the warehouses for the daily operation. Then at 11am, I verify the attendance of volunteers and classify everything that arrives to assemble the 700 daily packages. At noon, it may occur a problem, for example that a driver didn't arrive, or was stopped by a policeman, and such we have to solve immediately. At 3–4pm we are done with the deliveries and we have to clean the warehouses. At 4:30–5pm, the first drivers from stores arrive (there are 18) and we have to unload as fast as possible. At 6pm, I check if all trucks have arrived, what they will use for the next day, check so that none is skipping the day, review in detail eventual problems with the trucks (and in case of problems, if the repair shop can deliver it in time so we can use them the next day) and upload the files required for the alerts to be received in the system. At 6:30–7pm, all the trucks are moved from the warehouse to the office, so they are not at risk. At evening, there can be an emergency, for instance if a driver calls in sick. At that moment, I have to solve it even though it is midnight. The required characteristics for being head of operations is to have a great capability of organizing, solve problems fast, think in terms of solutions fast, be calm, be strict, be really organized, be resistant, be firm on the decisions made. These abilities and characteristics, I have learned here through the years. It was a personal development, and I continue to grow. When I started, I didn't even speak. So, I have grown gradually and acquired these abilities and characteristics thanks to my area boss, that now is our CEO. He started to teach and guide me to become an area leader. I did it step by step. (*Laura Carlón*, Head of Operations, APT)

Mexican Communities in Need ('Beneficiaries')

I am a social worker, having worked here since 2016. I coordinate beneficiary activities via working with their representatives. Their communities elect five representatives to our beneficiary committee, in which I and some other APT managers also are part of. There we work out problems that occur and have ongoing dialogue on how things go. Examples of problems are matching problems (e.g. donors have lots of carrots one week, while beneficiaries need something else) and a small number of persons re-selling donations, rather than eating them. In 98% of these cases, we solve this via respectful dialogue, in the rest of the cases we need to activate our written contracts. (*Grisel Flores*, Head of Beneficiary Relations, APT)

The Invisible Hand of APT ('Administration')

I've been working here for 14 years and seen APT growing to a success case. I am in charge of managing the material, financial and human resources of APT. I believe the most important elements of APT success is our *adaptability* relative to all stakeholders interacting with our institution. In my area, we have for instance adopted audits and controls in order to validate our operations. This, among other things, have radically improved our *transparency*, which allowed us to gain the confidence of the donors. Our MIS system, also allow us to have *traceability* of people and products. (*Mónica Lozano*, Head of Administration, APT)

The Visionaries of APT ('Management & Public Relations')

First thing in a day, I check my e-mails. Sometimes I check the surveillance cameras [16 cameras monitoring all key points in APT warehouses]. Then I open up the whole system and check the KPIs. Then I check if anything is a threat, or a problem, that I need to deal with immediately. If there is anything with the KPIs, I talk to leaders, just to ask them if there is anything I can do to support them in solving it. So, first I check the general rhythm of the day for APT as a whole, then I check for particularities. The main parts of what I do: 70% is coaching the leaders, 20% is checking and following up on KPIs, 10% is particularities, threats and problems. And that is the general pattern of my day. (*Bernardo Landeros*, CEO, APT)

I have two twins, 19 years old. I wake up, make breakfast for all, walk our dog and then go to APT. I am in charge of the team bringing the money into APT. My job is to make sure that relations with key stakeholders (e.g. board members, food donors, money donors, volunteer time donors, newspapers, social media) are good. Also, relations with government and law-makers are part of my work; we work close-up with them, especially in Mexico City, to design new policies. Usually, I have the contacts with the high-level executives of major companies (e.g. Walmart, Lala, Nestlé). With new relations, I usually go to them and start from scratch. I don't try to convince them, but try to make them see us as a corporate ally, not as a charity. We create social profit that increase their social impact. This approach has really worked well. After this, I usually invite them here, to see with their own eyes. Almost all leave convinced, saying 'how can we help'? Sometimes it is not easy for them to come. For instance, I had two CEOs that had corporate policies forbidding them to go to our area. For them, I recorded a video instead, and it worked. Another part of my work is international collaboration with food banks from other countries. Food banks all over the world have one common denominator – we are the leaders on what we do, no one else does what we do, we set the paths that other follow. (*Mariana Jiménez Cárdenas*, Head of Institutional Relations, APT)

All the time, I have to do public relations, to get new funding or other resources. I also meet with APT management once per month and with the Padres of Caritas in 4–5 board meetings per year. These relations are complex, as it is persons used to questioning everything. Very often, I have to talk with each board member individually before meetings, so that everything works out fine during the meeting. I also meet with Senators and Diputados, to discuss and affect laws and policy making. My vision with APT is *expansion*. In five years, we should serve 80 000 beneficiaries. We have used the land we bought to build another warehouse and we are a truly international food bank so we can be eligible for international funding. APT also is a provider of a good diet, not only give whatever food we get, but giving good and balanced food to create a healthy diet that is in line with all sustainability goals. (*Ana Bertha Pérez Lizaur,* President of the Board, APT)

System 2 Related Aspects of APT Success ('Organization as a System')

The first key aspect of 'APT as a system' is a very flat and highly action-oriented organization where donors, operations and beneficiaries take center stage and other functions are designed to support what's foregrounded (see Figure 20.3).

The second key aspect is a management information system (MIS) tailor-made by and for APT staff to serve the objectives and operations of APT in detail. APT have developed most sub-systems themselves, for example, the KPI system that visualizes KPIs per donor and coordinator in real time updated by the minute. Other sub-systems: APT have purchased licenses of and integrated with their MIS, for example a market-leading webfleet system to which APT is connected 24/7 and can monitor where drivers/trucks are, how they move, and what their stats are. Each area manager, CdeA coordinator and route driver operator at APT have individual daily objectives and quotas to achieve and their individual gradual progress during the day is traced in real time in the MIS system. APT managers are also integrated into the MISs of major donors, for example Walmart's system, where they provide monthly detailed reports (Walmart Global Donation Management, 2019). The third key aspect is APT's management philosophy:

We are very focused on simplifying what we do. There are always temptations in this sector to do more, many food banks "does everything." We are not a school. We are not a hospital. We are a food bank. This is not politically correct to say, but all this "impact talk" that is around today is harmful. They ask, do we reduce poverty, do we improve this, do we solve that… Wait! We are just a food bank, that's what we do. This talk is a problem. We have spent the last 6–7 years de-coupling us from the pressures it brings. The major pressure comes from donors but also from government, our board, funders, other institutions like ours and from society overall. We need to keep this out of our heads and always remind us and others why we are created. We do this in dialogue and via upholding boundaries. Boundaries are an especially big problem in our culture, as we are used to say "yes," "no problem" and "whatever you want," and that is not being responsible. In sum, the core of our business model is managing simplicity in a complex environment. Don't be lost in all the noise. Just identify the aspects that move the machine and then focus on that and put everything else aside. Key aspects of APT's business model are people, building leadership in people, our organizational culture, strict focus on goals and objectives, our tailor-made MIS, integrating new technology as it comes and having the discipline to work every day on these points. (*Bernardo Landeros*, CEO, APT)

DISCUSSION AND CONCLUSIONS

The APT case contributes to undermine the "underperformance hypothesis" of women entrepreneurs (Sheikh et al., 2018; Yousafzai et al., 2018a, 2018b). APT actors do this performatively, that is, not by emphasizing gender issues in discourse and dialogue to any large extent, but performatively by letting the actions and results speak for themselves. The women entrepreneurs and one male entrepreneur in APT lead an organization *topically focused* on one thing, to recover food that otherwise would be wasted and distribute it to people in need and *managerially focused* on one other thing, to deliver superior performance daily and systematically over long periods of time. With such strong focus, other variables are not allowed to take root; they are irrelevant or are made irrelevant. Grisel Flores, Head of Beneficiary Relations, formulates it distinctly:

> Man or woman, it does not matter here. This is an area where women have more opportunities, and we act on the existing ones or the ones we can create. Our success factors are teamwork, excellent communication, very clear and specific objectives and a heartily and constructive work environment. Some of this is an outcome of Bernardo's emancipatory style of leadership, we get a lot of trust from him. But we are all dedicated professionals here, we all bring important stuff to the table.

With such professionalism, APT fulfil their mission with clarity, efficiency, effectiveness and productivity. In more detail, the APT case highlights the importance of women entrepreneurs as social value creators with high societal impact in three main ways:

First, the APT case highlights that women entrepreneurs generate value via leadership traits "normally" assigned to women (i.e. dialogical, relational, relating, authentic, caring). The most important achievement of the leadership in this case is the way APT connects stakeholders. A key reason why APT is able to generate such high value on the societal level is their advanced integration of seemingly colliding logics. APT is excellent in relating to, and communicating with, stakeholders representing *different juridical forms* (i.e. charities, philanthropists, for-profit actors, not-for profit actors, governmental bodies, communities, cooperatives). APT is thereby able to connect all *sector types* and "glue stakeholders together," despite them having *high heterogeneity in end objectives* (i.e. poverty reduction, building sustainable food supply chains, improving food waste management, getting tax deductions, boosting civic sector idealism, creating a better world, implementing triple bottom line thinking and fulfilling the mission of a religious community).

Second, the APT case provides insights into the art of complexity reduction via management of paradoxes by women entrepreneurs (the "hybrid capacity" of APT, see introduction). APT is simultaneously extraordinarily human-centered in daily interactions (reduces people-related complexities), extremely management-oriented in their daily activities (reduces operations-related complexities) and very value driven in daily priorities (helps them fight discourse-related complexities brought upon them by "impact-talk" (see quote by Bernardo Landeros in section 'Findings' above) and never-ending and ever-changing "stakeholder wish lists" of what they think APT (also) should do.

Third, the APT case shows that *social value is something tangible emanating out of concrete practices*, rather than an abstraction or "something fluffy." APT do not appeal to emotions and "why don't you help a good cause" in their communication with high-end executives from potential and existing corporate donors; they communicate hardcore metrics and clear objectives relative to what they achieve, how they do it and why it matters – and then propose ways on how APT can be inserted as a strategic partner in their value chains. APT interact with companies with their own language and logic, without losing sight on who they are and their social mission. This "hybrid capacity" makes APT a radically overperforming organization and thereby an example of the importance of the two-system view on SVC (Sinkovics et al., 2015). The APT case provides two insights in this respect. First, that SVC-oriented organizations can integrate their internal systems with their stakeholders' systems to the same extent that for-profit actors can. Second, that benchmarking practices (to monitor, measure, analyze and compare the SVC generated in system 2 and relate this back to system 1) is both possible and highly preferable, in order to be perceived as a trustworthy actor. APT can become better though, to more explicitly focus on the link they generate to human rights, more specifically to what Wettstein (2012) coins as socio-economic human rights.

In summary, and connecting back to existing literature on non-monetary value creation by women entrepreneurs, I conclude that APT generates all the values on a societal level mentioned in the literature; community needs, role modelling, impact on other people's lives, influencing societal norms and attitudes towards women entrepreneurs, influencing institutional rules, improving overall society well-being and nurturing and improving family/social relations (Fisher et al., 2014; Welter & Xheneti, 2015; Angel et al., 2018; Sheikh et al., 2018; Yousafzai et al., 2018a, 2018b) On a critical note, APT generates more mixed value on an individual level. Employees indeed grow in APT, where individual values such as widened empowerment, personal development, agency and space for decision-making and thereby increased individual well-being is generated (Al-Dajani & Marlow, 2013; Gries & Naudé, 2011). But as "the cause" overflows all other aspects, there really is a price to pay for APT employees regarding, for instance, work–life balance (Jayawarna et al., 2011), as many of APT's employees testify that it is a 24/7 commitment that absorbs all/most of their waking hours and that the pay is lower both in relation to other comparable jobs and to the extra mile employees regularly (rather than exceptionally) deliver. This raises questions on the long-term sustainability of APT's business model.

ACKNOWLEDGMENTS

Thanks to *Mariana Jiménez Ojeda* (Técnica Académica, EDESI) for interview transcriptions from Spanish to English.

REFERENCES

Acs, Z. J., Boardman, M. C. & McNeely, C. L (2013). The social value of productive entrepreneurship. *Small Business Economics*, 40 (3), 785–796.

Al-Dajani, H. & Marlow, S. (2013). Empowerment and entrepreneurship: A theoretical framework. *International Journal of Entrepreneurial Behaviour and Research*, 19 (5), 503–524.

Angel, P., Jenkins, A. & Stephens, A. (2018). Understanding entrepreneurial success: A phenomenographic approach. *International Small Business Journal*, 36 (6), 611–636.

Dietz, A. S. & Porter, C. (2012). Making sense of social value creation: Three organizational case studies. *Emergence: Complexity and Organization*, 14 (3), 23–43.

Fisher, R., Maritz, A. & Lobo, A. (2014). Evaluating entrepreneurs' perception of success: Development of a measurement scale. *International Journal of Entrepreneurial Behavior & Research*, 20 (5), 478–492.

Flyvbjerg, B. (2006). Five misunderstandings about case-study research. *Qualitative Inquiry*, 12 (2), 219–245.

Gries, T. & Naudé, W. (2011). Entrepreneurship and human development: A capability approach. *Journal of Public Economics*, 95 (3–4), 216–224.

Hechavarría, D. M., Terjesen, S. A., Ingram, A. E., Renko, M., Justo, R. & Elam, A. (2016). Taking care of business: The impact of culture and gender on entrepreneurs' blended value creation goals. *Small Bus. Econ.*, DOI 10.1007/s11187-016-9747-4.

Jayawarna, D., Jones, O. & Macpherson, A. (2011). New business creation and regional development: Enhancing resource acquisition in areas of social deprivation. *Entrepreneurship & Regional Development*, 23 (9–10), 735–761.

Jones, T., Ram, M. & Villares-Varela, M. (2017). Injecting reality into the migrant entrepreneurship agenda. In C. Essers, P. Dey, D. Tedmanson & K. Verduyin (Eds.), *Critical Perspectives on Entrepreneurship. Challenging Dominant Discourses on Entrepreneurship*, 125–145. Abingdon, UK: Routledge.

Kantor, P. (2005). Determinants of women's microenterprise success in Ahmedabad, India: Empowerment and economics. *Feminist Economics*, 11 (3), 63–83.

Kim, J (2016). Narrative data analysis and interpretation: "Flirting" with data. In J. Kim (Ed.), *Understanding Narrative Inquiry: The Crafting and Analysis of Stories as Research*, 185–224. London: Sage.

Korsgaard, S. & Anderson, A. R. (2011). Enacting entrepreneurship as social value creation. *International Small Business Journal*, 29 (2), 135–151.

McGowan, P., Lewis Redeker, C., Cooper, S. Y. & Greenan, K. (2012). Female entrepreneurship and the management of business and domestic roles: Motivations, expectations and realities. *Entrepreneurship & Regional Development*, 24 (1–2), 53–72.

Mishler, E. G. (1995). Models of narrative analysis: A typology. *Journal of Narrative and Life History*, 5 (2), 87–123.

Morris, M. H., Miyasaki, N. N.; Watters, C. E. & Coombes, S. M. (2006). The dilemma of growth: Understanding venture size choices of women entrepreneurs. *Journal of Small Business Management*, 44 (2), 221–244.

Nicholls, A. (2009). We do good things, don't we? Blended value accounting in social entrepreneurship. *Accounting, Organisations and Society*, 34, 755–769.

OECD (2004). *Women's Entrepreneurship: Issues and Policies*, 2nd OECD Conference of Ministers Responsible for Small and Medium-Sized Enterprises (SMEs), Istanbul, Turkey, 3–5 June 2004.

Polkinghorne, D. E. (1995). Narrative configuration in qualitative analysis. *International Journal of Qualitative Studies in Education*, 8 (1), 5–23.

Sheikh, S., Yousafzai, S., Sist, F., Akdeniz, A. & Saeed, S. (2018). Value creation through women's entrepreneurship. In S. Yousafzai, A. Fayolle, C. Lindgreen, C. Henry, S. Saeed & S. Sheikh (Eds.), *Women's Entrepreneurship and the Myth of Underperformance: A New*

Look at Women's Entrepreneurship, 20–33. Cheltenham, UK and Northampton, MA, USA: Edward Elgar Publishing.

Sinkovics, N., Sinkovics, R. R., Hoque, S. F. & Czaban, L. (2015). A reconceptualisation of social value creation as social constraint alleviation. *Critical Perspectives on International Business*, 11 (3/4), 340–363.

The Global FoodBanking Network (2018). *The State of Global Food Banking 2018: Nourishing the World*. Chicago: The Global FoodBanking Network.

United Nations (2006). *The State of the World's Cities Report 2006/2007: 30 Years of Shaping the Habitat Agenda*. Nairobi, Kenya: United Nations Human Settlements Programme (UN-HABITAT).

United Nations (2014). *Poverty in Latin America*. New York, USA: United Nations Economic Commission for Latin America and the Caribbean. Infographic retrieved at http://www.cepal.org/en/infographics/poverty-latin-america, 9 January 2014.

Welter, F. (2019). *Entrepreneurship and Context*. Cheltenham, UK and Northampton, MA, USA: Edward Elgar Publishing.

Welter, F. & Xheneti, M. (2015). Value for whom? Exploring the value of informal entrepreneurial activities in post-socialist contexts. In G. McElwee & R. Smith (Eds.), *Exploring Criminal and Illegal Enterprise: New Perspectives on Research*, 253–275, Bingley, UK: Emerald Publishing Group.

Wettstein, F. (2012). CSR and the debate on business and human rights: Bridging the great divide. *Business Ethics Quarterly*, 22 (4), 739–770.

Wilson, F. & Post, J. (2013). Business models for people, planet (& profits): Exploring the phenomena of social business, a market-based approach to social value creation. *Small Business Economics*, 40, 715–737.

Yousafzai, S. Y., Fayolle, A., Lindgreen, A., Henry, C., Saeed, S. & Sheikh, S. (2018a). *Women Entrepreneurs and the Myth of 'Underperformance': A New Look at Women's Entrepreneurship Research*. Cheltenham, UK and Northampton, MA, USA: Edward Elgar Publishing.

Yousafzai, S. Y., Lindgreen, A., Saeed, S. & Henry, C. (2018b). *Contextual Embeddedness of Women's Entrepreneurship: Going beyond a Gender-Neutral Approach*. London: Routledge.

Zahra, S. & Wright, M. (2016). Understanding the social role of entrepreneurship. *Journal of Management Studies*, 53 (4), 610–629.

Sources

Alimento Para Todos:
Annual Report 2017, https://issuu.com/alimentoparatodosiap/docs/informe_anual_2017.
Development Model Report 2018.
Web page: https://www.apt.org.mx/en/, 27 April 2019.

BES Urban Lexicon (2012). *Metacity*. BES Urban Lexicon blog, http://besurbanlexicon.blogspot.com/2012/06/metacity.html, 11 June 2012.

Center for Economic and Social Rights, http://www.cesr.org/what-are-economic-social-and-cultural-rights, 20 November 2019.

Gilchrist, K. (2019). *Tackling food wastage can be a $2.5 trillion market opportunity for businesses*. CNBC, https://www.cnbc.com/2019/08/12/preventing-food-wastage-can-be-a-2point5-trillion-business-opportunity.html, 5 November 2019.

Instituto Nacional de Estadística y Geografía (INEGI), https://www.inegi.org.mx/app/areasgeograficas/?ag=09, 5 November 2019.

Lundberg, H., personal archive of about 4000 photos from the streets of Mexico City, shot 2007–2019.

MacroTrends, https://www.macrotrends.net/cities/21853/mexico-city/population, 21 November 2019.

McCarthy, J. (2016). *Italy passes law to send unsold food to charities instead of dumpsters*. Global Citizen, https://www.globalcitizen.org/en/content/italy-passes-law-to-send-unsold -food-to-charities/, 15 March 2016.

United Nations, https://www.un.org/sustainabledevelopment/sustainable-development-goals/ , 20 November 2019.

Walmart Global Donation Management, https://donations.walmart.com/GlobalDonations/ gdms/Public/landingPage, 6 May 2019.

Wikipedia:

https://en.wikipedia.org/wiki/Central_de_Abasto, 27 April 2019.

https://en.wikipedia.org/wiki/Walmart_de_México_y_Centroamérica, 27 April 2019.

21. Post conflict development and value creation through women's entrepreneurship: evidence from Swat, Pakistan

Musarrat Jabeen and Shandana Sheikh

INTRODUCTION

Conflict destroys infrastructure, damages the social fabric, and drives down the socio-economic strength of individuals (UN, 2009). Community and government agencies cease to provide safety nets and vital public services (Roos, 2019; Ahmed-Ghosh, 2003). In the context of post conflict countries, entrepreneurship seems to be the best option for countries to tie their hopes for accelerated economic development (Kokko, 2018).

Entrepreneurship significantly promotes post conflict development by enhancing social vitality and quality of life of conflict-affected people. A post conflict entrepreneur is committed in his entrepreneurial efforts with the objective of creating value for socio-economic well-being. Entrepreneurship contributes towards building sustainable peace and prosperity for individuals, families and communities (Hudock, Sherman, & Williamson, 2016). It is perceived as a realistic relief after the conflict owing to multiple positive impacts (Bruni, Gherardi, and Poggio 2004). Entrepreneurial ventures facilitate economic dynamics of the society which in turn help to face conflict (Calás, Smircich, and Bourne 2009); and to overcome the adverse effects of conflict (Marlow and Swail 2014; Ahmad, 2017).

Despite the central role of entrepreneurship in post conflict development, it has not received much attention by researchers and policy makers (Ahmad, 2017). In particular, the role of women entrepreneurs (Arshed, Carter, and Mason 2014), who play a critical role in promoting post conflict development and create opportunities for change, is largely ignored. Women become entrepreneurs to face the loss of men during and after the conflict; that highlights their challenging role compared to women living in peace conditions (Bozzoli, Brück, and Wald, 2013). Research shows that women are mostly recognized as dependents and victims in the context of post conflict development, ignoring their responsiveness to skill development institutions and their entrepreneurial actions to process the acquired skills for individual and societal development (Ayadurai, 2004; Webster, 2016). Thus, despite that women are agents of change and create multiple forms of value through their entrepreneurial activity, the predicament of women entrepreneurship remains an ignorant characteristic of post conflict development by the research and policy makers (Sorensen, 1998).

Women in post conflict development not only create value in monetary terms, they also create social value such as entrepreneurial networking to challenge the practices meant to keep aside women from economic empowerment (Lemmon, 2012). In post conflict development, women set the entrepreneurial norms through their intentions and actions (Ritchie, 2016). For example, a study by Ayadurai (2004) regarding women's post conflict role in Sri Lanka by the end of three decades-long civil war found women more entrepreneurial and more active compared to men and to the pre-violence period; thus, reflecting upon women's economic participation and their empowerment. Women are, most of the time, inclined to manage small business activities in traditional societies where their mobility is limited. Research on women in Afghanistan suggests that women working in the handicraft industry have small businesses based on dairy products, spinning wool and caring for young animals (WAFGAN, 2008). Accordingly, the sale of livestock and products increases the income of women and their families. Further evidence suggests that post conflict support for women's health, political and socio-economic rights in Sierra Leone increased confidence among women for entrepreneurship (USAID, 2009).

Women entrepreneurs encounter multiple challenges while creating value at multiple levels, though evidence of the role of women in a post conflict development context and militancy seems scarce (Bullough and Renko 2017; Hudock et al., 2016). Therefore, further research is desirable to recognize the contextual generics of post development and women entrepreneurship. Accordingly, this research study refines our perception to organize women entrepreneurship in a post conflict development context where gender inequality prevails, and the women entrepreneurs create value in the face of conflict. Analysing interviews of women entrepreneurs in the Swat region of Pakistan, a post conflict zone, this research aims to discuss the multiple realms of value that women create while also discussing the factors that aid such value creation.[1]

POST CONFLICT DEVELOPMENT AND VALUE CREATION THROUGH WOMEN ENTREPRENEURSHIP

Conflict is defined as a hostile engagement between or among disagreeing individuals and groups aspiring for incompatible goals or outcomes (Galtung, 1973). Post conflict development is the reconstruction of destroyed infrastructure and rehabilitation of conflict victims and the displaced to facilitate the development of livelihoods (Bullough and Renko, 2017; Deanna, 2006; Doern, 2009). An essential ingredient to post conflict development is a viable entrepreneurial environment that promotes policies and programs to initiate entrepreneurship (UN, 2009). Entrepreneurs are defined as people who are ingenious and creative in finding ways that add to their wealth, power, and prestige (Desai and Acs, 2007) during war or peace (Koltai and Muspratt, 2016). In conflict-affected countries, mostly grassroots-level people intend to create value to dispel the impact of conflict (Tobias and Boudreaux, 2011). Conflict-generated vulnerabilities motivate the entrepreneurs to create value in the new set of existing challenges and emerging opportunities organized by the state and supported by the society (Wang and Geale, 2015). In post conflict development, the entrepreneurs can identify products, services, processes and initiate businesses (Ahmad, 2017), by acquiring training provided by formal institutions (Bozzoli et al., 2013). Examples from the developing world suggest that institutions play a significant role in facilitating the creation of a favourable entrepreneurial environment and thus promoting development in a conflict-afflicted region (Ahmed-Ghosh, 2003). For example, in Swat, post conflict development was designed to counter the pre-conflict militant networks by setting new processes of Technical Education & Vocational Training Authority (TEVTA) for entrepreneurial activities (Ahmad, 2017).

UN resolution 1325 recognizes that the unique experiences of women in post conflict development can create socio-economic values (UNIFEM, 2000). Women are pressed to become entrepreneurs because of loss of men in conflict and they contribute value to the well-being of their family and community (Justino et al., 2012). In vogue, gender ideologies play the role to contain the socio-economic and political conduct of women (Bullough and Renko, 2017), however post conflict development opens opportunities for women that may counter the practices of gender inequality (Justino et al., 2012). Women entrepreneurs have been viewed as significant contributors in post conflict development (Dean, Larsen, Ford, & Akram, 2019). Value creation through women entrepreneurship evolves as a relatively dynamic process (Marlow and Swail, 2014) and is dependent on entrepreneurial trends prevalent in formal and informal institutions in post conflict regions (Calás et al., 2009). For example, in Sri Lanka, the civil war resulted in an increasing number of women becoming entrepreneurs to fulfil the lack of males in the workforce (Ayadurai, 2004). Post conflict support given to women in terms of education and health rights in Sierra Leone, increased confidence among women for entrepreneurship to contribute in peace building (Vernon, 2016). Moreover, in Uganda, women entrepreneurship became prevalent because of skill-learning, and networking which in turn was facilitated by the formal and the informal institutions in post conflict development (Sserwanga, Kiconco, Nystrand and Mindra, 2014).

Despite other socio-cultural constraints imposed on women across the world, entrepreneurship paves the way for women to become independent and promote their empowerment (Ahmad, 2017). As with other career options, entrepreneurship does not necessitate the acquisition of entrepreneurial education and training and thus women choose this career path as a way to create value for themselves and others around them in the face of conflict (Ritchie, 2016). Yet, research suggests that women in conflict-afflicted regions struggle to become entrepreneurial in the face of the challenges including inadequate resources, societal restrictions, family and household responsibilities and socio-cultural constraints (Bullough and Renko, 2017). This makes it compelling to highlight the value that accrues from the entrepreneurial activity of women, despite the challenges they face in the context of a conflict-afflicted region.

THE CASE OF SWAT

Value creation in entrepreneurship is mostly linked to monetary increase. Nevertheless, value creation is a greater entrepreneurial concept, and the only focus on economic outcome may ignore the significant human and societal features of the process (Bruni et al., 2004). In the context of post conflict development, researchers have discussed the critical role of entrepreneurship in addressing social needs and poverty reduction (McKeever, Anderson, and Jack, 2014). Further, the narrow approach of defining value creation follows the narrow benchmarks used to measure the women entrepreneurs, comparing their performance with men and calling them less successful than men (Dean et al., 2019). Moreover, research on women entrepreneurs has been organized focusing socio-economic hurdles and achievements (Marlow and Swail, 2014). However, further studies are required to identify the value creation through women entrepreneurship by combining three dimensions; first their socio-economic needs (Baumol, 1990); second their surrounding economic sufferings (Wang and Geale, 2015); third their role in national strategy against militancy (McKeever et al., 2014). In such contexts of post conflict development, the value creation by women entrepreneurship can be defined in terms of building sustainable peace through formal and informal institutions but may not be limited to these supporting mechanisms.

This research recognizes the crucial link between value creation and entrepreneurial environment (Day, 1987). It focuses on value creation beyond economic outcomes, which we refer to as improved ability and skills that reflect the benefit accrued to the individual entrepreneur, increased support of the society that reflects value accruing at the community level and increased number of women participating in entrepreneurship and moving towards empowerment, thus reflecting value accruing at the national level.

METHODOLOGY

To achieve the objectives of the research, a qualitative methodology is adopted herein as such methodological designs help to explore the multiple ways in which women create value, the nature of such value and the factors that facilitate its creation. Qualitative research aids in a detailed analysis of the data, allowing the researcher to harness the knowledge, attitudes and practices of the respondents, keeping in view their intentions and interconnections with the rest of the socio-economic system (Arshed et al., 2014; Hlady and Jouison-Laffitte, 2014; Dana and Dumez, 2015). The qualitative approach tolerates the backup of the entrepreneurship to be tested to reflect upon the characteristics of the eco environment in favour of post conflict entrepreneurial activities (Dana and Dana 2005). Moreover, qualitative research in post conflict environments has the ability to advance understanding of entrepreneurs' experiences and gives realistic data that quantitative survey-based approaches can't offer (Doern 2009). The two stories narrated in this chapter are based on qualitative data.

The context for the current research is Swat. The entrepreneurial challenges faced by women in Swat are due to the disappearance of traditional work groups because of displacement, death and divorce.[2] The militant trend heightened in 2009 when the Taliban took over Swat Valley and casted out government functionaries in Swat. Pakistan's army entered into the situation and liberated Swat from militants by applying military action during *Operation Rah-e-Raast* (Hamza, 2007). After the success of *Operation Rah-e-Raast*, the Pakistan army initiated the process of rehabilitation of the internally displaced people (IDPs) in Swat. The retreating Taliban and their allies destroyed bridges, government buildings, and in particular the female schools were blown. In this context, the Technical Education & Vocational Training Authority (TEVTA) was established in 2012 to impart entrepreneurial training to men and women; hence to empower them to start new businesses.

Sample

Trainees in Chakdra and Kabal registered in the TEVTA program since 2012 were contacted to take part in the research following purposive sampling. All the trainees attended a course of 12–18 months in any one of the following courses in health management, culinary arts, arts and craft, beautician, tailoring, knitting and computer skills. From the list of 300 trainees, 25 were selected for semi structured interviews, having businesses for three–four years. The interviews were conducted between September and November 2018. Each interview lasted 60 to 90 minutes. The interviews were conducted in the premises of TEVTA because the participants preferred it compared to their own homes in Swat. The participants were requested to discuss the various dimensions in which becoming an entrepreneur changed their life, or others around them. The TEVTA authorities introduced the lead researcher to the participants. The participants and the researcher were fluent in Urdu, the national language of Pakistan. The common language allowed the women entrepreneurs to speak their experiences. For the purpose of this chapter, the accounts of two women entrepreneurs have been selected to reflect the aspects of value created by women entrepreneurs in a post conflict region of Swat, Pakistan. Zaibu-Nisa (27, Chakdra, Swat) started her business in 2014 as a beauty artist after receiving training from TEVTA. She offers services that include skin care, haircuts, and bridal make up. Zaibu-Nisa has a family of nine: three brothers, three sisters, and her mother and father. Aneela (29, Batkhela, Swat) married ten years back, lost her husband in the Swat conflict in 2009. She had a nine-year-old son, and started her business in 2014.

FINDINGS

The thematic analysis of interviews suggests that women entrepreneurs created multiple dimensions of value on individual and society/community levels. On the individual front, women entrepreneurs reflect increased *entrepreneurial intentions, enhanced entrepreneurial skills and enhanced respect and recognition in the community.*

Entrepreneurial Intentions

Zaibun-Nisa's story reflects an original belief in herself and the assurance to fight against all odds to fulfil her intention. She explained how her intention and struggle kept her focused in her business. She believes that while support from family and contacts helps women make their own entrepreneurial intentions and realize their goals, it is her intention and hard work that has led to her success in her life and business. Before she started her business, she had not considered that she could run a business or do anything other than housework. Over time, her knowledge about the business and her self-belief in dealing with her skills grew. She had hardly communicated with anyone prior to starting the trade and did not know how to talk to clients for orders.

Aneela supported her own intention to participate in the training program, but she faced challenges when she first started her business. For instance, people would say awful things about her because she was working outside her home, and she wasn't initially sure about her abilities as a business woman. Over time, she changed the unhelpful opinions about her and working women in general by proving her skills and abilities as a businessperson.

Enhanced Recognition in Business and Community

The first challenge Zaibun-Nisa faced was that the women should not be self-employed. As she gained experience in business, her confidence also improved, and she began to serve the orders of clients at their places. Formerly, she would be scared to leave the house, fearing people's remarks, but she steadily overcame this fear and started believing in her ability to do business. A year after she started her business, Zaibun-Nisa started receiving acknowledgement for her work from the people in her community and others who heard about her skills of beauty. She did not do well from the first day she started her business, no demand of her skills was a challenge for her. The local women did not realize the skin problems that could be cured by beauty skills. To change this perception, Zaibun-Nisa went to every house in her community and talked about her business, explaining the benefits of beauty treatments.

With the passage of time, Zaibun-Nisa built her standing and her customers. She started off with a few clients. At first, her clients were in her village, where she could walk to their homes to offer services, but when the number increased, she rented a shop from which she sells her services, increasing her visibility and her clientele. Her practice in business taught her marketing and communication skills that help her to attract and retain customers. She made a panel with beauty pictures of women on it and information about the kind of services she offered. She also made business cards that she gives to her clients, so they can call her when they need her services and can refer other potential customers to her.

Aneela knew that she faced competition from male tailors in the market and she had to gain her customers' trust and good will. That she overcame by providing a mobile service of door to door orders collection. Aneela explains, "This has immensely helped me to expand my business since previously only ladies clothing was ordered but later I got orders for children Afghani designs prevalent in the area." Aneela's customers were not ready to register orders at her place. Aneela approached their doorsteps to get the orders and deliver the finished product to their place. She had to market her skills. When she first started the business, she provided some free service, for instance by mending or redesigning old clothes in an effort to build her name and credibility.

The findings suggest female entrepreneurs in Swat create value in several dimensions; improved ability and skills which reflect the benefit accrued to the individual entrepreneur, increased support of the society which reflects value accruing at the community level and increasing the number of women entrepreneurs which reflects value accruing to national building of a sustainable peace strategy. The findings of this research identify women entrepreneurs as a significant source of value creation in the context of post conflict development (see Figure 21.1).

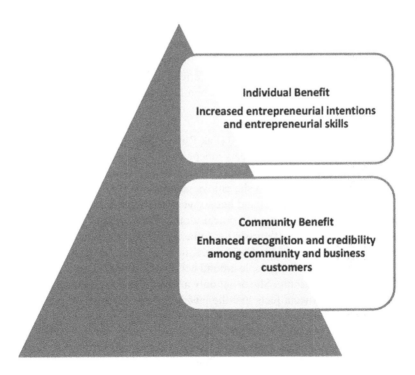

Figure 21.1   Dimensions of value creation in women's entrepreneurship

Zaibun-Nisa now has full power over her income from her business and uses it as she desires. She is not accountable to her father or brothers regarding how she spends her money or how she runs her business. A major part of Zaibun-Nisa's income is used to buy beauty items for the business and to pay rent for the shop. The income from her business also pays for her sisters and brothers' education, quality food, clothing, picnics and parties at restaurants. She bought some land next to her house as well. She has a feeling of contentment and attainment in being an entrepreneur, not only because she runs a successful business but also because the business has earned her respect both inside and outside her place. There is a difference in how her family and community counted her before and since she became a businesswoman. She noticed that she was valued more after becoming an entrepreneur. There were times that her three sisters and three brothers lacked a quality life, without taking excursions, or having a meal in some restaurant or items from some quality bakery. Zaibu-Nisa's thrust for a better quality of life led her to entrepreneurship, which has generated value for herself, her family, and her community. Zaibun-Nisa said that she is called by the family in decision-making situations. Zaibun-Nisa also narrated positive attitudes from her neighbouring families after she started the business. Now the community proudly tells other people about Zaibun-Nisa's business.

While becoming a successful entrepreneur, Zaibun-Nisa also made significant contributions to society. Zaibun-Nisa's success made other women start businesses. She teaches women the skills she learned from her business and encourages them to start their own businesses. She says to house-confined women, "If you are limited to your place, how would the people know what you can do? While going out would give you the confidence to earn." Two of the five women she has trained have started their own businesses. It gives Zaibun-Nisa a feeling of achievement and fulfilment. As a character model to the women, Zaibun-Nisa provides advice and support to those who ask her for help in any matter, personal or professional. She is known as the leader of the women in her village.

Aneela's business generates 25,000 (Pak Rupees) per month. She spends most of that on household expenses. She feels independent in being able to spend her own money, knowing that she does not have to answer to anyone about how much and where she spends the money, so she enjoys getting sweets from the bakery for her family or something for her son and her six-year-old nephew as her widowed sister lives with her. She likes making identical clothes for her sister and herself. Since Aneela's business started to flourish, her father as head of the family, asks her view on matters regarding the house. For Aneela, it is not important just to earn money from her business but to help people around her. Her widowed sister and her nephew are dependent on her earning. She is not only a support to herself but to another conflict victim as well. Aneela feels that the business earns her a lot of value from her family. As the only business woman in the home, she has to manage her time between the housework and her business. Her widowed sister helps her, preparing food for Aneela and her son. Aneela appreciates the help she receives from her family and believes that it plays an important role in her success as a businessperson.

At present Aneela is known as Darzi Baji ("the lady tailor") and is a basis of pride for her community. She has more than 100 customers, some of whom she visits on a regular basis, while others she visits in every neighbourhood. Word of mouth and referrals help her to expand her business, and tough work helps her earn a good reputation. Once Aneela was known as a victim of Swat conflict, she was limited to her residence, did not meet up with many people, and could not even see a doctor for health reasons, but now she goes out to meet customers, family, and friends. She has trained about 20 peers to have the same skills as she has to have a tailoring business. Her life has expanded, and she has benefitted her area in the post conflict development.

The institutional support is always found on the back of emerging entrepreneurial trends in post conflict development. However, the establishment of entrepreneurship is the art and science *specific* for each one.

DISCUSSION

Dominating ideologies describe business ownership and entrepreneurship only for men (Ahl, 2006), signifying that women are not fine to take on the task of entrepreneurship (Achtenhagen and Welter, 2005). However, in post conflict development, the new roles of women entrepreneurship are appreciated and accepted (Ayadurai, 2004). Women are found more entrepreneurial and more are working like the men worked in the pre-violence period, which indicates women's economic empowerment. This is very much likely due to the post conflict development in Sri Lanka (Roos, 2019). The capabilities and skills the women gain enable them to operate new roles in adverse situations for entrepreneurship (Hudock et al., 2016). The value creation by women entrepreneurs should be evaluated as a process expressing their new roles to counter conflict.

Notwithstanding the militant conflict, the participants in this study created value through new entrepreneurial intentions, acquisition of entrepreneurial training and initiation of new businesses in post conflict development (Day, 1987). They created value for themselves, for the society and for the state. The responsiveness of participants to entrepreneurial training is linked to the combination of security support by the Pakistan army and social support of informal institutions. However, this is unlikely in the Rwandan context wherein gender norms ascribing women in fixed roles constrain them in their entrepreneurial capacity (Deanna, 2006). Further, the women entrepreneurs work 'mutually' among themselves to disseminate and enhance the acquired skills to initiate and sustain entrepreneurship (Dean et al., 2019). Thus, enhancing the human capital of women entrepreneurs through entrepreneurial training programmes improves the ability for value creation, which is decisive in tackling anti women empowerment challenges (Bullough and Renko, 2017). In the post conflict development context, the formal and informal institutions co-exist for women's entrepreneurship, which is unusual in peace times (Sserwanga et al., 2014). In Swat the informal institutions came forward to align with the state institutions of Pakistan's army and TEVTA to support women entrepreneurship. This highlights the mutuality of formal and informal institutions working in post conflict zones for socio-economic change (Dean et al., 2019). This tendency was also advanced by UNDP's aid for women entrepreneurship in Swat (UNDP, 2020).

Female entrepreneurs mostly encounter problems in acquisition of skills, funds and social support to establish their business; but in processing a business they bring the social change that not only furnishes their business, but also facilitates incoming women entrepreneurs in post conflict development (Roos, 2017). Swat is a unique case of post conflict development contributed through women entrepreneurship enabled by the Pakistan army and the public institutions (UNDP, 2020). Publicity of experiences of successful women entrepreneurs in post conflict development can generate confidence among women in other conflict zones to create value in adverse circumstances (Justino et al., 2012). The trend will help to portray opportunities for value creation in building sustainable peace strategies to set aside the negative impacts of post conflict economic sufferings.

A post conflict development strategy must fully understand how conflict affects women and men differently, allocate capacity to address these unique needs, and ensure the full and equal participation of women in the development activities (Aldairany et al., 2018). The combined force of formal and informal institutions is desirable to acquire systemic entrepreneurship in peace and war times (Williams and Vorley 2015). Our study holds that in conflict-exposed states like Pakistan characterized by political instability and less economic development, formal and informal institutions can turn the post conflict challenges into opportunities by initiating entrepreneurial strategies and programmes. Our study contributes to post conflict development and entrepreneurship literature by investigating the two stories of women entrepreneurs. They were unique in their intentions to bring socio-economic change to counter the anti-women empowerment movement in Swat. The women contributed the three-dimensional values: value 1, benefits to the individual; value 2, benefits to the community and value 3, benefits to the state. The study predicts that the individual entrepreneurial trends found in this study will accumulate into group entrepreneurial trends.

NOTES

1. All names have been anonymized.
2. During the study it was found that women became separated or divorced through the Swat conflict. The reasons were either to continue with husbands (the followers of Taliban) or not. In this study the case of Aneela and her sister is quoted as they were divorcees in the aftermath of the Swat conflict in 2010.

REFERENCES

Achtenhagen, L. and Welter, F., 2005. (Re-) constructing the entrepreneurial spirit. In *Babson College Entrepreneurship Research Conference (BCERC)*. https://papers.ssrn.com/sol3/papers.cfm?abstract_id=1499374. Accessed on March 8, 2021.

Ahl, H., 2006. Why research on women entrepreneurs needs new directions. *Entrepreneurship Theory and Practice*, *30*(5), pp. 595–621.

Ahmad, S.B., 2017. Entrepreneurship in conflict zones insights on the startups in Syria. Brad Fled. https://ahmadsb.com/books/entre-in-conflict-zone/ENTREPRENEURSHIP-IN-CONFLICT-ZONES.pdf. Accessed on June 2, 2019.

Ahmed-Ghosh, H., 2003. A history of women in Afghanistan: lessons learnt for the future or yesterdays and tomorrow: women in Afghanistan. *Journal of International Women's Studies*, *4*(3), pp. 1–14.

Aldairany, S., Omar, R. and Quoquab, F., 2018. Systematic review: Entrepreneurship in conflict and post conflict. *Journal of Entrepreneurship in Emerging Economies*, *10*(2), pp. 361–383.

Arshed, N., Carter, S. and Mason, C., 2014. The ineffectiveness of entrepreneurship policy: is policy formulation to blame? *Small Business Economics*, *43*(3), pp. 639–659.

Ayadurai, S., 2004. An insight into the "constraints" faced by women entrepreneurs in a war-torn area: case study of the northeast of Sri Lanka. *Journal of Asia Entrepreneurship and Sustainability*, *2*(1), p. 1. http://www.lanka.net/centralbank/AnnualReport2004.html. Accessed on June 30, 2019.

Baumol, W.J., 1990. Entrepreneurship: productive, unproductive, and destructive. *Journal of Business Venturing*, *11*(1), pp. 3–22.

Bozzoli, C., Brück, T. and Wald, N., 2013. Self-employment and conflict in Colombia. *Journal of Conflict Resolution*, *57*(1), pp. 117–142.

Bruni, A., Gherardi, S. and Poggio, B., 2004. Entrepreneur-mentality, gender and the study of women entrepreneurs. *Journal of Organizational Change Management*, 17(3), pp. 256–268.

Bullough, A. and Renko, M., 2017. A different frame of reference: entrepreneurship and gender differences in the perception of danger. *Academy of Management Discoveries*, *3*(1), pp. 21–41.

Calás, M.B., Smircich, L. and Bourne, K.A., 2009. Extending the boundaries: reframing "entrepreneurship as social change" through feminist perspectives. *Academy of Management Review*, *34*(3), pp. 552–569.

Dana, L.P. and Dana, T.E., 2005. Expanding the scope of methodologies used in entrepreneurship research. *International Journal of Entrepreneurship and Small Business*, *2*(1), pp. 79–88.

Dana, L.P. and Dumez, H., 2015. Qualitative research revisited: epistemology of a comprehensive approach. *International Journal of Entrepreneurship and Small Business*, *26*(2), pp. 154–170.

Day, R.L., 1987. Relationships between life satisfaction and consumer satisfaction. In Samli, A.C. (Ed.), *Marketing and Quality-of-Life Interface*, pp. 289–311, Westport, CY: Greenwood Press.

Dean, H., Larsen, G., Ford, J. and Akram, M., 2019. Female entrepreneurship and the metanarrative of economic growth: a critical review of underlying assumptions. *International Journal of Management Reviews*, *21*(1), pp. 24–49.

Deanna, A. 2006. The burden of rapid development: A case study on women's economic empowerment in post-conflict Rwanda. https://www.issuelab.org/resources/21072/21072.pdf. Accessed on June 30, 2019.

Desai, S. and Acs, Z.J., 2007. A theory of destructive entrepreneurship. *Jena Economic Research Paper* (2007-085). https://www.econstor.eu/bitstream/10419/31786/1/583817904.PDF. Accessed on June 30, 2019.

Doern, R., 2009. Investigating barriers to SME growth and development in transition environments: a critique and suggestions for developing the methodology. *International Small Business Journal, 27*(3), pp. 275–305.

Galtung, J., 1973. Theories of conflict: definitions, dimensions, negations, formations. Hawaii: University of Hawaii. Retrieved from Transcend Organisation website: www.transcend.org. Accessed on June 15, 2019.

Hamza, H., 2007. Operation Rah-e-Raast: liberating Swat Valley from extremism. *South Asia Journal*. http://southasiajournal.net/7577-2/. Accessed on April 15, 2019.

Hlady-Rispal, M. and Jouison-Laffitte, E., 2014. Qualitative research methods and epistemological frameworks: a review of publication trends in entrepreneurship. *Journal of Small Business Management, 52*(4), pp. 594–614.

Hudock, A., Sherman, K. and Williamson, S., 2016. Women's economic participation in conflict-affected and fragile states. *Occasional Paper Series, 1*. Georgetown Institute for Women, Peace and Security, Washington, DC.

Justino, P., 2012. War and poverty. *IDS Working Papers, 2012*(391), pp. 1–29.

Kokko, S., 2018. Social entrepreneurship: creating social value when bridging holes. *Social Enterprise Journal, 14*(4), pp. 410–428.

Koltai, S.R. and Muspratt, M., 2016. *Peace through entrepreneurship: investing in a startup culture for security and development.* Brookings Institution Press. https://www.brookings.edu/book/peace. Accessed on March 15, 2020.

Lemmon, G.T., 2012. Entrepreneurship in postconflict zones. Council on Foreign Relations, New York. https://www.cfr.org/sites/default/files/pdf/2012/05/CFR_WorkingPaper12_Lemmon.pdf. Accessed on September 21, 2019.

Marlow, S. and Swail, J., 2014. Gender, risk and finance: why can't a woman be more like a man? *Entrepreneurship & Regional Development, 26*(1–2), pp. 80–96.

McKeever, E., Anderson, A. and Jack, S., 2014. Entrepreneurship and mutuality: social capital in processes and practices. *Entrepreneurship & Regional Development, 26*(5–6), pp. 453–477.

Ritchie, H.A., 2016. Unwrapping institutional change in fragile settings: women entrepreneurs driving institutional pathways in Afghanistan. *World Development, 83*, pp. 39–53.

Roos, A., 2017. A multiplicity of contexts: gender and locality in a contextualized view of entrepreneurship. *Journal of Asia Entrepreneurship and Sustainability, 13*(4), pp. 10–28.

Roos, A., 2019. Embeddedness in context: understanding gender in a female entrepreneurship network. *Entrepreneurship & Regional Development, 31*(3–4), pp. 279–292.

Sorensen, B. 1998. Women and post conflict reconstruction: Issues and sources. WSP Occasional Paper No. 3. *Programme for Strategic and International Security Studies*, http://www.unrisd.org/. Accessed on October 7, 2019.

Sserwanga, A., Kiconco, R.I., Nystrand, M. and Mindra, R., 2014. Social entrepreneurship and post conflict recovery in Uganda. *Journal of Enterprising Communities: People and Places in the Global Economy*, 8(4), pp. 300–317.

Tobias, J.M. and Boudreaux, K.C., 2011. Entrepreneurship and conflict reduction in the post-genocide Rwandan coffee industry. *Journal of Small Business & Entrepreneurship, 24*(2), pp. 217–242.

UN, 2009. United Nations policy for post conflict employment creation income generation and reintegration. https://www.refworld.org/pdfid/5227107a4.pdf. Accessed on February 6, 2019.

UNDP, 2020. Womenomics: women powering the economy of Pakistan. https://www.pk.undp.org/content/pakistan/en/home.html. Accessed on March 5, 2021.

United Nations Development Fund for Women (UNIFEM) 2000. Security Council Resolution 1325 Annotated and Explained. www.unifem.org. Accessed on January 6, 2019.

USAID, 2009. A guide to economic growth in post-conflict countries. https://reliefweb.int/report/world/guide-economic-growth-post-conflict-countries. Accessed on June 30, 2019.

Vernon, P., 2016. Bread and peace: linking economic development and peacebuilding. *GREAT Insights*, 5(1), pp. 4–6.

WAFGAN, 2008. Women's entrepreneurship and fair trade in Afghanistan. www.cw4wafghan .ca. Accessed on June 30, 2019.

Wang, C.C. and Geale, S.K., 2015. The power of story: narrative inquiry as a methodology in nursing research. *International Journal of Nursing Sciences*, 2(2), pp. 195–198.

Webster, N.A., 2016. *Gender and social practices in migration: a case study of Thai women in rural Sweden* (Doctoral dissertation, Department of Human Geography, Stockholm University).

Williams, N. and Vorley, T., 2015. Institutional asymmetry: how formal and informal institutions affect entrepreneurship in Bulgaria. *International Small Business Journal*, 33(8), pp. 840–861.

Index

Printed and bound by CPI Group (UK) Ltd, Croydon, CR0 4YY

16/04/2025

14658487-0004